Wealth and Complexity

Wealth and Complexity

Economically specialised sites in Late Iron Age Denmark

Edited by
Ernst Stidsing
Karen Høilund Nielsen
and Reno Fiedel

East Jutland Museum

Aarhus University Press

Wealth and Complexity. Economically specialised sites in Late Iron Age Denmark
East Jutland Museum Publications vol. 1

Graphic design: Jørgen Sparre
Typesetting: Ryevad Grafisk
Cover illustration: Aerial photo of Moeskær and the fields of Stavnsager (seen from southeast).
Photo: Michael Vinter.
Printed at Zeuner Grafisk, Denmark

ISBN 978 87 7124 324 6

AARHUS UNIVERSITY PRESS
Langelandsgade 177
DK-8200 Aarhus N
www.unipress.dk

Gazelle Book Services Ltd.
White Cross Mills, Hightown
Lancaster LA1 4XS, England
www.gazellebooks.com

ISD
70 Enterprise Drive
Bristol, CT 06010
USA
www.isdistribution.com

Published with the financial support of

Kulturstyrelsen
BECKETT-FONDEN
Den HIELMSTIERNE-ROSENCRONESKE STIFTELSE
Lillian og Dan Finks Fond
Landsdommer V. Gieses Legat

Contents

Foreword

Over the course of the last 30 years, many new settlements, in particular from the Late Iron Age, have been discovered as a result of energetic and persistent surveying of the landscape by metal-detector enthusiasts. Gudme, on the island of Funen, quickly became synonymous with these metal-rich sites, subsequently given the name 'central places'. With time, the flow of metal finds has increased and many new settlements have been added. Until 2001, the incoming and as yet manageable stream of discoveries could be followed via the publication *AUD* (*Arkæologiske udgravninger i Danmark* – Archaeological excavations in Denmark). However, a quick glance today at the website www.detectingpeople.dk reveals that, in August and September 2013 alone, 700 and 675 images of new detector finds were uploaded respectively; the number of finds is clearly growing enormously at the present time.

Only a few metal-rich settlements have been subjected to extensive investigation with large excavations and research projects being associated in particular with the settlement complexes of Gudme/Lundeborg, Sorte Muld and Tissø. A number of smaller sites, especially on Zealand, have also been examined in more detail and their character analysed.

As for Jutland, metal-detector finds have been much more modest in extent – sometimes even absent – for many years. Only around Aalborg/Nørresundby were relatively abundant finds discovered by metal detectorists at an early stage, with large numbers being recovered from Bejsebakken and Lindholm Høje in particular. Bejsebakken was subsequently excavated and the site is now in the process of being published. Recently, however, the situation across the rest of Jutland has changed markedly. Metal-rich sites have been identified in Vendsyssel, Thy and southwest Jutland as well as on Djursland, and new examples are continually being added.

These circumstances confront many museums with a new set of research problems: large areas requiring excavation, extensive cultural deposits and numerous metal finds. Major excavations, as seen at Gudme, Lundeborg, Tissø and Sorte Muld, are often not possible for financial reasons, unless the area is threatened by modern development or other landscape-changing activities. How can we gain an insight into the character of these sites and their significance relative to the rest of the settlement landscape while keeping costs down? The results of investigations in eastern Denmark cannot necessarily be applied to the situation in Jutland, which must be evaluated in its own context.

Stavnsager, located within Museum Østjylland's area of archaeological responsibility, is one of the metal-rich sites that has, for several years now, yielded metal finds across a large area. Over the last decade, a number of trials with various non-destructive survey methods have been carried out at Stavnsager and in adjacent areas, in collaboration with Dr Christopher Loveluck and his colleagues from the University of Nottingham. These have been followed up by trial excavations in order to establish a connection between the various survey data and the actual archaeological evidence present beneath the soil. On the basis of the experience gained at Stavnsager, Kulturhistorisk Museum Randers, subsequently Museum Østjylland, wished to establish a forum in which experience from sites of this kind in Jutland could be exchanged and various methods of survey and analysis, including non-destructive methods, could be discussed. The museum therefore arranged a seminar which was held on 28-29 September 2009 in Helligåndshuset in Randers. It was well-attended – with 89 participants and numerous contributions. The seminar concluded with an excursion to the Stavnsager area, where the modern agricultural landscape does not immediately convey an impression of the life that must have unfolded there in the Late Iron Age, Viking Age and Middle Ages.

Contributions to the seminar included presentations of new finds and sites, discussions of the term 'central place' and of social conditions in the Iron Age and introductions to a number of non-destructive survey methods. The main theme and the individual contributions were considered of such significance that the seminar organisers decided to publish a volume of proceedings. The individual articles were submitted in 2010 but, for various reasons, the editorial work was delayed and it was first in autumn 2013 that the finished manuscripts could be submitted to the publishers. We would like to thank the authors for their great patience during the editorial process.

Without Stavnsager, the seminar would never have taken place and this publication would not have been produced. In turn, our knowledge of the Stavnsager site is due, in no small amount, to the goodwill shown by Martha and Harry Rasmussen and Niels Rasmussen, on whose land the numerous excavations and the seminar excursion took place, and to the incredible resilience and persistence of Ove Madsen. Ove spent countless hours wandering across the fields at Stavnsager with a metal detector – often at the coldest, wettest times of year – and in the process discovered many excellent new metal finds. We owe them all a great debt of thanks.

Financial support for the seminar was kindly granted by *Kulturstyrelsen*, while *Museum Østjylland* and *Randers Kommune* provided the venue. Publication of the seminar proceedings was made possible by financial support from *Kulturstyrelsen, Lillian og Dan Finks Fond, Landsdommer V. Gieses Legat, Beckett-Fonden, Den Hielmstierne-Rosencroneske Stiftelse* and *Museum Østjylland*, for which we are very grateful.

We would also like to thank several other individuals and groups who provided great assistance and support in connection with the seminar and the editing and production of this publication: First and foremost the staff of Museum Østjylland, and Christopher Loveluck, who initiated the Stavnsager project. Thanks also to our patient and resilient translators, David Earle Robinson and Anne Bloch, and to Jørn Street Jensen and John Hines who provided bibliographical, terminological and archaeological expertise.

3rd October 2013
Ernst Stidsing
Karen Høilund Nielsen
Reno Fiedel

TOP | *The participants in the seminar 'Non-agrarian settlements and integrated survey and excavation strategy'.*

MIDDLE (left) | *The papers were presented at the archaeological seminar in Helligåndshuset, Randers, 28-29 September 2009.*

MIDDLE (right) and BOTTOM | *Field trip to Stavnsager, Moeskær and Hørning concluded the seminar.*

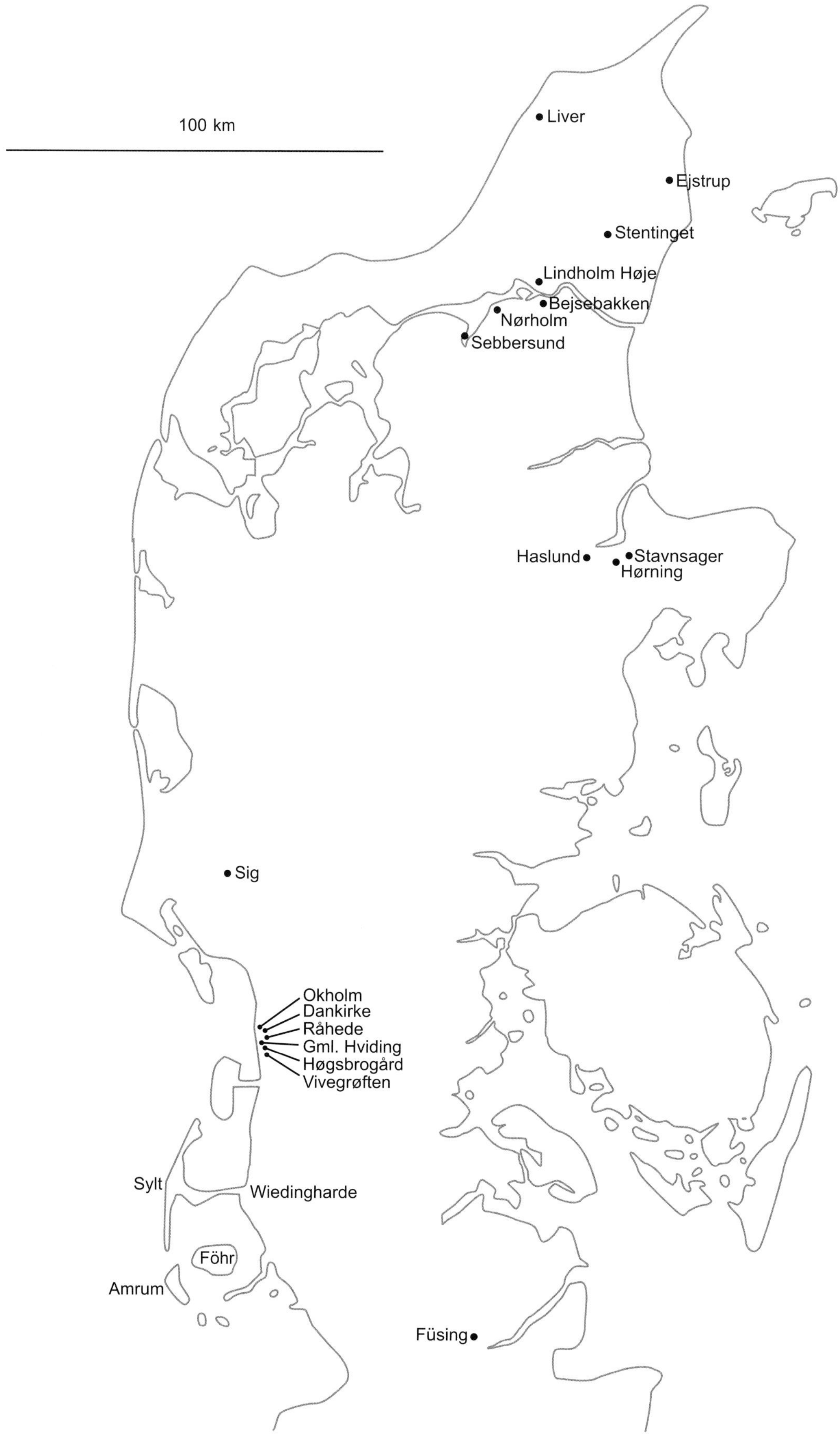

Central place sites presented in the papers.

Key issues concerning ‘central places’

Karen Høilund Nielsen

In 1986, John Collis wrote a paper entitled *Central Place Theory is Dead: Long Live the Central Place.* Although Collis admitted that the central place theory was one of the theoretical models that had helped ‘to change the archaeological paradigm from a limited historical and “culture” perspective to a more embracing socio-economic one, and thus to a total re-orientation of research methods of which regional survey and settlement sampling were the most obvious products’ (1986, 38), he concluded that it had actually only minor relevance for prehistoric and early medieval archaeology. It was only applicable as a background for the building of hypotheses, research planning and ‘mind models’ (Collis 1986, 39). At that time the concept of ‘central place’ was applied to a wide range of archaeological data sets from various prehistoric periods and had not yet become virtually synonymous with the metal-rich, so-called ‘productive sites’ of southern Scandinavia. There is, however, good reason to repeat Collis’s words as the term again appears to have become entirely devalued.

During the last two decades the term ‘central place’ has frequently been used by scholars to emphasise the significance of certain sites, both in Scandinavia and on the Continent. However, neither in history nor in archaeology is there any precise definition of an adequate central place model for the specific historical circumstances of the Late Iron Age and the Early Middle Ages (Drauschke 2010, 26; Hedeager 2002, 3; Skou Hansen 2003, 179). Thus, the term ‘central place’ can be seen applied both to a Jutish site yielding 20 metal artefacts and to the likes of Trier or Paris. It therefore seems very relevant to discuss the term and its applicability relative to Scandinavian metal-rich sites, with the aim either of finding a different nomenclature for these sites or defining a central place model with special relevance for this historic period – or both.

History of research[1]

‘Central place’ was introduced as a term and a concept in the 1930s and has subsequently had a chequered history within the fields of human geography, history and archaeology. In the former two, the term is closely related to trade and towns, while in Scandinavian archaeology it has acquired a rather different meaning focused on the settlements of the elite, with only scant reference to the original central place model of Continental historical geography.

A few critical voices have been raised in Scandinavia during the last decade, but only recent German publications have expressed more severe criticism of the Scandinavian model. In the following, I shall present and discuss the research history of the ‘central place’ as a concept and a term and discuss its implications for the Danish metal-rich settlements, using Stavnsager as an example.

Walter Christaller and central place theory

The term and concept of 'central place' were originally introduced by Walter Christaller in 1933 and never intended to be used in reference to pre-capitalist societies. It was proposed as a theoretical economic basis for a rational structure of the government services of a state, in this case a simplified redivision of the state administration of the German Reich (1932). However, it developed into an economic-geographic analysis of the regularity of the number, distribution, ranking, size and hinterland of towns, based on historical geography and exemplified by southern Germany. As a by-product, Christaller wrote the thesis *Die Zentralen Orte in Süddeutschland. Eine ökonomisch-geographische Untersuchung über die Gesetzmässigkeit der Verbreitung und Entwicklung der Siedlungen mit städtischen Funktionen*, which was published in Jena in 1933 (1933a; reprinted Darmstadt 1968). According to Christaller, the term 'Zentralort' was chosen as a *Notlösung* as he wanted a neutral term in place of town, village, castle etc. (Mitterauer 1971, 433). He also saw his model as universal and therefore not anchored in history (Müller-Wille 2010, 232; Schenk 2010, 11).

Christaller was searching for the regular spatial, functional and hierarchical structures according to which (modern) settlements were organised. The factors he used to determine the degree and rank of central importance included inter alia production and offering of centrally produced goods, trade, crafts, administration, cultural and religious institutions, organisation of economic and social life, transport and communication as well as a health system. If a formula could be generated describing where centres had actually emerged, it would then also be possible to predict where a new centre should be built. Although the basic ideas in Christaller's central place system were developed and put into practice in Germany before World War II, under the Third Reich, they have also been applied to German settlement-related structural planning from the 1950s onwards (Christaller 1933a; 1933b; 1940; 1941; Müller-Wille 2010, 232; Preston 2009) and his theories are still widely used in human geography (Grimm 2004, 560-61; Haggett 2001, 431-35; Mitterauer 1971; Wagstaff 1986).

The post-war era brought reorientation within many areas. In the 1960s, 'New Geography' was introduced, adopting a much more analytical and explanatory approach than the descriptive geography of earlier times. In many ways it was based on a way of thinking parallel to that of Christaller, namely the use of formulas to understand settlement structure. An important contribution was Peter Haggett's *Locational Analysis in Human Geography* (1965) and, inspired by this, 'New Archaeology' quickly followed suit (Collis 1986, 37). For scholars studying complex societies, 'central place' and 'central place theory' were the terms applied to what previously had been referred to as market towns, boroughs or cities. However, a series of new types of analysis and concepts also came to light and these were presented inter alia in *Spatial analysis in archaeology* by Ian Hodder and Clive Orton (1976).

The concept of central places was employed with respect to a number of archaeological cases dating from a whole range of periods, though with varying outcomes. Some examples were presented at a seminar in Oxford in 1982 and subsequently published in *Central places, Archaeology and History* edited by Eric Grant (1986). Together with successful examples came severe criticism levelled at attempts by archaeologists to shape their data to fit Christaller's theory, even though these data were, in the great majority of cases, too fragmentary to show more than that which already was obvious (Collis 1986, 37). An approach to the central place discussion in an archaeological context, connecting central places with places of power (magnate farms and manors, both secular and ecclesiastical), was also presented in this forum (Aston 1986; Austin 1986; Hooke 1986) and then taken up independently in Scandinavian archaeology.

Modified central place theory

Eric Grant (1986, 1) encouraged the formulation of much more applicable and testable central place theories when dealing with past societies represented by fragmentary data. A similar discussion was also taking place in historical studies (predominantly Austrian and German), where Christaller's theory was, at an early stage, modified in order to produce a model aimed at understanding and classifying Medieval towns and even earlier town-like settlements. Criticism of the traditional historian's approach had previously been expressed by Edith Ennen, who made the first attempt to orientate the historical concept of the town towards the central place concept used in human geography (Ennen 1965; Mitterauer 1971, 437, note 15). However, scholars such as Michael Mitterauer (history) and Dietrich Denecke (historical geography) were pivotal to this discussion in the early 1970s.

Mitterauer saw the introduction of the term and concept 'central place' not just as the introduction of a neutral term, but also as an opportunity to open up new perspectives and to ask different questions, especially as any discussion of the concept of the town had, to date, exclusively concentrated on questions of legal and constitutional history (Mitterauer 1971, 436). Mitterauer saw such a starting point as productive, especially when discussing early town-like settlements (Mitterauer 1971, 437); he also pointed out that central places were not necessarily either central or large settlements. Uninhabited central places were to be expected, especially in early periods. These included market places (fairs), cult places, assembly places, things or moots and strongholds without a permanent garrison. These were, in spite of their lack of settlement, all central facilities necessary for peaceful coexistence within a community; there are certain preconditions in the consciousness of a community which allow even uninhabited places to possess a central function (Mitterauer 1971, 444).

Mitterauer's approach thereby includes ideas relevant to archaeologists – and even prehistorians. However, he also warns that the further one goes back in time, the smaller the catalogue of central functions that can be identified; ultimately only a few basic components remain (Mitterauer 1971, 445). According to Mitterauer, only four main central facilities can be identified for the Early and High Medieval period – political, judicial, ecclesiastical and market-related (Mitterauer 1971, 455) – and these are interrelated. Furthermore, Denecke has observed that the quantifiable data on which the hierarchical classification of modern geography is based are unavailable for most historical periods and such analyses are therefore not possible. Instead, he suggests the use of a catalogue of (ranked) central functions (Denecke 1973, 42) and highlights the following functions and facilities as being important in historical eras: political and administrative offices and structures, judicial institutions, defensive institutions and strategic organisation, ritual and religious institutions, cultural institutions, welfare service and charitable institutions, structure and administration of the agrarian economy, craft and trade, trade institutions and communication. Each of these ten functions is then ranked internally (Denecke 1973, 4; Steuer 2007, 879). Denecke is, however, also fully aware of the impossibility of fulfilling all the criteria with respect to early historical periods (Denecke 1973, 48-49, 51).

Mitterauer also notes that settlement development can only be understood in the context of the entire cultural landscape (Mitterauer 1971, 466). In the development of regional social groups the potential for interaction is of immense importance. Consequently, any changes in central places would depend on lines of communication and alterations to these (Mitterauer 1971, 462). The establishment of new centres requires more than simply choosing a place for the performance of central functions; it also involves the establishment of tangible mental connections with this particular place (Mitterauer 1971, 447). Cult centres are more bound to their locality than is the case for power/political centres; consequently they are more difficult to move. There is a tendency for temporary cyclical markets to follow religious centres, whereas permanent trade centres, which are more dependent on political power, often follow the political centres and are thus easier to relocate (Mitterauer 1971, 465-66). A central place can, from its very beginning, develop as a poly-centre, whereby central functions or facilities are distributed over several different sites (Mitterauer 1971, 465).

Proto-towns and their formation

The use of the central place theory by historians has naturally focused on information derived from written sources. However, the growing number of urban archaeological excavations taking place in northern Europe has widened the perspective, and the discussion has become extended to include early periods of town history as well as urban facilities and functions for which there are no written sources and, as a consequence, the question of town formation.

The proceedings of the symposium *Vor- und Frühformen der europäischen Stadt im Mittelalter*, edited by Herbert Jankuhn, Walter Schlesinger and Heiko Steuer (1975), to which Denecke's paper was a contribution, included discussions addressing the development of the town during the Medieval period from a number of different angles. Several Scandinavian sites were featured, such as Eketorp, Helgö, Haithabu, Kaupang, Birka and Paviken, as well as actual Medieval towns both in Scandinavia and on the Continent.

Only a few months after this symposium, another meeting took place with the same main theme: *Frühe Städte im westlichen Ostseeraum*, although this covered a more limited geographical area. The organisers, *Sonderforschungsbereich 17, Skandinavien- und Ostseeraumforschung* in Kiel, had excavated in the Medieval towns of Kiel and Schleswig and wanted to discuss their findings with other scholars carrying out comparable excavations in neighbouring areas of Germany and in Scandinavia. The papers therefore concentrated much more on excavation results than on possible theories about urbanism. The only exception was a paper by Hans Andersson (1973), the only participant lacking an archaeological background. He presented the debate current among Scandinavian historians at that time with respect to the definition of a (Medieval) town and outlined his own ideas, based partly on Mitterauer and Christaller.

Britain too began to become involved in excavations and discussions of towns in the late 1960s, following 30 years of no research on the subject (Biddle 1976, 99). The British approach and background were rather different from those of the Germans. In his major paper on towns, Martin Biddle does not refer directly to Christaller's theories of central places, but instead takes his inspiration from Edith Ennen and her work on the European Medieval town (Biddle 1976, 100, passim; Ennen 1953; 1972).

In the wake of these developments in urban studies, the Danish Research Council launched a project called *Middelalderbyen* (The Medieval Town) in 1977. Throughout the course of the 1980s, this resulted in a series of monographs on a number of Danish towns, each of which included all available sources (Olaf Olsen in I. Nielsen 1985, 5). The monographs, although they did not discuss central place theory, dealt with all the criteria relative to such central places.

Centres of trade

While research in the 1970s focused on town formation, the 1980s this shifted towards one urban function, namely trade and its many faces. With the publication of Jørgen Jensen's *Oldtidens samfund: Dansk socialhistorie* in 1979, the concept of 'administered trade' was introduced into Danish post-Roman archaeology. This found particular response in Stig Jensens's discussion of Ribe and its predecessor(s), especially Dankirke with its rich finds of glass and glass beads (S. Jensen 1980). Discussion of trade was a natural consequence of the excavations then taking place in Ribe, Aarhus, Hedeby, Dorestad, Southampton etc., alongside research into the formation of pre-, proto- and Medieval towns.

Two publications from the 1980s are of crucial importance: *Dark Age Economics* by Richard Hodges (1982) and the multidisciplinary colloquia of the *Kommission für die Altertumskunde Mittel- und Nordeuropas* on the theme *Untersuchungen zu Handel und Verkehr* 1980-83, subsequently published under the same title (Claude 1985; Düwel et al. 1985a; 1985b; 1987; Jankuhn & Ebel 1989; Jankuhn et al. 1989).

Whereas Christaller's central place model and its modifications are based on human geography,

Hodges's analysis of the origins of towns and trade is founded on anthropological theories about trade and urbanism. These have their roots in the works of Karl Polanyi (1957), Paul Bohannan and George Dalton (1962), Carol Smith (1976) and Kenneth Hirth (1978), and even as far back as Gordon Childe's paper on the urban revolution (1950). Research in the German-speaking world is only mentioned very briefly (such as in the English translation of Ennen 1972 (Ennen 1979)).

Hodges's thesis presented an entirely new view of central places, emporia and the formation of early towns outside the Roman world. By adopting an archaeological approach, it subsequently had a major influence on Anglo-Saxon and northwest European research over a very long period because it was so firmly based upon recent and extensive archaeological fieldwork in the Early Medieval port sites of southern and eastern England, and some of their counterparts on the Continent. Previously the debate had been dominated by historians and anthropologists.

Hodges discusses not only central places, emporia and towns but also their development in the light of society as a whole: social changes, developments in transport, the introduction of coinage etc. He divides trading places into a number of types: i.e. gateways of types A and B, solar central places and competitive markets, each linked to their own type of society. The type B gateway corresponds to sites such as Dorestad from the time of early silver coinage, especially sceattas. A significant divergence relative to previous interpretations is that Hodges clearly understands the term 'central place' in quite a different way: i.e. central places cannot exist without a central power and all belong in the Late Viking Age and/or later. Whereas the German-speaking scholars tried to modify Christaller's model to fit pre-urban societies, Hodges was, perhaps unknowingly, adhering more closely to Christaller's original definition, although he makes no reference to him.

Hodges's relatively holistic analysis is dependent on ideas about trading systems and this probably also explains his rather different use of the central place concept. In Hodges's opinion, trade was the initial reason for the foundation of these sites. Furthermore, he concentrates on type B gateways and later site types, paying scant attention to 'premonetary' sites. A follow-up volume with a slightly different focus, *Primitive and Peasant Markets*, was published in 1988.

When he applied it in an archaeological context, however, Hodges's anthropologically based perspective was immediately opposed by some other scholars, and most severely by David Wilson in his paper in volume II of the *Untersuchungen zu Handel und Verkehr* (Wilson 1985, 255-56). Nonetheless, Hodges's work was, despite its faults, an eye-opener for many archaeologists, especially in northwestern Europe.

The six volumes of *Untersuchungen zu Handel und Verkehr der vor- und frühgeschichtlichen Zeit in Mittel- und Nordeuropa* (Claude 1985; Düwel et al. 1985a; 1985b; 1987; Jankuhn & Ebel 1989; Jankuhn et al. 1989) deal with a wide range of themes related to trade and transport in prehistory (predominantly the later stages), Antiquity and the Medieval period, with a geographical coverage corresponding to Europe and the western Mediterranean. The volumes deal with the methodological background in addition to providing detailed studies of a wide range of written and archaeological sources together with coins and place names. It could be said that they address the same aspects of trade as Hodges's thesis, or more. However, due to the division of the subject into a huge number of papers, each with different authors and spread across six volumes, any coherence is lost.

One of these papers – by Ulrich Köhler (1985) – on trade from an anthropological perspective is, however, worth mentioning here. It shows that the anthropological ideas so typical of Anglo-American archaeologists were also known to at least some German scholars and, as a consequence, became included in *Untersuchungen zu Handel und Verkehr*. With respect to central places and trading places, Köhler emphasises that, where there is no central power to maintain the 'market peace', markets are often held at sites of religious importance so that religious taboo secures the peace. This aspect is also touched upon by Mitterauer, albeit from another angle, but Köhler makes it clear that a central power is not indispensable.

Helgö, on the island of the same name in Lake Mälaren, is a Scandinavian site that became involved at an early stage in the discussion of the pre- and proto-towns due its unusual character. It was discovered in the 1950s and excavated in subsequent decades at a time when nothing comparable had been encountered. During the excavations, and subsequently, speculations with respect to the site have been legion and in 1988 an entire volume was devoted to a discussion of Helgö from a number of different angles (Lundström (ed.) 1988). This did not, however, result in a consensus being reached with respect to an interpretation of the site and this remains the case despite the growing number of publications dealing with the finds. The site is – to date – too unique.

Metal detecting, Gudme and the question of centrality

Many metal-detector sites came to light, especially in Denmark but also in Britain, during the 1980s (Vang Petersen 1991; Ulmschneider & Pestell 2003, 2), prompting debate about their origin and function, as they were clearly not traditional agrarian sites. The popularity of metal detecting in Denmark has its roots in the late 1970s. The number of metal objects recovered was initially relatively small and at first the significance of the finds was unclear. It also took some time for professional archaeologists and amateur archaeologists/metal detectorists to develop a modus operandi that took account of the interests of both parties. This does, however, seem to have been achieved now in Denmark. Within a few years, the number of finds recovered by metal detector grew enormously and the archaeological record for metal finds expanded to a previously unimaginable extent. Some chronological gaps were notably closed, particularly with respect to large parts of the Germanic Iron Age (AD 400-800). This had almost had the character of a revelation for a period which previously was so devoid of finds that migration to the level of desertion had been suggested. Suddenly, it was the period with the greatest number of metal finds. From the 'Dark Age' and the 'Migration Period Crisis', discussions now turned to other themes, concentrating in particular on early state formation – and with exactly the same prehistoric period.

A number of these sites were already known as a result of stray finds recovered by amateur archaeologists engaged in fieldwalking. This was true in particular for sites in the area in and around Aalborg and Nørresundby, especially Bejsebakken and Lindholm Høje (Christiansen 2008). But also Gudme and the adjoining area around Broholm Manor had, for almost two centuries, been renowned for its many finds of gold hoards. It was also here that the first real metal-detecting sensations occurred in Denmark. Not only the expected brooches saw the light of day, but gold and silver treasures, gold bracteates and Roman statues also numbered among the finds. The fact that Gudme had such an unusual character reinforced the idea that the local sites must have been unusual in terms of riches, power and ritual. The same was true of Sorte Muld on Bornholm, another well-known site, but the very different character of the finds resulting from the new investigations was most unexpected, especially their richness and the presence of thousands of small gold foil figures – so-called *guldgubber* (Adamsen et al. 2008; Watt 1991; 1992).

A series of settlement-related seminars, organised by Henrik Thrane and held mainly at Odense University's Institute of History from 1975 to the 1990s, also included several dedicated to Gudme. The first of these was in 1984 (Thrane (ed.) 1985), with successors in 1987 (Vang Petersen (ed.) 1989), 1989 (Thrane (ed.) 1990) and 1995 (Henriksen & Michaelsen (eds.) 1995). The proceedings of each of these seminars were quickly published and they include papers on a wide range of subjects, placing the Gudme sites in the context of the archaeological, historical and religious landscape. At an early stage, the coastal site at Lundeborg was linked with Gudme (see for example Thomsen et al. 1993). The proceedings of the first symposium were also published in a translated edition (only Thrane's paper appeared in a much more expanded version) in *Frühmittelalterliche Studien* in 1987 (Thrane 1987), which ensured Gudme's renown in international circles. Whereas the settlement seminars had aimed at establishing a local context for Gudme, an international conference held at Svendborg in 1991 had the intention of placing Gudme in a wider north European context (Nielsen et al. (eds.) 1994).

The many gold bracteates found at Gudme, together with the area's sacral place names, attracted particular attention, although some of the imported Roman artefacts also made an impact. As early as 1987, both Henrik Thrane and Karl Hauck had argued that Gudme, in the period AD 200-600, was a *Reichtumszentrum* and *Kultzentrum*, perhaps even the centre of a *Sakralkönigtum* for eastern Funen, whose religious and economic power could have stretched beyond its political and military might (Axboe 1991, 201; Crumlin-Pedersen 1992, 397-99; Hauck 1987, 172-75; Thrane 1987, 42-43; 1992). This idea is also supported by place-name studies (Kousgård Sørensen 1985). Even given a less grandiose interpretation, it was clear that during the Late Roman and Migration periods, and perhaps even later, Gudme was an aristocratic settlement and a central place (Fabech 1994, 176-78; Fonnesbeck-Sandberg 1991, 240-41; Thrane 1991b).

The research project *Fra Stamme til Stat i Danmark* (From Tribe to State in Denmark), launched by the Danish Research Council for the Humanities and carried out between 1984 and 1989 (Mortensen & Rasmussen (eds.) 1988; 1991), was another initiative that has left its mark on the understanding of the central place concept, at least in Scandinavian archaeology. Papers by Henrik Thrane on Gudme and Margrethe Watt on Sorte Muld brought the question of the central place sharply into focus (Thrane 1991a; Watt 1991). But it was a paper by Ulf Näsman (1991a) that placed the central place concept firmly on the agenda, not just in this particular sense, but in Scandinavian archaeology in general. It was in this context that the term and concept 'central place' were first used with reference to the metal-rich sites of southern Scandinavia (Fabech 1999a, 456; Näsman 1991a, 169-73).

Näsman describes central places as settlements with super-regional functions within the spheres of justice and religion, and as nodal points for the distribution of trade and craft products. Moreover, these centres formed a well-established phenomenon within the settlement structure of the Late Roman and Early Germanic Iron Ages. He also writes that the centres were, at the same time, also seats of magnates and places of worship, trade and specialised crafts servicing a larger region (Näsman 1991a, 169-70), but with a particular focus on trade – the distribution of commodities. Näsman defines Sorte Muld and Gudme as central places. Gudme is even described as a poly-centre, belonging to a superior level characterised by 'sacral settlement conglomerates'. Magnate farms with local central functions, such as Dankirke, Lejre and Nørre Sandegård, are placed on a lower level (Näsman 1991a, 171-73; 1991b, 327-28). Näsman had also discussed the subject at the symposium *Samfundsorganisation og Regional Variation* (Social organisation and regional variation) (Fabech & Ringtved (eds.) 1991). He concluded that it was unlikely that a central place in the Late Iron Age and Viking Age would take the form of one single physical centre, and that Dankirke, Uppåkra and Sorte Muld each represented only one of the qualities expected of such a centre (Näsman 1991b, 328).

In the presentation of his central place model, Näsman does not refer to the long-running discussion of the theory in Continental historical geography (see above). Gradually, though, the term drifted into everybody's consciousness as one that was applicable to these Gudme-like settlements and, with time, also to a much broader range of sites. A significant difference from the original central place model proposed by Christaller and his successors is, however, seen in the close ties with seats of the aristocracy.

Settlement, landscape and aristocratic central places

In 1993, a number of major settlement projects were launched under the direction of Charlotte Fabech, Steen Hvass, Ulf Näsman and Jytte Ringtved (Fabech et al. 1999, 13). Inspired by Ulf Näsman's paper (1991a), mentioned above, and in particular by Swedish human geography and place-name studies, one of the subjects addressed was central places.

Sweden has a long tradition of research into cultural landscapes. In his thesis *Centralbygd – randbygd* from 1974, Åke Hyenstrand analysed Sweden's settlement structure. Other scholars then took up the question, including Stefan Brink, who emphasised the importance of place-name studies in the analysis of past settlement structures. Brink saw place names, especially in certain regions of Sweden, as fossilised representations of the structure of the *bygd* (~settlement region) a thousand years ago or more. On this basis, he constructed a model of the ideal *bygd,* which is a sort of central place complex (Brink 1996; 1997; 1999, 434-35). In Denmark, the Gudme area is rich in old place names that indicate the ritual nature of the area and the landscape (Kousgård Sørensen 1985). However, this seems to be an exception, as Brink concludes that a comparable analysis of the Danish evidence would be exceptionally complex because too many Danish place names have been replaced or lost (Brink 1999, 425).

While place-name studies provide one idea of the settlement structure in the landscape, Fabech and Ringtved proposed an alternative model for a hierarchy or ranking-system for settlements and Late Iron Age central places, based on the archaeological record. This allocates sites to one of three levels, predominantly on the basis of finds of metal artefact (Fabech & Ringtved 1995, 14). Although they define central places on different levels, Fabech, in particular, concentrates almost exclusively on the elite level of central places in her later work. These elite central places are identified by the presence of archaeological finds such as imported gold objects, gold bracteates, gold foil figures, gold sword mounts, gold waste from workshops, silver scrap metal hoards, weapons, archaeological remains of halls, large settlements, large cemeteries, landing places and the like. These sites are situated on communication routes, close to resources, and are often poly-centric. Place names within the area of the central place are sacral and organisational (Fabech & Ringtved 1995, 19).

Central places are, in other words, constituted by the presence of a magnate's residence with associated workshops, halls, cult buildings, utility buildings, landing places etc., and they can vary in size from a single farm to a large constituent part of a hamlet or village (Fabech 1999a, 455). They are also linked to areas with sacral place names, surrounded by settlements with names indicating special buildings or functions (Fabech 1999a, 457). A central place in Fabech's (and Ringtved's) definition is thus the residence of the paramount leader and his concomitant specialists with a variety of functions including monopoly of force, economic management, craft production and ceremonial legitimisation of power. The manufacture of special wealth in such places served strategically to unite, link and control society, both economically and symbolically (Fabech 1999a, 456-57; 1999b, 42). The actual location of the central place was determined entirely by the political power responsible for it: in particular, by whether or not the individual who held power wished to develop the site into a centre within the political landscape, with its own perceived and recognised biography (Fabech 1999a, 458).

Support for this model – the cosmological legitimisation so to say – was provided by Lotte Hedeager. She described the similarities in the settlement structures of Gudme and Asgard, stating that Gudme was built as it was in order to mirror Asgard, in the same way as a Byzantine cathedral is a model of the Heavenly Kingdom (Hedeager 2001, 480; 2002, 4, 11-15).

Strictly speaking, Fabech and Ringtved equate central places with seats of magnates or magnate farm complexes (Fabech 1999b, 42-43; Fabech & Ringtved 1995, 18-20). This is a very different approach and a different definition to that of historical geography discussed above. In the latter, central places are urban phenomena of later periods or in other regions and are focused on central functions and services ('service centres'). Apart from a brief mention of Christaller (Fabech 1997, 154), references to the central places of historical geography are totally absent from Fabech and Ringtved's analyses. In fact, the two definitions of central place are so different that it is necessary to perceive them as two entirely different models, confusingly known by the same name: the Continental central place model and the Scandinavian 'central *bygd*' or 'magnate seat' model. There are of course some functional overlaps between the two, but the Scandinavian model presupposes a magnate residence at the site, whereas the Continental model does not. A number of other functions are also weighted differently.

The models of Scandinavian settlements and central places found new expression in Ulf Näsman's more comprehensive model of social development in southern Scandinavia which, in some respects, followed the route taken by Hodges (1982). Näsman concentrates on the political landscape and bases his model on analogies with Francia and the Anglo-Saxon kingdoms (Näsman 1998a; 1998b, 269-70). Included in his model are non-agrarian sites seen as the predecessors of emporia and early towns, although Näsman stresses that these central places are not urban communities (Näsman 2000, 46-47). In the model, central places are linked with the tribal confederations of the 4th to 7th centuries AD after which, around AD 700, a transition into kingdoms with emporia occurs (Näsman 1998a, 22-23; 1998b, 260-70). Näsman sees the central places, of which a residence of the elite was part and parcel, as representing a new economic and political organisation (Näsman 2000, 46).

Jens Ulriksen's study of specialised landing places and Lars Jørgensen's analysis of Tissø and comparative analysis of Gudme sites of supposed central place character are, on the other hand, approached from entirely different angles.

Ulriksen presents a group of sites that have metal finds, albeit in small numbers, in common with so-called central places, but which otherwise are of a much more humble character (Ulriksen 1990; 1998). All are clearly coastal settlements of a semi-permanent non-agrarian nature, situated with easy access to and from the sea. Ulriksen concludes that every large farm had its own specialised landing place on the coast, partly as a result of contemporary developments in boats and ships (Ulriksen 1998, 136). He divides the sites into three phases, of which the first is only represented by Lundeborg (primarily 3rd and 4th centuries AD). There is a significant increase in these sites from AD 520/30 onwards and around AD 680/700 trading sites or emporia begin to develop (Ulriksen 1998, 195). Ulriksen is inspired by Hodges (1982; 1988), but he also accepts Fabech and Ringtved's version of the central place concept (Ulriksen 1998, 13).

Jørgensen does not even include the central place concept in his analysis of Tissø and Gudme. For him these are magnate residences, the seats of the elite, comprising accommodation for the elite family, buildings for religious ceremonies and a separate settlement with workshops and trading facilities belonging to the manor (Jørgensen 1995; 1998; 2002; 2010). Jørgensen works retrospectively, looking backwards in time from the manorial estates of the Medieval period, and he interprets the development of social organisations on the basis of the buildings of the elite farms (Jørgensen 2001). In his opinion, a system that allowed the levying of tribute was a necessary prerequisite for the establishment of estates based on direct operations by tenant farms and the potential to force the population to pay estate dues and render their labour. The existence of this earlier phase, when the elite levied tribute, is argued for on the basis of the lack of utility buildings at the magnate farms in Gudme and the early phases of Tissø (Jørgensen 2001, 80-81). Jørgensen's ideas were criticised by Dagfinn Skre, who argues that it is unlikely that the magnate and his whole retinue could live at Gudme without storerooms for the tribute that would have been paid in kind. He believes that 'farms' consisting of hall buildings and lacking functional utility buildings were more likely intended for venues and religious gatherings (Skre 2010, 287). Mats Widgren has touched upon the same subject in his settlement hierarchy, which allocates settlements to one of four levels. Level D, in particular, covers the magnate farms discussed by Jørgensen. However, in Widgren's system these are ordinary large farms with secondary income from the control of crafts and trade and perhaps other dependent farms (Widgren 1998, 290-91).

Uppåkra and some critical remarks

Uppåkra, in western Scania, was the focus of major investigations during the course of the 1990s and subsequently. The results were presented in a large number of publications discussing various aspects of the finds and the fieldwork, although never resulting in a well-documented overview. Much effort was focused on the so-called 'cult-house' and its spectacular finds of gold foil figures, a glass bowl and a decorated metal beaker as well as a nearby sacrificial area yielding numerous finds of spearheads (Larsson (ed.) 2004). The area excavated is still much too small to enable a true impression to be gained of the structure of the site as a whole. On the basis of the Uppåkra project, Bertil Helgesson wrote his thesis *Samhälle, centra och regioner* (Helgesson 2002a), which includes a discussion of the concept and definition of a central place.

Bertil Helgesson's approach to a definition of the central place concept is slightly ambiguous. On the one hand he presents a detailed definition of such sites (Helgesson 2002a, 18-33), but on the other he concludes that: 'we lack a unitary definition. Perhaps we will never arrive at a definition and perhaps we do not need one' (Helgesson 2002b, 31). He makes no reference to the Continental definitions of the term, but bases his discussion on the archaeological finds and his own ideas about socially important central functions – namely specialised crafts, long-distance trade, cult, military power, communication routes, administration of justice and government – combined with references to Fabech and Ringtved (Helgesson 1998; 2002a, 16, 18, 143). He criticises the tendency to apply the term 'central place' to almost any site which is out of the ordinary and attempts in his work to restrict usage of the term to only the most obvious central places. These are then re-classified as magnate farms, sites with production and trade or strongholds (Helgesson 2002a, 29, 36-37, 143).

Helgesson criticises Fabech and Ringtved's model for having no temporal perspective and, accordingly, no discussion of how central places emerge and why they disappear. He is also critical of them for only including certain central functions, i.e. functions which can be expected to have been evenly spread over the entire region and therefore found at many more sites than those suggested (Helgesson 2002a, 20). This is also an aspect he questions in Näsman's model, in which both judicial and ritual functions and trade and production were characteristic of central places (Helgesson 2002a, 35-36).

Påvel Nicklasson shares Helgesson's view that the term 'central place' has been applied far too widely and that the changing nature of sites over time has been paid little attention (Nicklasson 2002, 120-21). Nicklasson also suggests a different interpretation of central places based on the very large number of sites that have now emerged and, in line with the magnate residence interpretation, he argues that central places were of military origin and accommodated the pirates of the period who based their economy on plundering (Nicklasson 2002, 120-21). This aspect has also been touched upon by Ulriksen (Ulriksen 1998, 221-22). Furthermore, Nicklasson reaches the conclusion that the real central places belong to the Late Viking Age and later periods, in line with Hodges (Hodges 1982, 52, 190; Nicklasson 2002, 122).

Back to the roots

Any discussion of central places has long been peripheral in German archaeology. Only with the west Slavonic settlement research of the early 1990s did the concept see increasing debate (Grimm 2004, 562; Gringmuth-Dallmer 1993) and German archaeology has only recently reacted against the Scandinavian central place concept.

The new debate in German archaeology focuses on the central place concept as presented by German and Austrian historical geography (cf. above), but also makes reference to the south Scandinavian theory of central places. Oliver Grimm's intention was to apply the Scandinavian framework to German research (Grimm 2006, 21-22), but it proved impossible to use the Scandinavian model with respect to, for example, German place names (Udolph 2010, 64-65). However, Grimm was well aware of the German concept of central places and also saw that this could contribute to Scandinavian research. Consequently, both Grimm and Steuer make reference to Eike Gringmuth-Dallmer (Grimm 2004, 562; Gringmuth-Dallmer 1993; 1999; Steuer 2007, 880-1), who suggested that for the central places of pre- and proto-historic periods only five basic functions were worth pursuing: authority, protection, resources, crafts/trade and religion. However, growing dissatisfaction with this concept has been expressed by scholars such as Winfried Schenk, who does not consider it a suitable explanatory tool for historical situations (2010, 13; see also Steuer 2007).

German applied studies on central places fall into two groups. One concentrates on the Late Roman and Early Medieval towns in, or close to the border of, the former Roman Empire. Consequently, discussions focus primarily on town-like settlements. The other group focuses on northern Germany, an area with no tradition of town-like settlements.

The application of the central place model to provincial areas of the Roman Empire was initiated by Jürgen Kunow in 1988 (Kunow 1988; 1989; 1992) and the idea has recently been taken up again by Marion Brüggler (2010). Brüggler analysed the provincial capitals and other comparable settlements of the Roman Empire and identified which central functions were found where, as well as which archaeologically identifiable structures were present. The most interesting discovery in relation to the Scandinavian central place debate is that, whereas the elite families of the Roman empire lived in, or had, a house in the town even though their estates were in the countryside, the situation was quite different in the Germanic provinces. Here, the native elite seems to have invested in rural religious centres rather than in monumental buildings in towns (Brüggler 2010, 18). Neither were theatres a feature of these provinces (Brüggler 2010, 17). However, Roman state administration stood as a shadow behind all of this and it must accordingly be taken into account, including the fact that the roads and transport routes were established by the Romans. Even a fair had to have the permission of the emperor. Fairs were often held in connection with religious feasts at sanctuaries and temples (Brüggler 2010, 19). Central places in the Roman Empire are thus more in line with the central places of the Medieval period, according to Hodges's typology (Hodges 1982, 52).

Jörg Drauscke addressed some of the same questions with respect to the Merovingian period, focusing in particular on the shift in central places that took place as a result of the transformed social organisation. He concluded that when imperial power faded, the Roman cities continued to function almost as before, but the bishops took control of some of them together with their central functions (Drauscke 2010, 33, 43). Other episcopal seats, some of them also royal seats, were also seen as central places, several with emerging cults of saints (Drauscke 2010, 34, 43). Later, craft centres emerged in the vicinity of the important resources and emporia on the northern and eastern fringe of the realm (Drauscke 2010, 43). Many of these emporia were located in the vicinity of their Roman predecessors, although with no direct continuity (Drauscke 2010, 42). In the Merovingian period, crafts were present both in the old Roman cities as well as in the villages, whereas during the Carolingian period craft activities declined in the Roman cities but continued in the villages. They then achieved dominance in conjunction with monasteries, canonical institutions and emporia along the North Sea coast and the eastern borders (Drauscke 2010, 39). Drauscke has, furthermore, also interpreted the seats of the landowning elite as central places, because it was here that accumulation and redistribution took place (Drauscke 2010, 31).

Other German contributions tend rather to follow in Scandinavian footsteps. Hauke Jöns (2010) applied Fabech's model to the Sievern area, whereas Jonathan Scheschkewitz's (2010) analysis of the coastal region between the rivers Ems and Elbe lies much closer to Ulriksen's ideas about the Roskilde Fjord area. There are, however, some significant deviations as the bracteates from the Sievern area are, for example, located in different circumstances than would be expected in relation to Fabech's model; the Sievern bracteates were found in areas of heath and mire, as is typical for Jutland, and not in connection with a (high status) settlement as seen in more easterly parts of southern Scandinavia. The finds analysed by Scheschkewitz also differ, to some extent, from those of Ulriksen. In a number of cases they are much earlier and the North Sea landscape is significantly different from that of Roskilde Fjord. The proximity of the Roman Empire and later the Frankish kingdoms also had an effect.

For Oliver Grimm, a central place must be seen in the light of the power structure of a region (Grimm 2004, 565) and must therefore include a magnate's residence with its hall (cf. Fabech above). But he also makes use of a number of other sources in order to identify political centres in Norway. These need not be a specific type of settlement; they may also be large boathouses, richly-furnished burials, strongholds, early church buildings, hoards, rune stones, place names and written sources (Grimm 2006, 27-28).

Recent German contributions to the debate thereby encompass an attempt to stay true to the German tradition, while also seeking inspiration from Scandinavian research. The situation is different in British archaeology. The central place discussion faded away at an early stage and when the metal-rich sites (termed in Britain 'productive sites') appeared as a consequence of metal-detecting activities, interest was initially concentrated on the large quantities of coins. Subsequently the discussion became directed towards other categories of finds from British metal-rich sites and their trade aspects. In a recent publication, *Early Medieval Markets and 'Productive' Sites* (Pestell & Ulmschneider (eds.) 2003), there is considerable focus on possible interpretations of British 'productive' sites (see also Ulmschneider 2002). However, this concentrates solely on finds dating from around AD 700 or later, i.e. the time when a revival of the international trade networks has been identified, based primarily on the emergence of silver coinage on a large scale (Blackburn 2003; Ulmschneider & Pestell 2003, 1, 5).

New discoveries in Germany may now be able to reorientate the debate. It is well known that Paderborn was established as a royal *Pfalz* by Charlemagne in AD 775/6. Situated in a fertile area with numerous springs at a point where major roads meet and cross the River Alme, an episcopal seat was established there in AD 805/6. Moreover, new finds in the vicinity offer additional perspectives on the site. A settlement including many *Grubenhäuser* was found and excavated at Balhorn, west of Paderborn (Bunte & Kröger-Köb 2007; Eggenstein et al. 2008; Ludowici 2010, 336). Finds in the area date from the Roman period onwards (Ludowici 2010, 336) and, according to written sources, Charlemagne used an area at Bad Lippspringe, northeast of Paderborn, as a place of assembly (Ludowici 2010, 336). The unique situation at Paderborn is that information from many sources, both written and archaeological, can be combined, making it possible to recognise the development of sites in the area into what Ludowici calls an 'area with a concentration of central functions', in other words a poly-centre (Ludowici 2010, 337). She also identifies a source that may shed light on the character of the site prior to Charlemagne becoming established in the area. The *Translatio S. Liborii* mentions that the first diocesan centres in northwestern Germany were founded at places specified as *populi frequentia* – visited by many people. The Church wanted diocesan centres to be established at places with large populations, usually a *civitas*, but these did not exist in the Saxon area (Ludowici 2010, 337 with further references).

The opportunity of confronting the written sources with the archaeological evidence for the Paderborn area allows analysis of the development of a so-called central place and the effect on the archaeological record of the political changes that took place.

Conclusion and perspectives

It is clear from the above that the Continental and the Scandinavian concepts of central places are very different and ought to have been described using different terms. Moreover, the two concepts each have a different focus: the Continental version is concerned with towns, while in Scandinavia more attention is given to elite residences. Whereas the central place discussion seems to have a natural place in regions with towns, it is questionable how far the idea is applicable to Scandinavia in the pre-urban period. Indeed, the question with respect to Scandinavia is whether central places, according to the Continental definition, existed at all until very late, i.e. the Late Viking Age and/or later. Furthermore, were any central functions that did exist located together in centres or poly-centres? Of course there may have been regional differences, like those seen in the general settlement structure of southern Scandinavia (cf. Holst this volume). It is therefore also questionable whether future research in southern Scandinavia should continue to be directed at central places of different kinds.

Instead of searching for, and trying to explain, central places, it would seem to me, on the basis of the above, more fruitful to deconstruct the whole idea and instead approach the interpretation of these metal-rich sites from the following two perspectives:

- Empirical analysis of metal-rich sites with a focus on functions directly reflected in the archaeological finds
- Application of probable models of interpretation for 'central' and communal functions in their widest sense above the level of the individual village

It may sound trivial, but I think it is important to keep these two approaches separate in future analyses in order to reduce preconceived opinions to a minimum. Too often it has been uncritically assumed that central functions would cluster together – as in the Continental version of the concept – ultimately converging to become towns. In Scandinavia, it has simply been taken for granted that central functions would be controlled by the elite and, accordingly, that there was an elite which held this power. Consequently, an analysis of functions identifiable in the archaeological record, on the one hand, and a discussion of possible central functions above village level, whether found separately or together, on the other, would be a more fruitful way forward. Moreover, the various aspects each need to be seen in their own chronological context, something which has too often been neglected in the past.

Empirical analysis

In order to understand the metal-rich sites of the later Iron Age, a systematic analysis of the archaeological and historical evidence pertaining the sites is necessary in order to establish the biography of each individual site. This analysis should include the internal structure of the site through time, its place in the landscape and its relationship to nearby agrarian settlements and the infrastructure, and should be aimed at identifying possible functions present at the site.

The next level of the analysis would be to compare the biographies of different sites in order to identify their differences and similarities.

Interpretative models

Dick Harrison criticises archaeologists and historians for not distinguishing places with central functions clearly enough from the nodal sites within a network; central functions are those which the elite wishes to control in the first instance (Harrison 1997, 25). Places possessing central functions (centripetal centres) have a catchment area and service the local population. They should be evenly spread relative to the general pattern of settlement; this is not the case for nodal sites within a network. The latter are supra-regional and related to inter-regional contacts and are therefore not centres in a regional perspective, but nodes in a supra-regional network (centrifugal centres). Networks are necessary for the distribution of material culture – and of ideas – and will often reflect trade in its widest interpretation, and even pilgrimage. However, these centres do not necessarily service the local areas in which they are situated and do not have to be evenly distributed. These two types of central function must therefore be analysed separately (cf. Harrison 1997, 25-27). Furthermore, the infrastructural complexity of central places is important, regardless of type, because the degree of complexity is also a measure of how difficult or easy it is to control them. Highly complex centres are easy to control, whereas this is much more difficult for low complexity centres, involving central functions spread across many different sites or centres (as in the Merovingian kingdom) (Harrison 1997, 27-28). The situation of settlements in the landscape is another aspect related to the infrastructure, i.e. whether they are related to agricultural resources, communication routes (both on land and on water), elevated areas etc. The driving strategy may be entirely pragmatic, but it is also possible that mental perceptions have had an influence. 'Centres' could additionally have been related to liminality (borders, gates, walls) (Harrison 1997, 28) – an aspect that, in practical terms, applies to many trading sites.

Consequently, an appropriate approach must be to look for functions related to (at least) two different types of network. These may overlap in real life, but each has an entirely different basis for its centrality.

Functions and sites of centripetal type

Functions of centripetal type, above the village level, could include rituals, solution of judicial disputes, marriage, exchange of livestock and 'economic specialities' (cf. Wolf 1966, 40) and defence of the region. Such transactions can be presumed to have taken place at locations other than the villages involved, but perhaps not all in the same place and not even at the same site on each occasion. On the other hand, fixed places and times would ease the operation of such a system. These places are likely to have been evenly distributed relative to the villages. Places of assembly, thing sites, 'sectional markets' and shrines are obvious examples (Brink 1996; 1997; Sanmark & Semple 2008; Wolf 1966). The situation can only be analysed against the background of relevant social models for the Late Iron Age. Initially, these functions were unrelated to the presence of an elite, but such a body may subsequently have taken control of one or more of them at some stage. If two opposing systems were in operation – for example a peasant society versus a warrior elite (cf. Holst this volume; Steuer 2007, 890) – it is more likely, though not necessarily certain, that some of the functions were controlled by the latter in areas where they had the upper hand.

Functions and sites of centrifugal type

Functions of centrifugal type could include supra-regional trade and exchange, pilgrimage and supra-regional social networks, through which goods, 'people' (e.g. through marriage) and ideas could be transferred. Network centres tend to define themselves relative to other centres of the same character located elsewhere, rather than to their hinterlands. The nodes of elite networks will be elite residences, whereas the nodes of a trading network are more likely to be gateway sites in liminal zones, probably also including coastal sites.

Luxury goods of types required by the elite to legitimise their social position were probably obtained by way of social networks. However, payments for military service on the Roman borders, the spoils of war, and the exploitation of areas following military aggression, could also have provided the status symbols needed – as could loot gained by piracy.

Trading sites or gateway communities are known from regions to the south of Jutland during the post-Roman period and their networks probably included southern Scandinavia, particularly from the 8th century onwards. For in-depth discussions of trading networks, see Bang (2008), Sindbæk (2005) and also Hodges (1988).

These two main types of function, centripetal and centrifugal, may not cover all – or any – of the functions present at the metal-rich sites. However, the empirical analysis should make it clear whether or not the metal-rich sites contain finds which do not fit the models. However, the degree to which the elite was implicated in these functions in the period under discussion remains to be ascertained.

One aspect not mentioned above relates to non-ferrous craft activities. Craftsmen may of course have been employed by the elite, but at a village level in a peasant society the situation could well have been different. Like the blacksmith, a craftsman working in copper alloys, silver and gold requires special skills. He also needs raw materials which cannot be extracted locally, not even within Jutland, unless his production is based purely on the melting down of old objects. If a farming family had bronze casting as an economic speciality, evidence for this should have been found in excavated villages; as yet this is not the case. Consequently, the possibility exists that there were part- or full-time craftsmen working elsewhere than in the traditional villages, but who were still part of the same closed regional exchange system that could secure their income. On the other hand, studies of Viking Age trading sites indicate that craftsmen travelled with tradesmen, resulting in products and waste from the same craftsman becoming very widely distributed (Ambrosiani 1981; 1982). This means that certain crafts may, at some stage and to some extent, have moved outside the closed regional system.

The Stavnsager complex

Stavnsager, Hørning and Krogsager form the corners of a settlement complex located southeast of Randers (fig. 1). The complex comprises an extensive settlement area at Stavnsager notable in particular for its large numbers of metal-detector finds, as well as other settlement traces such as remains of longhouses and *Grubenhäuser* (Høilund Nielsen & Fiedel 2001; Høilund Nielsen & Loveluck 2006; see also Fiedel this volume). Smaller quantities of metal-detector finds have been identified south of Krogsager and around Hørning. At

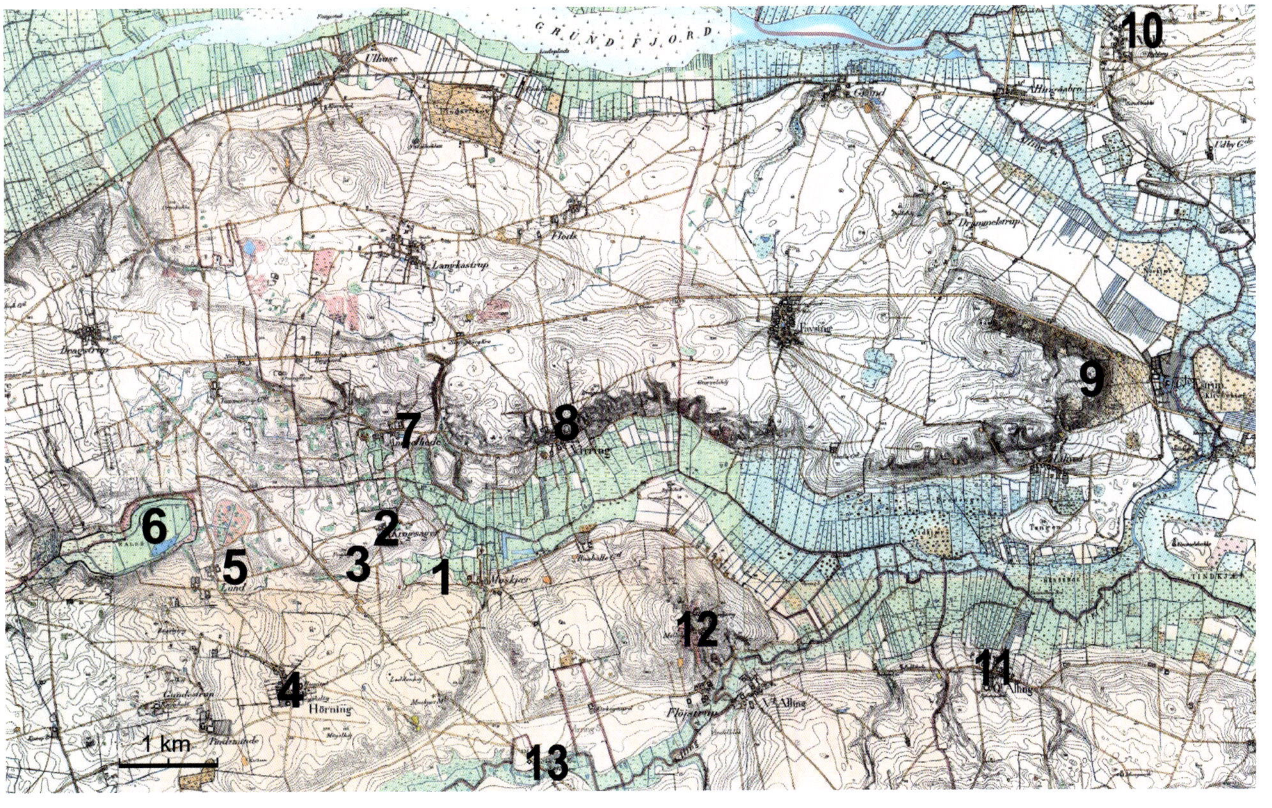

Fig. 1. | *Stavnsager and the surrounding landscape. Topographical map, 1:20 000, from 1883-90. In addition to the blue areas, the adjoining light green areas were most probably also open water in the early days of Stavnsager. 1. Stavnsager; 2. Krogsager; 3. Tinghøj; 4. Hørning; 5. Lund; 6. Hald Sø; 7. Ammelhede; 8. Virring (rune stone); 9. Helligbjerget (promontory); 10. Vejlby (rune stone, lost); 11. Øster Alling (rune stone); 12. Fløjstrup (rich female burial from c. AD 800, see Hedeager Krag 1999); 13. Sjellebro (ford, bridge, picture stone).*

Hørning, a 10th-century cemetery, a slightly later chamber grave with a barrow and an early wooden church built over the remains of the grave were also identified (Jeppesen & Schmidt 1996; Krogh & Voss 1961).

In order to discuss the Stavnsager complex in the light of the research strategy suggested above, the location of the site in the landscape will first be presented, followed by its chronology. Various categories of finds and historical data will then be discussed on basis of this time-space framework.

Landscape and communication

Stavnsager is located today on the floor of a valley landscape (fig. 1), rising significantly to the west with Hørning being situated on an elevated plateau. To the northwest, Krogsager occupies a similar position, and to the northeast, the terrain rises significantly, especially around the village of Virring where the entire neighbourhood can be surveyed from the church. West of Krogsager lies the lake Hald Sø, which has its outlet into the Oksenbæk (Trap 1963). Today, the valley is mostly pastureland, but it has previously been used for peat cutting. A stream – the Oksenbæk – flows from Ammelhede, located between Virring and Krogsager, through the entire valley until it joins the river Alling Å, just before it passes Helligbjerget, a prominent headland east of the inner valley.

Communication routes extending from the head of Randers Fjord down to the Bay of Aarhus are probably very ancient. There has been a ford at the crossing over Alling Å (Sjellebro) south of Hørning and Stavnsager at least since the Roman Iron Age. The first of several bridges was built in AD 752, confirming the importance and antiquity of the route (Dehn-Nielsen 1976, 77-78; Falktoft Andersen 1994, 155). So in terms of land transport, Stavnsager was well situated.

From the appearance of the landscape today, it is not obvious that the Oksenbæk would have been suitable for transport by boat or barge. However, analyses of sea-level change and land upheaval (Binderup 1996; Lidberg et al. 2007) indicate that the water level in the valley was most probably higher in relative terms during the Germanic Iron Age and Viking Age (fig. 2). A dendrochronological date for a track crossing the marshy area just north of Stavnsager does, however, indicate that the innermost part of the valley had silted up by around AD 1100 at the latest (Høilund Nielsen & Fiedel 2001, 78). This means that water transport may well have been possible for most of Stavnsager's lifetime,

Fig. 2. | *Land uplift at Stavnsager means that what was probably once shore is now cultivated land. However, in some winters the area is still so wet that it is possible to imagine what the area may have looked liked from the sea, i.e. from the northeast, 1500 years ago. Photo: Harry Rasmussen.*

but later problems in this respect may be one of several possible reasons for the settlement's decline.

There are no written documents dating from the Late Iron Age, but a much later source may provide some clues with respect to the settlement complex at Stavnsager. Between 1623 and 1625, Ole Worm, the very first Danish antiquarian, collected information of archaeological relevance from Danish clergymen (Jørgensen [ed.] 1974). The quality and character of the reports vary, but comments by the Reverend Jens Hansen Brun with respect to Virring and Essenbæk parishes are very informative. He writes (translated from the Danish of 1623 by John Hines): 'In much the same way it is said that Virring is a Variant of Vigring because there was once a Creek [*vig*] here, which in Olden Days they brought Ships into, because there was a Navigable Way to a Trading-Place which lay upon the Other Side with the name of Lundbye, as a Result of Which still today Anchor-rings and Complete Masts are found during Peat-cutting, although the Area is now but Meadows, Bogs, and Peat Soil.'

If this source can be trusted, it tells us that located opposite the village of Virring was a place by the name Lundbye, which it was possible to reach by boat. Today there is no place of this name here, but to the north of Hørning there is still a hamlet by the name Lund, although this is located some way from the presumed shore of the creek. The possibility remains that Lundbye was the name of a settlement that vanished long before 1623 and therefore does not survive on any extant maps. The archaeological site Stavnsager is located opposite Virring – perhaps it was the precursor of the vanished settlement known as Lundbye.

All in all, there is reason to believe that the Stavnsager settlement was, in its heyday, strategically well situated in the landscape, with access to both land and water transport routes.

Chronological framework

A chronological framework was established on the basis of the frequency of brooches per 25-year period, involving a total of c. 220 examples (fig. 3). There are virtually no finds of brooches pre-dating AD 400 and other artefact groups from earlier periods are just as rare. Although a large Early Roman Iron Age cemetery has been found west of Virring, to date there are no Late Roman Iron Age finds from the area. On the basis of the graph produced from the brooch analysis, combined with other research results from Stavnsager, a four-phase chronological model has been proposed (Fiedel et al. 2011; Høilund Nielsen 2009). In the present context, a fifth phase has been added to cover the Medieval finds dating from the period after 1100; phase 4 has also been subdivided.

The artefactual evidence for various functions

A very large proportion of the metal finds from Stavnsager is comprised of brooches or fragments

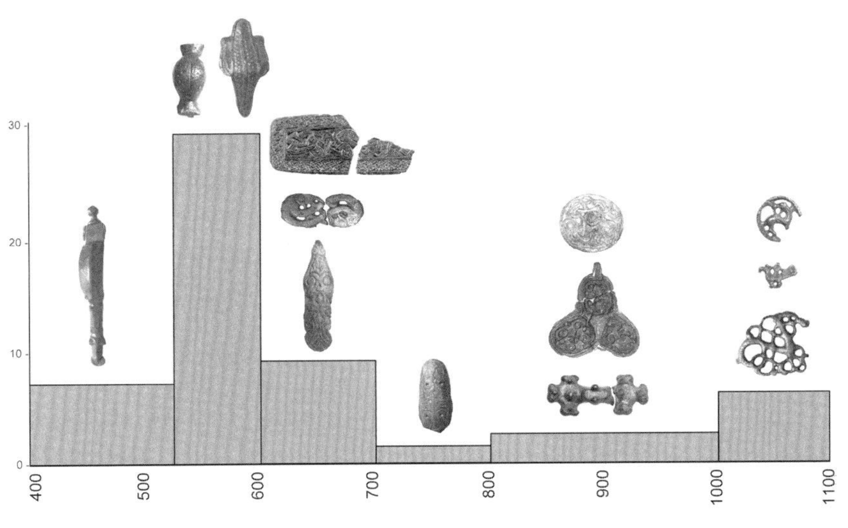

Fig. 3. | *The frequency of brooches (per quarter-century) found at Stavnsager. The most characteristic brooch types are depicted. Not to scale. After Høilund Nielsen 2011.*

of these. The huge quantities of brooches recovered from many metal-rich sites have never really been addressed in any of the models presented in past research. These brooches should, however, be able to contribute to an understanding of the sites as they constitute a significant proportion of the finds. They are often interpreted as the remains of workshop and metal-based craft activities.

It is assumed that the frequency of brooches reflects the extent of female presence as it has been established that the great majority of brooches at Stavnsager were lost accidentally. This is indicated by their general distribution (fig. 4) and their generally low level of damage – both of which are consistent with this conclusion (Høilund Nielsen 2011; Høilund Nielsen & Loveluck 2006, 71-74; cf. also Haldenby & Richards 2010). It is therefore unlikely that the many brooches found at Stavnsager, especially the very large number from phase 2, reflect the presence of craftsmen, or at best only to a minor degree. Unfortunately, male presence cannot be measured in the same way. Late Iron Age graves reveal that, whereas females were buried with their brooches and other dress accessories, males were accompanied by very little, except in the case of weapon burials. Consequently, unless there is evidence to the contrary, it will be assumed that at least as many males as females were present.

With respect to functional artefact groups (fig. 5), weapons are represented at Stavnsager by a number of metal fragments. To date, these are restricted to three phases during the lifetime of the site (fig. 5). Objects bearing religious imagery and symbols have also been recovered, but whereas those belonging to the Christian religion are fairly easily identifiable, the situation is more difficult with respect to pagan imagery. Foreign objects, present in small numbers at Stavnsager, fall into two groups: short-distance imports (objects that are foreign but still belong within the (southern) Scandinavian sphere) and long-distance imports (objects that have their origins outside Scandinavia).

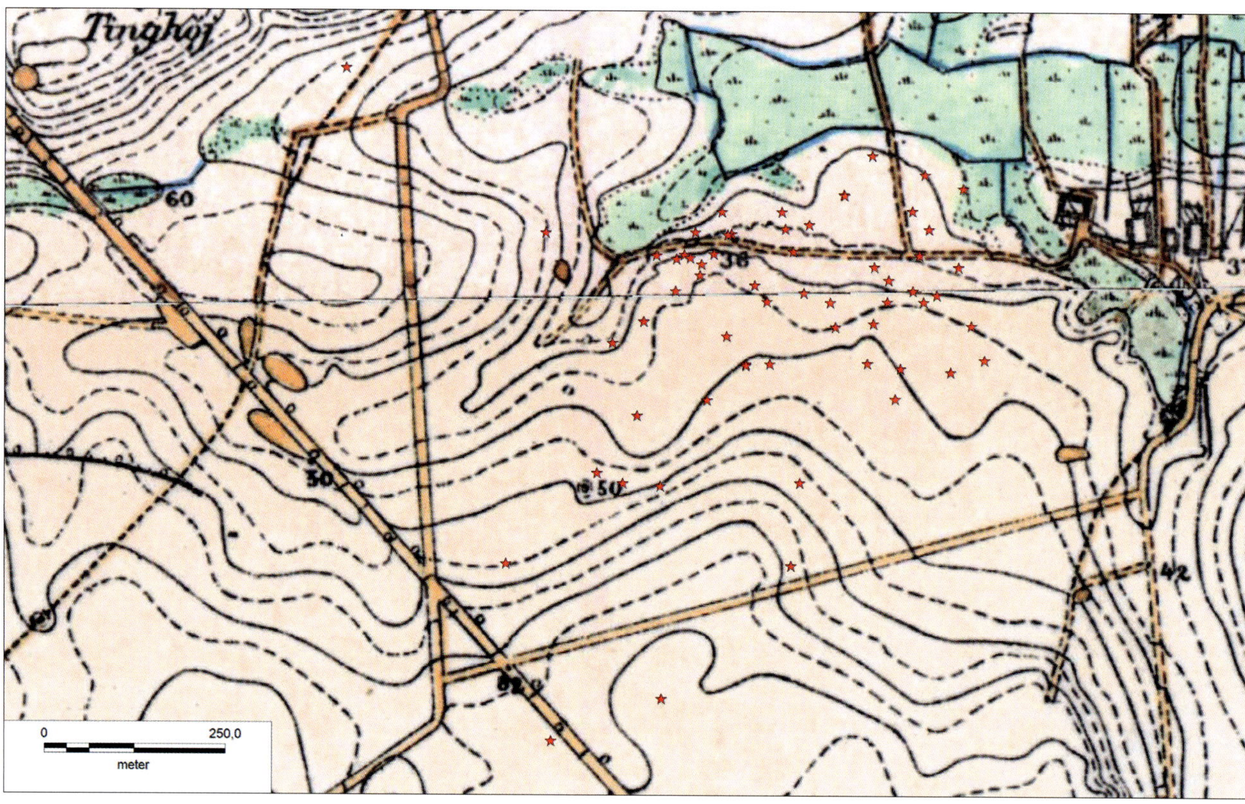

Fig. 4. | *The distribution of small equal-armed brooches (phase 2) at Stavnsager against the background of the topographical map, 1:20 000, from 1883-90. T.G. Poulsen.*

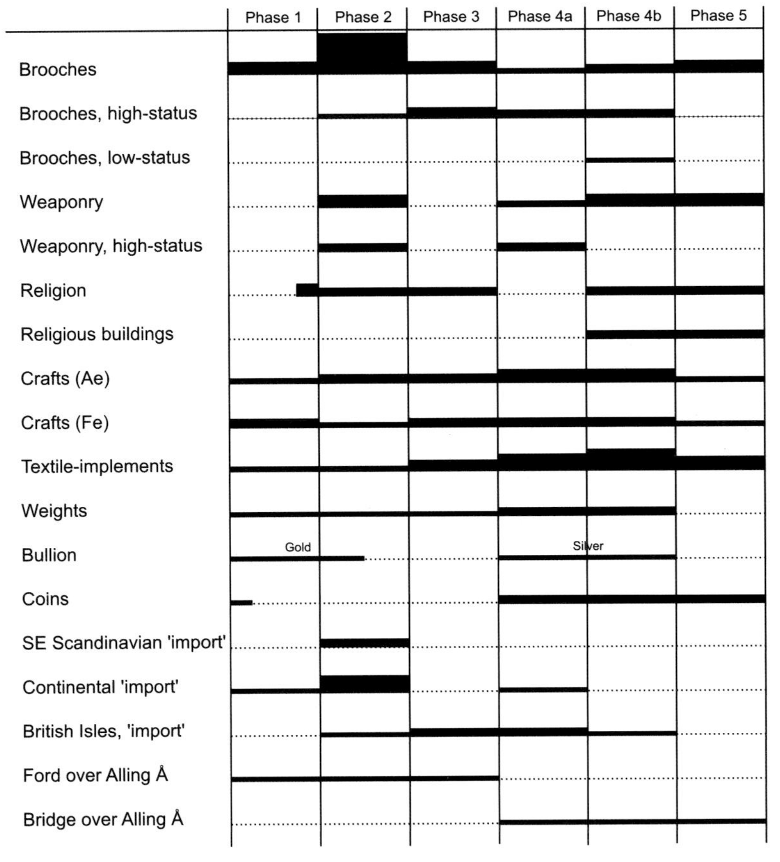

Fig. 5. | *The archaeological evidence for a number of functions identified at Stavnsager arranged by phase. K. Høilund Nielsen.*

As for trade-related artefacts, a number of weights have been found, but as yet no evidence of scales. Weights and scales could also have been used by craftsmen, but several factors suggest they relate more to trade than to crafts. Almost all the copper alloy used in the Late Iron Age was comprised of reused scrap metal (Jouttijärvi 2002, 37). Consequently, it was probably not necessary to weigh out the individual metals for alloys. However, for tradesmen engaged in a *Gewichtgeldwirtschaft* system, scales and weights were an absolute necessity.

Remains derived from metalworking are often hard to date. Iron slag, in particular, has been recovered during the excavations. There are also about 25 bronze-casting spruces and lumps of molten bronze. No (fired clay) moulds for any brooch have yet been located and it is therefore still uncertain whether any of the common, small equal-armed brooches recovered were produced on-site, although it seems very likely that some of them were at least repaired there. On the other hand, a number of other moulds and models suggest that craft activities took place to varying degrees throughout the lifetime of the settlement.

In a couple of cases iron slag has been found close to the marshy area, together with early phase 1 pottery. This indicates that the bog iron present in the area was exploited from the earliest days at Stavnsager. Bog iron was also used as a building material for the nearby Virring Church, dating from the late 11th century, which attests to the presence of the resource in the area (Schultz 1934, 206).

Furthermore, some of the *Grubenhäuser* were back-filled with fire-cracked stones, in some cases accompanied by debris from iron smithing (Fiedel et al. 2011). Large quantities of similar fire-cracked stones were found piled up to form a dike-like structure running along the edge of the marshy area (see Fiedel this volume). The earliest possible date for the *Grubenhäuser*, and the 'stone dike', is phase 2, but most of them are probably later, dating from phases 3 and 4.

Numerous fired clay loom weights and spindle whorls have been found, indicating textile production at the site. Many derive from the excavated

Grubenhäuser (see Fiedel this volume), which very often contain tools for textile production. Half of the *Grubenhäuser* containing loom weights also yielded spindle whorls. Although both loom weights and spindle whorls are likely to have been present at the site during all phases, the number seems to increase with the presence of the *Grubenhäuser*. This means that most date from phase 2 or more probably later.

Biography

The archaeological evidence for the various functions mentioned above is not distributed evenly through phases 1-5; there is significant variation. From the table in figure 5, it is clear that significant changes took place during phases 2, 4a and 4b, and the foundation of the site in phase 1 should perhaps be seen as the first significant change in the area.

Phase 1

Phase 1 is characterised by the presence of iron smelting and the rural settlement identified through excavation (see Fiedel this volume). It may have been the bog iron deposits in the area that attracted settlers in the first place, rather than agriculture. Bog iron could well have been exploited by people from a number of settlements, not just by local inhabitants, and could, therefore, have formed part of a closed regional exchange system (sectional market).

Brooches dating to this phase are of average type and not in any way socially conspicuous. Many take the form of very fragmented cruciform brooches (fig. 6), and it has been suggested that they represent scrap metal intended for the production of new brooches and other objects, probably in early phase 2 (Høilund Nielsen & Loveluck 2006, 72-74). A bow brooch with a casting fault should probably be seen in the same light (fig. 6).

The long-distance imports include five Late Roman coins and a fragment of a possible Continental Late Roman *Bügelknopffibel* (fig. 7). Furthermore, a sword pommel of Bifrons-Gilton type (fig. 8), dated to the first half of the 6th century

Fig. 6. | *The most characteristic brooch type of the Early Germanic Iron Age is the cruciform brooch. At Stavnsager most were found as fragments; for the better preserved items see Fiedel (this volume, fig. 13a). Centre right is of a bow brooch with a casting fault. Scale 1:1.*
Photo: Museum Østjylland.

(Menghin 1983), probably came from southeastern England and belongs either to late in this phase or phase 2. A small quantity of hack gold probably dates from late phase 1 and phase 2.[2]

Phase 2

In phase 2 the picture changes completely. The very large quantity of brooches, relative to earlier and later phases, is intriguing and suggests that a greater number of people passed through the site. Almost all the brooches are of average type, with the great majority being small equal-armed examples (fig. 9a), although there are several beak

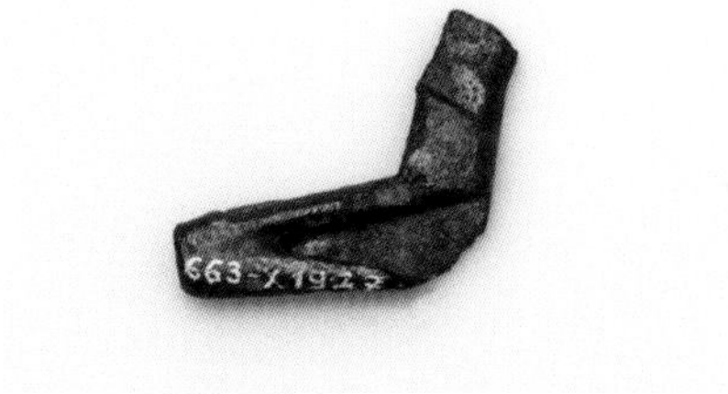

Fig. 7. | *Fragment of a possible Continental Late Roman* Bügelknopffibel. *Scale 1:1. Photo: Museum Østjylland.*

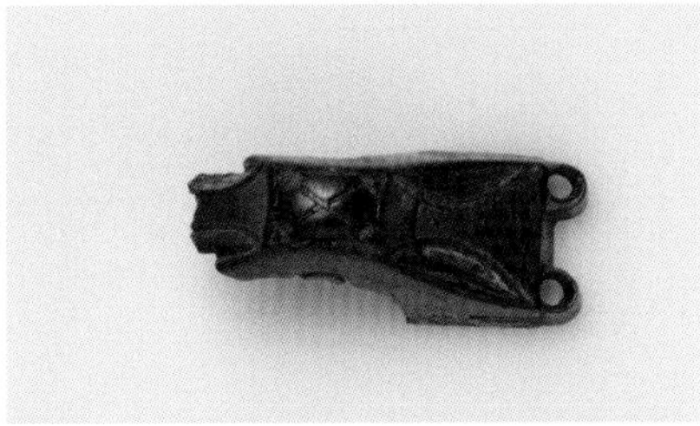

Fig. 8. | *A sword pommel of Bifrons-Gilton type. Scale 1:1. Photo: Museum Østjylland.*

brooches (fig. 9c), as well as some transitional types (fig. 9b). A large longhouse, dating from either late in phase 2 or early in phase 3, indicates that some of the inhabitants at Stavnsager were rising in the social scale.

A number of the tools related to textile production are possibly associated with this phase, but they are difficult to date. The same is true of the waste from copper alloy crafts. However, a number of the brooches from phase 2 show traces of repair to the pin anchor or the pin catch (fig. 10) and, as some of these repairs were not completed, the brooches could be from a craftsman's workshop. Two small equal-armed brooches were found in a secondary burial in an Early Roman Iron Age cemetery west of Virring (fig. 11). Neither has a parallel at Stavnsager. However, they are so similar in shape and style to those found at the site that a relationship seems plausible.

Other finds from phase 2 include several fragments of weapons, including two sword pommels, one of them Anglo-Saxon (although it could be slightly earlier), a small number of mounts and parts of buckles usually associated with sword belts and horse harness. Fragments of a bird mount could possibly derive from a shield (figs. 8 and 12). There is also a fragment of a high-status gold and garnet sword hilt mount (fig. 13) from late in the phase. Parallels are known from places as far apart as Vallstenarum on Gotland (Nerman 1969, fig. 523) and Staffordshire in Britain.[3]

Links with southeastern Scandinavia are clearly expressed via a number of finds. Beak brooches, which were introduced later than the small equal-armed brooches but belong within the same phase, are seen with several different pin constructions (fig. 14). Some resemble the small equal-armed brooches in this respect, others have pin constructions of a type predominantly used in southeastern Scandinavia (Høilund Nielsen & Loveluck 2006, 73) and at least some of them could also have been produced there. A contemporary of the beak brooches is a rare high-status brooch with (now lost) inlays, typologically related to the small equal-armed brooches (fig. 15). It has close parallels in Vallentuna in Uppland and Sävstaholm in Södermanland, and less close ones in Lejre on Zealand and Tác-Fövenypuszta in Hungary (Schilling 2009). A gold foil figure (fig. 17) belonging to this phase (cf. below) is also indisputably of southeast Scandinavian origin and is the only example of this specific type to be found outside Bornholm and Uppåkra (pers. comm. Margrethe Watt; Watt 2004, 173-75). All in all, it can be deduced that there was a significant eastern and southeastern Scandinavian contribution to the area during the later part of phase 2.

The number of objects related to trade is small, but a few short cylinder-shaped weights and a small quantity of hack gold may belong in this phase. Evidence of long-distance imports is also rare although rather widespread: an Anglo-Saxon sword pommel (fig. 8), some knobs from a Soester type large square-headed bow brooch (fig. 16), a Frisian Domburg brooch and what is possibly a Continental imitation of a cross-bow brooch. These are

A

B

C

Fig. 9. | *The most common and significant brooch types from phase 2 at Stavnsager. a. Small equal-armed brooches. b. Examples of transitional forms between small equal-armed and beak types. c. Beak brooches. Scale 1:1. Photo: Museum Østjylland.*

Fig. 10. | *Two brooches with repaired pin catches. Photo: Museum Østjylland.*

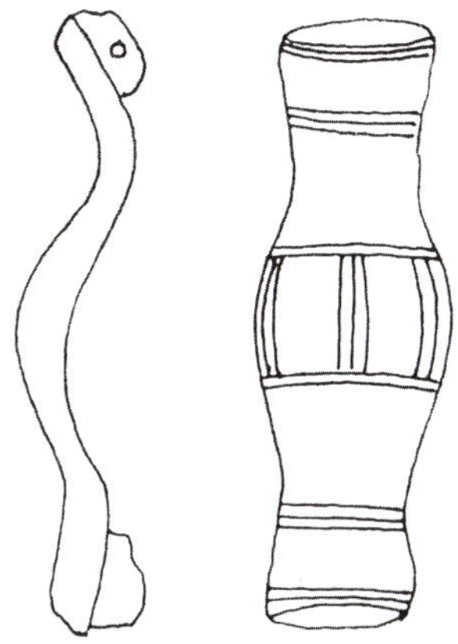

Fig. 11. | *One of two brooches found in a secondary burial in the Early Roman Iron Age cemetery at Virring. Scale 1:1. After M. Ørsnes 1966.*

Fig. 12. | *Fragments of weaponry and mounts. a. Strap end. b. Sword pommel. c. Fragment of a bird-shaped mount, possibly from a shield. d. Fragment of a bridle fitting. e. So-called T-shaped mount. f. Shield-on-tongue buckle. Scale 1:1. Photo: Museum Østjylland.*

Fig. 13. | *A fragment of a high-status gold and garnet mount, probably from a sword. Scale 2:1. Photo: Museum Østjylland.*

all personal accessories and it is unlikely that they were imported in their own right, being too rare and inconspicuous.

Imagery is also rare in this phase, but three peculiar objects do provide some insight. The images on these objects represent a man, a woman and a pig. A gold foil figure depicts a man carrying a steaming beaker in one hand and a staff in the other (fig. 17). The latter may be a staff of office (Watt 2004, 209) and the former may indicate that some kind of ceremony is represented. Based on the finds from Uppåkra and Sorte Muld, this figure

Fig. 14. | *Three different pin-anchor types found at Stavnsager. a. Single pin anchor. b. Double pin anchor. c. Tubular pin anchor. Photo: Museum Østjylland.*

Fig. 15. | *A large gilt brooch. The inlays have been lost, but were probably of semi-precious stone or glass. The brooch probably originated in eastern Scandinavia. Scale 1:1. Photo: Museum Østjylland.*

Fig. 16. | *Two knobs for a large square-headed bow-brooch of Continental type. Scale 1:1. Photo: Museum Østjylland.*

is clearly related to a ritual context (Adamsen et al. 2008; Larsson 2004).

A figure plaque depicts a woman pulling her plaits (fig. 18). She is dressed in a rather ornamental costume and adorned with a long bead necklace. The plaque has no pin construction or loop/eye and may have been used as a model for foil figures, although this interpretation is very hypothetical. This object cannot be securely assigned to phase 2, and could just as well be from phase 3, but phase 2 is the earliest possible date. The reason it was originally assigned to phase 3 is that some of the necklace beads are large and may depict the large crystal beads found in burials from phase 3. However, related motifs found in Continental contexts tend to indicate a 6th century date and thus phase 2, although this is of course inconclusive.

The figure plaque, although locally produced, suggests long-distance contacts. Parallels to the woman's dress and hair are found on ivory diptychs depicting the East Roman empress Ariadne and on a silver phalera from Eschwege/Niederhone, dating from just after AD 600 (Sippel 1987), showing a woman seated between animals. The Eschwege phalera is combined with two man-between-beasts phalerae with close links to other Scandinavian motifs. More distant parallels are seen in a group of bracteates, each depicting a woman en face (Pesch 2007, 128).

Fig. 17. | *A fragment of a gold foil figure,* guldgubbe, *of a type otherwise only found in Uppåkra and on Bornholm. Scale 4:1. Photo: Museum Østjylland.*

Fig. 18. | *A figure plaque depicting a woman pulling her plaits. She is dressed in an ornamental costume and adorned with a long bead necklace. The plaque has no pin construction or loop/eye. Scale 2:1. Photo: Museum Østjylland.*

Fig. 19. | *A small copper alloy pig. The hind part is missing. Scale c. 1.5:1. Photo: Museum Østjylland.*

A small copper alloy pig (fig. 19) possibly belongs in phase 2. At Sorte Muld on Bornholm, where parallels for the gold foil figure mentioned above have been found in great numbers, there were also foil figures of pigs (Watt 1992, 218-19). This suggests that the Stavnsager pig may have belonged to the same ritual world, although it is differently sculpted.

Altogether it seems unlikely that textile production and non-ferrous metal crafts were of any great significance at Stavnsager during phase 2. Trade-related objects are also too few to indicate this activity at the site. However, bog iron may have attracted attention as part of a sectional market, but this is unlikely to have left many traces. Of greater significance, however, is the large number of brooches present. Combined with the site's central position in the communication network, the many brooches could indicate that a place of assembly with either religious or judicial functions was established in the area. A religious aspect is suggested by the presence of the gold foil figure, the pig and the female figure plaque. These should be seen in combination with the place name Lund, and its location just south of the lake Hald Sø, which may indicate a ritual site (cf. Brink 1997, 416, 423, 431). A judicial function is another possibility; the name Tinghøj (Thing Mound), found between the lake Hald Sø and Krogsager, may indicate the existence of a thing site. The earliest known mention of Tinghøj is in 1688 (cf. Estrup 1907, 25). However, at that time the thing was held elsewhere, at a place used since at least 1594 (Estrup 1907, 26). This means that if a thing was ever held at Tinghøj, it was before 1594 – probably considerably before. Interpretations based on place names are of course rather speculative when it comes to dating these functions, but there is reason to believe that centripetal functions were present at Stavnsager during phase 2.

The above interpretations do not explain the significant southeast Scandinavian element seen in the material culture at Stavnsager. It is tempting to see the brooches and the gold foil figure depicting a man who is probably bearing a staff of office, both of eastern origin, together with the weapons, as an indication of the presence or intrusion of an eastern elite including both women, some of high status, and men who were both armed and mounted. Moreover, it is possible that the gold foil figure indicates the presence of foreign religious specialists. As the finds are few in number, perhaps the foreign elite only visited on a single occasion. In those days, kings received oaths of allegiance at the individual thing sites; only one of a number of possible reasons for a foreign elite to be present at a local place of assembly. But this does not mean that thing sites, as such, were controlled by the elite as they seem to have had an autonomous role in relation to the social hierarchy (Brink 1998, 300).

The brooch fragments originating from the Continent, especially Soest and Friesland, together with the motif on the female figure plaque, indicate that families at Stavnsager, or in the near vicinity, were members of a widely-connected network of personal relations extending from Friesland in the west across the Rhine-Lippe area to Thuringia in the east. The brooches possibly suggest marriage relations. The Soester-type brooch, in particular, signifies an elite level. The area around Soest was an important region for the extraction and exploitation of certain metals and salt, and a network based on marriage relations may have facilitated imports of these raw materials. At Stavnsager, centrifugal functions were, accordingly, only represented by personal connections.

Fig. 20. | *Plate brooch in the shape of a horned owl. An animal is depicted within its body. Scale 2:1. Photo: Museum Østjylland.*

Phase 3

In phase 3 the picture again changes significantly. The number of brooches returns to a more normal level, but those present are of a more select quality. Animals, including an owl (fig. 20) and other birds (fig. 21), and Animal Style II characterise brooches and mounts (fig. 22) and seem to reflect a new, perhaps pagan, imagery. No weapon components have

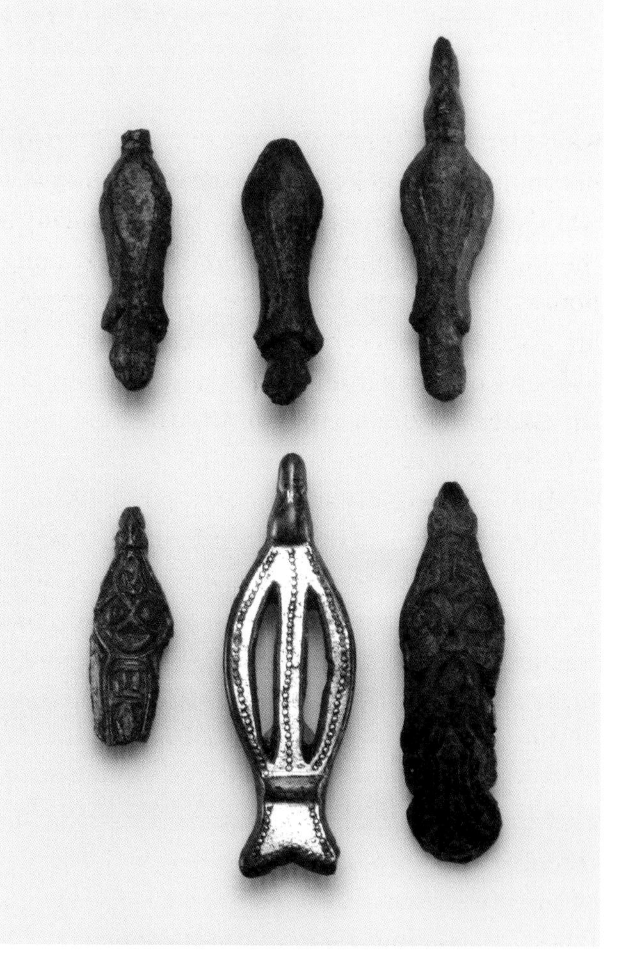

Fig. 21. | *A number of bird brooches. Upper row: possibly a local series. Lower row: three very different examples. Scale 1:1. Photo: Museum Østjylland.*

Fig. 22. | *A selection of mounts and rectangular brooches decorated in Style II. Scale 1:1. Photo: Museum Østjylland.*

Fig. 23. | *A fragment of a penannular brooch, probably from South Wales. Scale 1:1. Photo: Museum Østjylland.*

been identified from this phase to date. Craftwork in copper alloy and iron is represented and spindle whorls and loom weights also occur, especially in the increasing number of *Grubenhäuser*. Longhouses, dating from late phase 2 or early phase 3, are also in evidence, but these are now located at a greater distance from the wetland area, whereas the *Grubenhäuser* become concentrated closer to it (see also Fiedel this volume).

The only long-distance import from this phase is a brooch fragment originating from South Wales (fig. 23). It is unsure whether this reflects personal networks at this time, since typical indications of a trading network are absent, or whether it should be related to the subsequent phase in which a network of this kind appears to have emerged.

Altogether there are only slight indications of centripetal or centrifugal functions. The crafts represented may, of course, be taken as an indication of such functions, but the question is whether, at this stage, the finds represent more than would be expected at any settlement of a local magnate (or chieftain), who would surely have had craftsmen and textile producers in his household.

Judging from the style and quality of the brooches, the social position of the inhabitants seems to have improved. Any assemblies during this phase appear to have taken place elsewhere. Those of the previous period may, however, have served to increase the wealth and social position of the inhabitants. The extent to which this may have been due to a subordinate relationship to a possible foreign elite is, however, unclear.

Phase 4

Phase 4 brings yet another change at the Stavnsager settlement. An innovation is seen in the much clearer indications of trade, meaning that the site developed an identifiable centrifugal function. The bridge over Alling Å at Sjellebro was also built early during this phase. This must have made crossing significantly easier and also provided the opportunity to control traffic. A picture stone decorated with a Mammen-style mask was erected by the bridge in the late 10th century (fig. 24). Silver coins, so-called dirhems, are so far represented at Stavnsager by five whole coins, two halves and three quarters (fig. 25). There is also a small amount of silver bullion and some silver ingots (fig. 26). Recently, a very rare Carolingian silver coin, minted at Chelles between AD 793/94 and AD 813 (fig. 25), has also turned up (Moesgaard 2011). Moreover, about 15 weights, of globular, bipolar or cylindrical type, can also be attributed to this phase (fig. 27).

Traces of crafts, copper alloy and iron are also seen to increase and a number of moulds and models for ornamental rivet heads and a pendant relate to this phase (fig. 28). In terms of textile production, there are increasing numbers of loom weights and spindle whorls. Whether their number corresponds to that necessary for the household of a magnate's farm, or whether there was a surplus production which could either be exchanged for other goods or sold on, is impossible to say from this evidence alone. Another type of spindle whorl, made of lead, was introduced during this phase (fig. 29). These spindle whorls are even more common than those of fired clay, probably because they can be found using a metal detector. None were found in *Grubenhäuser*. There are 24 lead spindle

Fig. 24. | *The picture stone at Sjellebro. The northern side of the stone is decorated with a Mammen-style mask – an ornament characteristic of the Late Viking Age. Photo: R. Fiedel.*

Fig. 25. | *Silver coins from the Viking Age: a Carolingian coin minted at Chelles and some dirhems. Scale 1:1. Photo: R. Fiedel / K. Høilund Nielsen.*

Fig. 26. | *Silver ingots. Scale 1:1. Photo: Museum Østjylland.*

Fig. 27. | *A selection of weights of various types. Scale 1:1. Photo: Museum Østjylland.*

Fig. 28. | *Models and moulds for a pendant (fragment, lead) and ornamental rivet heads (copper alloy). Scale 1:1. Photo: Museum Østjylland.*

Fig. 29. | *Spindle whorls of lead. Scale 1:1. Photo: Museum Østjylland.*

whorls, but some of them are irregular and may have had different origins or functions. The weight and size of those convincingly identified as spindle whorls indicate spinning of a very fine thread (pers. comm. Ida Demant). They probably continue into early phase 5.

The evidence from brooches in the early part of this phase is much the same as that seen in the previous phase, although the brooches include a number of more unusual specimens, some of which display clear links to the new Carolingian style (fig. 30). Towards the end of the phase the picture changes: the group of brooches, especially those of Urnes style, still include some more select items, but these are accompanied by examples that are of very poor quality in every respect, especially in craftsmanship (fig. 31). It is also during the late phase 4 that Christian imagery makes an appearance. On this basis, phase 4 has been divided into sub-phases 4a and 4b.

Pagan imagery is rare in phase 4a, but two miniature swords may be considered as pagan objects (fig. 32). Christian imagery appears in phase 4b in the form of two pendant crosses and a Lamb of God pendant (fig. 33). The Urnes-style brooches and brooches bearing related motifs mentioned above also belong in this group. A small Urnes-style sculpture of a bird, probably a peacock, interlaced with a snake should also be seen in the context of Christian imagery (fig. 31).

The possible presence of armed men is indicated by two Carolingian mounts, one of silver (fig. 34). Such mounts are not unknown in southern Scandinavia, but they remain rare. They confirm an awareness of the Carolingian style that is also seen in brooches and pendants. In phase 4b a number of stirrup and harness mounts (fig. 35) attest to the presence of mounted warriors or at least mounted members of the household of a magnate's farm.

Fig. 30. | *Viking Age brooches and pendants. Scale 1:1. Photo: Museum Østjylland.*

With respect to long-distance imports, some metal fragments from the British Isles (fig. 36) are the only examples aside from the Carolingian mounts. Whereas the presence of the Carolingian mounts probably results from personal relationships, the fragments from the British Isles are more

Fig. 31. | *Urnes style: four brooches of very different quality. Upper left: a small figurine possibly formed of a peacock with an intertwining snake at its wings and tail. Scale 1:1. Photo: Museum Østjylland.*

Fig. 32. | *Miniature swords, one copper alloy, one silver. Scale 2:1. Photo: K. Høilund Nielsen / R. Fiedel.*

likely to be associated with the traces of trade at the site; they could even be the remnants of Viking plunder.

Phase 4b also sees some significant changes. Traces of settlement activities now appear at Hørning, west of Stavnsager. A cemetery was established on the site of the present churchyard. A burial mound for a woman from the elite was constructed at the cemetery, overlying some of the earlier graves. Not long afterwards, a wooden church was built such that the mound's chamber grave came to lie just inside the door of the church (Krogh & Voss 1961). Furthermore, contemporary *Grubenhäuser* have been identified to the northwest of the church (see Fiedel this volume). Given the example of Lisbjerg, further south, it is most likely that the magnate farm or manor to which the church belonged was located in close proximity to the church, rather than down at the Stavnsager settlement (cf. Jeppesen 2005). As yet it is impossible to say precisely when this elite family moved their main habitation to Hørning.

Interestingly, Virring Church, situated only a short distance away from Hørning, is also of very early date. However, it is a stone church, built shortly after the wooden church at Hørning. Significant features include the use of bog iron as a building material and clear Anglo-Saxon traits in the architecture (Schultz 1934), suggesting that some of the masons involved probably came from Britain. Again, this indicates that the elite fam-

Fig. 33. | *Pendant crosses and a Lamb of God pendant. Scale 1:1. Photo: Museum Østjylland.*

Fig. 34. | *A Carolingian silver mount. Scale 2:1. Photo: Museum Østjylland.*

Fig. 35. | *Copper alloy stirrup strap mount and bridle cheek pieces (fragments). Scale 1:1. Photo: Museum Østjylland.*

Fig. 36. | *Gilt copper alloy fragment from the British Isles. Scale 2:1. Photo: Museum Østjylland.*

ily who built this church must have had contacts abroad. Other churches in southern Scandinavia have architectural details of Anglo-Saxon origin, but they are rare and do not cluster in specific areas.

In phase 4, the presence of an elite family at Stavnsager/Hørning becomes increasingly clear and the same can be said of Virring, as demonstrated by its church. However, production and trade also seem to have increased at the site during phase 4, thus matching the description of Lundbye (~Stavnsager) noted by the local clergyman generations later.

Phase 5

The finds from phase 5 have not been analysed in detail. However, the wooden church at Hørning burned down and was replaced in the early 12th century by a Romanesque stone church, indicating that a family of position and wealth was still present in the area. Finds of buckles and mounts for books and belts, coins, a crossbow bolt, a bollock dagger, chapes and fragments of two spurs indicate continuing occupation of the area, although the trade element had disappeared, leaving just a farming community and the church.

A very interesting seal matrix of clerical type, dating from the 14th century and bearing the inscription *SIGILLUM SVENONIS [...]* (fig. 37), possibly belonged to a member of the Order of the Holy Ghost about a century before this order built a hospital in Randers (pers. comm. Michael Andersen; Høilund Nielsen & Fiedel 2001, 82). This seal matrix could suggest that the clerical staff at Hørning Church, or perhaps a local magnate, had connections with this order.

Conclusion

It is clear from this analysis of the biography of Stavnsager that the function of the site varied over time. The first settlers may have been attracted by bog iron deposits in the area which when extracted may have been redistributed via a so-called sectional market.

During phase 2, assemblies of either a religious or judicial character, or both, appear to have taken place in the area and on at least one of these occasions members of a foreign elite and their religious specialists from eastern and southeastern Scandinavia participated – perhaps for political reasons. During this phase at least, Stavnsager has the character of a site with centripetal functions.

Taking a long-term perspective, the inhabitants of Stavnsager appear to have enjoyed increasing socio-economic status, especially from late phase 2 and onwards, when personal connections with Thuringia, the Lippe/Rhine area and Friesland are indicated. This high status is supported by the better than average quality of the brooches and mounts dating from phases 3 and 4. The nature of the relationship between Stavnsager's inhabitants and the foreign elite has yet to be established. Neither has it been determined whether their increased socio-economic status was acquired by virtue of the assemblies. The Carolingian silver coin and mount, the burial beneath the church, the early church itself and so on, all suggest that the leading family belonged to the Jutland elite who were part of the politico-religious changes that occurred between the Viking Age and the Medieval period.

Fig. 37. | *Seal matrix of clerical type dating from the 14th century, bearing the inscription* SIGILLUM SVENONIS [...]. *Scale 2:1. Photo: Museum Østjylland.*

Early in phase 4, Stavnsager appears to join the group of gateway type B sites which became common during the 8th century and which are characterised by the presence of weights and scales as well as silver coins and hack silver. Based on the quantities of finds, Stavnsager was not a trading site on the scale of Dorestad and Ribe. Nevertheless it constituted a node in the trade network and thereby represented centrifugal functions. It is tempting to see the presence of trade at the site as having been promoted by the local magnate, but it could simply have been a consequence of the site's geographical position. However, the building of a bridge across the river Alling Å can only be understood as an investment by the local magnate. It seems likely that the later picture stone placed next to the bridge was most probably raised by the same family. Together with several rune stones in the surrounding parishes, Virring Church reflects the fact that a number of elite families were established in the region.

Future analyses of the Stavnsager complex, and the artefacts recovered from it, may change or enhance the interpretation of developments at the site. This study, however, clearly shows how important it is to maintain a chronological perspective and to keep analyses of centripetal and centrifugal functions separate from considerations of social development at the site. Similarly, in the analysis of centrifugal functions it is important to distinguish objects that may indicate trade from those that may reflect personal contacts.

Bibliography

Adamsen, C., U. Lund Hansen, F.O. Nielsen & M. Watt (eds.) 2008, *Sorte Muld*. Rønne.

Ambrosiani, K. 1981, *Viking age combs, comb making and comb makers in the light of finds from Birka and Ribe*. Stockholm.

Ambrosiani, K. 1982, Vikingatida kammar i öst og väst. Ett diskussionsinlägg. *Fornvännen* 1982, 180-83.

Andersson, H. 1973, Zentralorte, Ortschaften und Städte in Skandinavien – Einige methodische Probleme. In: H. Hinz (ed.), *Kiel Papers '72. Frühe Städte im westlichen Ostseeraum. Symposion des Sonderforschungsbereich 17 "Skandinavien- und Ostseeraumforschung", Christian Albrechts-Universität, Kiel, 8. bis 10. Maj 1972*. Kiel. 23-31.

Aston, M. 1986, Post Roman central places in Somerset. In: E. Grant (ed.), *Central places, archaeology and history*. Sheffield. 49-77.

Austin, D. 1986, Central place theory and the middle ages. In: E. Grant (ed.), *Central places, archaeology and history*. Sheffield. 95-103.

Axboe, M. 1991, Guld og guder i folkevandringstiden. Brakteaterne som kilde til politisk/religiøse forhold. In: C. Fabech & J. Ringtved (eds.), *Samfundsorganisation og regional variation. Norden i romersk jernalder og folkevandringstid. Beretning fra 1. nordiske jernaldersymposium på Sandbjerg slot 11.-15. april 1989*. Højbjerg. 187-202.

Bang, P.F. 2008, *The Roman bazaar. A comparative study of trade and markets in a tributary empire*. Cambridge.

Biddle, M. 1976, Towns. In: D.M. Wilson (ed.), *The archaeology of Anglo-Saxon England*. Cambridge. 99-150.

Binderup, M. 1996, Det fynske landskabs tilblivelse. In: O. Crumlin-Pedersen, E. Porsmose & H. Thrane (eds.), *Atlas over Fyns kyst i jernalder, vikingetid og middelalder*. Odense. 23-32.

Blackburn, M. 2003, Productive sites and the pattern of coin loss in England, 600-1180. In: T. Pestell & K. Ulmschneider (eds.), *Markets in Early Medieval Europe: trading and 'productive' sites, 650-850*. Macclesfield. 20-36.

Bohannan, P.J. & G. Dalton 1962, *Markets in Africa*. Evanston.

Brink, S. 1996, Political and social structures in early Scandinavia: a settlement-historical pre-study of the central place. *Tor* 28, 235-81.

Brink, S. 1997, Political and social structures in early Scandinavia 2. Aspects of space and territoriality – the settlement district. *Tor* 29, 389-437.

Brink, S. 1998, Land, bygd, distrikt och centralort i Sydskandinavien. Några bebyggelsehistoriska nedslag. In: L. Larsson & B. Hårdh (eds.), *Centrala platser – centrala frågor. Samhällsstrukturen under järnålderen: en vänbok till Berta Stjernquist*. Stockholm. 297-326.

Brink, S. 1999, Social order in the early Scandinavian landscape. In: C. Fabech & J. Ringtved (eds.), *Settlement and Landscape. Proceedings of a conference in Aarhus, Denmark, May 4-7 1998*. Højbjerg. 423-39.

Brüggler, M. 2010, Types, meaning and significance of "central places" in the Germanic provinces of the Roman Empire. *Neue Studien zur Sachsenforschung* 1, 14-25.

Bunte, T. & N. Kröger-Köb 2007, Balhorn in Merowinger- und Karolingerzeit. In: C. Grünewald & T. Capelle (eds.), *Innere Strukturen von Siedlungen und Gräberfeldern als Spiegel gesellschaftlicher Wirklichkeit? Akten des 57. Internationalen Sachsensymposions vom 26. bis 30. August 2006 in Münster*. Münster. 19-28.

Childe, V.G. 1950, The urban revolution. *Town Planning Review* 21, 3-17.

Christaller, W. 1933a *Die Zentralen Orte in Süddeutschland. Eine ökonomisch-geographische Untersuchung über die Gesetzmässigkeit der Verbreitung und Entwicklung der Siedlungen mit städtischen Funktionen*. Jena.

Christaller, W. 1933b, Grundsätzliches zu einer Neugliederung des Deutschen Reiches und seiner Verwaltungsbezirke. *Geographische Wochenschrift* I, 913-19.

Christaller, W. 1940, Grundgedanken zum Siedlungs- und Verwaltungsaufbau im Osten. *Neues Bauertum* 32, 305-12.

Christaller, W. 1941, Die zentralen Orte in den Ostgebieten und ihre Kultur und Marktbereiche. *Struktur und Gestaltung der zentralen Orte des deutschen Ostens*. Teil 1. Leipzig. 1-22.

Christiansen, T.T. 2008, Detektorfund og bebyggelse: det østlige Limfjordsområde i yngre jernalder og vikingetid. *Kuml* 2008, 101-43.

Claude, D. (ed.) 1985, *Untersuchungen zu Handel und Verkehr der vor- und frühgeschichtlichen Zeit in Mittel-*

und Nordeuropa, Teil 2: Der Handel im westlichen Mittelmeer während des Frühmittelalter. Göttingen.

Collis, J. 1986, Central place theory is dead: long live the central place. In: E. Grant (ed.), *Central places, archaeology and history.* Sheffield. 37-39.

Crumlin-Pedersen, O. 1992, Maritime aspects of the archaeology of Roman and Migration period Denmark. In: K. Hauck (ed.), *Der historische Horizont der Götterbild-Amulette aus der Übergangsepoke von der Spätantike zum Frühmittelalter.* Göttingen. 385-402.

Dehn-Nielsen, H. 1976, *348 oldtidsminder i Jylland.* København.

Denecke, D. 1973, Der geographische Stadtbegriff und die räumlich-funktionale Betrachtungsweise bei Siedlungstypen mit zentraler Bedeutung in Anwendung auf historische Siedlungsepochen. In: H. Jankuhn, W. Schlesinger & H. Steuer (eds.), *Vor- und Frühformen der europäischen Stadt im Mittelalter.* Göttingen. 33-55.

Drauscke, J. 2010, The search for central places in the Merovingian kingdom. *Neue Studien zur Sachsenforschung* 1, 26-48.

Düwel, K., H. Jankuhn, H. Siems & D. Timpe (eds.) 1985a, *Untersuchungen zu Handel und Verkehr der vor- und frühgeschichtlichen Zeit in Mittel-und Nordeuropa. Teil 1: Methodische Grundlagen und Darstellungen zum Handel in vorgeschichtlicher Zeit und in der Antike.* Göttingen.

Düwel, K., H. Jankuhn, H. Siems & D. Timpe (eds.) 1985b, *Untersuchungen zu Handel und Verkehr der vor- und frühgeschichtlichen Zeit in Mittel-und Nordeuropa. Teil 3: Der Handel des frühen Mittelalters.* Göttingen.

Düwel, K., H. Jankuhn, H. Siems & D. Timpe (eds.) 1987, *Untersuchungen zu Handel und Verkehr der vor- und frühgeschichtlichen Zeit in Mittel-und Nordeuropa. Teil 4. Der Handel der Karolinger- und Wikingerzeit.* Göttingen.

Eggenstein, G., N. Börste, H. Zöller & E. Zahn-Biemüller (eds.) 2008, *Eine Welt in Bewegung: Unterwegs zu Zentren des frühen Mittelalters.* (Katalog zur Ausstellung). München.

Ennen, E. 1953, *Frühgeschichte der europäischen Stadt.* Bonn.

Ennen, E. 1965, Die Stadt zwischen Mittelalter und Gegenwart. *Rheinische Vierteljahrsblätter* 30, 118-31.

Ennen, E. 1972, *Die europäische Stadt des Mittelalters.* Göttingen.

Ennen, E. 1979, *The medieval town.* Amsterdam/New York.

Estrup, J. 1907, Sønder Haldherreds Thingsteder. *Fra Randers Amt* 1907, 17-68.

Fabech, C. 1994, Reading society from the cultural landscape. South Scandinavia between sacral and political power. In: P.O. Nielsen, K. Randsborg & H. Thrane (eds.), *The Archaeology of Gudme and Lundeborg. Papers presented at a Conference at Svendborg, October 1991.* Copenhagen. 169-83.

Fabech, C. 1997, *Slöinge i perspektiv.* In: J. Callmer & E. Rosengren (eds.), *"... Gick Grendel att söka det höga huset ..." Arkeologiska källor til aristokratiska miljöer i Skandinavien under yngre järnålder. Rapport från ett seminarium i Falkenberg 16-17 november 1995.* Halmstad. 145-60.

Fabech, C. 1999a, Centrality in sites and landscapes. In: C. Fabech & J. Ringtved (eds.), *Settlement and landscape. Proceedings of a conference in Aarhus, Denmark, May 4-7 1998.* Højbjerg. 455-73.

Fabech, C. 1999b, *Organising the landscape: a matter of production, power and religion. Anglo-Saxon studies in archaeology and history* 10, 37-47.

Fabech, C., S. Hvass, U. Näsman & J. Ringtved 1999, 'Settlement and Landscape' – a presentation of a research programme and a conference. In: C. Fabech & J. Ringtved (eds.), *Settlement and landscape. Proceedings of a conference in Aarhus, Denmark, May 4-7 1998.* Højbjerg. 13-28.

Fabech, C. & J. Ringtved (eds.) 1991, *Samfundsorganisation og regional variation. Norden i romersk jernalder og folkevandringstid. Beretning fra 1. nordiske jernaldersymposium på Sandbjerg slot 11.-15. april 1989.* Højbjerg.

Fabech, C. & J. Ringtved 1995, Magtens geografi i Sydskandinavien. Om kulturlandskab, produktion og bebyggelsesmønster. In: H.G. Resi (ed.), *Produksjon og samfunn: om erverv, spesialisering og bosetning i Norden i 1. årtusen e. Kr.: Beretning fra 2. nordiske jernaldersymposium på Granavolden Gjæstgiveri 7.-10. mai 1992.* Oslo. 11-37.

Falktoft Andersen, I. 1994, *Vejviser til Danmarks oldtid.* København.

Fiedel, R., K. Høilund Nielsen & C.P. Loveluck 2011, From hamlet, to central place, to manor. Social transformation of the settlement at Stavnsager, eastern Jutland, and its networks, AD 400-1100. *Neue Studien zur Sachsenforschung* 3, 161-76.

Fonnesbech-Sandberg, E. 1991, Guldets funktion i ældre germansk jernalder. In: C. Fabech & J. Ringtved (eds.), *Samfundsorganisation og regional variation. Norden i romersk jernalder og folkevandringstid. Beretning fra 1. nordiske jernaldersymposium på Sandbjerg slot 11.-15. april 1989*. Højbjerg. 233-44.

Grant, E. 1986, Archaeology and the concept of central places. In: E. Grant (ed.), *Central places, archaeology and history*. Sheffield. 1.

Grant, E. (ed.) 1986, *Central places, archaeology and history*. Sheffield.

Grimm, O. 2004, Spangereid – Gudme/Lundeborg – Runder Berg. Zentralplätze der Spätkaiser- und Völkerwanderungszeit im überregionalen Vergleich. *Ethnographisch-Archäologische Zeitschrift* 45, 539-71.

Grimm, O. 2006, *Grossbootshaus – Zentrum und Herrschaft: Zentralplatzforschung in der nordeuropäischen Archäologie (1. – 15. Jahrhundert)*. Berlin.

Gringmuth-Dallmer, E. 1993, Frühe Zentren im südlichen Ostseegebiet zwischen Elbe und Oder. In: *Lokalne osrodki wladzy panstwowej w XI-XII wieku w Europie Srodkowo-Wschodnij*. Wrocław. 77-89.

Gringmuth-Dallmer, E. 1999, Methodische Überlegungen zur Erforschung zentraler Orte in ur- und frühgeschichtlicher Zeit. In: S. Moździocha (ed.), *Centrum i zaplecze we wczesnośredniowiecznej Europie Środkowej*. (Spotkania Bytomskie 3). Wrocław. 9-20.

Haggett, P. 1965, *Locational analysis in human geography*. London.

Haggett, P. 2001, *Geography. A global synthesis*. Harlow.

Haldenby, D. & J.D. Richards 2010, Charting the effects of plough damage using metal-detected assemblages. *Antiquity* 84, 1151-1162.

Harrison, D. 1997, Centralorter i historisk forskning om tidig medeltid. In: J. Callmer & E. Rosengren (eds.), *"... Gick Grendel att söka det höga huset ..." Arkeologiska källor til aristokratiska miljöer i Skandinavien under yngre järnålder. Rapport från ett seminarium i Falkenberg 16-17 november 1995*. Halmstad. 25-29.

Hauck, K. 1987, Gudme in der Sicht der Brakteaten-Forschung (Zur Ikonologie der Goldbrakteaten XXXVI). *Frühmittelalterliche Studien* 21, 147-81.

Hedeager, L. 2001, Asgard reconstructed? Gudme – a 'central place' in the North. In: M. de Jong & F. Theuws (eds.), *Topographies of power in the Early Middle Ages*. Leiden. 467-507.

Hedeager, L. 2002, Scandinavian 'central places' in a cosmological setting. In: B. Hårdh & L. Larsson (eds.), *Central places in the Migration and Merovingian periods: papers from the 52nd Sachsensymposium, Lund, August 2001*. Stockholm. 3-18.

Hedeager Krag, A. 1999, Silkevejen. *Skalk* 1999:6, 28-31.

Helgesson, B. 1998, Vad är centralt? – fenomen och funktion; lokalisering och person. In: L. Larsson & B. Hårdh (eds.), *Centrala platser – centrala frågor. Samhällsstrukturen under järnålderen: en vänbok till Berta Stjernquist*. Stockholm. 39-45.

Helgesson, B. 2002a, *Järnålderns Skåne: samhälle, centra och regioner*. Stockholm.

Helgesson, B. 2002b, Uppåkra in the 5th to 7th centuries: the transformation of a central place and its hinterland. In: B. Hårdh & L. Larsson (eds.), *Central places in the Migration and Merovingian periods: papers from the 52nd Sachsensymposium, Lund, August 2001*. Stockholm. 31-40.

Henriksen, M.B. & K.K. Michaelsen (eds.) 1995, *Gudme-Lundeborg – metodisk set. Rapport fra et symposium på Hollufgård den 28/2 1995*. Odense.

Hirth, K.G. 1978, Inter-regional trade and the formation of prehistoric gate-way communities. *American Antiquity* 43, 25-45.

Hodder, I. & C. Orton 1976, *Spatial analysis in archaeology*. Cambridge.

Hodges, R. 1982, *Dark Age economics. The origins of towns and trade AD 600-1000*. London.

Hodges, R. 1988, *Primitive and peasant markets*. Oxford.

Høilund Nielsen, K. 2009, Stavnsager 400-1100: Weiler, Zentralort, Herrenhof. In: S. Brather, D. Geuenich, & S. Huth (eds.), *Historia archaeologica: Festschrift für Heiko Steuer zum 70. Geburtstag*. Berlin. 415-33.

Høilund Nielsen, K. 2011, Stavnsager and the 'toffee-brooch' network – aspects of the metal-rich settlements of sixth-century southern Scandinavia. *Siedlungs- und Küstenforschung im südlichen Nordseegebiet*, 34. 307-20.

Høilund Nielsen, K. & R.A. Fiedel 2001, Stavnsager – spredte glimt af et jernaldersamfund gennem mere end 700 år – fra 400 til 1100 e. Kr.f. *Kulturhistorisk Museum Randers Årbog* 2001, 71-89.

Høilund Nielsen, K. & C.P. Loveluck 2006, Fortid og fremtid på Stavnsager – om de britiske undersøgelser august 2005 og de foreløbige resultater. *Kulturhistorisk Museum Randers Årbog* 2006, 63-79.

Hooke, D. 1986, Territorial organisation in the Anglo-Saxon West Midlands: central places, central areas. In: E. Grant (ed.), *Central places, archaeology and history*. Sheffield. 79-94.

Hyenstrand, Å. 1974, *Centralbygd-randbygd. Strukturella, ekonomiska och administrativa huvudlinjer i mellansvensk yngre järnålder*. Stockholm.

Jankuhn, H. & E. Ebel (eds.) 1989, *Untersuchungen zu Handel und Verkehr der vor- und frühgeschichtlichen Zeit in Mittel- und Nordeuropa, Teil 6: Organisationsformenn der Kaufmannsvereinigungen in der Spätantike und im frühen Mittelalter*. Göttingen.

Jankuhn, H., W. Kimmig, & E. Ebel (eds.) 1989, *Untersuchungen zu Handel und Verkehr der vor- und frühgeschichtlichen Zeit in Mittel- und Nordeuropa, Teil 5: Der Verkehr, Verkehrswege, Verkehrsmittel, Organisation*. Göttingen.

Jankuhn, H., W. Schlesinger & H. Steuer (eds.) 1975, *Vor- und Frühformen der europäischen Stadt im Mittelalter. Bericht über ein Symposium in Reinhausen bei Göttingen in der Zeit vom 18. bis 24, April 1972*. Vols. 1-2. Göttingen.

Jensen, J. 1979, *Oldtidens samfund: tiden indtil år 800*. (Dansk socialhistorie, 1). København.

Jensen, S. 1980, To sydvestjyske bopladser fra ældre germansk jernalder: jernalderbebyggelsen i Ribeområdet. *Mark og Montre* 16, 23-36.

Jeppesen, J. 2005, Stormandsgården ved Lisbjerg kirke: nye undersøgelser. *Kuml* 2004, 161-80.

Jeppesen, J. & H. Schmidt 1996, Rekonstruktion af stavkirken fra Hørning. *Kuml* 1993-94, 263-76.

Jöns, H. 2010, The Elbe-Weser region in northern Germany (the regions of Sievern and Stade in the first millennium AD). *Neue Studien zur Sachsenforschung* 1, 69-89.

Jørgensen, F. (ed.) 1974, Præsteindberetninger til Ole Worm, Vol. 2. København.

Jørgensen, L. 1995, The warrior aristocracy of Gudme: the emergence of landed aristocracy in Late Iron Age Denmark? In: H.G. Resi (ed.), *Produksjon og samfunn. Beretning fra 2. nordiske jernaldersymposium på Granavolden Gjæstgiveri 7.-10. mai 1992*. Oslo. 205-25.

Jørgensen, L. 1998, Fra nutidens pløjelag til jernalderens samfund – stormænd og håndværkere i Gudme. *Årbog for Svendborg & omegns Museum* 1998, 8-21.

Jørgensen, L. 2001, From tribute to the estate system, 3rd-12th century. A proposal for the economic development of the magnates' residences in Scandinavia based on settlement structure from Gudme, Tissø and Lejre. In: B. Arrhenius (ed.), *Kingdoms and regionality. Transactions from 49th Sachsensymposium 1998 in Uppsala*. Stockholm. 73-82.

Jørgensen, L. 2002, Kongsgård – kultsted – marked. Overvejelser omkring Tissøkompleksets struktur og funktion. In: K. Jennbert, A. Andrén, & C. Raudvere (eds.), *Plats och praxis: Studier av nordisk förkristen ritual*. Lund. 215-47.

Jørgensen, L. 2010, Gudme and Tissø. Two magnates' complexes in Denmark from the 3rd to the 11th century AD. *Neue Studien zur Sachsenforschung* 1, 273-86.

Jouttijärvi, A. 2002, Kobberlegeringer i jernalder og vikingetid. In: M.B. Henriksen (ed.), *Metalhåndværk og håndværkspladser fra yngre germansk jernalder, vikingetid og tidlig middelalder*. Odense. 27-40.

Köhler, U. 1985, Formen des Handels in ethnologischer Sicht. In: K. Düwel, H. Jankuhn, H. Siems & D. Timpe (eds.) 1985, *Untersuchungen zu Handel und Verkehr der vor- und frühgeschichtlichen Zeit in Mittel-und Nordeuropa. Teil 1: Methodische Grundlagen und Darstellungen zum Handel in vorgeschichtlicher Zeit und in der Antike*. Göttingen. 13-55.

Kousgård Sørensen, J. 1985, Gudhem. *Frühmittelalterliche Studien* 19, 13-38.

Krogh, K.J. & O. Voss 1961, Fra hedenskab til kristendom i Hørning: en vikingetids kammergrav og en trækirke fra 1000-tallet under Hørning kirke. *Nationalmuseets Arbejdsmark* 1961, 5-34.

Kunow, J. 1988, Zentrale Orte in der Germania inferior. *Archäologisches Korrespondenzblatt* 18, 55-67.

Kunow, J. 1989, Strukturen im Raum: Geographische Gesetzmäßigkeiten und archäologische Befunde aus Niedergermanien. *Archäologisches Korrespondenzblatt* 19, 377-90.

Kunow, J. 1992, Zentralität und Urbanität in der Germania inferior des 2. Jahrhunderts. In: H.v. Hesberg, H.J. Schalles, & P. Zanker (eds.), *Die römische Stadt im 2. Jahrhundert n. Chr.* Köln. 143-52.

Larsson, L. (ed.) 2004, *Continuity for centuries. A ceremonial building and its context at Uppåkra, southern Sweden*. Stockholm.

Lidberg, M., J.M. Johansson, H.-G. Scherneck, & J.L. Davis 2007, An improved and extended GPS-derived 3D velocity field of the glacial isostatic adjustment (GIA) in Fennoscandia. *Journal of Geodesy* 81:3, 213-30.

Ludowici, B. 2010, Overland routes as markers for central places: the Hellweg between Rhine and Elbe. *Neue Studien zur Sachsenforschung* 1, 335-40.

Lundström, A. (ed.) 1988, *Thirteen studies on Helgö*. Stockholm.

Menghin, W. 1983, *Das Schwert im frühen Mittelalter*. Stuttgart.

Mitterauer, M. 1971, Das Problem der zentralen Orte als sozial- und wirtschaftshistorische Forschungsaufgabe. *Vierteljahrschrift für Sozial- und Wirtschaftsgeschichte* 58, 433-67.

Moesgaard, J.C. 2011, Årets danefæ – sjælden karolingermønt fra klostret Chelles fundet i Stavnsager. *Årbog Museum Østjylland* 2011, 24-27.

Mortensen, P. & B.M. Rasmussen (eds.) 1988, *Fra stamme til stat i Danmark, 1: Jernalderens stammesamfund*. Højbjerg.

Mortensen, P. & B.M. Rasmussen (eds.) 1991, *Fra stamme til stat i Danmark, 2: Høvdingesamfund og kongemagt*. Højbjerg.

Müller-Wille, M. 2010, Comments on: Centrality and places. The central place Skiringssal in Vestfold, Norway (D. Skre). *Neue Studien zur Sachsenforschung* 1, 232.

Näsman, U. 1991a, Det syvende århundrede – et mørkt tidsrum i ny belysning. In: P. Mortensen & B.M. Rasmussen (eds.), *Fra stamme til stat i Danmark, 2: Høvdingesamfund og kongemagt*. Højbjerg. 165-78.

Näsman, U. 1991b, Nogle bemærkninger om det nordiske symposium "Samfundsorganisation og regional variation" på Sandbjerg Slot den 11.-15. april 1989. In: C. Fabech & J. Ringtved (eds.), *Samfundsorganisation og regional variation. Norden i romersk jernalder og folkevandringstid. Beretning fra 1. nordiske jernaldersymposium på Sandbjerg slot 11.-15. april 1989*. Højbjerg. 321-33.

Näsman, U. 1998a, Sydskandinavisk samhällsstruktur i ljuset av merovingisk och anglosaxisk analogi eller i vad är det som centralplatserna är centrala? In: L. Larsson & B. Hårdh (eds.), *Centrala platser – centrala frågor. Samhällsstrukturen under järnåldern: en vänbok till Berta Stjernquist*. Stockholm. 1-26.

Näsman, U. 1998b, The Justiniac era of south Scandinavia: an archaeological view. In: R. Hodges & W. Bowden (eds.), *The sixth century. Produktion, distribution, demand*. Leiden. 255-78.

Näsman, U. 2000, Power and landscape in Viking Age Denmark. In: E. Roesdahl & P. Meulengracht Sørensen (eds.), *Beretning fra nittende tværfaglige vikingesymposium*. Højbjerg. 40-56.

Nerman, B. 1969, *Die Vendelzeit Gotlands*. Stockholm.

Nicklasson, P. 2002, Central places in a peripheral area or peripheral places in a central area: a discussion of centrality in Halland, western Sweden. In: B. Hårdh & L. Larsson (eds.), *Central places in the Migration and Merovingian periods: papers from the 52nd Sachsensymposium, Lund, August 2001*. Stockholm. 111-23.

Nielsen, I. 1985, *Middelalderbyen Ribe*. Viby J.

Nielsen, P.O., K. Randsborg & H. Thrane (eds.) 1994, *The archaeology of Gudme and Lundeborg. Papers presented at a conference at Svendborg, October 1991*. København.

Ørsnes, M. 1966, *Form og stil i Sydskandinaviens yngre germanske jernalder*. København.

Pesch, A. 2007, *Die Goldbrakteaten der Völkerwanderungszeit – Thema und Variation. Die Formularfamilien der Bilddarstellungen*. Berlin/New York.

Pestell, T. & K. Ulmschneider (eds.) 2003, *Markets in Early Medieval Europe: trading and productive sites, 650-850*. Macclesfield.

Polanyi, K. 1957, The economy as instituted process. In: K. Polanyi, C.M. Arensberg & H.W. Pearson (eds.), *Trade and market in the early empires: economies in history and theory*. Glencoe. 243-70.

Preston, R.E. 2009, *Walter Christaller's research on regional and rural development planning during World War II*. (Metar 52). Berlin.

Sanmark, A. & S. Semple 2008, Places of assembly: new discoveries in Sweden and England. *Fornvännen* 2008, 245-59.

Schenk, W. 2010, "Central places" as a point of discussion from German geography in (pre)historical research. *Neue Studien zur Sachsenforschung* 1, 11-13.

Scheschkewitz, J. 2010, Water transport – specialized landing-places in the coastal areas of northwestern Germany in the first millennium AD. *Neue Studien zur Sachsenforschung* 1, 289-308.

Schilling, L. 2009, An Avar-period Germanic brooch from Tác-Fövenypuszta. In: D. Quast (ed.), *Foreigners in Early Medieval Europe: thirteen international studies on early medieval mobility*. Mainz. 261-271.

Schultz, C.G. 1934, Nogle tidligromanske landsbykirker, deres alder og forudsætninger. *Aarbøger for Nordisk Oldkyndighed og Historie* 1934, 195-236.

Sindbæk, S.M. 2005, *Ruter og rutinisering. Vikingetidens fjernhandel i Nordeuropa*. København.

Sippel, K. 1987, Ein merowingisches Kammergrab mit Pferdegeschirr aus Eschwege, Werra-Meissner-Kreis (Hessen). *Germania* 65, 135-58.

Skou Hansen, A. 2003, Centralpladser i romersk jernalder. *Kuml* 2003, 179-211.

Skre, D. 2010, Comments on: Gudme and Tissø. Two magnates' complexes in Denmark from the 3rd to the 11th century AD (L. Jørgensen). *Neue Studien zur Sachsenforschung* 1, 287-88.

Smith, C.A. 1976, Exchange systems and the spatial distribution of elites: the organisation of stratification in agrarian societies. In: C.A. Smith (ed.), *Regional Analysis*, 2. London. 309-74.

Steuer, H. 2007, Zentralorte. Archäologisch. In: *Reallexikon der germanischen Altertumskunde* 35. Founded by Johannes Hoops. 2nd ed. Berlin/New York. 878-914.

Thomsen, P.O., B. Blæsild, N. Hardt, & K.K. Michaelsen (eds.) 1993, *Lundeborg – en handelsplads fra jernalderen*. Svendborg.

Thrane, H. (ed.) 1985, *Gudme problemer. Beretning fra et bebyggelsesarkæologisk symposium på Hollufgård afholdt den 24.-25. oktober 1984*. Odense.

Thrane, H. 1987, Das Gudme-Problem und die Gudme-Untersuchung. Fragen der Besiedlung in der Völkerwanderungs- und der Merowingerzeit auf Fünen. *Frühmittelalterliche Studien* 21, 1-48.

Thrane, H. (ed.) 1990, *Gudme-rapport. Beretning fra det 3. Gudme-symposium, Hollufgård den 2. juni 1989*. Odense.

Thrane, H. 1991a, Gudmeundersøgelserne. In: P. Mortensen & B.M. Rasmussen (eds.), *Fra stamme til stat i Danmark, 2: Høvdingesamfund og kongemagt*. Højbjerg. 67-72.

Thrane, H. 1991b, Om Gudmes funktion. En tolkningsskitse. In: C. Fabech & J. Ringtved (eds.), *Samfundsorganisation og regional variation. Norden i romersk jernalder og folkevandringstid. Beretning fra 1. nordiske jernaldersymposium på Sandbjerg slot 11.-15. april 1989*. Højbjerg. 259-66.

Thrane, H. 1992, Das Reichtumszentrum Gudme in der Völkerwanderungszeit Fünens. In: K. Hauck (ed.), *Der historische Horizont der Götterbild-Amulette aus der Übergangsepoche von der Spätantike zum Frühmittelalter: Bericht über das Colloquium vom 28.11.-1.12. 1988 in der Werner-Reimers-Stiftung, Bad Homburg*. Göttingen. 299-380.

Trap. J.P. 1963, *Danmark. 7:2. Randers Amt*. 5th edition. København.

Udolph, J. 2010, The evidence of central places in place names. *Neue Studien zur Sachsenforschung* 1, 49-68.

Ulmschneider, K. 2002, Central places and metal-detector finds: what are the English 'productive sites'? In: B. Hårdh & L. Larsson (eds.), *Central places in the Migration and Merovingian periods. Papers from the 52nd Sachsensymposium, Lund, August 2001*. Stockholm. 333-40.

Ulmschneider, K. & T. Pestell 2003, Introduction: the study of Early Medieval markets. In: T. Pestell & K. Ulmschneider (eds.), *Markets in Early Medieval Europe: trading and productive sites, 650-850*. Macclesfield. 1-10.

Ulriksen, J. 1990, Teorier og virkelighed i forbindelse med lokalisering af anløbspladser fra germanertid og vikingetid i Danmark. *Aarbøger for Nordisk Oldkyndighed og Historie* 1990, 69-101.

Ulriksen, J. 1998, *Anløbspladser: besejling og bebyggelse i Danmark mellem 200 og 1100 e. Kr.: en studie af søfartens pladser på baggrund af undersøgelser i Roskilde Fjord*. Roskilde.

Vang Petersen, P. (ed.) 1989, *Skattefund og bebyggelse i Gudme-området på Fyn. Beretning fra det 2. Gudme-symposium, København den 6. marts 1987*. Odense.

Vang Petersen, P. 1991, Nye fund af metalsager fra yngre germansk jernalder. Detektorfund og danefæ fra perioden 1966-88. In: P. Mortensen & B.M. Rasmussen (eds.), *Fra stamme til stat i Danmark, 2: Høvdingesamfund og kongemagt*. Højbjerg. 49-66.

Wagstaff, M. 1986, What Christaller really said about central places. In: E. Grant (ed.), *Central places, archaeology and history*. Sheffield. 119-22.

Watt, M. 1991, Sorte Muld. Høvdingesæde og kultcentrum fra Bornholms yngre jernalder. In: P. Mortensen & B.M. Rasmussen (eds.), *Fra stamme til stat i Danmark, 2: Høvdingesamfund og kongemagt*. Højbjerg. 89-107.

Watt, M. 1992, Die Goldblechfiguren ("guldgubber") aus Sorte Muld, Bornholm. In: K. Hauck (ed.), *Der historische Horizont der Götterbild-Amulette aus der Übergangsepoche von der Spätantike zum Frühmittelalter: Bericht über das Colloquium vom 28.11.-1.12. 1988 in der Werner-Reimers-Stiftung, Bad Homburg*. Göttingen. 195-227.

Watt, M. 2004, The gold-figure foils ("Guldgubbar") from Uppåkra. In: L. Larsson (ed.), *Continuity for Centuries. A ceremonial building and its context at Uppåkra, southern Sweden*. Stockholm. 167-221.

Widgren, M. 1998, Kulturgeografernas bönder och arkeologernas guld – finns det någon väg till en syntes? The peasants of the human geographers and the gold of the archaeologists – is there a way to a synthesis? In: B. Hårdh & L. Larsson (eds.), *Central places in the Migration and Merovingian periods: papers from the 52nd Sachsensymposium, Lund, August 2001*. Stockholm. 281-96.

Wilson, D. 1985, Trade between England and Scandinavia and the Continent. In: K. Düwel, H. Jankuhn, H. Siems & D. Timpe (eds.), *Untersuchungen zu Handel und Verkehr der vor- und frühgeschichtlichen Zeit in Mittel- und Nordeuropa. Teil 3: Der Handel des frühen Mittelalters*. Göttingen. 255-69.

Wolf, E.R. 1966, *Peasants*. Englewood Cliffs.

Notes

1 The analysis formed part of my research project, 'From Stavnsager to Constantinople. The adaptation of southern Scandinavia to a changing world, AD 450-600', funded by The Danish Research Council for the Humanities and based at the Institute of History and Civilisation at the University of Southern Denmark.

2 After this chapter was written, four gold bracteates were found at Stavnsager. They date from late phase 1. See Fiedel this volume, figure 13a.

3 Cf. http://www.staffordshirehoard.org.uk (accessed 14.10.2013) and http://finds.org.uk/staffshoardsymposium (accessed 14.10.2013).

Füsing – a metal-rich site in the vicinity of Haithabu/Schleswig dating from c. AD 700-1000

Andres Siegfried Dobat

Since the 1980s, when the metal detector turned Danish settlement archaeology upside down, productive or metal-rich sites have been a prominent feature of research into Early Medieval (Late Iron Age and Viking Age in Danish terminology) societies in Scandinavia. The large number of sites that have been discovered since then – and which are still being discovered – have radically changed our perception of the socio-political and economic constitution and development of this period.

In Scandinavian discussions, many of these sites are traditionally referred to as *specialised settlements* or *central places*, implying their prominent or at least somewhat distinct role within economic, religious, military and/or political networks. However, the Early Medieval settlement landscape appears to have been extremely heterogeneous as well as regionally and functionally varied. The group of productive or metal-rich sites covers a wide variety of very different settlement categories: seats of petty kings, residences of local or regional elites, agrarian villages, manors, specialised production sites, trading places and sites for craft/production (Böhme 2001; Christiansen 2008; Høilund Nielsen 2005; Holst 2010; Jørgensen 2009; Skre 2007, 445-69).

This complex picture of the Early Medieval settlement landscape continues to confront us with many questions. What led to the concentration of metal finds on these sites compared to other settlements? What was the socio-political background for the regional differences in the Scandinavian settlement landscape? And what role(s) did individual sites play within their regional setting and in relation to each other?

The metal-rich settlement site of Füsing in Schleswig-Holstein, northern Germany, is significant for the current discussion of such questions. Since 2003, the site has been subject to continuous archaeological investigation.[1] Intensive metal-detector surveys have resulted in a substantial number of finds dating from the 7th to the 10th century, and a geomagnetic survey has revealed a dense building structure, consisting predominantly of *Grubenhäuser*.

As the site was initially discovered during a period when the use of metal detectors was illegal in Schleswig, and as the investigations since then have been conducted within the framework of a research project, the site provides unique opportunities for an experimental approach to surface survey methods and their further development.

In its geographical setting, a few kilometres from one of the major Scandinavian emporia, Haithabu, and the Medieval town of Schleswig, the site provides unique opportunities to study the relations between an emporium and a later town as well as their contemporary regional surroundings within a narrow geographical frame of reference (for Haithabu, see Hillberg & Carnap-Bornheim 2007; Jankuhn 1986). The results of such investigations can thus be expected to contribute to an understanding of the long-term development of economic and socio-political networks in Early Medieval Scandinavia.

In the following, I will provide an overview of the current research on Füsing. I hope to give some insights into the potential benefits – and the limitations – of integrated survey methods in the study of metal-detector sites.

Regional setting

Füsing is situated in the southeastern corner of Angeln. Positioned on a sandy plateau, the site is surrounded to the west and the south by Schlei Fjord and to the north by the river Füsinger Au. Seen from Schlei Fjord, the settlement area occupied an extremely prominent position, highly visible even from a considerable distance. From the settlement plateau it is possible to survey most of the inner part of Schlei Fjord, including the natural entrance to the Haddebyer Noor or the area of High Medieval Schleswig (figs. 1 and 2).

Schlei Fjord, which penetrates the Jutland peninsula from its eastern coast, connected Füsing to an important waterway (Brandt 2006). The settlement was, however, located some distance from the shore of the fjord, and the spatial pattern of surface finds suggests that the site was linked to water-borne traffic via Füsing Au.

The archaeological evidence indicates that the adjacent hinterland was comparably densely settled, at least from the 9th century AD onwards. The dense population of the hinterland during the 10th century is supported indirectly by the concentration of Early Medieval place names and Romanesque churches in this particular part of the region.

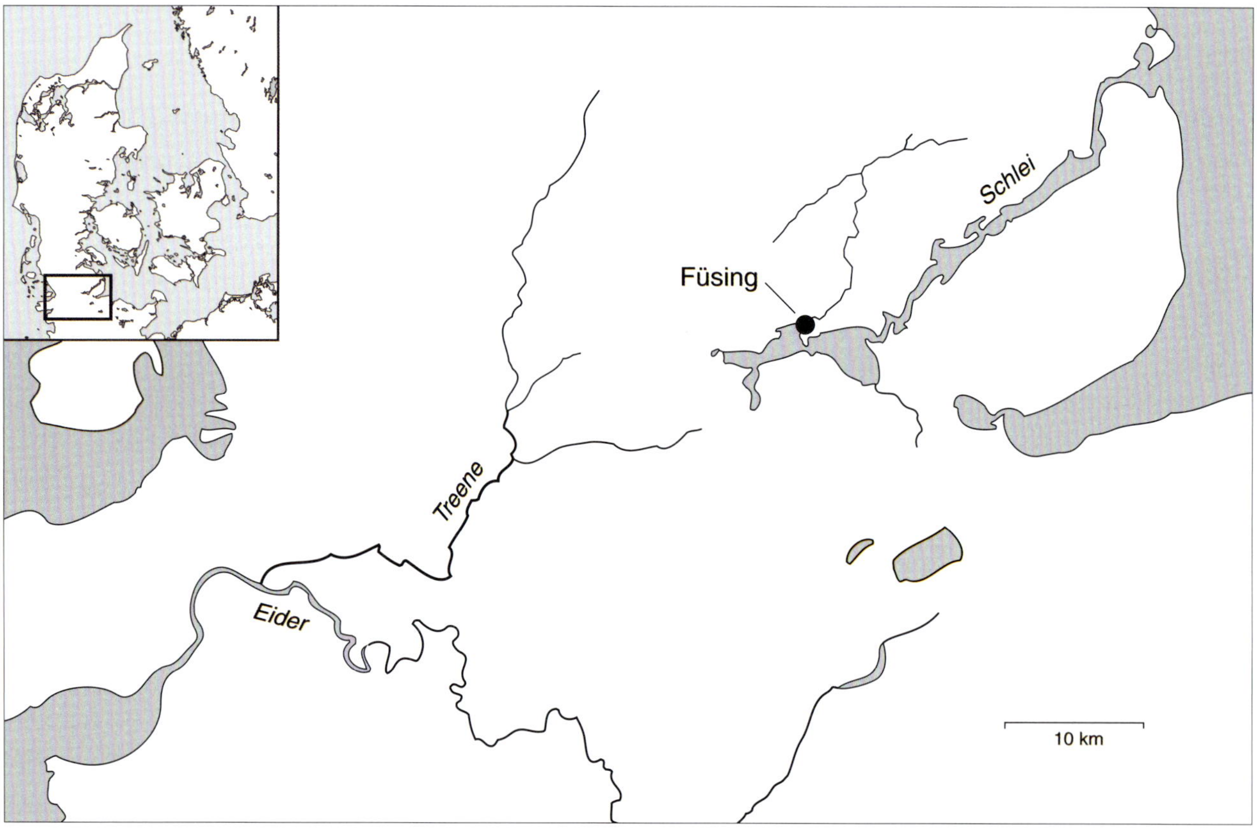

Fig. 1. | *The Schleswig isthmus with Füsing on the northern shore of Schlei Fjord and the mouth of the Füsinger Au. J. Kirkeby.*

Fig. 2. | *View of the site (in the centre) and the inner part of Schlei Fjord from the northeast in August 2006. Upper left: Haddeby Noor and the settlement area of Haithabu. Upper centre: the area of Medieval Schleswig. Photo: E. Schlosser Mauritsen.*

Methodological background for the discovery and the metal-detector surveys

Füsing was included in a pilot project studying the maritime cultural landscape of Schlei Fjord during the Early Medieval period because settlement indications had been recorded at the site in the 1960s (Dobat 2003). Methodologically based on comparable earlier studies in Scandinavia (Carlsson 1987; Ulriksen 1994), the project involved recording possible evidence of landing places and was intended to provide the basis for a subsequent field study.

Some of the 'probable landing-place' sites identified during the pilot project were the subject of metal-detector surveys in 2003. At Füsing, the initial survey resulted in the discovery of the first metal artefacts including scrap metal and fragments of dress accessories. This clearly illustrated the potential of the site and led to successive surveys conducted up to the present day.

Excavations of settlements on heavily cultivated soils have demonstrated that metal-detector finds generally tend to correlate with certain archaeological structures recorded below the plough soil. Repeated surveys may thus result in meaningful distribution patterns, allowing the structural or organisational aspects of the sites to be assessed (Gregory & Rogerson 1984; Helgesson 2002; Jørgensen 2003). However, previous projects have also revealed the various problems connected with the generation of surface-find assemblages and the consequences for their later study. Metal-detector surveys, in particular, carry the risk of providing a biased representation of artefact scatters, since areas with a high ratio of finds are generally prospected more thoroughly than areas where finds appear to occur less regularly. Repeated reconnaissance may confirm or even strengthen the appearance

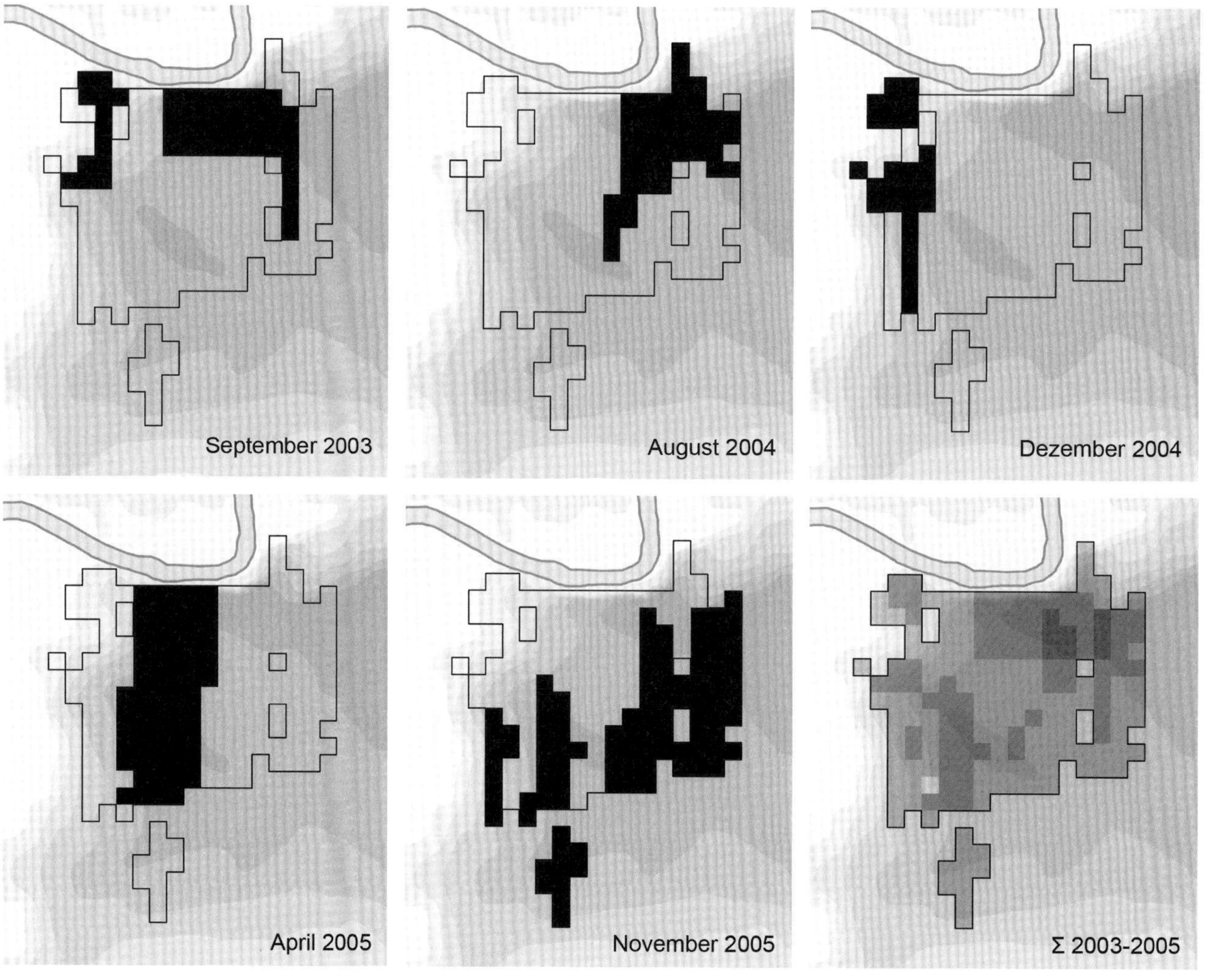

Fig. 3. | *Spatial extent of the metal-detector surveys conducted during the five individual campaigns between 2003 and 2005, and the total sum of survey intensity on the site. Light grey: surveyed once; grey: surveyed twice; dark grey: surveyed three times. Cf. figure 4. Contour interval 1 m. J. Kirkeby.*

of artefact concentrations or supposed peripheral areas, generating a highly biased representation of the outer limits or the internal structure of, for instance, a settlement complex (cf. Paulsson 1999, 51; Watt 2000, 6).

In response to this problem, a systematic working approach was adopted during the metal-detector surveys at Füsing. From the outset, the surveys were conducted by experienced specialists and under the supervision of the research group. A digitally-fixed 20 m grid system was established (figs. 3 and 4). The geo-referencing thus ensured its analogous positioning, even in the context of repeated surveys within the same area. During the actual surveys, which sometimes involved more than ten metal detectorists, each participant was assigned a certain number of plots (each 400 square metres in size) to survey (cf. also Gregory & Rogerson 1984).

The finds

As a result of the annual metal detector surveys at Füsing between 2003 and 2006, around 400 artefacts of Early Medieval date have been recorded, the majority consisting of non-ferrous metals. The finds were distributed over an area covering around 7.5 ha of the moraine plateau, with two obvious focal points: one in the northern part along the riverbank, and another around the

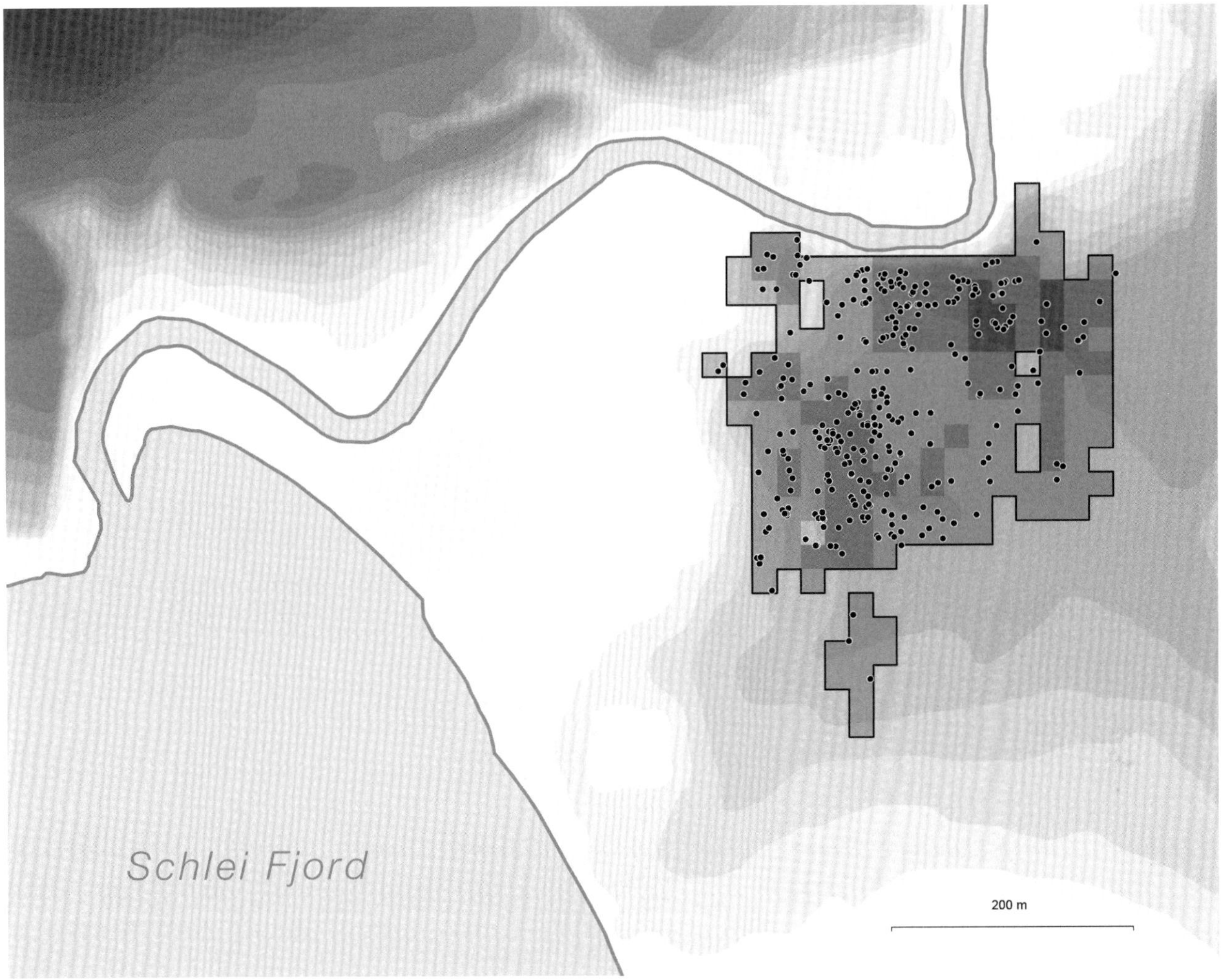

Fig. 4. | *Distribution of all surface finds from the site and the spatial extent and intensity of metal-detector surveys within the individual plots of the grid system. Cf. figure 3. K. Lambert Johansen and J. Kirkeby.*

elevated ground in the southern part of the settlement area (fig. 4).

Costume accessories such as brooches, pendants and various types of copper-alloy fittings represent a significant component of the assemblage. The majority are rather common Scandinavian objects, paralleled in the broad spectrum of especially south Scandinavian grave and settlement assemblages from the second half of the 7th to the 10th century. A few costume accessories are obviously foreign, such as a number of 8th- and 9th-century equal-armed brooches of probable Frisian origin and several other objects of Continental provenance.

Most of the assemblage consists of functionally unidentifiable pieces of bronze, lead and silver, which probably represent scrap metal. Its massive occurrence on the site has to be seen as reflecting craft activity. This is supported by the evidence of other artefacts such as numerous ingots and models of lead and bronze as well as a single patrix die for stamping sheet metal. The working of iron is demonstrated by various pieces of slag, and a small number of loom weights indicate textile production. Most of the artefacts that can be directly linked with craft activities were found in the northern part of the settlement. Several weights of copper alloy or lead, and of various shapes, may be related to the weighing of silver in a non-monetary currency system.

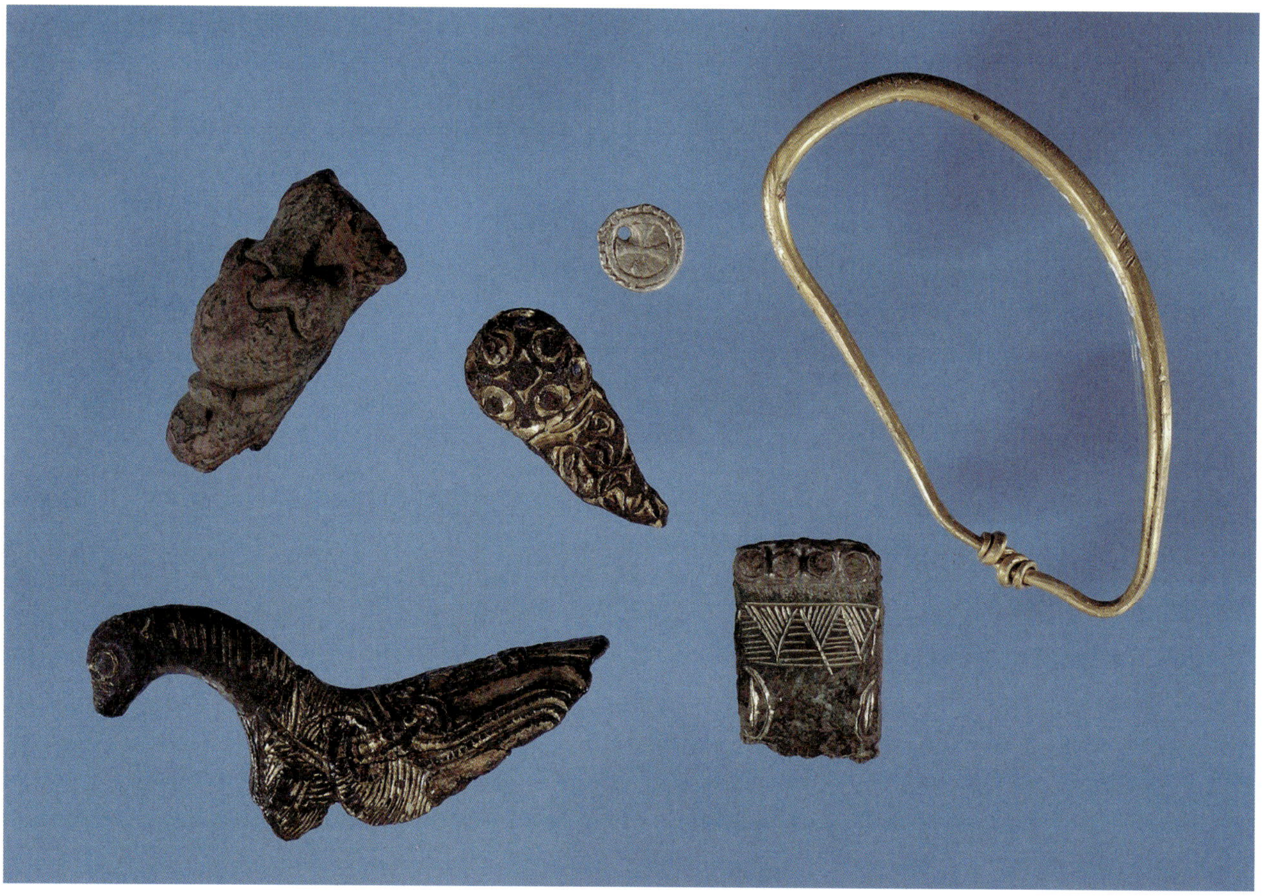

Fig. 5. | *Selection of finds of special character from Füsing: animal-head-shaped hasp (top left); fragment of a mount from a harness bow (bottom left); Carolingian mount with glass inlay and ornamentation in Tassilokelch style (centre); Carolingian strap-end with silver and gold plating (bottom right); tremissis with secondary perforation and cross-shaped ornament (top centre); gold arm ring with maximum diameter of 73 mm (top right). Photo: A.S. Dobat.*

Silver is present at Füsing in the form of a dirhem, minted in late 8th-century Baghdad, a small ingot and several pieces of melted silver. Also recovered was a gold tremissis coin, which was, however, used secondarily as a pendant (fig. 5). The piece must have been minted around the middle or second half of the 7th century, presumably somewhere in the area of present-day Holland.

A small group of artefacts attracts particular attention due to their exclusive character or their qualitative manufacture (fig. 5). One example is an 8th-century gilt mount of Continental origin but unknown function with glass inlay and elaborate ornamentation in Tassilokelch style. Similar pieces appear to have been produced in aristocratic workshops and are generally seen as being related to the elite of the Carolingian Empire. A comparable social background can be presumed for a gold arm ring, presumably originating from a disturbed hoard within the settlement area. The most spectacular finds, however, are a massive animal-head-shaped hasp and a fragment of a gilt mount from a harness bow. The latter can only be compared with a very exclusive group of Danish harness bows, which are conspicuous as being of the highest standard and represent the most complex examples of figurative metalwork in Early Medieval southern Scandinavia (Dobat 2006). Equivalent harness bows are known from a small number of 10th-century graves or hoards, all of which appear to have been associated with the aristocratic sphere of the Jelling dynasty.

Geomagnetic surveys and aerial photography

In 2005, a geomagnetic survey was conducted by the Department of Geophysics at the Institute of Geological Sciences, Kiel University, using a high-resolution fluxgate magnetometer (fig. 6). The survey covered most of the presumed settlement area and resulted in the identification of a large number of more or less well-defined positive geomagnetic anomalies (figs. 7 and 8). On the basis of the general appearance of Early Medieval settlements in the region (Meier 1994; Tummuscheit 2011), most of these anomalies probably represent *Grubenhäuser*. Around 110 such features could be distinguished rather clearly, mostly in the northern part of the settlement area. The spatial distribution of the probable *Grubenhäuser* thus corresponds with the concentration of surface finds along the riverbank, where most of the artefacts directly connected with craft activity were found. An aerial photograph, which was taken during the extremely dry summer of 2006, conveys the same picture of the spatial distribution of probable *Grubenhäuser* (fig. 9).

On the other hand, in the area around the elevated ground in the central and southern part of the settlement area, where a concentration of metal-detector finds indicates another focal point of the settlement activity, relatively few structures can be discerned by geomagnetic survey and aerial photography (cf. figs. 4 and 9). This can presumably be explained in terms of the limits of geomagnetic survey and aerial photography with respect to the identification of less substantial features possessing a low degree of geomagnetic incongruity, such as postholes. On this basis, the central area of the settlement can be assumed to have been structured in a different way, presumably consisting mainly of post-built constructions.

This view receives support if we take a closer look at the metal-detector finds. A distribution

Fig. 6. | *The department of Geophysics at the Institute of Geosciences, Kiel University, conducting the geophysical survey on the site in autumn 2005. Photo: A.S. Dobat.*

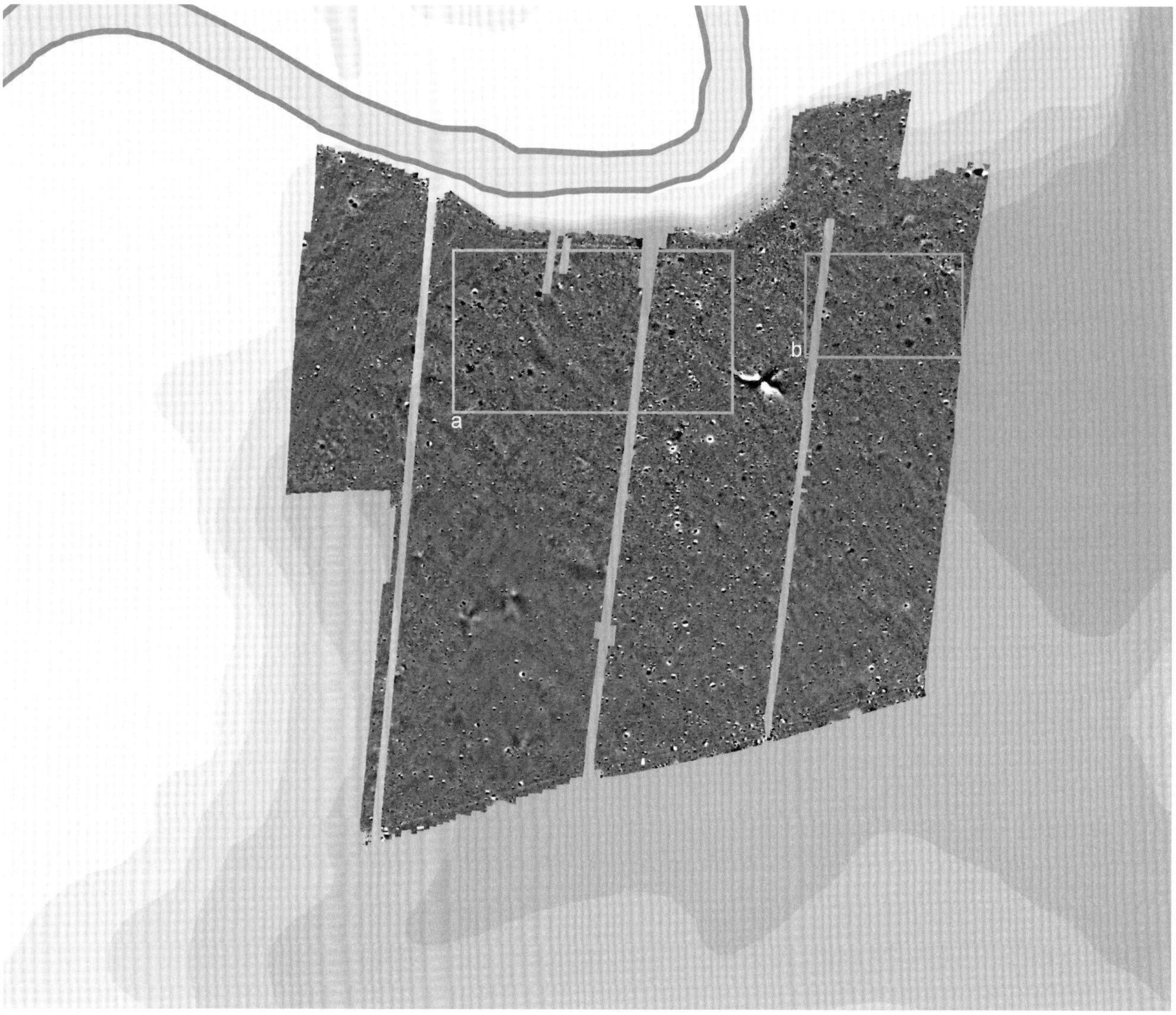

Fig. 7. | *Results of the geophysical survey; see also the detail of the framed area b in figure 8. H. Stümpel.*

map showing all artefacts directly related to craft activity reveals a clear overlap between these finds and the distribution of *Grubenhäuser*, whereas artefacts containing precious metals are for example distributed more randomly over the entire area – with a higher concentration in the central part of the settlement.

The site thus appears – and this is a working hypothesis – to have been structurally divided into two parts, one dominated by *Grubenhäuser* along the riverbank, possibly a workshop area, and the other, a residential area, presumably with longhouses, occupying the elevated part of the settlement plateau.

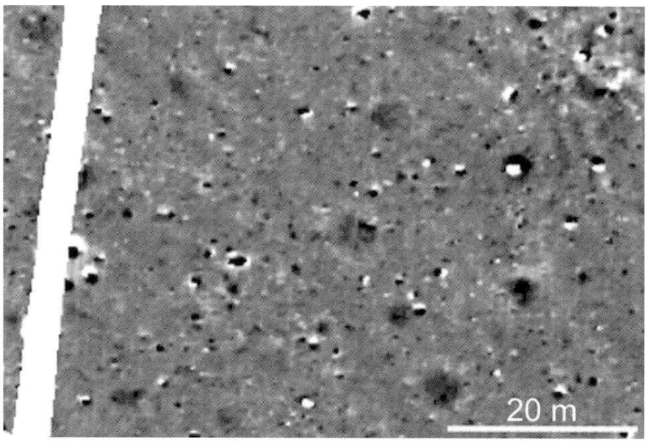

Fig. 8. | *Results of the geophysical survey. Detail b in the eastern part of the settlement area; for the positioning of the section see figure 7. H. Stümpel.*

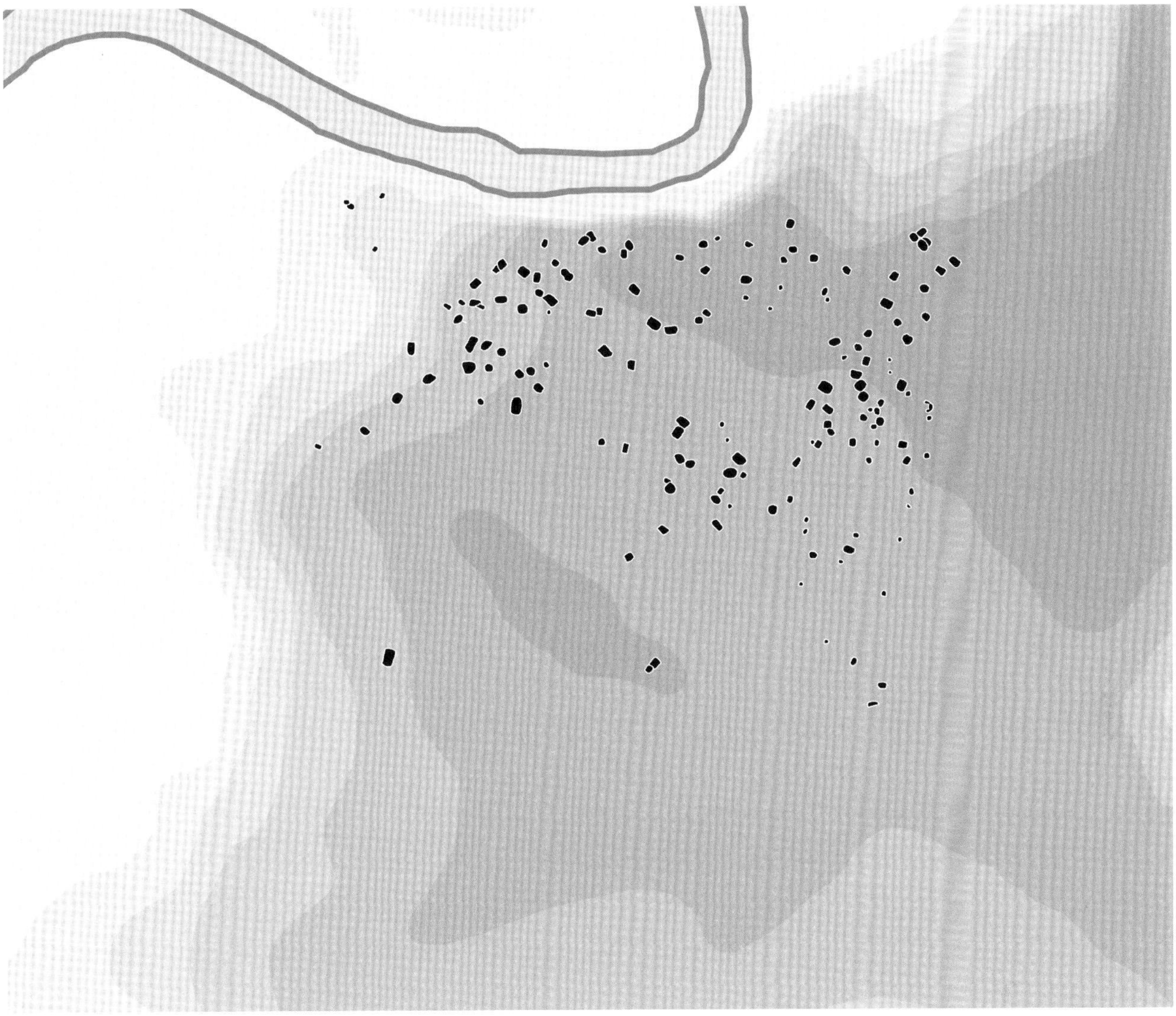

Fig. 9. | *Combined drawing and interpretation of the anomalies revealed by aerial photography and geophysical measurements. J. Kirkeby.*

Structure and function of the site

Despite their preliminary nature, the results of these investigations provide some insights into the structure and function of the site. Having applied a wide range of surface survey methods, we are in the privileged situation of being able to draw on the results of three independent survey methods: metal detector, air reconnaissance and geomagnetic survey. Most important for an understanding of the site, and in particular with regards to appraisal of its function and structural appearance, is the potential for viewing the metal-detector finds against the preliminary picture of the underlying structural features (cf. figs. 4 and 9).

The fixed-plot system applied in the metal-detector surveys proved its worth not only during the final analysis of the finds assemblage, but already during the actual field surveys (figs. 3 and 4). As a means of reconstructing the movements of each individual participant, it ensured complete coverage of the settlement area at a similar intensity. At the same time, it constituted the basis for a controlled enlargement of the research area in the form of corridors or single plots extending beyond the fringes of the settlement activities, as defined at that point in the research. The 20 m grid system thus constituted a prerequisite for the establishment of a representative pattern for the distribution and density of the artefact scatter, even after repeated reconnaissance of particular areas. It would be unrealistic to expect a similar systematic approach to be applied at every metal-detector site. In most cases, and especially in Denmark, methodological standards are defined by local amateurs. Nevertheless, a systematic metal-detector survey should be the very first step in any investigation of such sites, and amateur and professional archaeologists alike should seek to ensure that the survey is systematic in one way or another and thereby improve the data value of the finds.

According to the finds assemblage, settlement activities began at Füsing around AD 700, at the latest. The relatively large number of *Grubenhäuser* and the massive occurrence of fire-cracked stones may be signs of permanent occupation. There are no indications of continuous occupation at the site after AD 1000, when the settlement seems to have been abandoned. To date, Füsing is the only site in the region, apart from Haithabu, where indications of primary settlement have been discovered for the period between the 7th and early 8th century AD. The results at Füsing therefore support the hypothesis of a continuous settlement history in the region.

The finds from Füsing are predominantly related to craft activities. The working of non-ferrous metals, including the production of highly prestigious jewellery, appears to have been of particular importance. *Grubenhäuser* can also be considered as being associated with craft activities. At Füsing, this conclusion is further supported by the spatial correlation of the geomagnetic anomalies and functionally specific artefact types. The various foreign artefacts reflect the embedding of the site into a supra-regional network of communication, while the geographical orientation of Füsing relative to natural communication corridors already hints at the significance of trade/exchange activities. Füsing Au linked the site to a regional communication route embracing most of the southern part of the Angeln region.

The regional setting of Füsing close to the narrow section of the fjord and the ramparts at Reesholm may suggest some sort of military or administrative function, at least on a seasonal or intermittent basis, though this is not directly evident from the finds assemblages.

As regards the role of the settlement in social terms, the small group of artefacts of exclusive character is of particular significance. They are all high-status objects belonging to the very upper strata of the social hierarchy in Early Medieval Scandinavia, suggesting the site's associations with an aristocracy enjoying close relations to the Jelling dynasty of the 10th century. The relation of the site to the aristocracy is further substantiated by 12th- and 13th-century historical references, indicating the region's original status as part of the royal lands (*patrimonium* or *kongelev*). This is supported by the special status of the Medieval village of Füsing in the organisational apparatus of the bishopric in Schleswig and its special juridical status (*birk*), well into the High Middle Ages.

As indicated by a barrage dating from around AD 737, the narrow section of Schlei Fjord at Reesholm immediately south of Füsing was highly significant strategically (Kramer 1994). This massive structure must be seen in connection with the Danevirke defensive ramparts as intended to prevent hostile forces from crossing the fjord. Evidence from place names also points towards later defensive structures at this location. An historical reference implies the existence of a tollbooth at the narrow section of the fjord during the Late Medieval period (Radtke 1981; Unverhau 1990, 37). Although not evident in the finds assemblage, it is thus conceivable that Füsing, at least periodically, fulfilled some military and possibly administrative functions.

A comparative approach

In a regional context, in addition to the emporium of Haithabu, Füsing can be compared with the late 9th- and 10th-century settlement of Kosel West, which is similarly dominated by *Grubenhäuser*. Here, there is some evidence of craft activity such as metal-working and textile production, and imported goods indicate close relations with Haithabu as well as participation in mercantile activity. Regarding the quantity and wealth of the assemblage of metal objects, together with the spatial extent of the occupation and the number of probable *Grubenhäuser*, Füsing does, however, represent a rather isolated phenomenon, at least in the immediate vicinity of Haithabu.

In the regional surroundings of Ribe, the Early Medieval emporium in the southwestern part of Jutland, a number of places have been recorded with equally significant assemblages indicating craft and mercantile activities. Some of these places around Ribe were obviously dependent somehow on the activities at the emporium. Others not only functioned synchronously with Ribe, but they also seem to have taken over its function as a mercantile and production centre when Ribe obviously lost its significance as a trading place from around AD 900 (Feveile 2001; 2006, 52; Jensen 1992).

In a supra-regional perspective, we find some correspondences in the characteristic appearance of a variety of different site categories. One group comprises the so-called landing places, of which a considerable number have been investigated in coastal landscapes all over southern Scandinavia (Callmer 2002; Carlsson 1987; Ulriksen 1994). The majority of such coastal sites have been found to date to a period extending from the 7th century well into the Middle Ages. However, with regard to their topographical situation, the spatial extent of their settlement indicators and the qualitative character of some of their artefacts, Füsing does not seem to fit into the picture of typical landing places in the Baltic region.

Füsing can also be compared with the extremely heterogeneous group of settlements that are generally referred to as central places or aristocratic manors (Henriksen 2000; Høilund Nielsen 2005; Holst 2011; Jørgensen 2003; Larsson & Hårdh 1998; Skre 2007, 445-69). The majority of these sites must presumably be interpreted as primarily representing manorial estates. Nevertheless, many seem also to have had a wide spectrum of central functions. As residences of social elites, their variety as regards complexity and size, as well as the composition of the finds assemblages, reflects a complex socio-political hierarchy. Whereas the significance of the majority of sites and their residents was presumably confined to their local or regional context, others can be presumed to have constituted the centres of larger political units, chiefdoms, petty kingdoms or kingdoms. With regard to the present state of the evidence from Füsing there is, however, no definite substantiation of the permanent presence of aristocratic elites, and there are no indications of the site having had any political or religious significance.

Finally, as another potential approach for establishing the possible background of the settlement at Füsing, account can be taken of Hovgården on the island of Adelsö, situated directly north of Birka, and Skiringsal/Husby at the Viksfjord, in the northern hinterland of Kaupang. The evidence provided by place names, prestigious finds and huge hall buildings at both sites has been interpreted as indicating the existence of royal manors in connection with emporia (Brunstedt 1998; Skre 2007, 223-48).

Discussion and perspectives

Based on the present state of evidence, Füsing can be said to combine the characteristics of various forms of settlements known in southern Scandinavia. It presumably served as a focal point for craft activities and, to some extent, also the exchange and distribution of commodities of particular importance for the settlement landscape of the southwestern part of Angeln. As such, it may have been organisationally linked to aristocratic elites – who were either residents of the site itself or maintained organisational connections to the site somehow from an elite residence in the hinterland.

The evidence presently available, coupled with a comparative review of other settlement types, prompts the following working hypothesis: Füsing was a manorial estate and the seat of a regional elite. It served as a regional central place for various functions, including communication, production and trade/exchange. As such, the site was of particular significance for southwestern Angeln. The settlement may temporarily have served as a royal manor associated with the emporium of Haithabu.

As outlined in the introduction, Füsing possesses special research potential by virtue of its regional context, situated close to the emporium and emergent town of Haithabu/Schleswig. Like earlier investigations in the region (Meier 1994, 194; Müller-Wille 2002, 38), the investigations at Füsing underline that, at least until around AD 1000, the settlements in the Schlei region were characterised by a wide-ranging economical foundation, extending far beyond the scale of agrarian subsistence. They were integrated into networks of exchange that were of a more or less decentralised character and involved both a regional and a supra-regional sphere.

Until around AD 1000, Füsing and Haithabu coexisted as focal points of production and possibly also exchange activities. This co-existence can be interpreted in different ways: It can be regarded as reflecting either a functional specialisation or an orientation towards different economic spheres. While Haithabu must be seen primarily in a supra-regional context with particular focus on Continental relations, Füsing seems to have been focused primarily on its regional hinterland.

The site could have functioned as nodal point, linking supra-regional and regional exchange networks. As such, it would have played an important role in the circulation of imported goods that reached the area via Haithabu and were then distributed further out into the hinterland. Furthermore, the craft activities on the site may also have been closely linked with Haithabu such that certain products were manufactured to be sold at the emporium, as is the case in the regional environs of 8th- and 9th-century Ribe (cf. Feveile 2006). Seen from this perspective, the discovery of Füsing raises many new questions of significance, not only from a regional point of view, but also regarding the long-term development of economic and socio-political networks in Early Medieval Scandinavia in general.

Although the investigations already completed at the site provide some insights, proper excavations should be embarked upon if we are to gain a full understanding of its settlement structure, its function and its implications for regional social and economic structures. A detailed understanding of the functional and structural background, and a representative picture of the site, can only be reached through excavation.

In this respect, I would argue that the previous metal-detector and geomagnetic surveys constitute both a help and a challenge. They provide an initial insight into the overall structure of the site and the architectural features we must expect to encounter. Accordingly, they allow us to target our excavation efforts on specific features, such as *Grubenhäuser* or other identifiable structures, without having to localise them through trial trenches. This approach, however, carries the risk of producing a biased picture, because a lack of geomagnetic anomalies, as I have tried to show above, cannot necessarily be taken as indicative of the lack of settlement features.

Future excavations at Füsing must therefore pursue two strategies: 'focused excavations', in direct continuation of the geomagnetic survey and targeted on specific areas; and 'trial excavations' following in the wake of the metal-detector survey, hopefully resulting in a more representative picture of the settlement structure at the site and ultimately thereby providing the basis for further excavations of wider areas.

Through adoption of this strategic approach, I hope eventually to be able to contribute to the discussion of the questions outlined above and to arrive at a more detailed interpretation of the settlement at Füsing and the implications of the site in its regional and supra-regional contexts.

Bibliography

Böhme, H.W. 2001, Gedanken zu den frühen Markt- und Handelsplätzen in Südskandinavien. In: E. Pohl, U. Recker & C. Theune (eds.), *Archäologisches Zellwerk. Beiträge zur Kulturgeschichte in Europa und Asien* [Festschrift Helmut Roth]. Rahden/Westfalen. 483-98.

Brandt, K. 2006, Portage at the base of Jutland during the Viking Period and the Middle Ages. In: C. Westerdahl (ed.), *The Significance of Portages*. Oxford. 53-64.

Brunstedt, S. 1998, Hovgården på Adelsö – Kungsgård och politisk Maktcentrum. In: P. Bratt (ed.), *Forntid i ny dager – Arkeologi i Stockholmstrakten*. Stockholm. 214-21.

Callmer, J. 2002, North-European trading centres and the Early Medieval craftsman. Craftsmen at Åhus, north-eastern Scania, Sweden ca. AD 750-850. In: B. Hårdh & L. Larsson (eds.), *Central Places in the Migration and Merovingian Periods*. Stockholm. 125-57.

Carlsson, D. 1987, Äldre hamnar – ett hotat kulturarv. *Fornvännen* 82, 6-17.

Christiansen, T.T. 2008, Detektorfund og bebyggelse. Det østlige Limfjordsområde i yngre jernalder og vikingetid. *Kuml* 2008, 101-43.

Dobat, A.S. 2003, The maritime hinterland of Hedeby. Berichte des 54 Sachsensymposiums in Schwerin. *Jahrbuch Bodendenkmalpflege Meckenburg-Vorpommern* 51, 419-35.

Dobat, A.S. 2006, Bridging mythology and belief – Viking Age functional culture as evidence for the belief in divine intervention. In: K. Jennbert, A. Andrén & C. Raudvere (eds.), *Old Norse Religion in Long-term Perspectives. Origins, Changes, Interactions*. Lund. 184-88.

Feveile, C. 2001, Okholm – en plads med håndværksspor og grubehuse fra 8.-9. århundrede. *By, Marsk og Geest* 13, 5-32.

Feveile, C. 2006, Ribe på nordsiden af åen, 8.-12. århundrede – oversigt og tolkning. In: C. Feveile (ed.), *Det ældste Ribe: Udgravninger på Nordsiden af Ribe Å 1984-2000*. 1.1. Højbjerg. 13-63.

Gregory, T. & A.J.G. Rogerson 1984, Metaldetecting in archaeological excavation. *Antiquity*, 58, 179-84.

Hillberg, V. & C. von Carnap-Bornheim 2007, Recent archaeological research in Haithabu. In: J. Henning (ed.), *Post Roman Towns – Trade and Settlement in Europe and Byzantium, 1. The Heirs of the Roman West*. Berlin/New York. 199-218.

Helgesson, B. 2002, *Järnålderns Skåne. Samhälle, centra och regioner*. Stockholm.

Henriksen, M.B. 2000, Lundsgård, Seden Syd og Hjulby – tre fynske bopladsområder med detektorfund. In: M.B. Henriksen (ed.), *Detektorfund – hvad skal vi med dem? Dokumentation og registrering af bopladser med detektorfund fra jernalder og middelalder*. Odense. 17-60.

Høilund Nielsen, K. 2005, "...the sun was darkened by day and the moon by night ... there was distress among men ..." – on social and political development in 5th- to 7th-century southern Scandinavia. *Studien zur Sachsenforschung* 15, 247-85.

Holst, M.K. 2010, Inconstancy and stability: large and small farmsteads in the village of Nørre Snede (Central Jutland) in the first millennium AD. *Siedlungs- und Küstenforschung im südlichen Nordseegebiet* 33, 155-79.

Jankuhn, H. 1986, *Haithabu. Ein Handelsplatz der Wikingerzeit*. Neumünster.

Jensen, S. 1992, Metalfund fra vikingetidsgårdene ved Gl. Hviding og Vilslev. *By, marsk og geest* 3, 27-40.

Jørgensen, L. 2003, Manor and market at Lake Tissø in the sixth to eleventh centuries: The Danish productive sites. In: T. Pestell & K. Ulmschneider (eds.), *Markets in Early Medieval Europe: Trading and 'Productive' Sites, 650-850*. Macclesfield. 175-207.

Jørgensen, L. 2009, Pre-Christian cult at aristocratic residences and settlement complexes in southern Scandinavia in the 3rd – 10th centuries. In: U. von Freeden, H. Friesinger & E. Wamers (eds.), *Glaube, Kult und Herrschaft. Phänomene des Religiösen im 1. Jahrtausend n. Chr. in Mittel- und Nordeuropa. Akten des 59. Internationalen Sachsensymposions und der Grundprobleme der frühgeschichtlichen Entwicklung im Mitteldonauraum*. Bonn. 329-54.

Kramer, W. 1994, Ein Seesperrwerk des 8. Jahrhunderts in der Schlei. *Archäologie in Deutschland* 3, 20-21.

Larsson, L. & B. Hårdh (eds.) 1998, *Centrala Platser Centrala Frågor. Samhällstrukturen under järnåldern*. Stockholm.

Meier, D. 1994, *Die wikingerzeitliche Siedlung von Kosel (Kosel-West), Kreis Rendsburg-Eckernförde*. Neumünster.

Müller-Wille, M. 2002, *Frühstädtische Zentren der Wikingerzeit und ihr Hinterland. Die Beispiele Ribe, Hedeby und Reric.* Stuttgart.

Paulsson, J. 1999, Metalldetektering och Uppåkra. Att förhåla sig till et detektormaterial. In: B. Hårdh (ed.), *Fynden i centrum: Keramik, glas och metal från Uppåkra.* Stockholm. 41-58.

Radtke, C. 1981, Die Oldenburg an der Schleimündung. *Offa* 38, 341-65.

Skre, D. 2007 (ed.), *Kaupang in Skiringssal.* Aarhus.

Tummuscheit, A. 2011, *Die Baubefunde des frühmittelalterlichen Seehandelsplatzes von Groß Strömkendorf.* Schwerin.

Ulriksen, J. 1994, Danish sites and settlements with a maritime context, AD 200-1200. *Antiquity* 68,261, 797-811.

Unverhau, H. 1990, *Untersuchungen zur historischen Entwicklung des Landes zwischen Schlei und Eider im Mittelalter.* Neumünster.

Watt, M. 2000, Detektorfund fra bornholmske bopladser med kulturlag. Repræsentativitet og metode. In: M.B. Henriksen (ed.), *Detektorfund – hvad skal vi med dem? Dokumentation og registrering af bopladser med detektorfund fra jernalder og middelalder.* Odense. 79-98.

Notes

1 The investigations at Füsing are being carried out by the Department of Prehistoric Archaeology at the University of Aarhus in co-operation with the Archäologisches Landesmuseum and the Landesamt Schleswig-Holstein. The discovery and subsequent investigation of Füsing was dependent on the support of many individuals, groups and organisations, particularly the Clausen, Holtorf and Pedersen families. The metal-detector surveys would not have been possible without the enthusiastic contributions of Sønderjyske Amatørarkæologer and Metalldetektor AG, Archäologisches Landesamt Schleswig-Holstein. I would like to thank the many people who gave their expertise and advice, especially my friends and colleagues at the Department of Prehistoric Archaeology at the University of Aarhus, the Archäologisches Landesmuseum and Landesamt Schleswig-Holstein, as well as the Department of Geophysics at Kiel University. For the financial support I received while working on the site I am indebted to HM Queen Margrethe II's Archaeological Foundation.

Centrality and trade on the North Frisian Islands during the Migration period

Martin Segschneider

The islands Sylt, Föhr and Amrum lie close together off the west coast of the southern part of the Jutland peninsula (fig. 1). They all consist of moraine cores to which saltmarshes, dunes and sand spits are attached. Whereas Sylt and Amrum face the open North Sea, Föhr lies sheltered by the other islands, in the midst of the Wadden Sea. The outer islands had to be passed by anyone sailing north or south along the west coast of Jutland, making them the perfect place from which to control traffic and trade (Segschneider 2007). Due to their setting, it can be assumed that chieftain's farmsteads with associated landing places existed on the islands during the Migration period.

However, centrality on the North Frisian Islands during the Migration period is not an easy topic to write about. Few excavations have been carried out to date and the use of metal detectors is only in its infancy. Nevertheless, it proved possible to gather interesting new evidence during the course of the last decade through investigations carried out on behalf of the Archaeologisches Landesamt Schleswig-Holstein; the results of these will be presented here.

Fig. 1. | *Migration period sites on Sylt, Föhr, Amrum and the mainland area opposite. Large dots: sites referred to in the article; white areas: moraine and dunes; shaded areas: marshes. After Kersten & La Baume 1958, Kossack et al. 1974 and Segschneider 2004.*

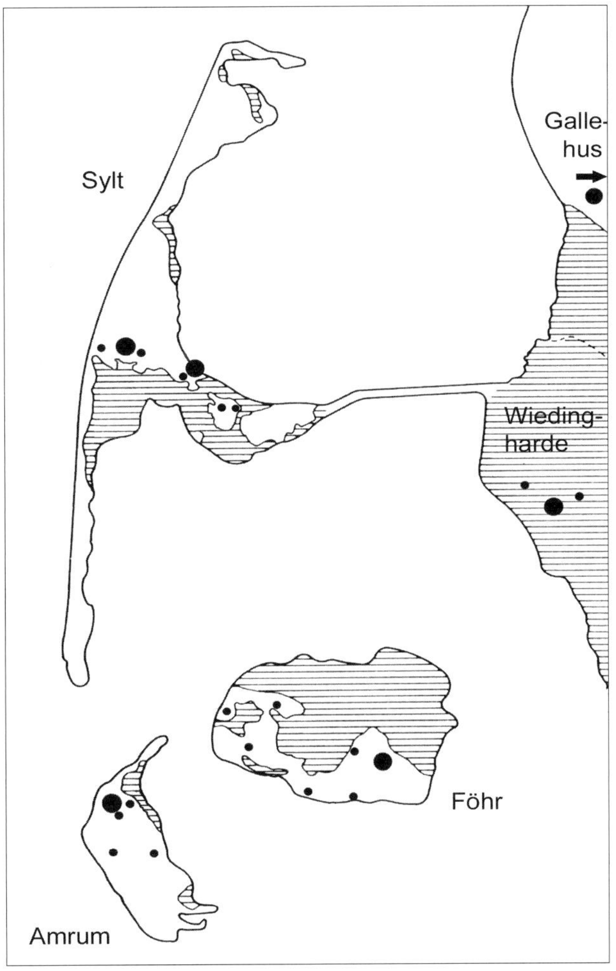

Amrum

Along the west coast of Amrum, winter storms continually uncover special settlement traces beneath the Medieval dunes in two dune valleys (fig. 2). They belong to a large landing place, at

Fig. 2. | *Two* Grubenhäuser *on Amrum in the northern part of the market area excavated in autumn 2008. Photo: M. Segschneider.*

least 200 x 150 m in extent. To date, the archaeological structures exposed by wind and rain include seven *Grubenhäuser*, ditches, pits and a four-poster granary. In the southern valley, clay-turf walls, built into a layer of white sand, give the impression of marked-out plots typical of those used for trading purposes in market areas (Segschneider 2002a). The occupation layer in both valleys, blackened by charcoal dust, contained many finds: some 20 Frankish glass beaker sherds, around 70 glass beads, thousands of richly decorated pottery sherds, iron rivets and slag, parts of broken bronze brooches, animal bones and mussel shells (Ethelberg 2003, 301-304; Segschneider 2002a; 2002b; 2009). A small pit used for the deposition of burnt animal bones, together with a large fragment of a crucible, shows that ritual activities also took place here. There can be no doubt that these finds accumulated during seasonal marketplace activities, and this is consistent with the fact that the poorly-built *Grubenhäuser* show almost no trace of use, and have no hearth. Taking into account the topography of the coastline and the presumed trade route for Frankish glasses to the north (Hansen 1993), it is logical that such a landing place and beach market evolved just here between AD 400 and 550. Trading ships sailing along the coast presumably landed here for a stopover, so that some of the Frankish glass beakers (or just sherds?) ended up on the island. Judging from the small proportion of the settlement that has been uncovered so far, at least 100 *Grubenhäuser* are estimated to have been built here. Such a large marketplace with direct connections to the long-distance trade route running along the west coast of Jutland would have been under the control of powerful chieftains. The settlements of Dejbjerg and Dankirke, both of which have yielded many Frankish glass beaker sherds (Egeberg Hansen 1996; Lund Hansen 1984), could obviously have had a connection with the marketplace on Amrum (Segschneider 2002a; 2002b). They provide a good idea of how a chieftain's settlement in the vicinity of a marketplace would have been structured.

Urn graves are relatively numerous among Migration period finds at Amrum. These were all inserted into existing Bronze Age barrows. Some of these are located quite close to the marketplace (Kersten & La Baume 1958, 125-6, 184-5), others contain numerous glass beads and one has a Frankish glass sherd (Segschneider 2002a, 128). However, it has not been possible as yet to locate any large settlement with superior buildings/halls, like those seen at Dejbjerg or Dankirke. The dunes on the western side of the island may have covered any remains of such a settlement, but it could equally well have been located on one of the neighbouring larger islands (Segschneider 2002a, 128). LIDAR images show a dike running from the market place on Amrum to the east, ending at a hill called 'Borag' on the shore of the Wadden Sea. This is one of the closest points to the island of Föhr, with only some 5 km of tidal flats separating the two islands here, so what was happening on the other side?

Föhr

For many years, only few settlement traces were known from the moraine part of the island of Föhr. Most belonged to the Migration period, a time represented archaeologically by urn graves in Alkersum, Süderende, Hedehusum, Goting and Nieblum and settlement traces in Dunsum and Goting (Kersten & La Baume 1958).

But one day in June 2006 everything changed. Esben Schlosser Mauritsen flew over the island as part of a project aimed at detecting Viking Age settlements along the west coast of Jutland. Prior to this, there were no known anomalies visible from the air, so this was just to check whether there might be anything worth noticing – and there was. Following a long period of drought, the vegetation on the sandy soil showed crop-marks very clearly, even on grasslands. Abundant settlement traces appeared in several locations (Mauritsen et al. 2009).

A site near Wrixum revealed the presence of *Grubenhäuser*, wells, ditches, roadways and even longhouses arranged as farmsteads (fig. 3). The longhouses were surrounded by ditches in the shape of more or less rectangular courtyards with rounded corners. Within these, two or three *Grubenhäuser*, and sometimes a well, were present. Depending on the moisture remaining in the ground, even fine details were visible in some areas, though in others the settlement traces remained obscured.

In order to obtain a more even overall picture, it was decided that a geophysical survey should be conducted in collaboration with the Institute of Geosciences at Kiel University. The survey was carried out in the following years and included the use of both geomagnetism and georadar. The results were again very convincing (fig. 4) and they form part of a diploma thesis written by Tina Wunderlich (2008). The homogenous sand is very suited to geomagnetism survey and very clear patterns were apparent. Due to the fired clay present in many anomalies (as revealed by cores), an image showing sharp contrasts and only minor disturbance is produced. Judging from the amount of magnetised material in the remains of the northern and southern houses, the settlement presumably burnt down. The house in the middle also shows a fairly clear system of postholes. All three longhouses have straight walls and appear to be at least 50 m long. This would make them the largest examples found in Schleswig-Holstein to date. They can be related to houses excavated in Flögeln, Lower Saxony, which date from the Late Roman Iron Age or the Migration period (Zimmermann 1992). Around them, *Grubenhäuser*, wells and ditches form complexes which, as had already been revealed by the aerial photos, apparently formed farmsteads together with the longhouses. According to the aerial photos, the settlement extends out further to the west. To the southwest, there seems to be a contemporary single farmstead with another very large building, enclosed within an angular courtyard/ditch, together with two *Grubenhäuser*.

Fieldwalking nearby to the west revealed black-burnished pottery with curved rims, giving a preliminary date for the settlement of the 4th and 5th

Fig. 3. | *The Wrixum site on an aerial photo from 2006 showing various settlement traces/vegetation anomalies (enhanced contrast). North is to the left. Photo: E. Schlosser Mauritsen.*

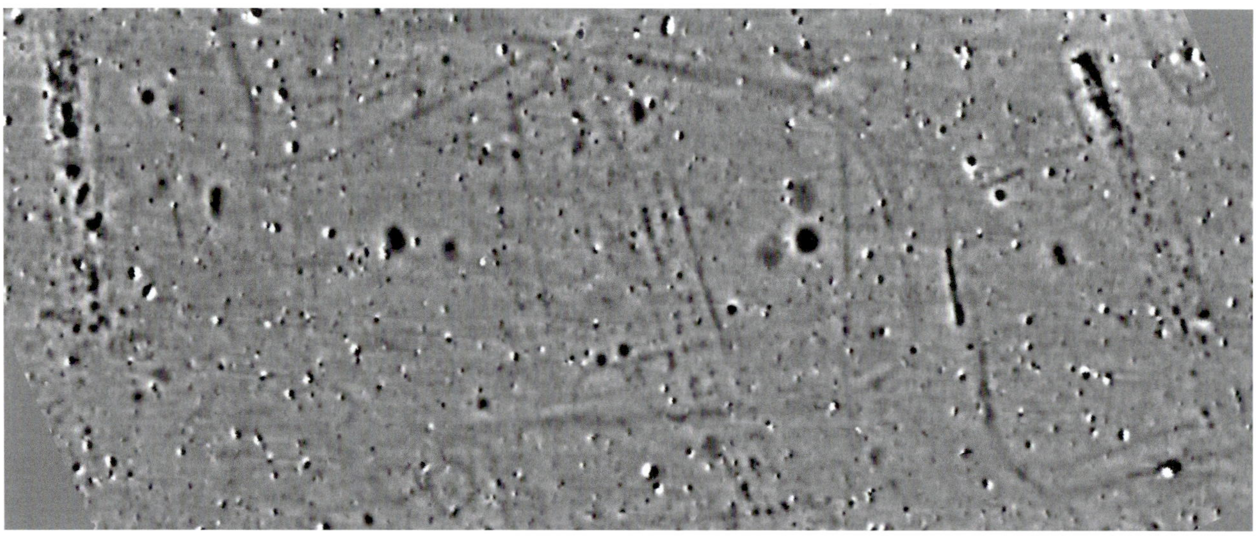

Fig. 4. | *Geomagnetic image showing the eastern half of the Wrixum site in 2008. It measures approximately 150 x 70 m; north is to the left. Longhouses,* Grubenhäuser, *wells, ditches and postholes are visible, although obscured by black and white dipole anomalies caused by scrap metal pieces. H. Stümpel and T. Wunderlich, Institute of Geosciences, Kiel University.*

century AD. Taking into account the size of the longhouses, it is possible that the newly discovered site near Wrixum represents a superior settlement from the Migration period. If so, its chieftain might have been in charge of the trading place on Amrum. But only proper excavations will provide a precise date and fully reveal the character and importance of this promising settlement.

Sylt

Sylt is the largest of the three islands. Again, knowledge of Migration period settlements and graves here was rather scant up until the middle of the 20th century (Kersten & La Baume 1958). Later, the Archsum project added some sites on the Archsum moraine core (Kossack et al. 1974). Nearly 30 years later, between 2003 and 2007, when an industrial area was about to be built on a former military airfield north of Tinnum, several traces of a large settlement were detected. Among these was a longhouse destroyed by fire, about a dozen *Grubenhäuser* and several pits and ditches. So-called red ash located nearby originates from extensive salt production using peat, which was extracted from the Wadden Sea. The area was levelled in the 1940s and only some of the deeper structures survived, in particular where they had been overlain by younger settlement layers. The finds include abundant pottery, a cruciform bronze brooch, amber and glass beads, bone pins and so on. The longhouse that had burnt down revealed a full series of pottery, including imitations of glass vessels (fig. 5). Remarkably, the settlement had access to the Wadden Sea through a tidal channel running to the south.

It proved possible to detect another Migration period settlement located close to the saltmarsh at Keitum. Construction activities led to the discovery of some *Grubenhäuser*, the stone pavement of a house, settlement layers, pits and ditches. Preservation conditions were again rather poor, but it was still possible to locate further sherds of pottery, which imitated glass vessels. This seems to be a common feature of important Migration period settlements on the Jutland peninsula (Stidsing

Fig. 5. | *Miniature pottery from a burnt-down longhouse (right) and from a* Grubenhaus *(left), Tinnum/Sylt. Some of the pots were obviously intended to imitate prestigious Frankish glass vessels. Photo: L. Hermannsen, Archäologisches Landesamt Schleswig-Holstein.*

2008). But what do we know about the original glass vessels? A complete glass vessel, presumably dating from the 6th century, was found in a barrow in Westerland as early as 1766 (Kersten & La Baume 1958, 631). This has long been a famous part of the collection now housed by the National Museum of Denmark in Copenhagen. It shows that complete Frankish glass vessels were owned by wealthy inhabitants of the island, as suggested by the marketplace on Amrum. These were prestigious items used in drinking ceremonies and were well known to the inhabitants of the islands.

Wiedingharde

Finally, these discoveries must be considered in the context of the mainland. One might wonder why the area of the Wiedingharde, formerly named Horsbüllharde, is included in an article about the North Frisian Islands. Up until the Late Middle Ages, however, it was in fact a saltmarsh island, later surrounded by a ring dike (Segschneider 2004, 58-9). Analysis of pottery from the settlements of Emmelsbüll-Toftum and Horsbüll showed clearly that the inhabitants had strong links with the islanders across tidal channels (Segschneider 2004, 88). A fragment of a Frankish glass vessel also reveals the area's connection to the islands and the open sea. As the Migration period sites in the Wiedingharde lie not too distant from the find site of the famous golden horns at Gallehus, one could argue that the islands, saltmarshes and this part of the mainland moraine were all linked by tidal channels. In my opinion, one should not rule out the possibility that the settlements on the islands and the area around Gallehus belonged to a single regional system that existed around AD 500. Due to the special geographical circumstances, centrality could have functioned for purposes related to cult, trade, supervision, warfare and so on in many different ways and places in this region.

Bibliography

Ethelberg, P. 2003, Gården og landsbyen i jernalder og vikingetid (500 f. Kr. – 1000 e. Kr.). In: P. Ethelberg, N. Hardt, B. Poulsen & A.B. Sørensen (eds.), *Det Sønderjyske Landbrugs Historie. Jernalder, vikingetid og middelalder*. Haderslev. 123-373.

Egeberg Hansen, T. 1993, Glashus. *Skalk* 1993:5, 3-7.

Egeberg Hansen, T. 1996, Et jernalderhus med drikkeglas i Dejbjerg, Vestjylland. *Kuml* 1993-1994, 211-37.

Lund Hansen, U. 1984, Dankirke. Die Gläser. In: *Reallexikon der germanischen Altertumskunde* 5. Founded by Johannes Hoops. 2nd ed. Berlin/New York. 249-53.

Kersten, K. & P. La Baume 1958, *Vorgeschichte der nordfriesischen Inseln*. Neumünster.

Kossack et al. 1974:Kossack, G., O. Harck & J. Reichstein 1974, 10 Jahre Siedlungsforschung in Archsum auf Sylt. *Bericht der Römisch-Germanischen Kommission* 55:2, 261-427.

Schlosser Mauritsen, E., M. Segschneider & T. Wunderlich 2009, Siedlungsprospektion mit Luftfotografien und Geomagnetik auf der nordfriesischen Insel Föhr. *Archäologische Nachrichten aus Schleswig-Holstein* 2009, 20-23.

Segschneider, M. 2002a, Fränkisches Glas im Dünensand. *Archäologisches Korrespondenzblatt* 32:1, 117-36.

Segschneider, M. 2002b, Trade and centrality between the Rhine and the Limfjord around 500 AD. The beachmarket on the North Frisian island Amrum and its context. In: B. Hårdh & L. Larsson (eds.), *Central places in the Migration and Merovingian periods: papers from the 52nd Sachsensymposium, Lund, August 2001*. Stockholm. 247-56.

Segschneider, M. 2004, Die Marschen der Insel Föhr und der Wiedingharde, Kreis Nordfriesland. Eine siedlungsarchäologische Studie. Dissertation, Kiel University. http://macau.uni-kiel.de/receive/dissertation_diss_00001782 (accessed 30.09.2013).

Segschneider, M. 2007, Sylt. In: *Reallexikon der germanischen Altertumskunde* 30. Founded by Johannes Hoops. 2nd ed. Berlin/New York. 50-54.

Segschneider, M. 2009, Grubenhäuser und Glasperlen – ein Landeplatz der Völkerwanderungszeit in den Norddorfer Dünen. In: G. Quedens (ed.), *Amrum 2008. Jahreschronik einer Insel*. Amrum. 142-44.

Stidsing, E. 2008, Imitationer af Frankiske glasdrikkebægre fra yngre jernalder. *Kulturhistorisk Museum Randers Årbog* 2008, 30-37.

Wunderlich, T. 2008, Anwendung von Potentialmethoden zur Verbesserung des Nutzsignals und der Interpretation magnetischer Feldmessungen in der Archäometrie. Diploma thesis, Kiel University.

Zimmermann, W.H. 1992, Die Siedlungen des 1. bis 6. Jahrhunderts nach Christus von Flögeln-Eekhöltjen, Niedersachsen. Die Bauformen und ihre Funktionen. *Probleme Küstenforschung im südlichen Nordseegebiet* 19, 1-360.

At the geestland edge southwest of Ribe: On the track of a centre of wealth during the 1st millennium AD

Claus Feveile

As has been the case in so many places across Denmark over the last c. 25 years, hundreds of metal finds dating from the Iron Age, Viking Age and Middle Ages have been recovered around Ribe with the aid of metal detectors. A fair proportion of the finds were discovered in places where past discoveries, aerial photographs or actual excavations suggested there might be something worth finding; in other cases metal detectors have led – and continue to lead – to the discovery of previously unknown sites.

Up until 2008, Antikvarisk Samling in Ribe was a museum with a very small geographic area of archaeological responsibility. As such, museum staff were able to acquire very detailed insights into the archaeological sites and monuments within the area. They employed four approaches in particular: examination, review and presentation of all known finds and ancient monuments prior to 1984 (Jensen (ed.) 1998); annual campaigns of aerial photography, especially from 1984 until the mid-1990s, though subsequently they were more sporadic; since 1982, reconnaissance of all the planted windbreaks that have been ploughed out for replacement – to date more than 375 km of windbreaks have been examined in this way in the area around Ribe (Jensen 1985), and finally, a combination of rescue and research excavations.

The sum of all these diverse observations has clearly demonstrated that the area to the southwest of Ribe, comprising the present-day parishes of Vester Vedsted and Hviding, has a quite remarkable concentration of settlements from the Iron Age, Viking Age and the Early Middle Ages, both quantitatively and qualitatively. Besides the discoveries made during the many modern excavations, one only needs to think of the Vester Vedsted hoard from the 10th century, with its c. 1 kg of gold and a little silver, or the ground-breaking excavations at Dankirke in the 1960s where the contents of a burnt-down building, together with those of a nearby cultural layer, have contributed to the almost mythical character of the site.

Since the middle of the 1980s, metal-detector archaeology has contributed to this picture in many ways, supplementing our knowledge and, not least, recovering astonishing finds time after time. Not many archaeologists make extensive use of metal detectors themselves, but I am one of the few. I therefore know what a huge investment of labour and effort is required and how small the detecting head is relative to a large field, in respect of which an archaeologist may say 'we would just like you to take a look at this …'. This article could not have been written without the enormous contributions – both in time and effort – made by the detectorists, and many heartfelt thanks are therefore due to the museum's detector team: Jens Christian Lau, Gunnar Larsen, Henrik Christiansen and Flemming Gadgaard.

Professional research efforts as regards Ribe have so far been concentrated on the town's 'Viking

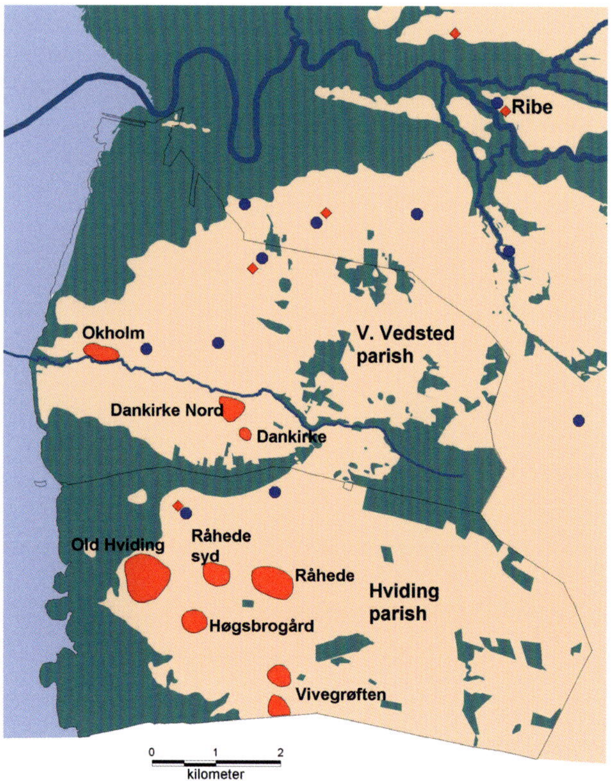

Fig. 1. | *The area southwest of Ribe, showing wetland areas and arable land. The estimated extent of the metal-detector sites mentioned in the text is given; other sites from the Late Roman/ Early Germanic Iron Age are shown in blue, and sites from the Late Germanic Iron Age, Viking Age and Early Middle Ages are shown in red.*

Age', i.e. the trading or market place dating from the 8th and 9th centuries AD. This decision is completely justified, as the latter is, without parallel, the most important individual archaeological site in southwestern Jutland. However, this focus has resulted in otherwise very exciting and remarkable sites being rather unfairly neglected. As a consequence, the interplay between the market place/ town and the settlements of the surrounding area is neither well studied nor well understood. It is therefore my hope that attention will, in the future, be focused on these 'satellite sites' around Ribe – sites which were either a pre-requisite essential to the founding of Ribe, or significant partners contemporaneous with the market place and the town. In this respect, the area to the southwest of Ribe, the present-day Vester Vedsted and Hviding parishes, will undoubtedly come to play a very central role.

In the following, an outline of a number of the sites located to the southwest of Ribe will be briefly presented, supplemented by some remarks of a more methodological nature (fig. 1).

Dankirke

The Dankirke settlement is comprised of two discrete parts: the wealthy farm towards the south, which was excavated by the Danish National Museum in the 1960s, and an apparently ordinary farmstead settlement in an area to the northwest, usually referred to as 'Dankirke North'. The excavations at Dankirke will not be dealt with further here – they have already been presented in a preliminary form (Jarl Hansen 1985; 1990), while a more detailed analysis and presentation of the extensive finds is still awaited. It should be noted, however, that there are two unusual circumstances relating to this site that have led to it being attributed the status of a rich chieftain's or magnate's farmstead. One concerns the remains of a burnt-down building which, on excavation, revealed a very rich finds assemblage. The other concerns a cultural layer formed in association with the settlement that was preserved up until the time of the excavation solely because it lay as the fill of a natural depression (fig. 2). When Dankirke is compared with other settlements, it is necessary to imagine how the site would have appeared as an excavation object had the building not burnt down and if natural conditions had not happened to result in the preservation of the cultural layer. What interpretation would, I wonder, have been placed on these otherwise very ordinary buildings, albeit oriented in an untraditional way?

In this respect it is also interesting to take a look at the results of the metal-detector surveys that have been carried out, both on the scheduled (i.e. protected) part, where the excavations took place, as well as on numerous occasions on the site of Dankirke North. An estimated 100-150 hours of surveys have been completed since 1992.

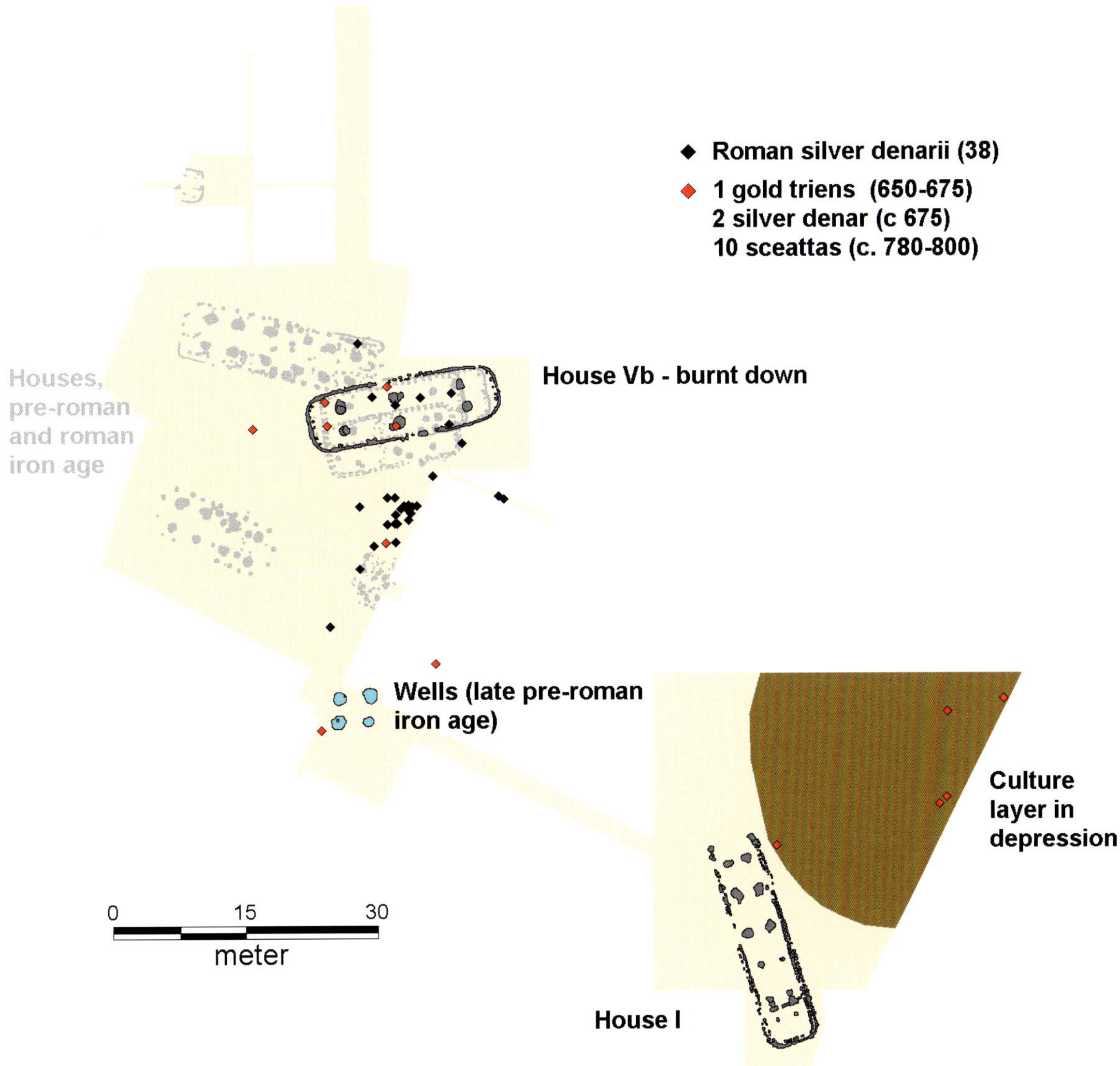

Fig. 2. | *Dankirke. Simplified plan of the excavations. After Jarl Hansen 1990, with additions.*

The results for both areas were astonishing relative to what was expected: There were virtually no finds – and nothing over and above the commonplace. Surveys on the scheduled part, the location of the 'chieftain's' farmstead, have yielded one Roman denarius, a fragment of a cruciform brooch and a piece of a silver arm ring from the Viking Age. At Dankirke North, there were similarly very few finds and these were of quite commonly occurring artefacts. It is possible to argue that this situation could be due to ploughing not having been particularly destructive such that the cultural layer was only disturbed to a limited extent, but this is in no way the case. As early as the 1960s, a significant part of the now scheduled Dankirke was subjected to deeper ploughing (Jarl Hansen 1990, 213), and in the middle of the 1980s, when the land changed hands, the same happened in parts of Dankirke North. If we were to rank sites today according to the metal finds recovered by metal detector, Dankirke would be somewhere close to the bottom of the list.

Okholm

Okholm is the settlement name for the westernmost part of the village of Vester Vedsted and the find site of a hoard discovered in 1859. A farmhand quarrying sand found buried treasure including arm and neck rings, ingots and ornaments, all of gold, together with a small number of dirhems and fragments of silver ornaments (Jørgensen & Petersen 1998, 298-99). The hoard has been dated to the middle of the 10th century AD. In the 1960s, Okholm was drawn into the hunt for the earliest location of Ribe in a joint excavation project involving Mogens Bencard of Antikvarisk Samling, Ribe, and Hans Jørgen Madsen of Moesgård Museum. Though it quickly became apparent that the site had nothing whatsoever to do with Ribe and its predecessors, the excavations were significant for the time and yielded several intriguing finds. They were most recently followed up by a series of rescue and research excavations in 1995-96, which investigated a number of *Grubenhäuser*, dating in particular from the 8th and 9th centuries, with clear links to trade and crafts. Together, the two excavation campaigns have revealed important evidence of a special site with numerous *Grubenhäuser* and traces of both glass bead manufacture and bronze casting. The finds included, for example, imported Rhenish and Frisian pottery and also coins: a single Roman bronze coin, two sceattas from the 8th century and three Nordic penninge from the 9th century, plus a couple of special coins from the 11th century. A grave from the late 6th century was also investigated (Bencard 1969; Feveile 2001; Høilund Nielsen 1998; Nielsen 1998).

As regards metal-detector surveys, not much time has been invested in the fields around the excavated areas – no more than an estimated 20-30 hours. The first attempts did not yield any finds and so there has been little interest in continuing to survey the area; there are other much more productive sites in the vicinity. Whether these first impressions represent the real nature of the site, however, it is difficult to say with certainty. I am not convinced that a few hours of survey can provide a truly indicative picture of a site, and further efforts should certainly be invested in the Okholm area in the future. On the other hand, it should be borne in mind that at other sites which were 'discovered' in an equally short time, many hours of further metal-detecting have only confirmed the good results encountered in the first few hours. Perhaps, then, the impression of Okholm as a site at which there is next to nothing to be found by metal-detector is not mistaken.

Gammel Hviding

This site comprises a large but still partially ill-defined area to the west of Gammel Hviding Church (fig. 3). It was discovered by aerial photography in 1984 when Stig Jensen recognised the clear outline of a 'Trelleborg house' in the cereal crop. This led to a major research and rescue excavation in the years 1986-94, involving the investigation of a c. 2.5 ha area located 300-400 m west of the church, running directly up to the boundary between the wet salt marsh and the dry, higher sandy geestland. In the first year of excavation, a metal-detector survey of the topsoil was initiated prior to its removal from the excavation site (Jensen 1987a), together with areas in the immediate vicinity. In 1995, a smaller area was excavated just west of the planting by the church. Collectively, these excavations demonstrated that there was scattered settlement in the large area towards the west throughout large parts of the Pre-Roman and Early Roman Iron Age. After this, there was a lull until some time most likely in the 7th or early 8th century AD. From then on, and until the middle of the 12th century, there was probably continuous occupation within the excavated area. Up until the second half of the 10th century, however, the traces are generally poorly preserved. Often only wells, deep pits and postholes from pairs of roof-bearing posts are preserved. Between the time of the 'Trelleborg house' and the middle of the 12th century, the settlement traces are much better preserved, and a series of main phases can be identified. To date, only a few aspects of the excavations have been presented in preliminary articles. These include the metal-detector finds resulting from the surveys carried out during the first years (Jensen 1987a; 1987b; 1990). A thorough analysis is still lacking; it is therefore conceivable that the 'phases' shown could require revision on a number of points (fig. 4).

Fig. 3. | *Gammel Hviding. West of the church, two excavated areas are marked in grey while all the recorded metal-detector finds (after 1998) are shown in black.*

Metal detectors have been employed more or less annually at Gammel Hviding since the middle of the 1980s. At a very conservative estimate, at least 1500-2000 hours in total have been invested in these surveys. The finds to date lie spread over an area of c. 700 x 700 m, and though we probably now know the main extent of the site, we are still unsure about the boundaries of the finds distribution towards the south and east; they are clearer towards the north and especially the west, where the salt marsh constitutes a natural finds boundary, at least in preservation terms (table 1 and fig. 5).

The metal-detector finds include a few pieces from the Early and Late Roman Iron Age, together with a number of fragments of brooches from the Early Germanic Iron Age. The excavation to the west uncovered a *Grubenhaus* and a pit from the Early Germanic Iron Age, presumably representing the westernmost parts of a village, as reflected in the scattered finds of brooches to the east of the large excavated area. The Late Germanic Iron

Fig. 4. | *The four main phases of the farmstead at Gammel Hviding, c. AD 1000 to the 12th century. Final analysis and interpretation of the excavation results will probably add further elements to the individual phases, and possibly also another main phase, but is unlikely to change the relative chronology.*

Age is also only relatively sparsely represented, but the finds do include two coins from the early 8th century, both sceattas of Continental runic type, a bird brooch of Ørsnes type D5 and a small (oval) tortoise brooch. The great majority of the metal finds belong to the period extending from the 9th century up to and including the 12th century. There is a rich selection of Scandinavian find types: ornaments, articles for everyday use and various fittings (Klæsøe 2005). There is also a selection of dirhems from the 9th to the10th century and German coins from the 10th to the 11th century; these are accompanied by several ingots and pieces of hack silver.

In addition to these scattered stray finds, there was a concentration of hack silver and fragments of dirhems within an area of c. 15 x 15 m that must be interpreted as a ploughed-up hoard (Moesgaard 2007, 134).

Imported finds are also prominent, especially Carolingian-Ottonian enamel brooches, of which there are 30 examples (Baastrup 2007; 2009; and later finds); there are also a couple of Carolingian coin brooches and a quatrefoil Råhede-type brooch, all from the 9th century (Feveile 2011a, fig. 5.2). The transition between the Viking Age and the Middle Ages is represented by several bird brooches and a number of Urnes-style brooches. The point on which Gammel Hviding differs from other metal-rich sites is in its many foreign, imported ornament types. By and large, these types must be considered as simple and common in the areas of their origin – and are perhaps attributed too great a significance when they appear in Scandinavia. The number of enamel brooches found in Denmark is steadily increasing and every year new finds are added, both from new find sites and from those which have

<table>
<tr><th>Gl. Hviding</th><th>Early Roman Iron Age
1-200</th><th>Late Roman Iron Age
200-400</th><th>Early Germanic Iron Age
400-550</th><th>Late Germanic Iron Age
550-800</th><th>Viking Age
800-1050</th><th>Medieval
1050-1200</th><th>Total</th></tr>
<tr><td rowspan="3">Jewellery</td><td rowspan="3">10</td><td colspan="2">16</td><td colspan="2">1</td><td></td><td rowspan="3">82</td></tr>
<tr><td rowspan="2"></td><td rowspan="2">16</td><td rowspan="2">6</td><td colspan="2">16</td></tr>
<tr><td>17</td><td></td></tr>
<tr><td>Jewellery, imported</td><td></td><td></td><td></td><td></td><td>35</td><td></td><td>35</td></tr>
<tr><td rowspan="3">Personal, keys, box, mounts</td><td rowspan="3"></td><td rowspan="3"></td><td rowspan="3"></td><td colspan="2">1</td><td></td><td rowspan="3">11</td></tr>
<tr><td rowspan="2"></td><td colspan="2">9</td></tr>
<tr><td>1</td><td></td></tr>
<tr><td>Riding gear incl. strap-distributors</td><td>1</td><td></td><td></td><td>1</td><td colspan="2">13</td><td>15</td></tr>
<tr><td>Strap-ends, buckles</td><td></td><td></td><td>2</td><td></td><td>6</td><td></td><td>8</td></tr>
<tr><td>Weight lead/ bronze</td><td></td><td></td><td></td><td colspan="3">38</td><td>38</td></tr>
<tr><td rowspan="2">Hacksilver/-ingots</td><td rowspan="2"></td><td rowspan="2"></td><td rowspan="2"></td><td rowspan="2"></td><td colspan="2">27</td><td rowspan="2">29</td></tr>
<tr><td>2</td><td></td></tr>
<tr><td>Bronze ingots, casting sprues</td><td></td><td></td><td></td><td colspan="3">12</td><td>12</td></tr>
<tr><td>Coins</td><td></td><td colspan="2">3 (Roman)</td><td>2 (Sceattas)</td><td>21 (Dirhams)
7 (German)</td><td>1</td><td>34</td></tr>
<tr><td>Rune stick</td><td></td><td></td><td></td><td></td><td>1</td><td></td><td>1</td></tr>
<tr><td rowspan="4">Total</td><td rowspan="4">11</td><td colspan="2">19</td><td colspan="2">2</td><td></td><td rowspan="4">265</td></tr>
<tr><td rowspan="3"></td><td rowspan="3">18</td><td colspan="3">50</td></tr>
<tr><td rowspan="2">9</td><td colspan="2">65</td></tr>
<tr><td>90</td><td>1</td></tr>
</table>

Table 1.

previously yielded this kind of brooch. In 10-15 years, it will probably become clear that these rather unremarkable brooches are present at a great many sites. The tendency towards concentrations of find sites around Ribe, Aalborg and Roskilde is probably more the result of a long tradition of the use of metal detectors in these areas, rather than any cultural-historical factor or factors. Whether southwestern Jutland – including the part south of Gammel Hviding – will ultimately demonstrate a higher proportion of finds due to its proximity to northwestern Europe and its relatively early exposure to Christian influences, with which these kinds of brooches are linked (Wamers 2004, 46), only the future can tell.

Råhede

In 1998, about 2 km directly east of Gammel Hviding Church, Stig Jensen discovered the remains of a large 'Trelleborg house' during aerial reconnaissance. It lay on the top of a small ridge that provided open views to the north, south and west. Subsequent aerial survey has identified numerous buildings dating from the Early Middle Ages. No excavations have yet been carried out at this location.

Shortly after Råhede was discovered, metal detectors were employed at the site. The presence of a 'Trelleborg house' and its proximity to Gammel Hviding alone was enough to attract the attention of detectorists. In the first years, however, efforts were somewhat half-hearted as only a few scattered finds were forthcoming. The site

Fig. 5. | *Gammel Hviding. A selection of metal-detector finds.*

was subsequently left alone, and only since exploration resumed in 2004 has it yielded a large number of finds. The lack of finds resulting from the preliminary investigations at Råhede prompts caution when expressing an opinion about sites that have rarely produced finds, such as Dankirke and Okholm, discussed above. Sometimes many hours of work must be spent conducting trials over a much greater area than perhaps was imagined in the early stages before the finds really begin to emerge. An estimated 300-400 hours have been invested in metal-detector surveys at Råhede (table 2).

The earliest finds are from the Early Germanic Iron Age and consist of a few fragments of cruciform brooches. These are followed by two beak brooches – a very unusual brooch type for this part of the country. The great majority of the finds can, however, be ascribed to the later part of the Viking Age and the Early Middle Ages (fig. 6).

The differences between Råhede and Gammel Hviding are especially striking in terms of the relationship between local and imported ornament types; there are many more imported examples at Gammel Hviding than at Råhede. This is strange, considering the very short distance between the two sites and also the fact that they probably both include material from large parts of the Late Germanic Iron Age, the Viking Age and the early Middle Ages. Are we seeing the difference between

Fig. 6. | *A selection of metal-detector finds from Råhede.*

<table>
<tr><th>Råhede</th><th>Early Roman Iron Age
1-200</th><th>Late Roman Iron Age
200-400</th><th>Early Germanic Iron Age
400-550</th><th>Late Germanic Iron Age
550-800</th><th>Viking Age
800-1050</th><th>Medieval
1050-1200</th><th>Total</th></tr>
<tr><td rowspan="2">Jewellery</td><td rowspan="2"></td><td colspan="2">4</td><td rowspan="2">3</td><td colspan="2">10</td><td rowspan="2">28</td></tr>
<tr><td></td><td>2</td><td>8</td><td>1</td></tr>
<tr><td>Jewellery, imported</td><td></td><td></td><td></td><td></td><td>5</td><td>1</td><td>6</td></tr>
<tr><td rowspan="2">Personal, keys, box, mounts</td><td rowspan="2"></td><td rowspan="2"></td><td rowspan="2"></td><td rowspan="2"></td><td colspan="2">3</td><td rowspan="2">10</td></tr>
<tr><td>1</td><td>6</td></tr>
<tr><td>Riding gear incl. strap-distributors</td><td></td><td></td><td></td><td></td><td colspan="2">5</td><td>5</td></tr>
<tr><td>Strap-ends, buckles</td><td></td><td></td><td></td><td></td><td>2</td><td>1</td><td>3</td></tr>
<tr><td>Weight lead</td><td></td><td></td><td></td><td colspan="3">9</td><td>9</td></tr>
<tr><td>Gold ingot</td><td></td><td></td><td></td><td></td><td>1</td><td></td><td>1</td></tr>
<tr><td>Hacksilver/-ingots</td><td></td><td></td><td></td><td></td><td colspan="2">6</td><td>6</td></tr>
<tr><td>Bronze ingots</td><td></td><td></td><td></td><td colspan="3">4</td><td>4</td></tr>
<tr><td>Coins</td><td></td><td colspan="2">1 (Roman, copper)</td><td></td><td>1 (Dirham)</td><td></td><td>2</td></tr>
<tr><td>Patrix die</td><td></td><td></td><td></td><td></td><td>1</td><td></td><td>1</td></tr>
<tr><td>Bronze droplets</td><td></td><td></td><td></td><td></td><td colspan="2">>50</td><td>>50</td></tr>
<tr><td rowspan="3">Total</td><td rowspan="3"></td><td colspan="2">5</td><td></td><td colspan="2">24 + >50</td><td rowspan="3">125</td></tr>
<tr><td rowspan="2"></td><td rowspan="2">2</td><td colspan="3">13</td></tr>
<tr><td>3</td><td>19</td><td>9</td></tr>
</table>

Table 2.

<table>
<tr><th>Høgsbrogård</th><th>Early Roman Iron Age
1-200</th><th>Late Roman Iron Age
200-400</th><th>Early Germanic Iron Age
400-550</th><th>Late Germanic Iron Age
550-800</th><th>Viking Age
800-1050</th><th>Medieval
1050-1200</th><th>Total</th></tr>
<tr><td rowspan="3">Jewellery</td><td rowspan="3"></td><td colspan="2">2</td><td colspan="2">1</td><td></td><td rowspan="3">16</td></tr>
<tr><td rowspan="2"></td><td colspan="2">2</td><td colspan="2">1</td></tr>
<tr><td>4</td><td>4</td><td></td><td>2</td></tr>
<tr><td>Jewellery, imported</td><td></td><td colspan="2">1</td><td></td><td>3</td><td></td><td>4</td></tr>
<tr><td>Personal, keys, box mounts</td><td></td><td></td><td></td><td></td><td>1</td><td></td><td>1</td></tr>
<tr><td>Weight lead/ bronze</td><td></td><td></td><td></td><td colspan="3">4</td><td>4</td></tr>
<tr><td rowspan="2">Coins</td><td rowspan="2"></td><td colspan="2">2 (Roman)</td><td colspan="2">1 (Sassanid drachma)</td><td rowspan="2"></td><td rowspan="2">4</td></tr>
<tr><td></td><td></td><td></td><td>1 (Dirham)</td></tr>
<tr><td>Hoard</td><td></td><td></td><td>141</td><td></td><td></td><td></td><td>141</td></tr>
<tr><td rowspan="4">Total</td><td rowspan="4"></td><td colspan="2">5</td><td colspan="2">2</td><td></td><td rowspan="4">170</td></tr>
<tr><td rowspan="3"></td><td colspan="2">2</td><td colspan="2">1</td></tr>
<tr><td rowspan="2">145</td><td colspan="3">4</td></tr>
<tr><td>4</td><td>5</td><td>2</td></tr>
</table>

Table 3.

25 years and 1500-2000 hours of detector survey at Gammel Hviding and 6-8 years and 300-400 hours of corresponding work at Råhede – or are other factors involved?

Råhede South

Located approximately halfway between Gammel Hviding and Råhede, a small number of metal artefacts have been found at Råhede South since work began there in 2008. No more than an estimated c. 100 hours of detector survey have been carried out. Reconnaissance has been conducted in the vicinity, focusing on a number of windbreaks, and this has revealed the presence of settlement from the Early Iron Age as well as the Middle Ages; there are no definite finds from the intervening period. It was almost by chance that the site came to be partially surveyed by metal-detector, yet within the course of a few hours a German coin from c. AD 1000 was found as well as an Urnes-style brooch and a bird-shaped brooch from the early Middle Ages. Subsequent surveys did not yield nearly such impressive finds.

Høgsbrogård

At Høgsbrogård, a series of crop marks were observed relating to presumed pits and similar structures, but no building foundations could be recognised. An old *sb.* number (i.e National Museum site number) refers to the find of a Roman coin. These observations led to the area being subjected to a metal-detector survey for the first time in the winter of 2008-09. To date, finds have been recovered from an area measuring about 300 x 300 m with no definite boundaries; an estimated c. 200 hours were spent on surveys in 2009 and the spring of 2010 (table 3). The finds are evenly distributed in date from the Late Roman Iron Age to the early Middle Ages. The overview (table 3) includes all the finds from a hack silver hoard dating from the Early Germanic Iron Age, though only about half of these originate from the plough soil and were found by metal detector (fig. 7). The rest of the hoard lay in a feature beneath the plough soil. A minor excavation in connection with the hoard revealed settlement traces from the Early Germanic Iron Age (Feveile 2011b). The metal detector finds show, furthermore, that metal items were lost regu-

Fig. 7. | *The Høgsbrogård hoard. Photo: J. Lee.*

larly during the course of the Late Germanic Iron Age, Viking Age and early Middle Ages without it being clear at the moment whether these represent a continuous occupation.

Vivegrøften

Aerial photographs showing traces of at least 15-20 longhouses have revealed the presence of a village from the Roman/Germanic Iron Age at Vivegrøften in the southern part of Hviding parish. The site was first detected from the air by St. Joseph at the end of the 1960s, and a minor excavation carried out in 1969 by Olfert Voss revealed the well-preserved remains of a building from the Early Germanic Iron Age (Jensen 1980). A metal-detector survey was carried out on the field containing many building foundations in 2009 without leading to the discovery of very many finds (only two or three brooches and a ring-shaped piece of gold), and the metal detectorists began to talk about going home. A few hundred metres to the south they could see a field that 'looked promising' – not least because it contained a small but striking elevation and it was known that there were a few scattered and undated crop marks. After just a few hours it was clear that the field contained many finds – and much more than had been anticipated. The extent of the site is not yet securely defined, but the concentration of finds appears to lie within an area of c. 400 x 400 m. However, this does not correspond to the area within which the aerial photographs had revealed traces of longhouses and 'ordinary' village settlement. An examination of the chronological distribution of the metal finds at Vivegrøften reveals a completely different distribution than that seen previously in the region to the southwest of Ribe (table 4). The great majority of the finds can be dated to the Late Roman and Early Germanic Iron Age, with more than 20 brooches dating from this time. As an extra bonus more than 15 glass beads and numerous of the very scarce (apart from in Ribe's 8th-century cultural layer) glass mosaic tesserae were found on the surface of the field during the course of the metal-detector survey. The later finds, somewhat fewer in number, are evenly distributed in time through the Late Germanic Iron Age, Viking Age and early Middle Ages. A find very much in a class of its own is a small pyramid with inlaid semi-precious stones on a background of honeycomb silver and gold foil. The piece originates from a sword baldric and is of a type known, in particular, from England, including the Sutton Hoo graves (Carver 1998, plate IV); there are also numerous examples of corresponding mounts from the Continent. In Denmark, however, there are only three finds of this type: this example from Vivegrøften, a less well-preserved one from Gammel Hviding (fig. 8) and one from Sandegård on Bornholm (Watt 2006, fig. 13). As far as I have been able to discover, the only similar examples from the rest of Scandinavia are from Valsgärde grave 7; these are of a slightly different type without inlays (Arwidsson 1977, Tafel 15).[1]

Methodological considerations

Are metal-detector surveys nothing more than simple treasure hunting or can we archaeologists use the results professionally? At the beginning of the 1980s, the view was that the metal detector was 'The work of the devil' (Fischer 1983). Are we now saying it is a gift from Heaven? There are certainly those who do not share the latter view, but attitudes to the metal detector and its use have nevertheless changed decisively in a positive direction. This is partly a result of the special Treasure Trove legislation in Denmark, which ensures that virtually all finds are submitted to museums, but especially because there are numerous cases of successful collaborations between museums and the many metal detectorists (Henriksen 2006). This is a form of collaboration that we have also been able to export to Scania, northern Germany and Norway.

Is it at all possible to use the locations of metal-detector finds for intra- or inter-site analyses? In Ribe, for example, we have never had a tradition of recording precisely where and how areas have been surveyed by metal detector. We do not divide the fields up into small grids; we do not record from year to year where we have surveyed and how many times we have gone over the same area. In 1998 the positions of finds began to be recorded using GPS. Before then we generally have much less precise descriptions of find sites: 'north of the excavation trench' would be a typical example. This means that we do not know which areas have been surveyed or how many times we have covered the same ground. On several occasions, I have observed 'holes' or 'gaps' in the scatters of survey points. It is impossible to tell whether these are of cultural-historical relevance and reflect a real absence of finds, or simply mark areas that have not been surveyed at the same intensity as adjacent areas. What should be recorded and what should be retained? How significant are the conditions for preservation? To make a very general comparison between finds from southwestern Jutland and those from eastern Denmark, as presented on metal-detector club websites, it appears that conditions of preservation for metals are generally poorer in the former area. The same conclusion is also indicated by an analysis of more than 2000 metal finds from southern Jutland (Brinch Madsen 1998; Brinch Madsen et al. 2004). This study examined finds in various categories (settlements, graves, and hoards), types of corrosion and soils. In particular, finds from settlements were found to be heavily affected by corro-

<table>
<tr><th>Vivegrøften</th><th>Early Roman Iron Age
1-200</th><th>Late Roman Iron Age
200-400</th><th>Early Germanic Iron Age
400-550</th><th>Late Germanic Iron Age
550-800</th><th>Viking Age
800-1050</th><th>Medieval
1050-1200</th><th>Total</th></tr>
<tr><td rowspan="3">Jewellery</td><td rowspan="3"></td><td colspan="2">14</td><td></td><td colspan="2">2</td><td rowspan="3">33</td></tr>
<tr><td rowspan="2"></td><td colspan="2">3</td><td rowspan="2">3</td><td rowspan="2"></td></tr>
<tr><td>8</td><td>3</td></tr>
<tr><td>Jewellery, imported</td><td></td><td></td><td></td><td></td><td>1</td><td></td><td>1</td></tr>
<tr><td rowspan="2">Personal, keys, box, mounts</td><td rowspan="2"></td><td rowspan="2"></td><td rowspan="2">1</td><td rowspan="2"></td><td colspan="2">2</td><td rowspan="2">5</td></tr>
<tr><td></td><td>2</td></tr>
<tr><td>Riding gear incl. strap-distributors</td><td>1</td><td></td><td></td><td>1</td><td colspan="2">3</td><td>5</td></tr>
<tr><td>Strap-ends, buckles</td><td></td><td></td><td></td><td>1</td><td></td><td></td><td>1</td></tr>
<tr><td>Weight lead</td><td></td><td></td><td></td><td colspan="3">1</td><td>1</td></tr>
<tr><td>Hacksilver/-ingots</td><td></td><td></td><td></td><td colspan="3">8</td><td>8</td></tr>
<tr><td>Coins</td><td></td><td colspan="2">5 (Roman)</td><td></td><td>1 (Dirham)</td><td></td><td>6</td></tr>
<tr><td>Ring gold</td><td></td><td colspan="2">1</td><td></td><td></td><td></td><td>1</td></tr>
<tr><td rowspan="3">Total</td><td rowspan="3">1</td><td colspan="2">20</td><td colspan="3">9</td><td rowspan="3">61</td></tr>
<tr><td rowspan="2"></td><td colspan="2">3</td><td colspan="2">7</td></tr>
<tr><td>9</td><td>5</td><td>5</td><td>2</td></tr>
</table>

Table 4.

sion, especially those from the Germanic Iron Age (which was also represented by the least number of finds). Brinch Madsen et al. (2004) conclude that soil type and whether a find was discovered prior to or after modern agricultural developments involving the heavy use of chemical fertilisers both play a significant role – in unison – as regards the appearance of metals. In my view, this conclusion also perhaps extends to the matter of the survival of more fragile artefact types. Its consequences also need to be considered with respect to our ability to recognise different find types, as well as to our interpretation of finds in general. At Stavnsager, for example, the many fragments of cruciform brooches are interpreted as evidence for the deliberate collection, cutting up and melting down of older ornaments (Høilund Nielsen & Loveluck 2006, 70-71). In contrast, I have always understood the many fragments at for example Gammel Hviding as being the result of the degradation of previously more complete artefacts – a degradation that I believe takes place in the plough soil where many of the artefacts have, in my view, lain for centuries. That which remains is often just the solid core – the head plate of the brooch with its pin catch for example. The less robust brooch types, such as those from the Late Roman Iron Age, are by and large absent from our metal-detector assemblages. My guess is that, due to the fragility of the metal, they are now so degraded that they are no longer recognised – or they simply no longer exist. If my view

Fig. 8. | *Pyramidal fittings, to the left from Gammel Hviding, to the right from Vivegrøften.*

is correct, the absence of certain date-conferring finds for a period can, therefore, be explained to some extent by preservation conditions. Perhaps this is of no great consequence when comparisons are made within a narrow geographic area, but between different regions and provinces, or between sites located on different soil types, it can be of crucial significance.

In several parts of Denmark – and this includes to some degree the Ribe area – only a small number of sites have been subjected to metal-detector survey and often at very variable intensity, whereas other areas appear as complete blanks on a distribution map of metal-detector finds. This is a classic archaeological problem, and a situation we have to live with. However, all things being equal, it also means that we are far too easily led to believe that find-rich metal-detector sites were also important sites in the society of their time. This is doubtless true of a number of 'first division' examples, such as Tissø, Haithabu, Gudme and Sorte Muld. But can the same be said of the next 'layer' of sites? I believe we will only be able to answer this question when we have achieved the same level of insight into a large number of comparable sites within a given area. Often, however, we are forced by many different factors to limit our efforts to a few or perhaps even a single site within each of our study areas. This is a limitation dictated both by the possibility of access for metal detectorists, the enthusiasm of museums (or lack of it) with respect to finding new sites, limitations imposed on local museums and the possibility of financing other methods of investigation.

As professional archaeologists, we are perhaps too enthused by the finds recovered by metal detectorists so that sites where good finds are encountered, often by chance, are quickly highlighted as being central places with far-reaching contacts. Experience in this respect from south-western Jutland, particularly concerning the finds from Hviding parish, shows how dangerous it is to concentrate on a single site selected on the basis of the first exceptional finds from a parish or a district. In Hviding, metal-detector archaeology began in the mid-1980s at Gammel Hviding, west of the church, on the basis of one aerial photograph. Had there been sugar beet or grass on the field that particular year and not cereals – and on the other hand, had we invested all our energy in that single site – it would be unlikely that we would know about Råhede, Høgsbrogård or Vivegrøften. And I wonder what still remains hidden – what we still do not understand or have yet not found. Why is Vivegrøften so rich in metal finds from the Germanic Iron Age when we can apparently find nothing whatsoever at the locus classicus, Dankirke? And can we be at all sure that Dankirke and Dankirke North are 'detector negative'? I do not feel convinced with respect to either question. The data foundation is much too uneven from site to site. At the moment we are comparing metal-detector sites where several thousand hours have been expended over many years with sites where the metal detector has scarcely been taken out of the box, for example at Okholm. Such comparisons cannot stand up to close critical scrutiny.

A centre of wealth emerges

Problems with the very heterogeneous data foundation will not, however, prevent me from sketching a picture of the situation here in the area south-west of Ribe during the 1st millennium AD. Let me just refer to this as a working paper – future investigations must correct any errors as necessary.

The earliest layer of sites included Dankirke, Høgsbrogård and Vivegrøften, where the majority of the finds date from the Late Roman Iron Age and the Germanic Iron Age. We can at present only guess at the internal relations between these three sites, all of which have generated numerous metal finds. The same is also true of the relations between the many contemporaneous settlements lacking metal finds. Is metal really absent or have we just not spent enough time looking for it? Dankirke apparently ceased being a special site in the middle of the 6th century, whereas the metal-detector finds from both Høgsbrogård and Vivegrøften show continued activity through the Late Germanic Iron Age and the Viking Age. Dankirke has previously been linked with the founding of Ribe shortly after

Fig. 9. | *Three Carolingian coin brooches from the 9th century. The one on the left is from Råhede; the other two are from Gammel Hviding.*

AD 700 (Jensen 1991; Jensen & Watt 1993) on the basis of, among other things, 13 coins dating from the 7th and 8th centuries that constituted the latest finds from the 1960s excavation. I have previously argued that these coins are not an expression of continued settlement but rather the result of the burial of perhaps two hoards (Feveile 2006). Together, these three sites display a wealth that apparently distinguishes them from the majority of coeval settlements across a very large area. At present, it is necessary to go northwards to Dejbjerg, or perhaps Billum to the west of Varde, in order to find evidence for corresponding wealth among finds recovered (Egeberg Hansen 1996; Frandsen 1996; 2001). The reason why Vester Vedsted and Hviding parishes stand out so conspicuously is uncertain. At Brokær, just north of Ribe, remains of graves have demonstrated the presence of a princely environment that is a few centuries earlier (Ethelberg 2003, 274ff; Rasmussen 1995). And at Dankirke, a special level in the social hierarchy is represented by some fittings from a Late Pre-Roman ceremonial wagon (Jarl Hansen 1985). This suggests that there was also wealth in the area in earlier periods.

Although the metal-detector finds from the 6th to the 8th century are not so conspicuous as those from the periods both before and after, there is, nevertheless, little doubt that the area to the southwest of Ribe also represented a very special environment during these centuries. The two pyramidal fittings from Gammel Hviding and Vivegrøften have already been mentioned. Found in Enderup, midway between Gammel Hviding and Vester Vedsted, a fragment of a brooch from the early 7th century similarly belongs to an aristocratic environment (Høilund Nielsen 1997). It is also worth noting that all four beak brooches found in southwestern Jutland came from two sites in Hviding parish: Råhede and Høgsbrogård.

Stig Jensen has previously pointed out that the pre-requisites essential for the establishment of the market place at Ribe were to be found in the preceding magnate's environment at Dankirke. In a way, I agree with him. We have to look to the southwest of Ribe; I am not willing to identify one particular site, let us say for example Dankirke, as the 'origin' of Ribe. I believe that the entire area around Vester Vedsted and Hviding should be identified as a collective power centre, central place, centre of wealth, or some such similar category, and that it was here that Ribe had its local starting point – just as it was from here that, from the early 8th century onwards, the trading place was controlled and originally established jointly with Frisian contacts. The actual residence of power did not move at all; it remained outside Ribe all along, though it was of course represented in the town in some form or other. It was the trading function, the controlled site or location where exchange took place that was positioned on the bank of the river Ribe Å, where access both to and from the sea and to and from the hinterland was controllable – but this was not the seat of power.

The rich sites at Vester Vedsted and Hviding continued to be occupied throughout the Late Germanic Iron Age and the entire Viking Age: Okholm, Råhede and Gammel Hviding, in particular, according to the present picture sketched by the archaeological record. But to 'rank' the sites in any way would appear to be a risky business. What should we rate highest: 1 kg of gold at Okholm, or examples of foreign contacts as seen in particular at Gammel Hviding? Perhaps these closely-spaced sites should be seen as several parts of the same lineage or dynasty, regardless of the social layer they represent: a south Danish royal family, members of the king's retainers or another branch of society's elite (fig. 9)?

Conclusion

Metal-detector archaeology has played, and continues to play, a very important role in discussions concerning central places, chieftain's residences and magnate's farmsteads as well as in the delimitation of such environments relative to more ordinary agrarian settlements. As a technique in itself, it cannot stand alone but must be combined with a number of other investigative methods in order to produce a credible picture of past societies. I will continue to be enthused by every new metal find that turns up, but at the same time I also urge caution with respect to the drawing of conclusions until a more adequate data foundation has been built up.

Bibliography

Arwidsson, G. 1977, *Valsgärde 7*. Uppsala.

Baastrup, M.P. 2007, Vikingetidens og den tidlige middelalders emaljefibler fra Sydvestjylland. *By, marsk og geest* 19, 5-16.

Baastrup, M.P. 2009, Småfibler af karolingiske og ottonske typer i Danmark. *Aarbøger for nordisk Oldkyndighed og Historie* 2005, 209-55.

Bencard, M. 1969, Grubehuse i Okholm. *Mark og montre* 1969, 26-36.

Carver, M. 1998 (rev. ed. 2007), *Sutton Hoo. Burial Ground of Kings?* London.

Egeberg Hansen, T. 1996, Et jernalderhus med drikkeglas i Dejbjerg, Vestjylland. *Kuml* 1993-94, 211-37.

Ethelberg, P. 2003, Gården og landsbyen i jernalder og vikingetid (500 f. Kr. – 1000 e. Kr.). In: P. Ethelberg, N. Hardt, B. Poulsen & A.B. Sørensen, *Det Sønderjyske Landbrugs Historie. Jernalder, vikingetid og middelalder.* Haderslev. 123-373.

Feveile, C. 2001, Okholm – en plads med håndværksspor og grubehuse fra 8.-9. århundrede. *By, marsk og geest* 13, 5-32.

Feveile, C. 2006, Sceattaerne fra Dankirke – skatte eller enkeltfund? *Nordisk Numismatisk Unions Medlemsblad* 2006:1, 3-9.

Feveile, C. 2011a, Korsfibler af Råhedetypen. En upåagtet fibeltype fra ældre vikingetid. *Kuml* 2011, 143-60.

Feveile, C. 2011b, The Høgsbrogård Hoard – a scrap metal hoard from the Early Germanic Iron Age in southwest Jutland. *Arkæologi i Slesvig – Archäologie in Schleswig. Sonderband. Det 61. Internationale Sachsensymposium 2010*. Neumünster. 269-81.

Fischer, C. 1983, Den har fanden skabt. *Skalk* 1983:1, 8-14.

Frandsen, L.B, De rige kvinder i Billum. *Mark og montre* 1996, 48-53.

Frandsen, L.B. De stenrige grave i Billum – jordfæstegrave fra ældre romersk jernalder. *Mark og montre* 2001, 19-32.

Henriksen, M.B. 2006, The metal detector – friend or foe for the archaeologist? Aspects of metal detector archaeology in Denmark. In: K.M. Hansen & K.B. Pedersen (eds.), *Across the western Baltic. Proceedings from an archaeological conference in Vordingborg.* Vordingborg. 217-26.

Høilund Nielsen, K. 1997, Et ornamenteret fibel-fragment fra Enderup ved Hviding. *By, marsk og geest* 9, 9-16.

Høilund Nielsen, K. 1998, En gravplads fra Okholm – lokal eller fremmed befolkning? *By, marsk og geest* 10, 7-21.

Høilund Nielsen, K. & C.P. Loveluck 2006, Fortid og fremtid på Stavnsager – om de britiske undersøgelser august 2005 og de foreløbige resultater. *Kulturhistorisk Museum Randers Årbog* 2006, 63-79.

Jarl Hansen, H. 1985, Fragmenter af en bronzebeslået pragtvogn fra Dankirke. *Aarbøger for nordisk Oldkyndighed og Historie* 1984, 217-43.

Jarl Hansen, H. 1990, Dankirke. Jernalderboplads og rigdomscenter. Oversigt over udgravningerne 1965-70. *Kuml* 1988-89, 201-47.

Jensen, S. 1980, To sydvestjyske bopladser fra ældre germansk jernalder. *Mark og Montre* 1980, 23-36.

Jensen, S. 1985, Hvad 100 km læhegn gemte. *Mark og montre* 1985, 49-54.

Jensen, S. 1987a, Plough-layer archaeology. *Arkæologiske udgravninger i Danmark* 1986, 9-19.

Jensen, S. 1987b, Hvidings vikinger. *Skalk* 1987:1, 3-8.

Jensen, S. 1987c, Overgangshuset. *Skalk* 1987:6, 3-8.

Jensen, S. 1990, Metalfund fra vikingetidsgårdene ved Gl. Hviding og Vilslev. *By, marsk og geest* 3, 27-40.

Jensen, S. 1991, *The Vikings of Ribe.* Ribe.

Jensen, S. 1998 (ed.), *Marsk, land og bebyggelse. Ribeegnen gennem 10.000 år.* Vol. 1-2. Højbjerg.

Jensen, S. & M. Watt 1993, Trading sites and central places. In: S. Hvass & B. Storgaard (eds.), *Digging into the past. 25 Years of Archaeology in Denmark.* Copenhagen/Højbjerg. 195-201.

Jørgensen, J. & P.V. Petersen 1998, *Guld, magt og tro. Danske skattefund fra oldtid og middelalder. Gold, power and belief. Danish gold treasures from Prehistory and the Middle Ages.* København. 1998.

Klæsøe, I.S. 2005, Et sælsomt spænde fra Ribe-egnen. *By, marsk og geest* 17, 5-13.

Madsen, H.B. 1998, Oldsagernes bevaringsgrad. In: S. Jensen (ed.), *Marsk, land og bebyggelse. Ribeegnen gennem 10.000 år.* Vol. 1. Højbjerg. 43-52.

Madsen, H.B., J.H. Andersen & L.B. Andersen 2004, Deterioration of prehistoric bronzes as an indicator of the state of preservation of antiquities in the Danish agrarian landscape: preliminary results. In: T. Nixon (ed.), *Preserving archaeological remains* in situ? *Proceedings of the 2nd conference 12-14 September 2001.* London. 50-57.

Moesgaard, J.C. 2007, Møntskatten fra Danelund og møntvæsenet i Sydvestjylland i vikingetid og tidlig middelalder. *Aarbøger for nordisk Oldkyndighed og Historie 2004*, 107-56.

Nielsen, L.C. 1998, *Ekskurs 3: Okholm.* In: S. Jensen (ed.), *Marsk, land og bebyggelse. Ribeegnen gennem 10.000 år.* Vol. 2. Højbjerg. 173-84.

Rasmussen, B.M. 1995, Brokær. Ein Reichtumszentrum der römischen Kaiserzeit in Südwestjütland. *Acta Archaeologica* 66, 39-109.

Wamers, E. 2004, Kristne gjenstander i tidligvikingtidens Danmark. In: N. Lund (ed.), *Kristendommen i Danmark før 1050. Et symposium i Roskilde den 5.-7. februar 2003.* Roskilde. 43-59.

Watt, M. 2006, Detector sites and settlement archaeology on Bornholm. A survey of 'productive sites' from the Iron Age and the Viking Age 1996-1999. *Journal of Danish Archaeology* 14, 139-67.

Notes

1 Thanks to Karen Høilund Nielsen and Anne Jørgensen for their help in tracking down similar examples in Scandinavia.

The metal detector site of Sig Syd

Jens G. Lauridsen

In the spring of 2005, Varde Museum was presented with a couple of fine artefacts found by metal detector in an area close to the village of Sig, c. 7 km northeast of Varde. These comprised a large trefoil brooch from the Viking Age and a small St. Clement figure, presumably a book clasp. The submission of these finds resulted from cooperation between the museum and the only amateur metal detectorist within the Museum's area of responsibility at that time. Museum staff had for some time supplied Michael Kristiansen with maps and information about places that could be interesting to survey with a metal detector, and this partnership bore fruit. Personal circumstances, however, led to the museum not receiving any finds for a number of years. In 2008, when autumn ploughing began at Sig Kapelbanke, the metal detecting recommenced, resulting in Michael Kristiansen becoming a frequent visitor to the museum. And his finds prompted great enthusiasm among museum staff as they included many fine and rare artefacts. Varde Museum had its first 'metal-rich' site and, judging from the nature of the finds and their quality, this must have been an important settlement.

History

Sig Kapelbanke, originally known as Thorstrup Kapel, was not chosen as a subject for metal-detector survey merely by chance. This south-facing foothill, extending out from Varde moraine hill in Varde river valley, has been the site of two chapels, the first Romanesque, the second a Gothic building. The presence of both buildings was demonstrated by K. Høgsbro Østergård through excavations in 1935. In the meadow below the chapels there was formerly a sacred spring, St. Biritti's or, subsequently, St. Gertrud's spring, which apparently had a long period of use. The spring was investigated in 1936 by H.K. Kristensen, revealing finds of pottery from the Renaissance and also from the Early Iron Age (Danmarks Kirker 19:3, 1441-42; Kristensen 1938, 24-34; Østergaard 1938, 17-23). The extent to which the spring was used in the intervening periods is something we will never know as it has now been eroded away by the river.

In connection with investigations prior to the laying of a gas pipeline in the 1980s, Esbjerg Museum carried out an excavation a little to the southwest of Sig Kapelbanke in the autumn of 1982 (ESM 1090). This revealed part of a settlement from the Roman Iron Age and apparently also traces of a Late Viking Age or Early Medieval settlement (Christiansen 1987).

At the instigation of the former National Forest and Nature Agency,[1] Lene B. Frandsen of Varde Museum carried out an investigation here in 1991. The aim was to establish the extent of the cemetery belonging to the lost chapels (fig. 1) and to define its limits in connection with a planned extended scheduling. The limits were found and the sched-

Fig. 1. | *Thorstrup Kapel seen from the air. Photo: Museet for Varde By og Omegn.*

uled area around the chapels was extended to the south (Frandsen 1992).

On a subsequent visit to the site, the museum became aware that white calcined bone and pottery had been ploughed up directly south of the newly established scheduled area. A grant from the *Keeper of National Antiquities' Archaeological Secretariat*[2] in 2002 made it possible to mount an excavation.[3] It turned out that the area contained Pre-Roman Iron Age urn burials and massive settlement traces from the Early and Late Iron Age as well as parts of a settlement from the Medieval period (fig. 2). Furthermore, the presence of a cultural layer up to 0.5 m in thickness, together with traces of ironworking, was established on the edge of the excavated area to the south. Metal-detector surveys prior to the removal of the topsoil had yielded various metal artefacts, including the bronze terminal of a knife handle, a lead spindle whorl, pieces of melted bronze, a fragment of a scutiform mount and a copper sterling struck in Randers in c. AD 1420-1440 in the name of Eric of Pomerania. The investigation's aim was to recover the urns, and its limited resources did not permit a closer examination of the settlement traces.

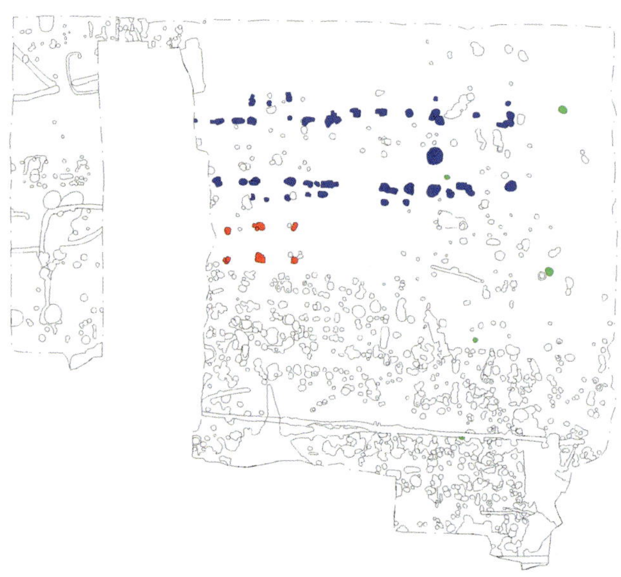

Fig. 2. | *Excavation trench, 2002. Green: urns from the Pre-Roman Iron Age; blue: longhouse from the Medieval period. J.G. Lauridsen.*

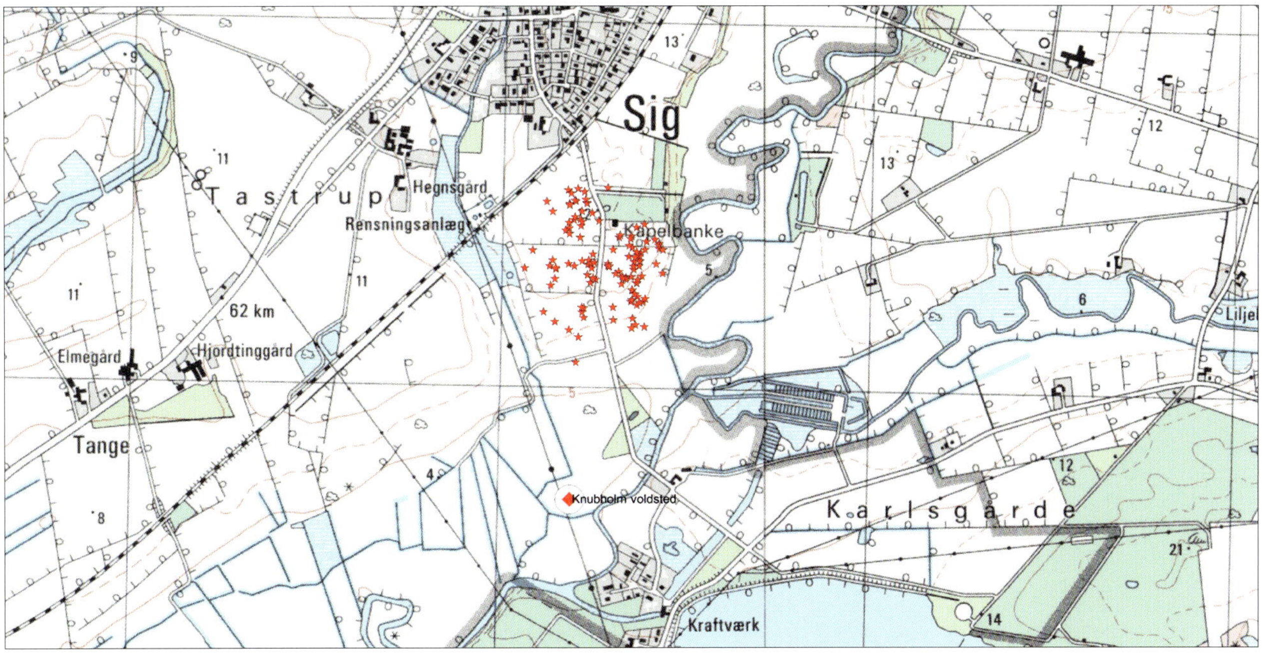

Fig. 3. | *Map showing the distribution of finds. J.G. Lauridsen.*

Less than 500 m from the southernmost extent of the metal-detector finds on the edge of the river Varde Å lie the remains of Medieval Knubholm, a castle mound that is still under intensive active cultivation. The exact date of the site is not yet known, but the Medieval finds from Sig Syd can probably be linked with Knubholm and traffic between the castle mound, the settlement and Thorstrup Kapel.

The metal-detector finds

The site was subjected to metal-detector survey by Michael Kristiansen in the autumn of 2008, the spring of 2009 and the autumn of 2009. The fields were not ploughed in the autumn of 2009. As a consequence, the resulting assemblage comes from only two seasons of ploughing. The finds distribution (fig. 3) reveals an extent for the site of c. 500 x 500 m. However, the accuracy of this picture remains to be determined.

Most of the artefacts recovered from Sig Syd have parallels in Scandinavia and they vary greatly with respect to type and date. The metal artefacts date from the 3rd to the 13th century AD with a main emphasis in the 8th to 10th centuries. A number of finds cannot be more closely dated. This applies for example to weights and spindle whorls, which occur in several different forms, as well as to the many fragmented artefacts that cannot be identified to type.

A number of finds are clearly associated with trade and crafts (fig. 4). These now include nine weights, three cut silver coins, of which two are dirhems, and a coin that has not yet been identified but is probably of Magnus the Good (AD 1042-1047). In addition to these, there is a quantity of melted lead, bronze and bronze scrap, including a fragment of an imported Roman bronze. There are also various silver pieces, one of which weighs 12 g.

A number of different artefacts have links with harness and riding equipment, including whole and fragmented bronze rings and a small number of pins and strap distributors, strap ends and stirrup fittings – finds which also shed light on traffic and transport (fig. 5). Only few finds bear witness to weaponry: a chape from a knife or a sword scabbard and the fragment of a presumed mouthpiece, similarly from a sword scabbard, together with fittings of various other kinds. On being cleaned, the mouthpiece was found to bear the remains of fine gilt ornamentation (fig. 6).

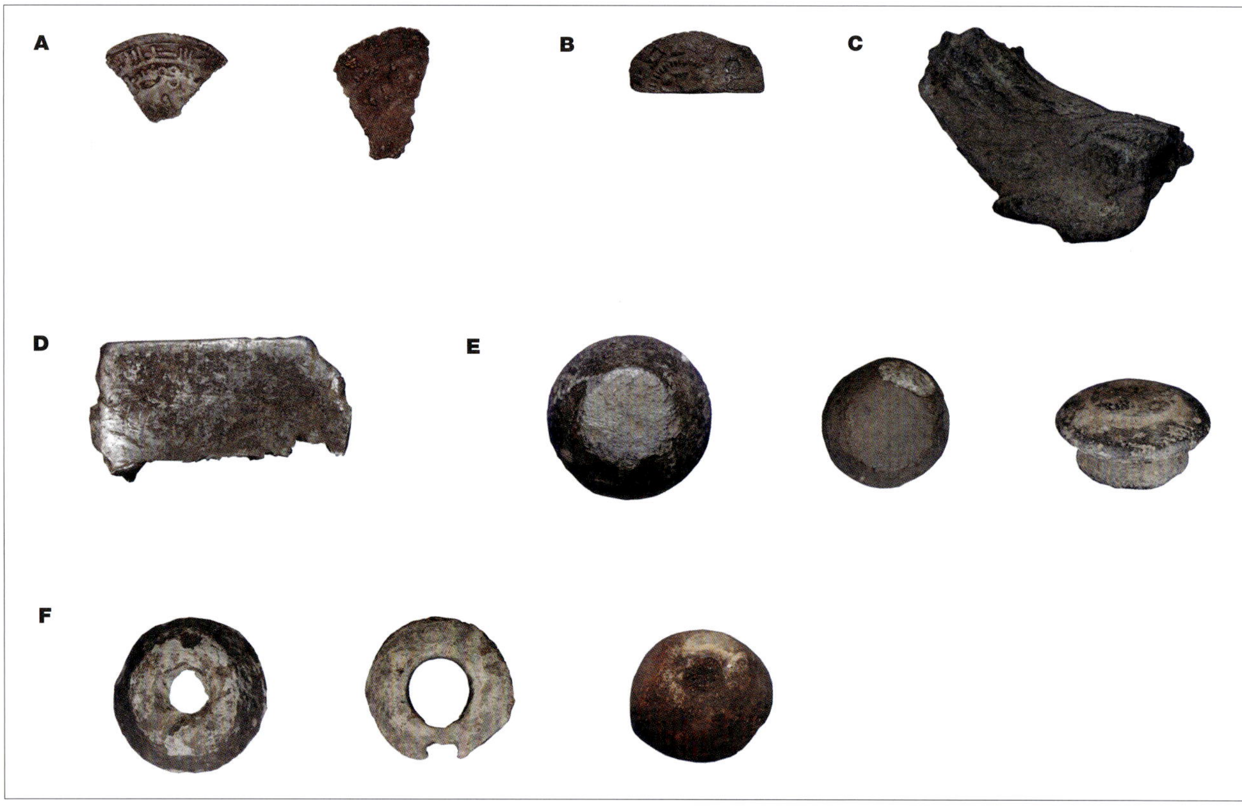

Fig. 4. | *Trade-related finds: a. dirhems; b. silver coin; c. Roman bronze fragment; d. silver fragment; e. weights; f. spindle whorls. Scale 1:1. Photo: L.C. Bentsen.*

Fig. 5. | *Harness and riding equipment: a. mounts; b. strap ends; c. strap distributor; d. stirrup fittings. Scale 1:1. Photo: L.C. Bentsen.*

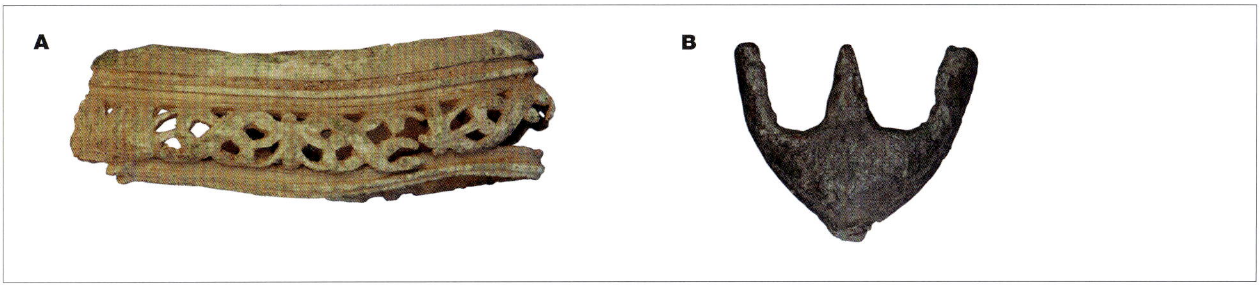

Fig. 6. | *Sword/dagger sheath fittings: a. chape; b. mouthpiece. Scale 1:1. Photo: L.C. Bentsen.*

In addition to these, there were also finds of personal accessories such as costume ornaments and brooches of various kinds (fig. 7).

A number of artefacts are of such a character that they can be classed as extraordinary (fig. 8). These include Carolingian-Ottonian enamel brooches: an enamel brooch with cross motif of Wamer's type 3, brooches with several settings, a cross-shaped brooch with a central setting and subsidiary settings on each arm of the cross, a disc brooch with a central setting surrounded by pits, the latest of the types, and a brooch that is so poorly preserved it could not be identified to type (Baastrup 2009). There is also an Anglo-Saxon stirrup strap mount (Pedersen 1999, 143-44; Williams 1997, 2; style identified by Gabor Thomas 2009) and a strap end of bronze formed as an elongated plastic animal head in the Ringerike Style with round eyes and long backward-flaring nose lappets. All of these artefacts date from the Viking Age. Furthermore, the finds include a very large weight, weighing 198 g and made of lead encased in bronze. The flat sides of the weight are decorated with an equal-armed cross, the arms of which have lily-shaped terminals; the cross is covered with dot and circle ornamentation.

One very special piece is a flat, rectangular sheet of gold with rounded corners with the figure of a man etched on its smooth and slightly arched upper surface (fig. 9). This piece is a *guldgubbe*, i.e. a gold foil figure, of an individually manufactured form, and it is the westernmost example of its type found in Denmark. According to Margrethe Watt (pers. comm. 2009), there are just under 100 known examples of such individually manufactured *guldgubber* in Scandinavia.

Several of the aforementioned artefacts bear witness to contacts extending beyond Scandinavia: the Arabic dirhems, the Carolingian-Ottonian enamel brooches, which reveal links with Christian contexts on the European Continent (Baastrup 2005, 228-29), and the ornamented stirrup strap mount, which suggests links with the British Isles. The latter is Anglo-Saxon niello work of high quality in Trewhiddle style, from the 9th to 10th century AD. This fitting formed just a small part of an exclusive set of equipment that must have been magnificent in its entirety, with all the other fittings executed in the same style. It has parallels in the silver work seen in Anglo-Saxon hoards such as that from Poppleton, near York (Thomas 2006).

Location

The location of a metal-rich site such as that outlined above is unlikely to be purely a matter of chance. If we look at the historical map evidence (fig. 10), it is clear that the Varde Å runs directly adjacent to Thorstrup Kapel/ Sig Kapelbanke. Furthermore, several other streams are seen to join Varde Å in the same location. This was a fluvial crossroads, and as such it suggests the role of rivers as transport and traffic routes through the landscape. Varde Å is a large river with access to the Wadden Sea – perhaps another factor that was important in the choice of location. It was a route that functioned throughout several centuries.

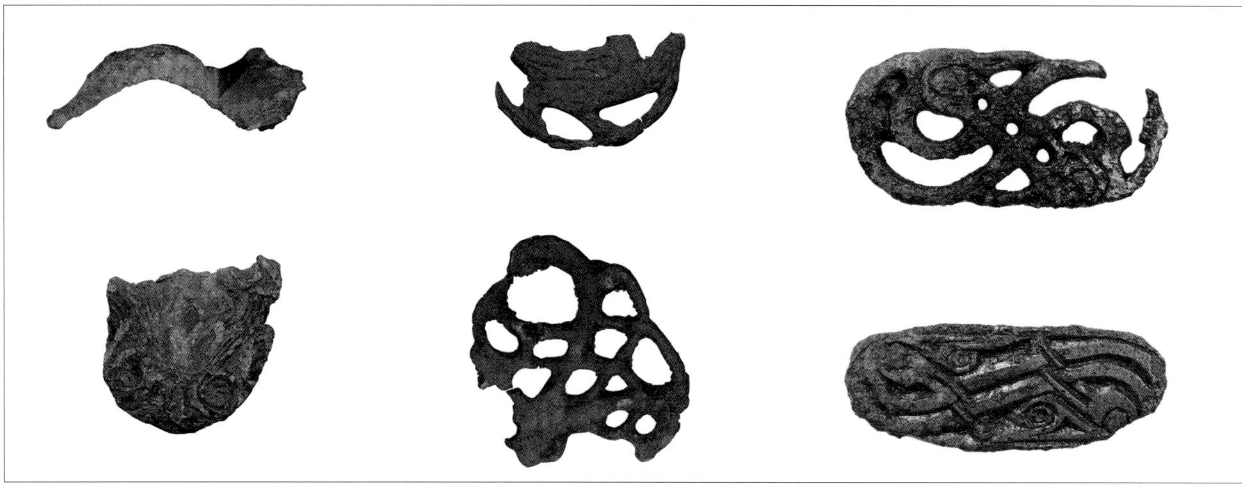

Fig. 7. | *Personal accessories: fragments of brooches. Scale 1:1. Photo: L.C. Bentsen*

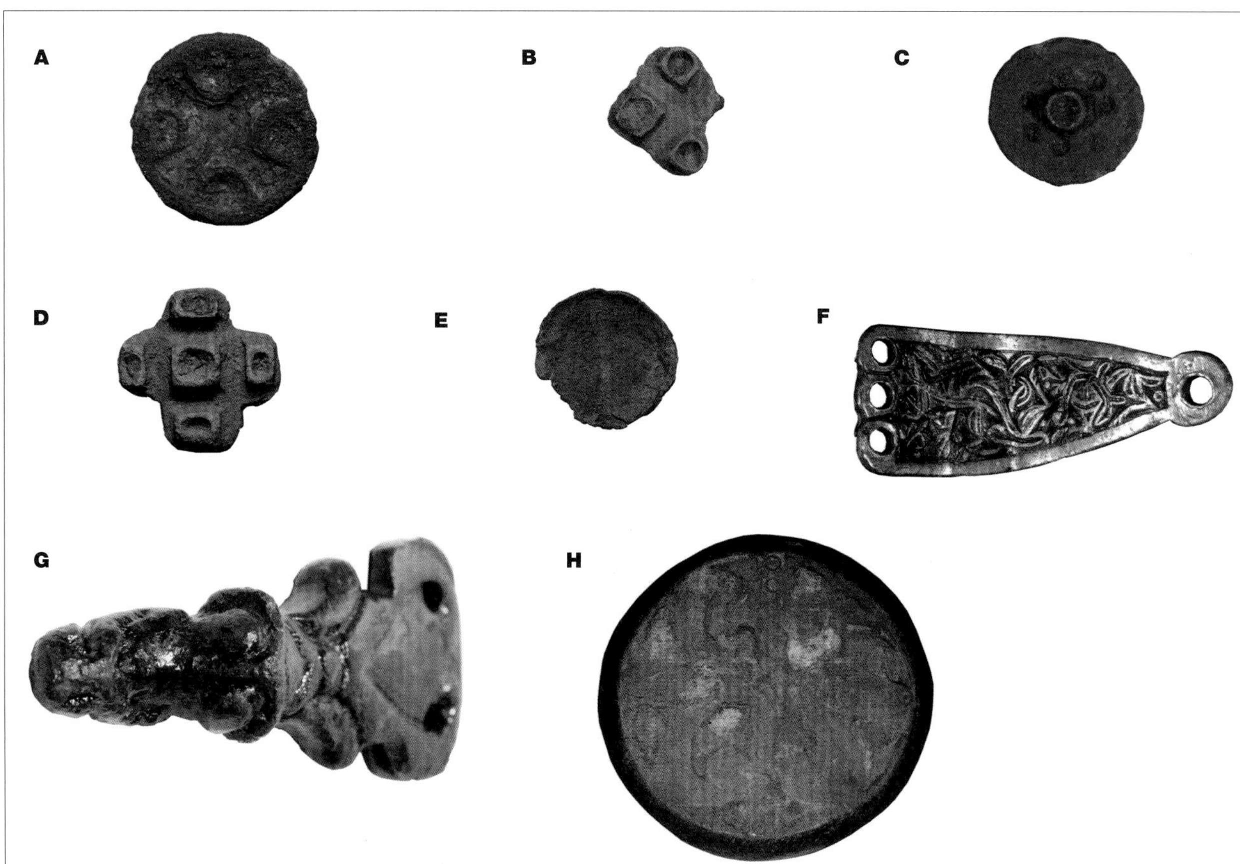

Fig. 8. | *Exceptional finds (a.-e. Carolingian-Ottonian enamel brooches): a. Wamer's type 3; b. a fragment of a brooch with several settings; c. a disc brooch with a central setting surrounded by pits; d. a cross-shaped brooch with settings; e. an unidentified fragment of a brooch; f. Anglo-Saxon stirrup strap mount; g. strap end of bronze; h. large weight. Scale 1:1. Photo: L.C. Bentsen.*

Fig. 9. | *Gold foil figure. Scale 3:1. Photo: L.C. Bentsen.*

Preservation/degradation

A number of the metal-detector finds are so well preserved that several of the artefacts still retain their original surface. In a single instance, a Carolingian brooch still has an iron pin on its back and remains of the enamel can be seen on the front. This must bear witness to the fact that the soil in which the artefacts lie is, or was, relatively untouched. Signs of degradation of otherwise well-preserved cultural layers are visible at the site. At several points across the area there are quantities of ploughed-up pottery on the surface. These are not just small fragments – in some places very large sherds have been dragged up out of the soil. The urn graves are, as mentioned above, further examples of continuous attrition. The colour of the topsoil and its composition reveal where the cultural layers have been ploughed up, something that is particularly apparent on the fields directly to the south and southwest of Sig Kapelbanke. Cultivation at the site is intensive, as it is across most of Denmark. To the east and the south, cereals are the primary crop, but on a large part of the northwestern area potatoes are grown. We know that potato cultivation in particular, like that of maize, rape and Christmas trees, is very destructive of hidden (i.e. buried) archaeological remains. Between the potato rows, at intervals of a specific number of metres, there are also longitudinal, deeper ploughed furrows containing pebble gravel, known in Danish as *stenstrenge*, that are a direct consequence of potato cultivation.

How do we deal with these extensive metal-rich sites, which will be cultivated ever more intensively in the future? When will ploughing have disrupted the hidden archaeological remains to such an extent that it will be impossible to interpret them in an excavation? Greater attention should be drawn to the increasing destruction of our cultural heritage by agriculture. Perhaps attempts should be made to reach agreements with individual land-

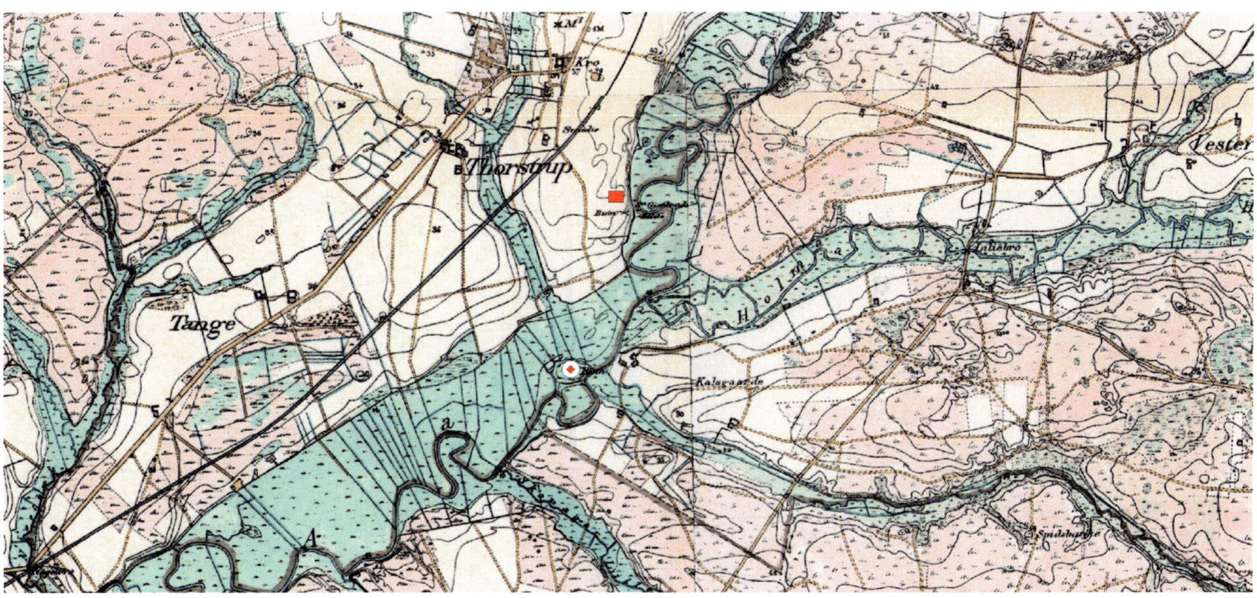

Fig. 10. | *Topographical map of the area (1:20 000, from 1883-90) – note the river courses. Red rectangle: Thorstrup Kapel/Sig Kapelbanke; red diamond: Knubholm.*

owners that would guarantee less damaging forms of cultivation on areas with well-preserved archaeological features and cultural layers. As it is, we are increasingly losing the potential to interpret these sites, as well as many others.

Bibliography

Baastrup, M.P. 2009, Småfibler af karolingiske og ottonske typer i Danmark. *Aarbøger for Nordisk Oldkyndighed og Historie* 2005, 209-55.

Christiansen, H. 1987, 1506 Sig sb. 106 (Torstrup sogn). In: *Danmarks længste udgravning. Arkæologi på naturgassens vej 1979-86*. København. 390.

Danmarks Kirker 19, Ribe amt, Vol. 3. Torstrup, Horne, Hodde, Tistrup. København 1988-1991.

Frandsen, L.B. 1992, Sig Kapelbanke – eftersporing af en middelalderlig kirkegård. *Fra Ribe Amt* 25:3, 417-21.

Kristensen, H.K. 1938, Sankt Gertruds Kilde i Torstrup. *Fra Ribe Amt* 9:3, 24-34.

Østergaard, K.H. 1938, Kapelbanken i Thorstrup Sogn. *Fra Ribe Amt* 9:3, 17-23.

Pedersen, A. 1999, Riding gear from late Viking Age Denmark. *Journal of Danish Archaeology* 13, 1996-97, 133-60.

Thomas, G. 2006. Reflections on a '9th-century' Northumbrian metalworking tradition: a silver hoard from Poppleton, North Yorkshire. *Medieval Archaeology* 50, 143-64.

Williams, D. 1997, *Late Saxon stirrup-strap mounts. A classification and catalogue*. York.

Notes

1 Now part of the Danish Agency for Culture

2 Now part of the Danish Agency for Culture.

3 Sig Syd, VAM 1471.

Stavnsager – small glimpses of something big

Reno Fiedel

In Jutland – the Danish mainland – c. 15 km southeast of Randers lies the hamlet of Moeskær (fig. 1), in the middle of a peaceful old-world landscape. The area is today a mixture of arable land, meadows and woods. Settlement takes the form of single farms or small groups of houses and farms – villages in an old-fashioned sense. Only one major road traverses the area and the hum of traffic can barely be discerned in Moeskær, and only when the wind is in a certain direction. In brief, it is an idyllic spot on the Danish map (fig. 2). But it was not always this way: Archaeological investigations reveal that there was widespread settlement and lively activity here through 700 years of the Late Iron Age, Viking Age and Early Middle Ages.

Stavnsager is the old name for a plot of land on the western edge of Moeskær. Initially, it only referred to the first excavations at Moeskær but subsequently it was adopted as the site name for the entire study area. The Stavnsager complex (KHM 0663)[1] comprises today the entire Moeskær-Krogsager-Hørning area, as defined by metal-detector survey.

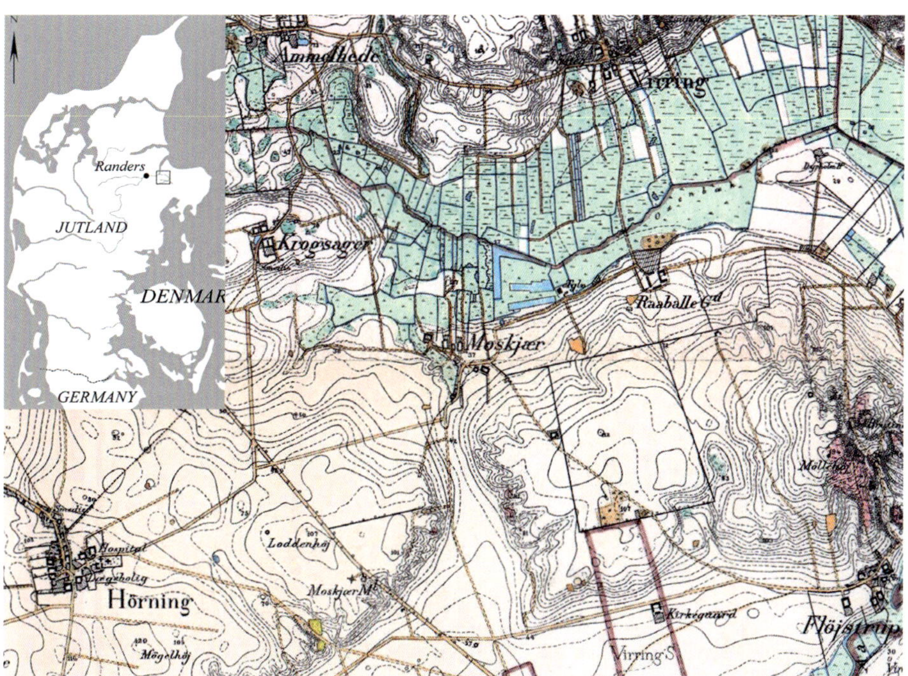

Fig. 1. | *The study area: the triangle between Moeskær, Krogsager and Hørning. After the Danish Geodata Agency's scans of topographical maps from the 1880s.*

Fig. 2. | *The landscape from Virring Church, looking towards Hørning Church, which can just be glimpsed at the top of the picture. The buildings on the edge of the picture to the left are Moeskærgård farm. Stavnsager's central settlement area extends out from the farm to the area between the long shelter belts. Photo: R. Fiedel.*

In the Iron Age and Viking Age it was possible for people to travel by water from the coast to the Moeskær settlement, more than 15 km inland. They could have sailed via the northern route, in through present-day Randers Fjord and onwards along now dried-out watercourses, but navigation might also have been possible via an eastern route following the now reclaimed Kolindsund (fig. 3).

The Iron Age settlement was concentrated around the small hamlet of Moeskær. It lay on the southern edge of a stretch of meadowland that slopes evenly to the north from 12 to 7.5 m a.s.l. The meadowland lies in a small inlet in the Oksenbæk river valley, in which the Oksenbæk runs from east to west to meet the river Alling Å, which then flows into Grund Fjord and Randers Fjord. To the south, southeast and west the settlement is bordered by a softly rounded, undulating moraine landscape.

The soil at the site is primarily fine yellow moraine sand, especially on the southern, more elevated part of the settlement area, while the northern lower part includes both moraine gravel and clay.

The investigations

In 1983, Kulturhistorisk Museum Randers was contacted by the landowner Harry Rasmussen after he had found pottery and organic material during

Fig. 3a. | *Soil map visualising the possible navigation routes to Stavnsager. After the Geological Survey of Denmark and Greenland:* Jordartskort over Danmark, *1989.*

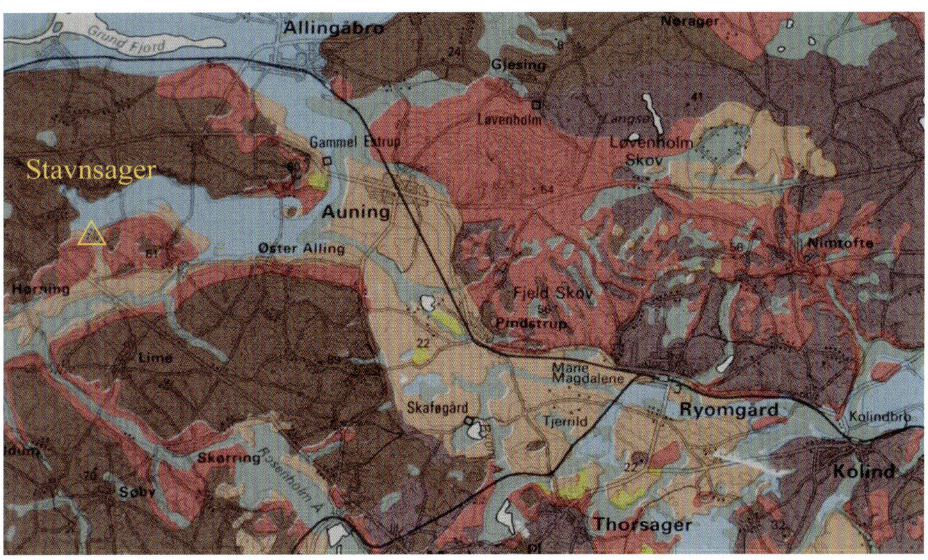

Fig. 3b. | *Close-up of the problematic area on the Kolindsund route. After the Geological Survey of Denmark and Greenland:* Jordartskort over Danmark, *1989.*

drainage work. Between 1983 and 1990, there were several further reports of finds at Moeskærgård. Each time, the museum followed these up with site visits and sometimes small trial excavations of a few square metres. These minor excavations turned up numerous traces of iron production and flax retting pits (KHM 232/83, 038/86, 281/86, 240/90 and 0017). One slightly more extensive investigation of a partially wood-built stretch of road was carried out in 1992 (KHM 0179).

It was not until 1993, however, with the discovery of Neolithic structures during sub-soiling operations in advance of windbreak planting, that attention became focused in earnest on the Moeskær area. The investigation of an earthen long-barrow dating from the Funnel Beaker culture took place between 1994 and 1996 (Fiedel 2006, 45-47) – a period during which museum staff spent a great deal of time in the area. When the landowner presented his collection of surface finds found in the area, which proved to date from the Viking Age, the decision was made to cut a single evaluation trench in the autumn of 1994, and from 1995 onwards small areas began to be opened up by machine (fig. 4).

In 1995, two excavations, with a combined area of c. 1500 m², revealed the existence of seven

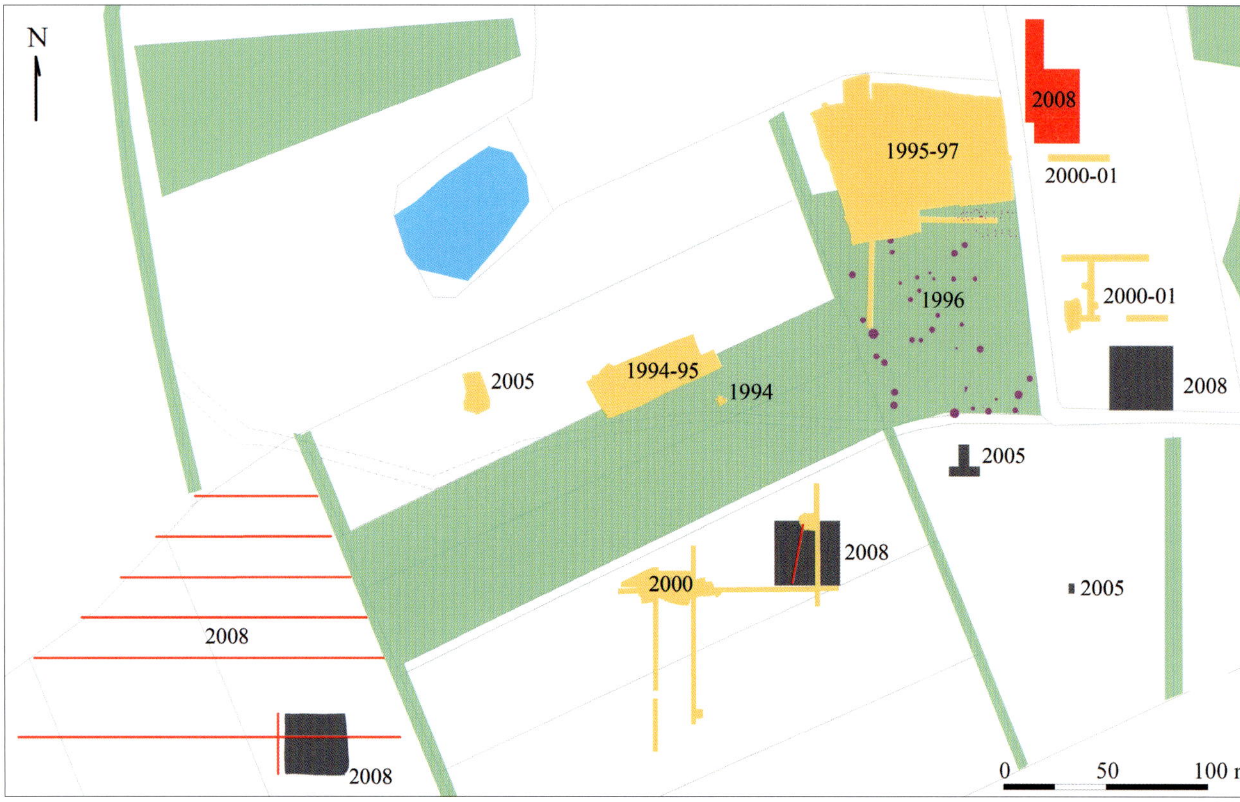

Fig. 4. | *Investigations at Stavnsager 1994-2008. Yellow: Kulturhistorisk Museum Randers (KHM) investigations; purple: sub-soiled* Grubenhäuser*; grey: British investigations; red: GPR (ground-penetrating radar) investigations by Y. Salmon, Israel. Landscape types: green: forested areas; blue: lake. R. Stidsing/R. Fiedel.*

Grubenhäuser, two wells and a large number of postholes. The study area lay next to a low-lying stretch of meadowland, and a north-south oriented trench revealed the presence of a bank-like concentration of heat-shattered stones running close to and alongside the meadows. In places, this layer was more than 1 m in thickness and it lay over layers interpreted as sections of road running alongside the meadowland (fig. 4).

In 1996, about 3000 m² of settlement area were investigated. About 900 features were exposed, from which it was possible to identify traces of at least seven longhouses, three *Grubenhäuser*, a grave – possibly surrounded by a ditch with associated fence – and a few scattered sections of fence. In addition, two large circular features became visible on the surface, which could represent wells or watering holes for cattle. The northern part of the surface, out towards the meadowland, in an extension of the excavation trench from 1995, was found to be covered by a compact layer of heat-shattered stones.

With the expansion in 1997 of the trench from the previous year, a further six longhouses, three small buildings, a section of fence, a possible *Grubenhaus*, four wells and an inhumation grave were revealed (fig. 4).

That same year, the land to the south of the excavation was sub-soiled. Over an area of 10 000 m² it was subsequently possible to observe the remains of 38 *Grubenhäuser*, a large number of postholes, several of which could securely be assigned to two longhouses and what may have been a stretch of road in the upturned subsoil. All the features were surveyed and plotted, in preparation for later investigation of the basal layers of the *Grubenhäuser* (fig. 4).

In December 2000, the museum had the opportunity to carry out a further trial excavation. In this, another longhouse, a well and three *Grubenhäuser* were investigated, together with a large number of postholes (fig. 4).

In 2005, a small trench was investigated at the find site of a gold foil figure, a so-called *guldgubbe*. Remains were found here of postholes, a *Grubenhaus* and a section of fence, but nothing was discovered that could be directly associated with the gold figure (fig. 4).

Prior to 2010, we knew of only one area of concentrated settlement, i.e. that west of Moeskær. However, during drain-laying works around the village of Hørning in summer 2010 it became apparent that – as expected – there were settlement traces here too (KHM 2534). Further geophysical and geochemical investigations and/or actual excavations are now necessary in order to ascertain the nature of this settlement (fig. 12).

The limited extent of the investigations over the years was due partly to a lack of funding and partly to the fact that the landowner, out of concern for his arable production, was not interested in large, longer-term excavations in the area.

In addition to Kulturhistorisk Museum Randers's own excavations, an area of 3000 m² was investigated in collaboration with foreign archaeologists in 2005 and 2007/2008 (fig. 4). These excavation areas comprised five trenches (1-5) and were control excavations (ground-truthing) related to geophysical and geochemical investigations (superimposed survey techniques) over areas of, respectively, 5.2 and 16 ha (including 4 ha to the east of Hørning Church). They were carried out by Chris Loveluck's team as part of the international Stavnsager Project (Loveluck & Strutt with Clogg, this volume; Strutt 2006; 2007).

In 2008, selected areas were also surveyed with georadar equipment loaned by the University of Haifa (Loveluck & Salmon 2011; Salmon this volume) (fig. 4).

Fig. 5. | *The Moeskær area seen from the west. The area of concentrated Iron Age settlement is marked in yellow. The red-framed area has been sub-soiled and could not be investigated. Blue: potential navigation area; brown: identified road routes. R. Fiedel.*

The settlement at Moeskær

We now have knowledge at various levels of the existence of longhouses, *Grubenhäuser* and a few small post-built buildings, wells, wheel tracks and stretches of road – in one place stabilised with planks. The heaps of heat-shattered stones found in several places within the area are remarkable. Most striking of these is a 6-700 m long, in places bank-like, accumulation at the transition between dry land and the wetland (meadow) area. Traces of iron production were found at two locations close to the wetland area, and in one area pits were investigated that had been used for drying of flax fibre.

The distribution of metal finds and our investigations to date demonstrate a delimited settlement concentration during the entire Late Iron Age in the area to the west of Moeskær.

A multi-phased settlement from the Early Germanic Iron Age located in the immediate vicinity of the inner part of the wetland area has also been investigated. There is a single longhouse and numerous *Grubenhäuser* dating from the Late Germanic Iron Age, whereas the Viking Age is represented by

Grubenhäuser and possible traces of curved house walls in the trenches excavated by the British team.

In the centre of this concentrated settlement/ activity area lies a large piece of land which was sub-soiled in advance of afforestation. A site visit in 1994, after it had been planted with trees, revealed ploughed-up fire-reddened earth and heat-shattered stones over large parts of the area, but with the greatest concentration in the eastern part. The western part did not have large quantities of stones, but here it was possible to see on the surface the contours of two northwest-southeast oriented and longhouses aligned parallel to each other. The heat-shattered stones and the fire-reddened soil in the eastern part can tentatively be interpreted as traces of ploughed-up *Grubenhäuser* (fig. 5).

Fig. 6a. | *The 1996-97 trench seen from the southwest. To the north, this borders on the prehistoric wetland area. Photo: R. Stidsing.*

Fig. 6b. | *House sites from the Early Germanic Iron Age under excavation. Photo: R. Stidsing.*

Longhouses

Stavnsager's earliest settlement dates from the Early Germanic Iron Age and is located alongside the wetland area to the north. Where identifiable, the longhouses are of traditional type with straight longitudinal sides and rounded gables. The standard length varies between 17 and 20 m, although a few examples are around 30 m. Their width varies between 5.5 and 6 m. Of the c. 20 more or less fragmented longhouses, three are oriented north-south whereas the others lie approximately east-west, i.e. parallel to the wetland area (fig. 6a & b).

In the Late Germanic Iron Age, the settlement shifted southwards, further away from the wetland area and consequently higher up in the terrain. Only one longhouse has been investigated from this period. This is oriented southeast-northwest and has slightly curved side walls and straight gables. It is 6 m wide and at least 27 m long; the western part has been ploughed away (fig. 7).

The sub-soiled remains of two longhouses in the afforested area west of the longhouse excavated in 2001 should presumably be considered as belonging to the later settlement. The British team recorded undated curved sequences of posts in trench 4 and these could originate from longhouses from this period or later.

Small buildings

In three locations alongside the wetland area, sets of posts were found that can be interpreted as remains of small square buildings or sheds with a floor area of between 4 and 15 m².

Fig. 7. | *Longhouse from the Late Germanic Iron Age investigated in 2000. Photo: R. Fiedel.*

Grubenhäuser

A total of 70 *Grubenhäuser* have so far been located and surveyed in the settlement area to the west of Moeskær. Of these, four were merely observed and were not excavated after ploughing in 1999. In the case of 38 presumed *Grubenhäuser* found in the area sub-soiled in 1997 (fig. 8a), the ploughed-up material was dug through and date-conferring and function-related finds were recovered from the individual features. In 2010, a control excavation of two of the *Grubenhäuser* revealed undisturbed fill preserved up to a depth of 0.5 m. All in all, rather more than a third of all the *Grubenhäuser* have been investigated by traditional excavation (fig. 8b).

The sunken parts of the *Grubenhäuser* vary in size from small circular features with a diameter of around 2 m to large rectangular sub-surface features measuring 4.5 x 5.5 m. The fill of the *Grubenhäuser* was found to contain pottery dating from the Late Germanic Iron Age and the Viking Age. Since we have only seen the floor layer horizon in relatively few buildings, it is possible that there are also *Grubenhäuser* from the Early Germanic Iron Age in the area. The buildings, some with several occupation phases, have in many cases been used for textile production. Metal casting and forging of iron also took place inside some of them. The *Grubenhäuser* were concentrated within a c. 150 m wide westsouthwest-eastnortheast-oriented belt, beginning c. 50 m from the wetland area and located parallel to it.

The stone concentration alongside the wetland area

One of the more intriguing finds is a marked accumulation of heat-shattered stones that can be followed along the 7.5 m contour line over a distance of 6-700 m. It runs in an east-west direction alongside the wetland area which was navigable at the time and which today is a low-lying expanse of wet meadowland. Furthest to the west – in the area of the Early Germanic Iron Age village located alongside the wetland area – the stone accumulation almost has the character of a bank. However, the stones were deposited on solid ground, so the intention cannot have been reclamation of the wetland area. It seems more likely that this feature provides a clear indication of a well-organised society involved in the large-scale consumption of heat energy in relation to various forms of production; these resulted in a waste product in the form of heat-shattered stones. As the stones could not be used for road building or similar purposes, they were dumped on the edge of terra firma in order to stabilise the surface running down towards the

Fig. 8a. | *Part of the sub-soiled area where the archaeological structures and features are clearly evident. The* Grubenhäuser *are marked with ranging poles. Photo: R. Fiedel.*

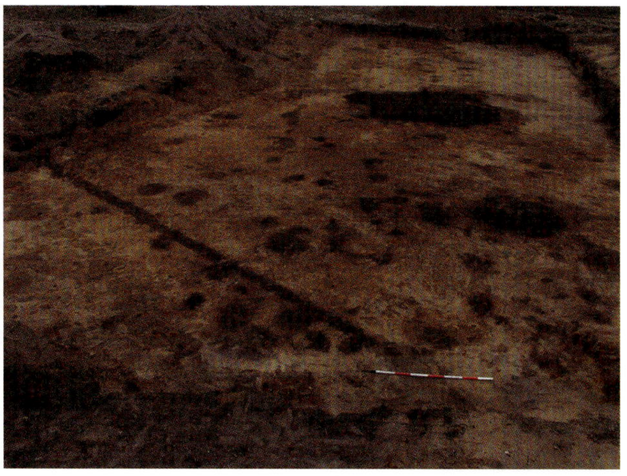

Fig. 8b. | *'The gold fogey trench', 2005.* Grubenhaus *surrounded by postholes and sections of fence. Photo: R. Fiedel.*

Fig. 9a. | *The stone border lies under the dark, charcoal-rich area along the northern limit of the excavation. Photo: R. Stidsing.*

Fig. 9b. | *Section showing the position of the stone border down towards the low-lying area. Two wells can be seen at the base of the section trench. Photo: R. Fiedel.*

Fig. 9c. | *The stone border covered by dark, charcoal-rich soil and with underlying stratigraphy. The top of a well, dated to the Early Germanic Iron Age on the basis of a fibula, can be seen to the lower left. Photo: R. Fiedel.*

Fig. 10a. | *Exposed part of the wood-reinforced road in the wetland area. Photo: F. Christiansen.*
Fig. 10b. | *Section through the road which appears higher in the terrain further to the south. Photo: R. Fiedel.*

wetland area. These heat-shattered stones partially overlay the Early Germanic Iron Age settlement and must therefore have accumulated during the Late Germanic Iron Age and thereafter (fig. 9a, b and c).

Land and water routes

In several places, after sub-soiling or recent conventional ploughing, the contours of stretches of road could be seen on the surface. In a few instances sectioning here has revealed the existence of deep wheel tracks. The gauge of the carts that used the roads was between 1.1 and 1.2 m.

Particularly striking evidence of land transport is seen in the form of a c. 3 m wide wooden road surface (with two dendrochronological dates of, respectively, AD 1091 and 1106) in a depression in the terrain (fig. 10a). This 'corduroy road' was formed of trunks, branches and occasional plank-like pieces of wood laid transversely. The wooden section extended over a distance of 18 m, after which the

Fig. 11a. | *The U-shaped ditch is partially covered to the north by later dark, charcoal-rich layers. Photo: R. Fiedel.*

Fig. 11b. | *The small grave during excavation. Photo: R. Stidsing.*

road continued to the south with a cobbled surface (fig. 10b). To the north of the depression the road fans out into several wheel tracks resembling sunken roads.

There is much to suggest that, at least during the Germanic Iron Age and the Early Viking Age, it was possible to travel to the settlement – or somewhere very close to it – by water. Perhaps not in large vessels, but in flat-bottomed boats or barges that could be poled the final stretch from open water in through the reed bed. The establishment of the wooden causeway definitively severed the water route into the central area, suggesting that the inner part of the wetlands gradually developed into a mire during the course of the 2nd millennium AD.

Wells

A total of nine wells have been investigated: six in the Early Germanic Iron Age area, one by the Late Germanic Iron Age area and two in the British team's trench 3. On excavation, four of the wells were still water-bearing. All were built of vertical cloven planks, sharpened to a point at one end and hammered into the subsoil. In some cases, timber had been reused from buildings and carts. The vertical planks were supported externally by horizontal timbers or tree trunks. The construction consisted in all cases of a large outer well frame encompassing an inner well lining, from which the water was drawn. In one case the inner well lining was formed of a hollowed-out tree trunk. The location of the wells does not necessarily say anything about their date. Only two could be dated: one to the Early Germanic Iron Age – on the basis of a cruciform brooch and pottery – and another to the Viking Age (AD 746) by dendrochronology (Christensen 2009).

Flax production

The lining of the Viking Age well possibly also functioned as a retting pit used for processing flax, either as its primary or secondary function. This interpretation is supported by a nearby area containing pits used for drying flax fibre.

Iron production

There would have been access to bog iron ore in the extensive areas of meadowland alongside the watercourses Oksenbæk and Alling Å. Iron slag has been found in two locations close to the wetland area at Moeskær, suggesting that the production of iron took place here during the Germanic Iron Age.

Graves

There are no known cemeteries in the vicinity of Moeskær. Geochemical analyses carried out by the British team did reveal a high concentration of phosphorous and calcium near trench 1 that could possibly indicate a cemetery area, but as yet no further traces have been found.

The only grave investigated to date is a small inhumation grave located in the area of the Early Germanic Iron Age settlement. This was enclosed within a U-shaped section of fence, the opening of which faced out towards the wetland area, but the fence cannot be securely linked with the grave (fig. 11a). The grave was small, presumably that of a child, and the body was buried in a slightly scorched wooden coffin made from a hollowed-out tree trunk. Two small pottery vessels (Early Germanic Iron Age) accompanied the child and the bones of a small animal were also found in the grave (fig. 11b).

The settlement at Hørning

In 2010, there was an opportunity, for the first time in 50 years, to carry out an archaeological investigation close to Hørning Church. This was of great interest even though all that was involved was the laying of a drain that followed the course of the old hand-dug drain pipe. Since the sensational discoveries made during the restoration of the church, namely a demolished burial mound and associated wooden church (Krogh & Voss 1961), there had been no further opportunity to obtain new archaeological information in the area.

The course of the drain ditch (G1-G5), together with trench G6, resulted in the uncovering of an area of 9000 m^2. Excavation revealed the presence of c. 250 postholes, 70 pits and two *Grubenhäuser*. In trenches G1, G2 and G6 a large number of field furrows were recorded that could be dated to the Middle Ages.

None of the postholes could be put into a constructional context and almost all were without finds. Some very large, deep postholes were discovered in G2 and G3, but these also lacked finds.

The most interesting area was that in the angle formed between trenches G4 and G5, where the *Grubenhäuser* were located. These buildings stood 6 m apart; one was totally excavated while the

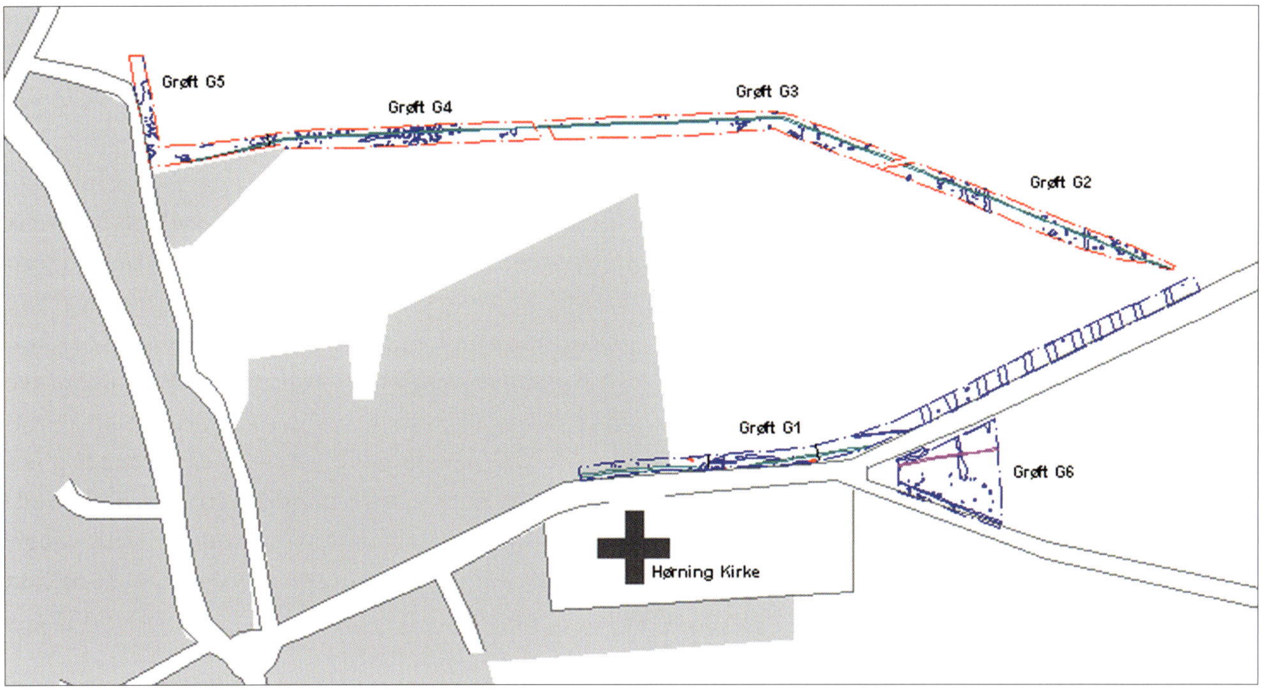

Fig. 12. | *The investigated area to the north of Hørning Church. The* Grubenhäuser *were found in the bend between trenches* (grøft) *4 and 5. R. Stidsing.*

other, due to its location in a field boundary, could only be sectioned longitudinally. Both were of the type with a post at each gable and both yielded finds of pottery and loom weight fragments. The *Grubenhäuser* can be dated, on the basis of rim sherds of hemispherical vessels, to the Viking Age. A corresponding rim sherd was found in a group of postholes just to the north of them.

Consequently, there is evidence of workshop activity within 200 m of Hørning Church. Due to the nature of the terrain, the *Grubenhaus* settlement could only have extended to the south and west, i.e. beneath the present day village of Hørning (fig. 12).

Metal-detector surveys in the area

Stavnsager is the first area where Kulturhistorisk Museum Randers has embarked on a systematic search for metal finds. The metal-detector surveys were all carried out by one person, Ove Madsen, and they have taken place each spring and autumn for almost 20 years. Consequently, Stavnsager cannot be said to be a conventional metal-detector site in the sense that metal-detectorists locate a find area where, subsequently, archaeological excavations are perhaps carried out. At Stavnsager the archaeological investigations came first and were followed up with metal-detector surveys.

The metal-detector surveys began in the autumn of 1994. In that first year the finds included four equal-armed brooches. At the time these were presumed to have come from ploughed-up graves dating from the Germanic Iron Age. The detector survey was continued in 1995 when the yield was 11 equal-armed brooches and beak brooches. Since then, the number of finds has increased significantly each year.

In the early years, the detector surveys were carried out immediately west of Moeskær, which we now know to be the location of the concentrated settlement area. Subsequently, the surveys were extended to include the triangle formed between Moeskær, Krogsager and Hørning – an activity area covering more than 100 ha.

Due to the limited extent of the excavated area, much of the work on the Stavnsager Project has been based on the dating and distribution of the metal-detector finds. This will continue to be the case until an even greater area can be surveyed by magnetometer and subjected to geochemical analysis. Since 1999, Karen Høilund Nielsen has studied the metal finds from Stavnsager, resulting in a number of articles dealing with their dating and distribution (Høilund Nielsen 2006; 2009; 2011; Høilund Nielsen & Fiedel 2001; Høilund Nielsen & Loveluck 2006; see also Høilund Nielsen this volume).

The metal finds

The earliest metal finds – dating from the Early Germanic Iron Age – are relatively few in number and often heavily fragmented, perhaps representing scrap metal. Nearly all these finds are of the same brooch type, the cruciform brooch.

Of the many hundreds of metal finds from Stavnsager, a great proportion can be dated to the early part of the Late Germanic Iron Age. In terms of quantity, 'cheap brooches' – in the form of small equal-armed brooches and beak brooches – dominate. However, more special brooches, parts of weapons and even a fragment of a gold foil figure, a so-called *guldgubbe*, are among the finds from the period.

In the subsequent period, the number of brooches decreases but the variation in type increases: small tortoise brooches, bird brooches, S-shaped brooches and plate brooches all belong

Fig. 13a. | *Selection of finds from the Early Germanic Iron Age; bracteates are 20 % oversized to scale. Photo: Museum Østjylland.*

Fig. 13b. | *Selection of finds from the Late Germanic Iron Age. Photo: R. Fiedel.*

to this category, together with a number of unique pieces with religious features.

The Viking Age finds include circular disc brooches, equal-armed brooches and trefoil brooches as well as a number of unique specimens. From the end of the period there are Urnes-style brooches, small bird brooches and pieces bearing religious (Christian) motifs.

Finally, dating from various periods, there are finds of silver ingots, hack silver and gold, coins and objects relating to weighing and measuring.

Some of these finds are illustrated below (fig. 13a-f). For more information, see the aforementioned articles by Karen Høilund Nielsen.

Summary

The Stavnsager area has provided considerable evidence of activity during the Germanic Iron Age and Viking Age in the form of roads, mask and rune stones, noble graves and gold finds (Høilund Nielsen & Fiedel 2001).

Combined with evidence from the museum's fieldwalking and systematic metal-detector surveys, Karen Høilund Nielsen's examination and analysis of the metal finds and, not least, the British team's geophysical and geochemical investigations, analyses and control excavations (ground-truthing) reflect a high degree of activity and means that today we are able to obtain an impression of de-

Fig. 13c. | *Selection of finds from the Viking Age. Photo: R. Fiedel.*

velopments in the area over the course of seven centuries.

In the Early Germanic Iron Age, the settlement at Moeskær was of regular agrarian character. Village life unfolded alongside the wetland area, and iron was also produced. There are no remains of *Grubenhäuser* or traces of workshop activity from this period. As mentioned above, a great number of fragments, large and small, of cruciform brooches have been found from this period.

In the Late Germanic Iron Age, the habitation area moved further to the south, away from the wetland area. Large longhouses and numerous workshop buildings spread out across a wide area, and the quantity and diversity of metal finds from this period increase dramatically. Weapons, equestrian equipment and objects of a religious character represent new elements in the finds. Furthermore, a number of these finds also reveal contacts with distant areas.

The finds suggest a hierarchical society, in which control was based on an armed force: a chieftain and his housecarls. The settlement at Moeskær also became involved in production and trade, with the potential for water travel as a precondition. At intervals, markets and religious festivals would have been held.

It was during this period that the Moeskær settlement reached its greatest extent. Whether this blossoming grew out of the early village community or was the consequence of a new external organisation, it is impossible to say.

During the Viking Age, significant settlement and workshop production continued in the Moeskær area; with time, however, the power centre apparently became displaced towards Hørning.

Hørning had two faces during the Viking Age: one pagan, the other Christian. Beneath the present Hørning Church the remains have been found of a pagan cemetery, together with a pagan grave in a burial mound. The mound was demolished and a wooden church erected on the site. These initiatives took place at a time of religious change, when Harold Bluetooth and Svein Forkbeard were

Fig. 13d. | *Finds of foreign origin. Photo: R. Fiedel.*

Fig. 13e. | *Paganism and Christianity. Photo: R. Fiedel.*

Fig. 13f. | *Selection of gold and silver finds. Photo: R. Fiedel.*

exploiting religion for political purposes, resulting in great unrest and instability. With Hørning as its centre, the area was now only a pawn in a much greater political game. The religious, social and political changes within the Moeskær-Krogsager-Hørning triangle would have required a powerful local magnate who had the influence and strength to force through a religious change – and build a church (Fiedel et al. 2011).

We have not yet found the magnate's residence, but perhaps we have made contact with Viking Age Hørning in recent investigations in the area northwest of the village.

A central place – or ...?

For a number of years now the Stavnsager complex has, for the want of a better term, been referred to as a 'central place'. The results of these investigations suggest a site that was more than just an 'ordinary' settlement. There was settlement continuity here throughout the Germanic Iron Age and Viking Age, and during this period it developed from a local agrarian society to an outward-looking, network-oriented society with crafts, trade and contacts with distant places. The organisation and governance changed with time from a village chieftain to a regionally significant magnate with far-reaching contacts. Whether this magnate's family became established in the Moeskær area and subsequently moved to Hørning, or whether they themselves were subjugated in the Viking Age by even more powerful rulers in Hørning, it is impossible to say.

Regardless of the term used – and a clearer definition of the term 'central place' is definitely to be desired – future work on the Stavnsager complex and its surroundings can make a significant contribution to our understanding of life in eastern Jutland during the Germanic Iron Age and Viking Age as compared with the contemporary, showier settlements on the Danish islands.

Bibliography

Christensen, K. 2009, Dendrokronologisk datering af prøver fra brønd fra Stavnsager ved Hørning. (WM2277). Rapport fra Trædaterings-laboratoriet. Højbjerg.

Fiedel, R.A. 2006, Kendte og ukendte gravhøje i Hørning sogn. *Kulturhistorisk Museum Randers Årbog* 2006, 27-48.

Fiedel, R., K. Høilund Nielsen & C. Loveluck 2011, From hamlet, to central place, to manor: social transformation of the settlement at Stavnsager, eastern Jutland, and its networks, AD 400-1100. *Neue Studien zur Sachsenforschung* 3, 161-76.

Høilund Nielsen, K. 2006, Analyse og bearbejdning af metalfundene fra centralpladsen Stavnsager. Unpublished report. Kulturhistorisk Museum Randers.

Høilund Nielsen, K. 2009, Stavnsager, 400-1100. Weiler, Zentralort, Herrenhof. In: S. Brather, D. Geuenich & C. Huth (eds.), *Historia Archaeologica. Festschrift für Heiko Steuer zum 70. Geburtstag*. Berlin. 415-433.

Høilund Nielsen, K. 2011, Stavnsager and the 'toffee-brooch' network – aspects of the metal-rich settlements of sixth-century southern Scandinavia. *Siedlungs- und Küstenforschung im südlichen Nordseegebiet* 34, 307-20.

Høilund Nielsen, K. & R. Fiedel 2001, Stavnsager – spredte glimt af et jernaldersamfund gennem mere end 700 år – fra 400 til 1100 e. Kr.f. *Kulturhistorisk Museum Randers Årbog* 2001, 71-89.

Høilund Nielsen, K. & C.P. Loveluck 2006, Fortid og fremtid på Stavnsager – Om de britiske undersøgelser august 2005 og de foreløbige resultater. *Kulturhistorisk Museum Randers Årbog 2006*, 63-79.

Krogh, K.J. & O. Voss 1961, Fra hedenskab til kristendom i Hørning. En vikingetids kammergrav og en trækirke fra 1000-tallet under Hørning kirke. *Nationalmuseets Arbejdsmark* 1961, 5-34.

Loveluck, C. & Y. Salmon 2011, Exploring an Early Medieval harbour and settlement dynamics at Stavnsager, Denmark: a geo-archaeological dialogue. *Antiquity* 85:330, 1402-17.

Strutt, K. 2006, *Results of a Geophysical Survey at the site of Stavnsager, Jutland, Denmark, July-August 2005* (SREP 1/2006), Archaeological Prospection Services of Southampton.

Strutt, K., 2007, *Results of a Geophysical Survey at the site of Stavnsager, Jutland, Denmark, September 2007* (SREP 13/2007), Archaeological Prospection Services of Southampton.

Notes

1 KHM 0663 Stavnsager, Hørning parish, Sønderhald district. The main field activities have taken place in the area of Moeskærgård, owned by Harry Rasmussen and his family. Many thanks are due to him and his family for their hospitality, patience and still growing interest in the archaeological project. Thanks are also due to a dozen members of Randersegnens Amatørarkæologer and not least to our skilful detectorist, Ove Madsen, for his extensive work. Many professional archaeologists have been involved in this long-running project; key figures have been Ragna Stidsing, Karen Høilund Nielsen and Christopher Loveluck. My sincere thanks to all of them.

Haslund Øst – a newly discovered metal-detector site

Ernst Stidsing

In conjunction with an archaeological excavation initiated by Kulturhistorisk Museum Randers in 2007 near Haslund, members of the metal-detector club Tellus carried out a detector survey of the fields adjacent to the village church. The club members had discovered that metal artefacts dating from prehistory and Medieval times were often to be found in the vicinity of churches. This proved also to be the case at Haslund Church. Between the appearance of the first find in 2007 and the end of 2009, more than 50 objects were recovered. Of these, 35 can be securely dated to the period from the Early Germanic Iron Age to the High Medieval Period (c. AD 400-1300). This total would not astonish any archaeologist with even a passing knowledge of metal-detector sites, but it is large enough – and the finds are of such a character and quality – for the site to stand out

Fig. 1. | *The central find site, southeast of Haslund Church. Photo: Museum Østjylland.*

relative to the usual finds spectrum found in relation to agrarian society in eastern Jutland.

Haslund lies about 5 km south of Randers and about 15 km west of Stavnsager, near Hørning. Its name belongs to the earliest layer of place names, dating from the time prior to the Viking Age (Hald 1965). The village of Haslund, and consequently also the site, lies on the edge of a large plateau that grades down towards wetland areas to the west, south and east of the village. The finds were located on a relatively steeply sloping field lying immediately east of the church (fig. 1). The area that produced the finds is no more than 200 x 200 m (4 ha) in total.[1]

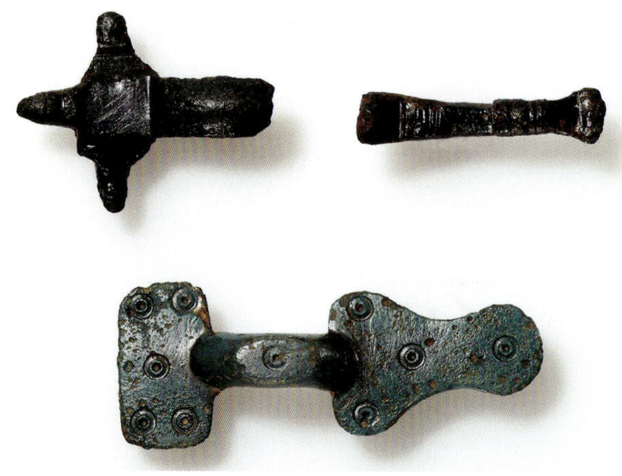

Fig. 2. | *Artefacts from the Early Germanic Iron Age. Scale 1:1. Photo: Museum Østjylland.*

The finds

Of the rather more than 30 artefacts that can be linked with the aforementioned period, only three can be dated to the Early Germanic Iron Age: two fragments of cruciform brooches and a brooch of a special and distinctive type (fig. 2). This small, elongate brooch has a rectangular head plate, a solid bow with an oval platform and a tongue-shaped foot plate with outline and roundels, like some of the great square-headed brooches (Parfitt & Anderson 2012, 73). The brooch is decorated with ring-and-dot punch marks. Parallels to this piece are rare; those that have been found are dated to the Early Germanic Iron Age.

The Late Germanic Iron Age is much better represented, with no fewer than 15 pieces (all brooches), i.e. just less than half of the total number of finds, being dated to this period. Six of these are beak brooches, of which four belong to the earlier sub-type G2, dated by Ørsnes to his phase 1, and two are of the later sub-type G3, which are mainly dated by Ørsnes to his phase 2 (Ørsnes 1966). Unusually, one of the beak brooches of sub-type G1 is gilt (fig. 3). The assemblage also includes two small equal-armed brooches of type F, dated by Ørsnes to his phase 1, and two S-shaped brooches that can be linked with his types L and J. One of these, the best preserved, is tin coated and has an animal head at both terminals (fig. 3). Finally, the assemblage includes two disc brooches of type I, as well as an exceptionally well-preserved and very small (3 cm long) tortoise brooch, of type N, decorated with an animal figure (fig. 3). Two disc brooches belonging to a type with a central setting surrounded by pits, dated to the 8th century AD, were also discovered by metal detector (fig. 3).

Fig. 3. | *Selected artefacts from the Late Germanic Iron Age. Scale 1:1. Photo: Museum Østjylland.*

About a dozen artefacts can be dated to the Viking Age or the early High Medieval Period. These include two keys, while the remainder are brooches or fragments of brooches. One of these fragments has a flat front decorated with a field of five curved lines forming four bands: a trapezoid, almost triangular field following the curve is decorated with hatching where the field is widest and is separated by a bar from a gilt interlacing pattern in the narrow part of the field. These two elements perhaps represent parts of the body and tail of a bird (fig. 4). A poorly-preserved disc brooch is decorated with a quadripartite interlacing pattern enclosing a central, flat depression, perhaps for an inlay (fig. 4). Two brooches are of the bird-shaped type. One of these is simple, with marking of the wings and the suggestion of feathers on the tail, whereas the other has clearly marked tail feathers and a transition from tail to body, as well as transversely fluted legs with marked front and rear talons. It also has upraised wings with the suggestion of feathers, a 'dotted' (feather-covered) neck and a marked head with a curved beak and eye, which almost extends up to form a neck crest or comb. The head, tail and outermost part of the wing are connected by interlacing (fig. 4). The brooch is related to Anne Pedersen's bird brooches in Ringerike and Urnes styles – with a bird-shaped brooch from Stavnsager as a close parallel – and to a proto-type that Pedersen terms 'stylised birds'. The brooches date from the second half of the 11th century and beginning of the 12th century (Pedersen 1999). An unusually well-preserved Urnes-style brooch also belongs in this late part of the Viking Age. Both the pin anchor and the pin catch are preserved (fig. 4).

The site has also produced an enamel brooch of a type that is referred to by Maria Baastrup as an Anglo-Saxon/southern Scandinavian cloisonné brooch (Baastrup 2005). It is slightly more than 3 cm in diameter and has a scalloped gilt edge, along which there are five circular settings containing blue glass. The motif is a central cruciform figure in dark blue enamel. At the end of each arm of the cross there is a circular cell filled with yellowish enamel. These circular cells are linked by way of a cell wall to a central cell filled with green enamel. The areas between the arms of the cross are filled with enamel of a turquoise colour. During production, the middle cell wall in two of the arms of the cross appears to have become displaced (fig. 5) (Stidsing 2009). Baastrup dates this type to the end of the 10th century and the 11th century (Baastrup 2005).

Fig. 4. | *Selected artefacts from the Viking Age/Early Middle Ages. Scale 1:1. Photo: Museum Østjylland.*

Silver artefacts are exclusively represented by a small polyhedral bead weighing just over 6 g. The faces of the bead are decorated with ring-and-dot punch marks. The piece, of a form also known from other sites, is interpreted as a weight from the Viking Age, but it could also have been the terminal knob of a Permian ring (fig. 6).

Several artefacts can readily be assigned to the High Medieval period: two pendants of so-called 'Lamb of God' type, dating from the 12th and 13th centuries, and a small lead cross, just less than 4 cm in length, with a suspension hole in one arm (fig. 7).

One of the more unusual artefacts is a small animal figure in bronze. The animal cannot be unequivocally identified, but it resembles a horse.

Fig. 5. | *Enamel brooch. Scale 1:1. Photo: Museum Østjylland.*

Fig. 6. | *Polyhedral bead. Scale 1:1. Photo: Museum Østjylland.*

The head is well proportioned with the suggestion of ears. The neck, with indication of a mane, and chest are, however, greatly oversized relative to both the head and the body. The body is equipped with four rather short legs and a short stubby tail. The type, known in its hundreds from Norway but represented by only a few examples found in Denmark, is very heterogeneous both with regard to form and weight; these pieces are referred to as 'Haakon V's brass horses', and they have been dated to Haakon V's reign, i.e. the beginning of the 14th century (Brøgger 1921). They have been interpreted as weights adjusted relative to the weight of 1 mark, corresponding to c. 214 g. The weights are found adjusted to various multiples of a mark. The horse from Haslund has a weight of 15 g; this corresponds to about a fifteenth of a mark. It is therefore unlikely that it has been adjusted relative to the Norwegian mark, but it is still possible that it is a weight (fig. 8).

Fig. 7. | *Artefacts from the Middle Ages. Scale 1:1. Photo: Museum Østjylland.*

Haslund Øst from a local perspective

There are several locations near Haslund Øst with chronological links to the finds from this metal-detector site. A gold bracteate from the Early Germanic Iron Age was found at Lindkær, 7 km from

Fig. 8. | *Weight. Scale 1:1. Photo: Museum Østjylland.*

Haslund, and there is a 13th-century golden altar from Ølst Church, 5 km to the southeast of Haslund. In addition to these, finds from Frederiksdalvej, Tebbestrup and Over Hornbæk deserve more detailed mention (fig. 9).

Frederiksdalvej

In 1990-91, Kulturhistorisk Museum Randers investigated the exceptionally well-preserved remains of a village at the site of Frederiksdalvej 1. The village dated from the Late Pre-Roman Iron Age and the beginning of the Early Roman Iron Age and comprised 14 individually fenced-in farmsteads (Christiansen 1995). The site, which lies 800-900 m northeast of Haslund, does, however, precede Haslund Øst chronologically and probably constitutes part of a village complex in the area. Accordingly, in 2007-08, the museum investigated a larger settlement, Frederiksdalvej 3, some few hundred metres further to the south and a few hundred metres to the east of Haslund. This had settlement phases from the Early and Late Germanic Iron Age, the Viking Age and the High Medieval period (Poulsen 2008). A metal-detector survey was carried out at the site prior to the excavation, although only of areas that were suitable: A large part of the area, which lay fallow prior to excavation, and was covered with tall grass and other vegetation, could therefore not be surveyed. This operation yielded three Lamb of God ornaments and a gilt brooch decorated in th e Viking Age Borre style. It was without doubt the prospect of further finds that prompted the metal detectorists to return repeat-

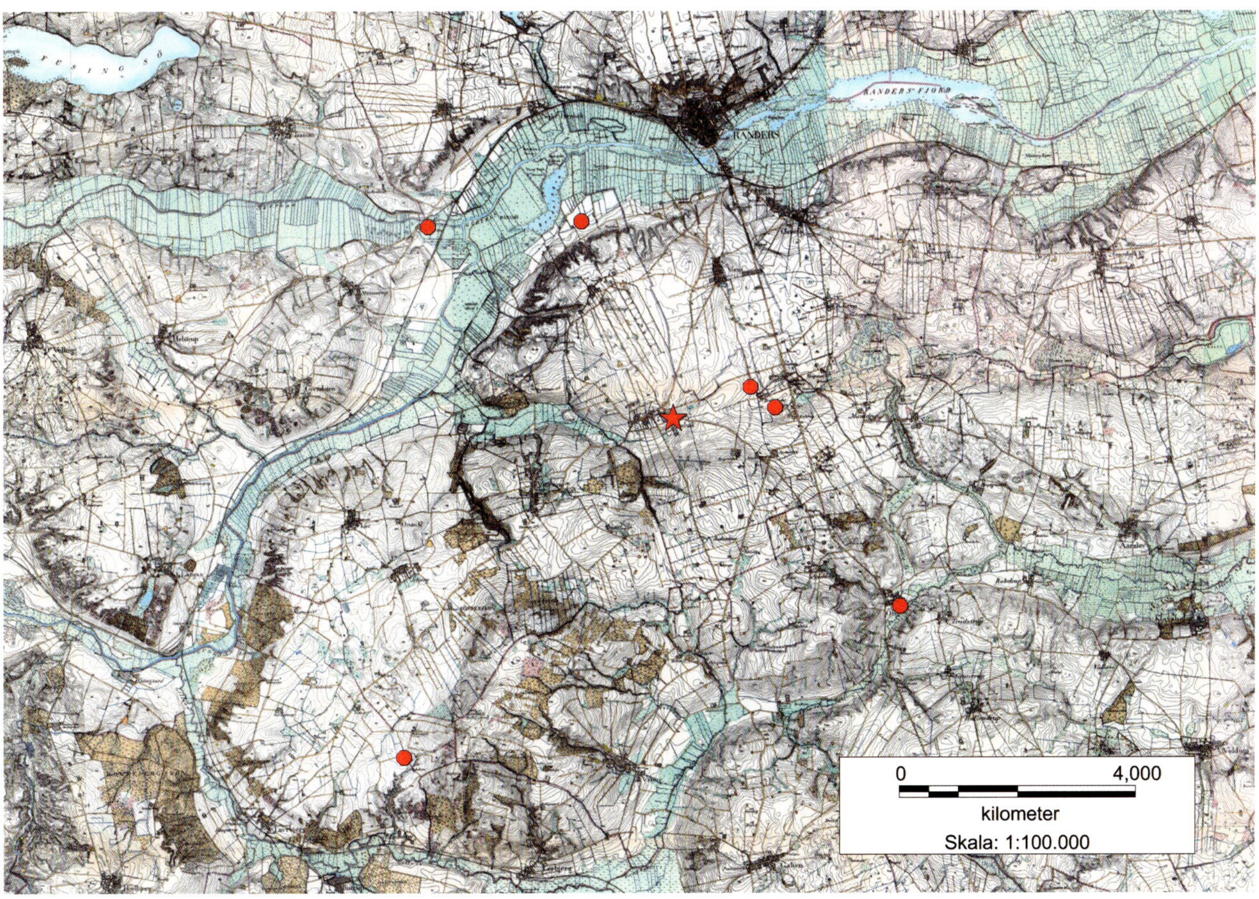

Fig. 9. | *Contemporary find spots in the vicinity: For the Over Hornbæk and Lindkær bracteates, respectively northwest and southwest of Haslund, for the arm ring north of Haslund as well as the Frederiksdalvej villages to the east and Ølst southeast of Haslund. The find spots for the bracteates from Over Hornbæk and the gold arm ring from Tebbestrup are, however, uncertain.*

edly and carry out further surveys of the features revealed by the excavation, despite no artefacts from the relevant periods being recovered (fig. 9). In 2008 and 2009, the investigations continued in a neighbouring area known as Frederiksdalvej 4, only a couple of hundred metres from the settlement at Frederiksdalvej 3 and c. 1500 m east of Haslund. Ten farmsteads were investigated here, including eight farms from the Early Germanic Iron Age. The village was probably somewhat larger than this, however, as an area in the middle of the excavation had been disturbed by an old clay pit. Detector surveys were also carried out at this site both prior to and during the investigation, but nothing was found that could be dated securely to the relevant period.

Tebbestrup

In 1856, an arm ring was found in Tebbestrup Kær. The find spot cannot be relocated precisely but it lies about 3 km northwest of Haslund. The arm ring consists of two parts, hinged together on the reverse; it is hollow and made of sheet gold with applied gold filigree wire and beads. The two halves of the ring terminate in two opposing animal heads, each with an open jaw, in which lies the ring's complicated locking mechanism. It can be dated to the Early Germanic Iron Age and is so far unique in Denmark. It is thought to have been produced in the area around the Black Sea (Jørgensen & Vang Petersen 1998).

Over Hornbæk

If we move a little further away – just over 4 km northwest of Haslund – we reach Over Hornbæk, where five gold bracteates, a silver-gilt great square-headed brooch and a couple of amber beads were found in 1847. However, the bracteates from Over Hornbæk were found on the other side of the river Gudenå – and this is probably rather too far from the environment at Haslund for them to be directly related to this.

Conclusion

Considering the c. 50 finds recovered so far, ranging in date from the Early Germanic Iron Age until sometime in the High Medieval period – a period of almost 1000 years – Haslund Øst cannot be categorised as a large settlement. Both Haslund village and the archaeological site lie on the edge of a large plateau that slopes down towards wetland areas to the west, south and east. There is no immediate difference between the topography of the site and that on the extremes of the plateau, a c. 2 x 1 km area. However, it is not suggested here that this is a site which, in terms of area, matches the large, well-known detector sites – just that the topography does not exclude this possibility. In order to discover whether the site has a greater extent than the c. 4 ha which have so far yielded finds, it is necessary for the metal detectorists to discover the boundaries of the site. That is, they need to survey areas extending away from those in which finds have been made. Another possibility would be to carry out archaeological investigations of both the site itself and the local areas immediately adjacent to it. Archaeological investigations are necessary if an understanding is to be acquired of the environment reflected in the finds from Haslund Øst, as this assemblage differs significantly from that of an ordinary village and from those of the large and exceptionally find-rich central places or detector sites. Correspondingly, archaeological investigations at Haslund Øst will also facilitate an understanding of the interplay between this site and the surrounding agrarian settlements.

Bibliography

Baastrup, M.P. 2009, Småfibler af karolingiske og ottonske typer i Danmark. *Aarbøger for Nordisk Oldkyndighed og Historie* 2005, 209-55.

Brøgger, A.W. 1921, *Ertog og Øre: Den gamle norske vegt.* Kristiania.

Christiansen, F. 1995, Frederiksdalvej – en boplads fra ældre jernalder. *Kulturhistorisk Museum Randers Årbog* 1995, 103-10.

Hald, K. 1965, *Vore Stednavne.* København.

Jørgensen, L. & P. Vang Petersen 1998, *Guld, magt og tro. Danske skattefund fra oldtid og middelalder.* København.

Parfitt, K. & T. Anderson 2012, *Buckland Anglo-Saxon Cemetery, Dover. Excavations 1994. Canterbury.*

Pedersen, A. 2001, Rovfugle eller duer. Fugleformede fibler fra den tidlige middelalder. *Aarbøger for Nordisk Oldkyndighed og Historie* 1999, 19-67.

Poulsen, T. G. 2009, "Trædbacket" arkæologiske undersøgelser af en tidlig middelalderlig landsby ved Frederiksdalvej. *Kulturhistorisk Museum Randers Årbog* 2008, 46-57.

Stidsing, E. 2010, To fibler af fremmed oprindelse. *Kulturhistorisk Museum Randers Årbog* 2009, 76-79.

Ørsnes, M. 1966, *Form og stil i Sydskandinaviens yngre germanske jernalder.* København.

Notes

1 KHM accession nos. 0515 and 2750.

Central places in abundance?

The eastern Limfjord area in the Late Iron Age and Viking Age

Torben Trier Christiansen and Torben Sarauw

Traces of large settlements from the Late Iron Age and Viking Age lie densely in the Aalborg area (fig. 1). Parts of some of these settlements, at Lindholm Høje and Bejsebakken, were excavated as early as the 1950s (Ramskou 1953; 1955; 1957; Ørsnes 1966, 256). Finds of brooches and other metal artefacts indicated that these settlements were perhaps of a special character. When metal detectors were introduced at the end of the 1970s, it was here, of course, that local detector enthusiasts began their activities – and with great success; there was a dramatic increase in the number of finds of metal artefacts from these sites in subsequent years (e.g. Christiansen 2008; Vang Petersen 1991). For a long time these two sites stood out as being markedly more affluent than the other ordinary rural settlements in the region, and on this basis they were interpreted as central places (Johansen 1994, 23).

Detail was added to the picture during the course of the 1980s and 1990s as a consequence of private detectorists continuing their work and regularly submitting finds from an increasing number of sites along the eastern Limfjord. Furthermore, investigations of a trading and craft site at Sebbersund in 1990-93 added new aspects to the overall settlement picture (Birkedahl Christensen & Johansen 1992).

It was first after the very extensive excavations conducted at Bejsebakken in 1999 and 2000 that it was possible to obtain a more complete insight into what lay hidden at one of the large detector sites in terms of features and underlying structures. The interpretation of Bejsebakken is therefore important for a general understanding of the detector sites in the eastern Limfjord area, including the interaction between coastal and inland sites.

The continuing increase in the number of finds, a direct result of the many skilled detectorists residing in the Aalborg area, has led to the present situation where we now know of 11-12 sites rich in metal finds along the eastern Limfjord (fig. 1). Against this background, the settlements at Bejsebakken and Lindholm Høje now appear much less distinctive than was previously the case. It seems obvious that not all the densely-spaced metal-rich sites within the region can be interpreted as central places relative to a larger area. A subtler approach to the phenomenon is required.

As yet, the many detector finds lack the support of further investigations at several of the sites. However, it is now obvious that almost all the prominent *bakkeøer* – 'hill islands' – along the eastern Limfjord hosted settlements during the Late Iron Age and Viking Age, where the circulation of metals was much greater than at contemporary inland settlements. However, finds of gold, silver and luxury imported goods, which would indicate the permanent presence of a social elite elevated markedly above the ordinary population of the area, are very few and far between.

In 2009, the first investigations were carried out on Nørholm, the find-rich hill adjacent to

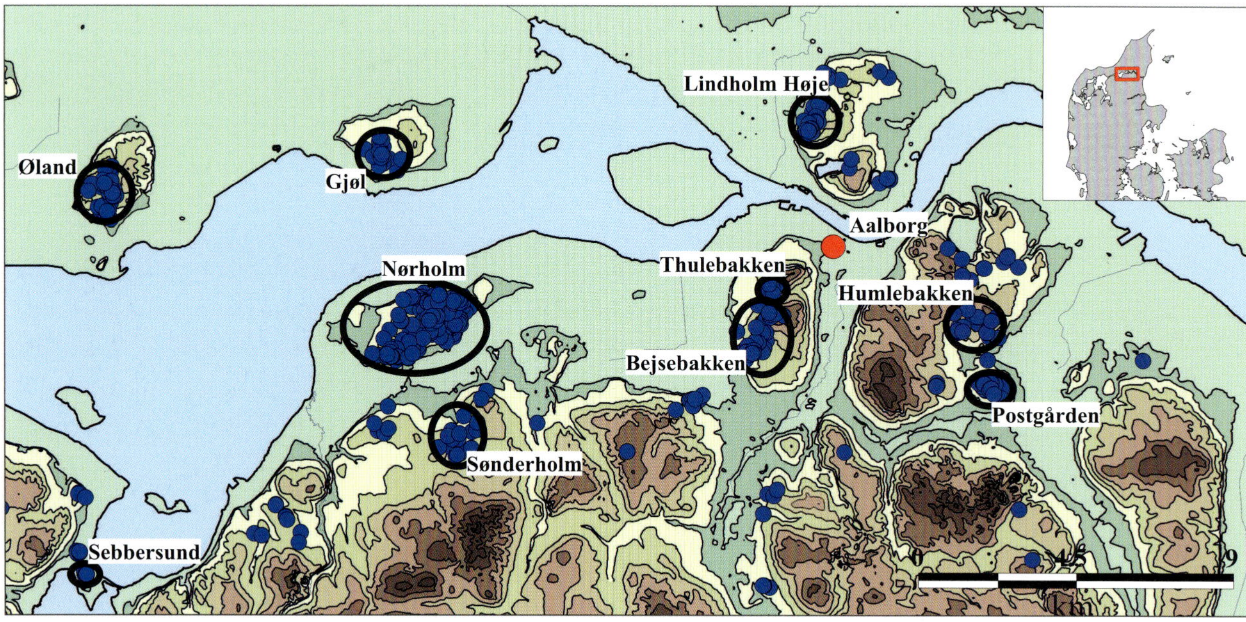

Fig. 1. | *All detector finds from the prehistoric period in the eastern Limford area. The pale green areas represent raised seabed.*

Bejsebakken. In the following, the results of these investigations, together with the preliminary interpretations of Bejsebakken (Sarauw forthcoming), will be outlined in brief to provide a basis for a discussion of the overall settlement structure in the region at that time.

Bejsebakken

Bejsebakken lies immediately southwest of Aalborg on an elongated 'hill island' – the Hasseris *bakkeø* (figs. 1 and 2). From the top of the hill, where the Late Iron Age settlement lay concentrated, there is a wide vista over the Limfjord, which here almost has the character of the broad arm of a river, and of the surrounding 'hill islands'. To the west and east of Bejsebakken, the rivers Hasseris Å and Østerå run through what today is an area of raised seabed and a former branch of the fjord. In the Late Iron Age and Viking Age, these areas were probably

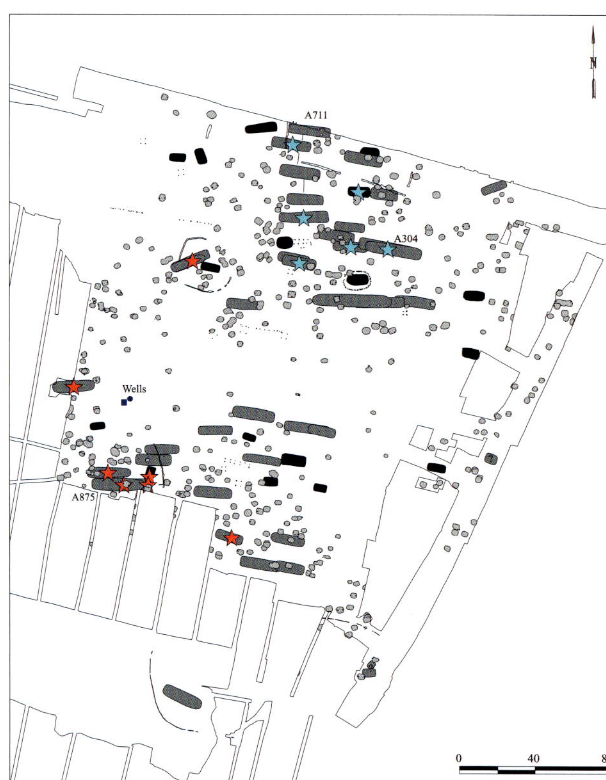

Fig. 2. | *Distribution of three-aisled longhouses and* Grubenhäuser *at Bejsebakken. The dendrochronologically-dated well and the well-preserved fence ditches are also marked. Three-aisled longhouses containing sherds from hemispherical vessels are marked with red stars, while blue stars denote longhouses containing pottery from the Late Roman/Early Germanic Iron Age.*

wetter than they are today, but they could have been used for grazing and as a source of raw materials; peat for example could be obtained for use in building construction and as fuel.

The settlement from the Late Iron Age and Early Viking Age is concentrated on a plateau lying c. 54-57 m above sea level (fig. 2). A total area of c. 8 ha has been investigated on Bejsebakken, but the Late Iron Age settlement is concentrated within a c. 230 x 230 m area corresponding to just less than 5 ha. Within this area there are records of a total of 422 *Grubenhäuser*, of which a majority have been investigated. In addition to these are 57 three-aisled longhouses, 12 structures thought to be bases for haystacks, two wells, 13 possible graves, various pits, cultural layers etc. Extensive settlement traces from the Late Neolithic period were also detected (Sarauw 2006; 2008a; 2008b).

In the northeastern part of the area the subsoil consists of sand and clayey sand, whereas further to the south and west there is chalk. The chalk areas, which also occur on the other 'hill islands', were however avoided as far as possible by settlements in the prehistoric period.

Three-aisled longhouses seem to fall within two main concentrations. These are located, respectively, to the north and south of an east-west oriented find-free area measuring c. 160 x 30 m that, to the east, appears to expand both to the north and the south. The evidence of low settlement intensity in this area appears genuine, reflecting a conscious choice made in the prehistoric period – probably because the area had a special function. There is, therefore, nothing in the topography or the composition of the subsoil that precludes the exploitation of this area for settlement. Its special function probably extends back to the founding of the settlement in the Late Roman/Early Germanic Iron Age. It is also respected in subsequent settlement phases, the last of which dates from the Early Viking Age. Similar settlements with 'common areas' or greens are exemplified by Sædding, where the green is of almost identical dimensions to that at Bejsebakken (Stoumann 1980, 96).

The three-aisled longhouses can be dated typologically and with the aid of pottery (fig. 2). Furthermore, these dates are partially confirmed by the radiocarbon dates. The northern concentration is, with a few exceptions, assigned to the end of the Late Roman/Early Germanic Iron Age, whereas the southern concentration is broadly assigned to the Late Germanic Iron Age/Early Viking Age. The dating of the southern concentration is also supported by dendrochronological dates from a well located in the same area (AD 655 and AD 682).

The three-aisled longhouses in the individual areas appear to have several common features and it is possible to distinguish several phases. An example in the northern concentration is the series comprising A711, A429 phases I and II, A266 and A370 (fig. 3). The five longhouses are mostly 15-20 m in length and stand side-by-side, forming a north-south row. Together with their obvious typological similarities, this suggests that they represent a single farmstead that was renewed at intervals. One of the longhouses can be dated on the basis of its pottery to the Late Roman/Early Germanic Iron Age. The three radiocarbon dates obtained from A429 allow a weighted average for the date of the building to the period AD 436-537. An example from the southern concentration, where sherds of hemispherical vessels were found in several of the longhouses, comprises a distinctive longhouse with three phases (fig. 3; A910, A944 and A875). The three radiocarbon dates obtained from A875 result in a weighted average of AD 782-886. Two of the house phases lay almost directly on top of each other, while the third – A910 – lay a little to the north. All the longhouses had six or more pairs of roof-bearing posts in their construction, of which the final sets were located in the gables. The length of the longhouses varied between 18.5 and 23 m, and there was a tendency for the distance between the roof-bearing posts to decrease towards the gables.

In the northern building concentration there was also a chieftain's farmstead in three phases, dated to the second half of the 5th century AD (fig. 4). In phase III, the longhouse occupied an area of c. 200 m^2, corresponding to a length of 33.5 m and a width of 5.5-6.5 m. The western end of the building contained a hearth, possibly used in more

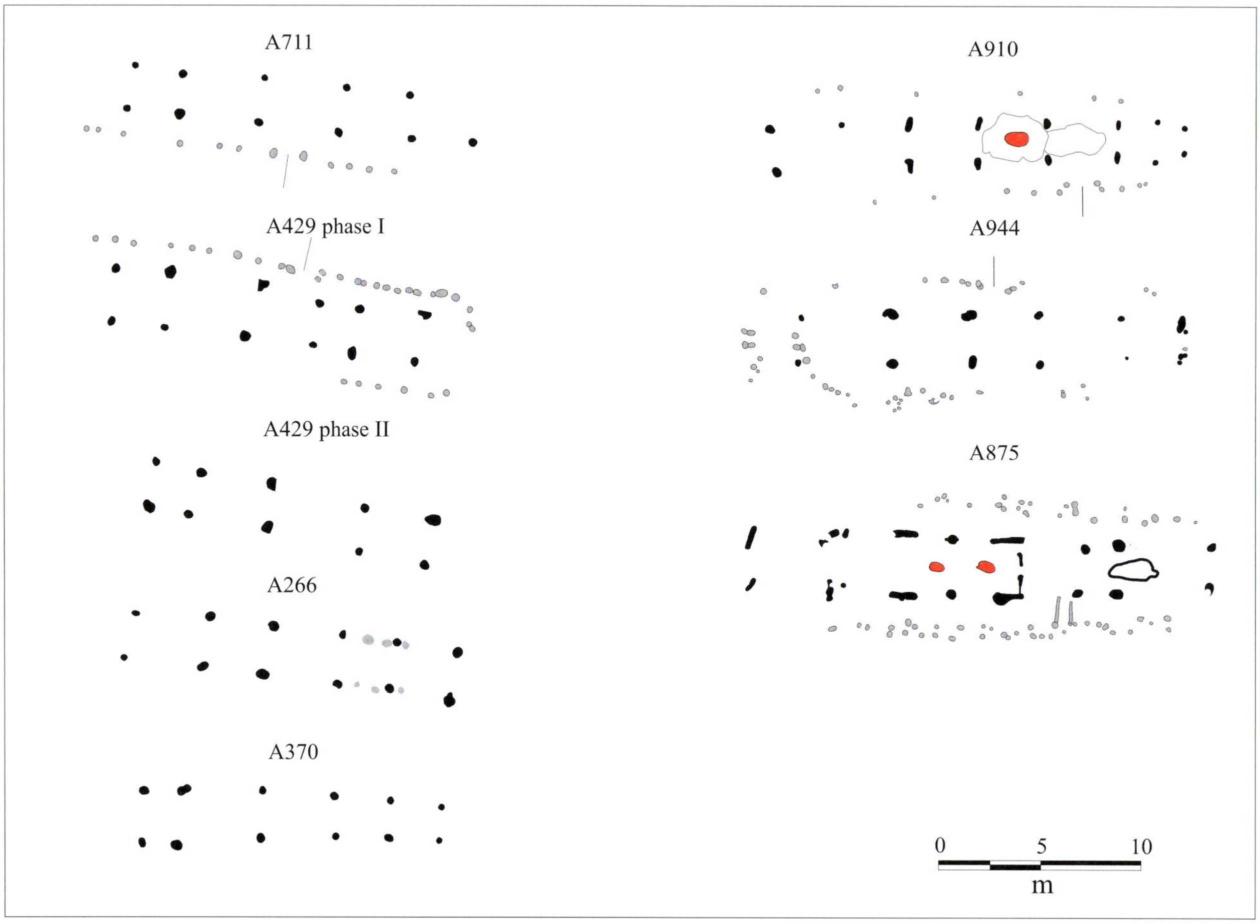

Fig. 3. | *Examples of typological series of three-aisled longhouses from the northern (left) and southern (right) concentrations. The location of the longhouses is shown in figure 2.*

than one phase, where deposition of several lambs had taken place (Jacob Kveiborg pers. comm.). The final phase contained a large number of iron artefacts, primarily spearheads, of which several had been deliberately destroyed. In addition, there were a few sherds of glass from a green pedestalled glass beaker of Snartemo type decorated with glass threads.

Another distinctive building lay immediately south of the chieftain's farmstead. It was a small three-aisled structure, no larger than 11 x 5.5-6 m, but was nevertheless fenced in, with the enclosure located directly up against the building (fig. 4). It is tempting to see it as part of the chieftain's farmstead. The fenced enclosure suggests that the building had a special function, over and above those activities related to the subsistence economy.

There are parallels to this building at several other sites, in environments where chieftain's farmsteads, prestige objects and weapons played an important role (e.g. Helgesson 2004; Herschend 1995).

About 400 *Grubenhäuser* have been investigated in total. However, the extent of the settlement to the north was not established and *Grubenhäuser* were also present in the southern trial trenches. An estimate suggests that the actual total could well have been twice the above figure (Sarauw forthcoming). Many of the *Grubenhäuser* lie concentrated in small clusters, within which the individual buildings exhibit great typological similarities in their construction, thereby suggesting some form of horizontal stratigraphy.

In most of the *Grubenhäuser*, many of which are oval or broadly oval, there are only traces of

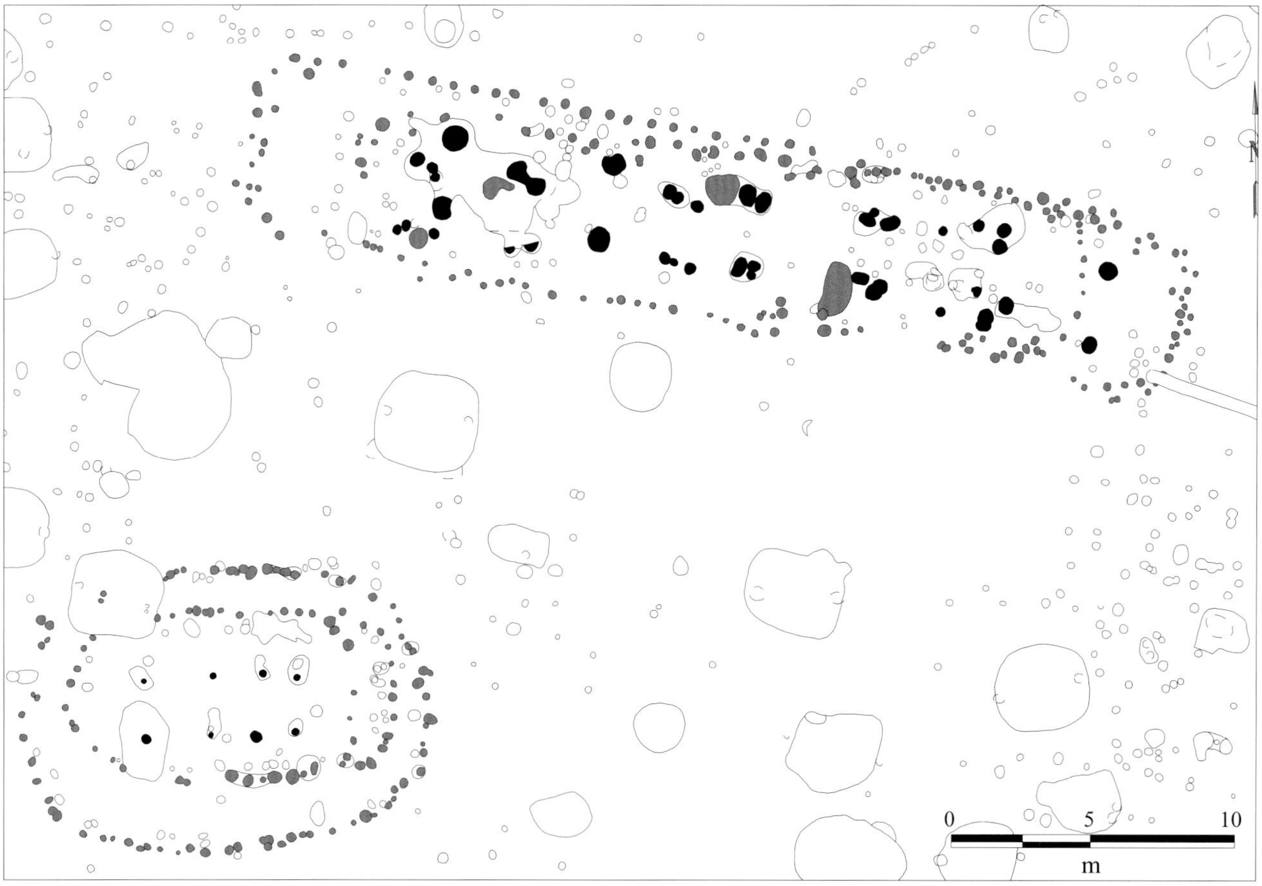

Fig. 4. | *Chieftain's farmstead with three phases and a possible cult building.*

the roof-bearing posts. These *Grubenhäuser* are, accordingly, of the simple type seen at many other sites, especially in northern Jutland and Sweden (e.g. Meier 1994; Ohlsson 1976; Strömberg 1978), but also on Zealand (Thomsen 2009, 503).

Artefacts connected with textile production have been found in almost a quarter of the *Grubenhäuser* at Bejsebakken. In particular, loom weights and spindle whorls are common, but sewing needles, spindle hooks and fragments of wool combs have also been recovered on a few occasions (fig. 5). In several cases, oval pits are seen at a basal level in the *Grubenhäuser*, which are thought to be connected with weaving (Zimmermann 1981, 134ff). One *Grubenhaus* functioned as a smithy or a jeweller's workshop, as shown by the traces of a possible anvil. The discovery of hammerscale, slag, parts of casting moulds and fragments of garnet at its basal level seems to confirm this interpretation.

The fill layers of the *Grubenhäuser* contained large quantities of artefacts which provide an indication of the many different crafts and the trade that must have taken place on the site. For example, there are iron ingots, artisans' tools – in the form of files and drills, weights and the arm of a balance or scales.

The fact that Bejsebakken, with its central location in the Limfjord area and the northern Jutland region, was part of a greater North European network is shown by finds of various brooch types that seem to have their main centres of distribution in other Scandinavian areas. This applies, for example, to a brooch type with a rectangular head plate and a spade-shaped/semi-circular foot (fig. 6a), which is known from Uppåkra (Hårdh 2003, 53-54) and southwestern Norway (e.g. Kristoffersen 2006, 73), and two iron brooches with S-shaped terminals (fig. 6c), which have their main area of distribution in Sweden and Finland (e.g. Kivikoski 1939, 90ff;

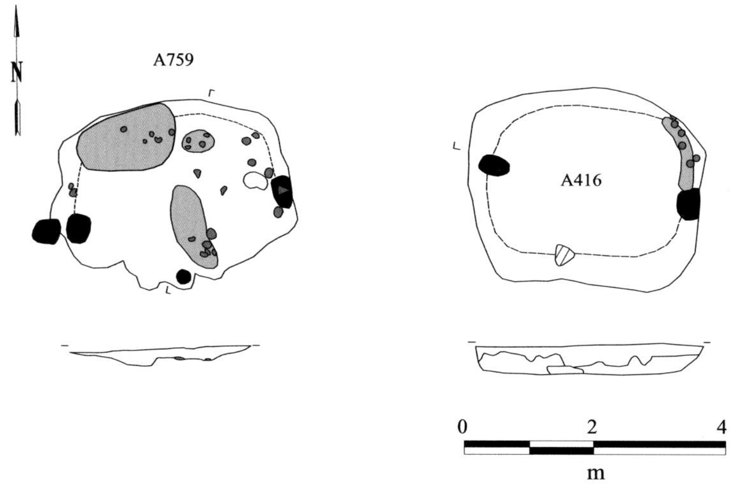

Fig. 5. | *Examples of two* Grubenhäuser *that have functioned as weaving huts. Pits are shown in pale grey, loom weights in dark grey and the red triangle denotes a spindle whorl.*

Fig. 6. | *A selection of brooches found primarily in the* Grubenhäuser *at Bejsebakken. A. Brooch with rectangular head plate and spade-shaped/semicircular foot. B. Disc brooch. C. Iron brooch. D. Plate brooch with backplate of iron. E. Tortoise brooch. F. Oval openwork brooch. Scale 1:1. Photo: J. Slot-Carlsen.*

Lehtosalo-Hilander 1982, 89ff; Strömberg 1971, 252).

For dating purposes, and in relation to the other detector sites, it is the brooches in particular that are of interest as we are now able to see a connection between stray finds and those recovered from datable contexts (table 1). The 1999-2000 investigations yielded 27 brooches, of which 22 were found in *Grubenhäuser*, although primarily in secondarily deposited layers. As is apparent from table 1, the most common finds were rectangular brooches with a backplate of iron and applied decorated plates of bronze (fig. 6d). A massive 81.5 % of the brooches resulting from the investigations are assigned to the Late Germanic Iron Age, whereas this figure for the stray finds is only 52.7 % (fig. 7). These figures clearly indicate that the majority of the *Grubenhaus* settlement should be dated to the Late Germanic Iron Age. The occurrence of the many stray finds of artefacts and coins from the Middle Ages at Bejsebakken is due to the use of the area for the deposition of refuse from the town of Aalborg during the latter period. This is also apparent in the fill layers of the *Grubenhäuser*: Clay pipes and window glass have been found in several of these, but as a consequence of animal activity.

If, in conclusion, a preliminary picture of the settlement development at Bejsebakken is to be sketched, the following can be said: Towards the north there was a modest settlement consisting

Dating	Brooch type	Stray finds	1999-2000
Late Roman Iron Age	Various types	7	1
Early Germanic Iron Age	Cruciform brooches	14	1
	Other types	9	1
Late Germanic Iron Age	Small equal-armed brooches	1	
	Bird brooches	24	
	Beak brooches	19	2
	Oval plate brooches	10	2
	Rectangular plate brooches	12	12
	Circular plate brooches	4	1
	Small oval 'tortoise' brooches	6	2
	Other types	11	3
Viking Age	Oval 'tortoise' brooches	1	
	Disc brooches	4	1
	Equal-armed brooches	9	
	Trefoil brooches	8	
	Urnes brooches	8	
	Other types	6	1
All periods	Others/unidentifiable	12	
	Total	165	27

Table 1. | *Distribution of stray finds of brooches and brooches of known context at Bejsebakken.*

of three-aisled longhouses, founded at the end of the Late Roman or Early Germanic Iron Age, with which, at the end of the 5th century, a chieftain's farmstead became linked. In the Late Germanic Iron Age, the settlement moved southwards, where it appears to have remained until the Early Viking Age. A fix-point for this settlement is provided by two dendrochronological dates of, respectively, AD

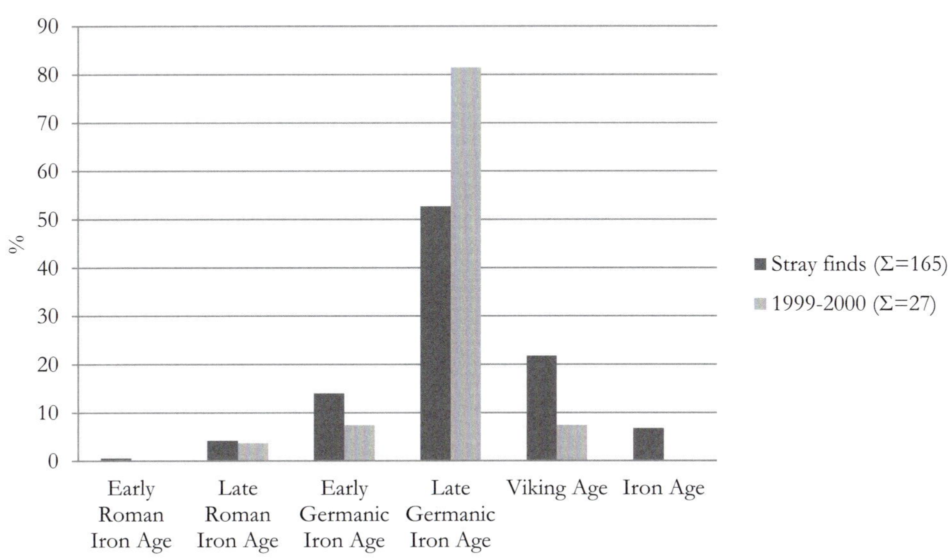

Fig. 7. | *Histogram showing the percentage distribution per period of stray finds of brooches and brooches of known context from the investigations carried out in 1999 and 2000.*

655 and AD 682 from the same well. The farmsteads are not traditional examples as we know them from settlements in southern and central Jutland with fences, roofed areas in the yard, structures interpreted as bases for haystacks, various utility buildings and *Grubenhäuser* (e.g. Nørbach 2003). Fences and possible haystack structures are only seen to a limited extent. Furthermore, the degree of preservation of the three-aisled longhouses demonstrates that remains of fences would have been detected in so far as these had been constructed in the traditional way using wooden fence posts. This situation may be due to differences in the local vegetation and thereby in the contemporary livestock composition and husbandry practices. This assumption is supported by the results of analyses of both pollen and plant macro-remains, which reveal that the local area was not characterised by woodland. On the contrary, heather was used as fuel (Hambro Mikkelsen 2001) and the area around Bejsebakken was relatively open, being dominated by pastures, meadows and fallow fields (Enevold 2010).

The great abundance of *Grubenhäuser* should therefore not be seen as representing numerous successive phases of buildings belonging to traditional farmstead units – there are too many for this to be the case. Only 38 of the buildings from all phases are thought to constitute actual longhouses or dwelling houses; of these, 21 are assigned to the Late Germanic Iron Age. Preliminary analyses show, furthermore, that a very large number of *Grubenhäuser* contain sherds of hemispherical vessels, which are traditionally dated to AD 700-1000 (Madsen 1991, 219-20). Stig Jensen has, however, pointed out that hemispherical vessels have in several cases been found in contexts containing rectangular plate brooches decorated in style C (Jensen 1982, 122). This applies first and foremost at Lindholm Høje, introducing the possibility that, in northern Jutland, hemispherical vessels occur from the middle of the Late Germanic Iron Age, corresponding to c. AD 650. The record from Bejsebakken appears to support this, as the rectangular plate brooches are found in corresponding contexts here.

A preliminary working hypothesis, which awaits, however, the results of the ongoing pottery and artefact analyses, is that a large proportion of the *Grubenhäuser* at Bejsebakken should be assigned to the middle and the end of the 7th century AD. This proposal is not contradicted by the other finds. The long-distance trade that commenced around AD 700 is, accordingly, only weakly reflected in the finds. For example, sherds from soapstone vessels are only found in limited quantities.

One must therefore imagine a situation where, within a 50-100 year period, there were many *Grubenhäuser* here at the same time, and a form of specialised textile production apparently had a prominent role in the community. Contemporary with the *Grubenhäuser* were a few longhouses, from where some form of control was probably exercised over production and the other aspects of trade and craftwork apparently linked with the site. There is a great deal to suggest that Bejsebakken – in the light of the quantity of metal finds from the Late Germanic Iron Age relative to other contemporary settlements, its central location relative to the Limfjord and the north-south traffic on land as well as the extensive textile production – was of regional significance for trade, textile production and crafts. By the Early Viking Age, the site had outplayed its role relative to the town of Aalborg, where new investigations have revealed the existence of a *Grubenhaus* settlement radiocarbon-dated to AD 632-888 (Vrængmose Jensen & Bergmann Møller 2010).[1]

Nørholm

About 9 km west of Bejsebakken lies the former island of Nørholm. The area between these two distinctive hills comprises exclusively low-lying raised seabed. Today, it hosts drained fields, but in the Iron Age these were wet meadowlands. The raised seabed encircles the whole of the massive Nørholm hill, which is 40 m high and has an area of 480 ha. Only 400 m of shore meadows to the north separate the hill from the Limfjord. The narrow eastern part of the Limfjord broadens at this point to form the 2.5 km wide broad Gjøl Bredning and, towards the west, the 7.5 km wide Nibe Bredning. On the opposite shore lie the north coast's striking hills, the former islands of Gjøl and Øland.

For several years, Nørholm has been the most productive detector site in the region. To date, a total of 327 prehistoric treasure trove finds have been recorded from the hill, scattered over an area of approximately 340 ha. If the distribution of the datable finds is considered, the beginnings of a pattern can be discerned (fig. 8). Towards the southwest, at Mellemholm, a very marked concentration of finds from the Early Iron Age can be seen; these are dominated by brooches from the Roman Iron Age. Towards the southeast, at Østergård near the foot of the hill, a concentration of finds from the Germanic Iron Age is apparent, and towards the northeast, just south of Nørholm, there is an area dominated by metal finds dating from the Viking Age. With regard to topography, the concentrations of finds are seen running down the sides of the Nørholm hill and also on the more obvious topographic locations, such as local plateaus.

With respect to type spectrum, the finds from Nørholm closely resemble those from the other sites in the region and demonstrate, collectively, great continuity through the prehistoric period and into the Middle Ages. The number of finds also increases steadily with time and during the whole of the Iron Age and Viking Age the assemblages are markedly dominated by brooches (figs. 9 and 10), mostly of commonly occurring types. There are a few finds of a foreign nature, especially amongst those from the Viking Age. Finds other than brooches included 12 imported coins, a little hack silver and a single weight. In general, however, the traces of actual trade are very limited. Similarly, luxury ornaments and precious metals are few and far between.

Despite the extensive detector activity, very few actual archaeological investigations have been carried out on the hill. This is due to a very large part of the area being agricultural land that has been unaffected by construction works. The only investigations conducted prior to 2009 concerned the excavation of parts of a settlement from the Early Iron Age located near the foot of the hill on the south side. In addition to this, a grave from the

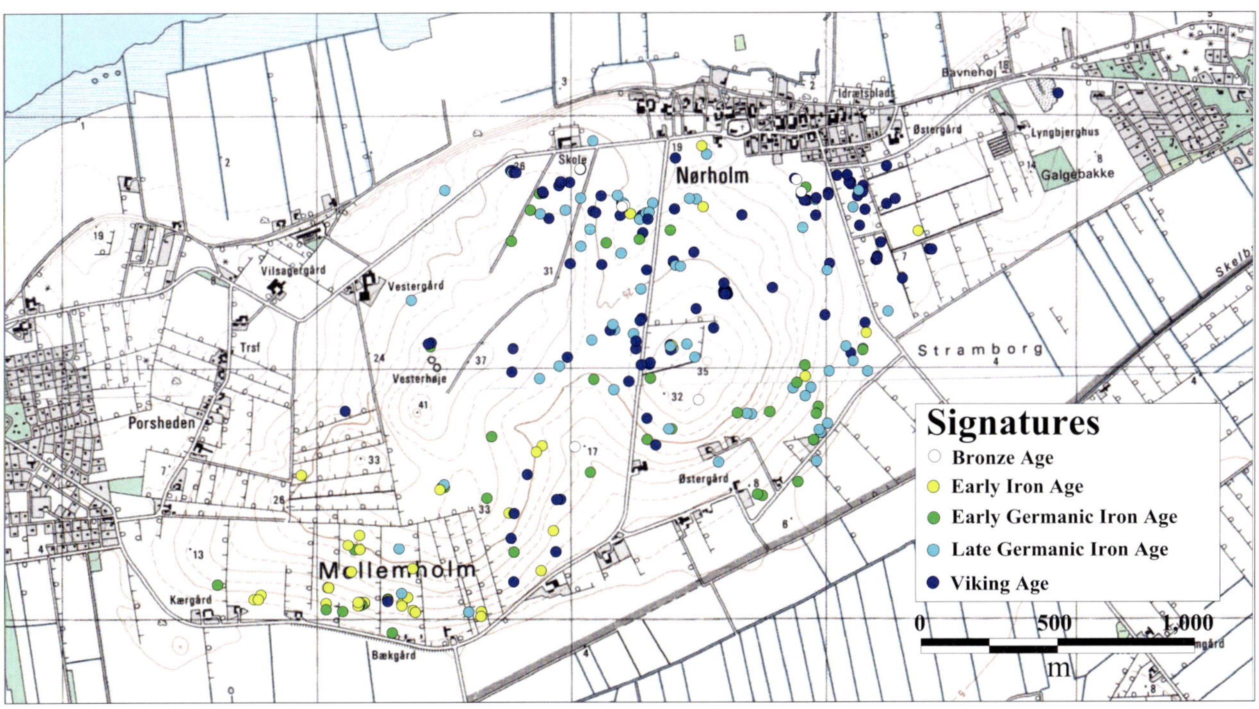

Fig. 8. | *The distribution of detector finds from Nørholm dated to the Bronze Age, Iron Age and Viking Age.*

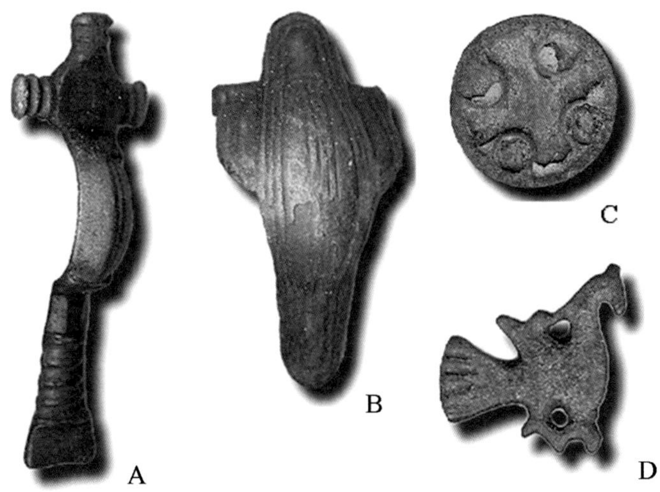

Fig. 9. | *Examples of brooches found by metal detector on the Nørholm 'hill island'. A. Cruciform brooch. B. Beak brooch. C. Enamel brooch with cross motif. D. Bird brooch. Scale 1:1. Photo: J. Slot-Carlsen.*

Roman Iron Age containing smith's tools was investigated at Østergård on the southeastern side, and a few trial excavations have been carried out without producing any finds worthy of mention.

After the harvest in 2009, Nordjyllands Historiske Museum finally had the opportunity to carry out a modest trial excavation on Nørholm (fig. 11). First of all, a limited series of trial trenches was laid out at Mellemholm, near the foot of the hill on its south side. Over several years, a number of brooches from the Roman and Early Germanic Iron Age have been handed in from this area, possibly indicating the presence of a cemetery suffering plough damage. The preliminary investigation resulted in the localisation of two graves in the chalky subsoil on a small plateau – a small, 65 cm long child's grave and an inhumation grave containing a well-preserved skeleton; both had been disturbed by ploughing.

Some trial trenches were also laid out in a couple of the most find-rich areas on the extensive hilltop. No traces of prehistoric settlement were found here, however, perhaps as a consequence of the chalky subsoil.

Finally, trial trenches were laid out at Østergård, near the foot of the hill on the southeastern side, where several fine artefacts had been found by detector. The trial trenches contained densely packed settlement traces in the form of postholes, pits and a couple of *Grubenhäuser*. Despite the sandy sub-

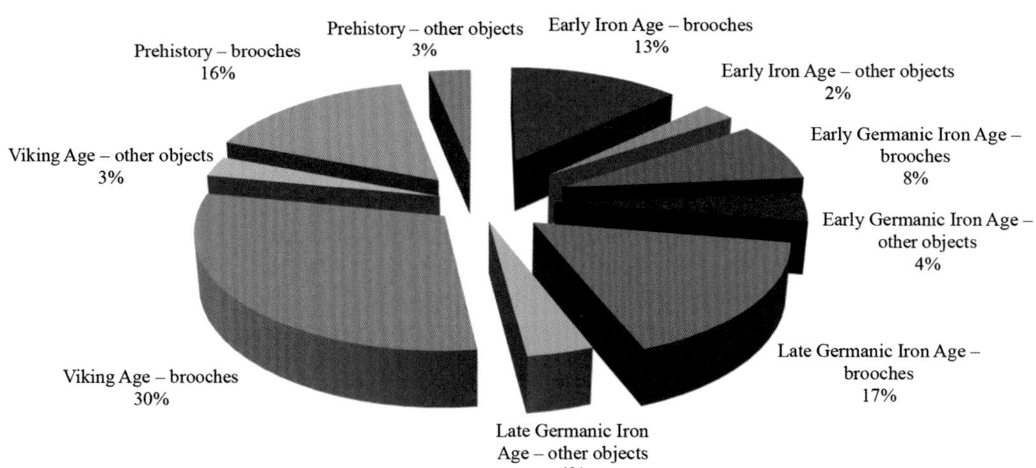

Fig. 10. | *Detector finds from Nørholm.*

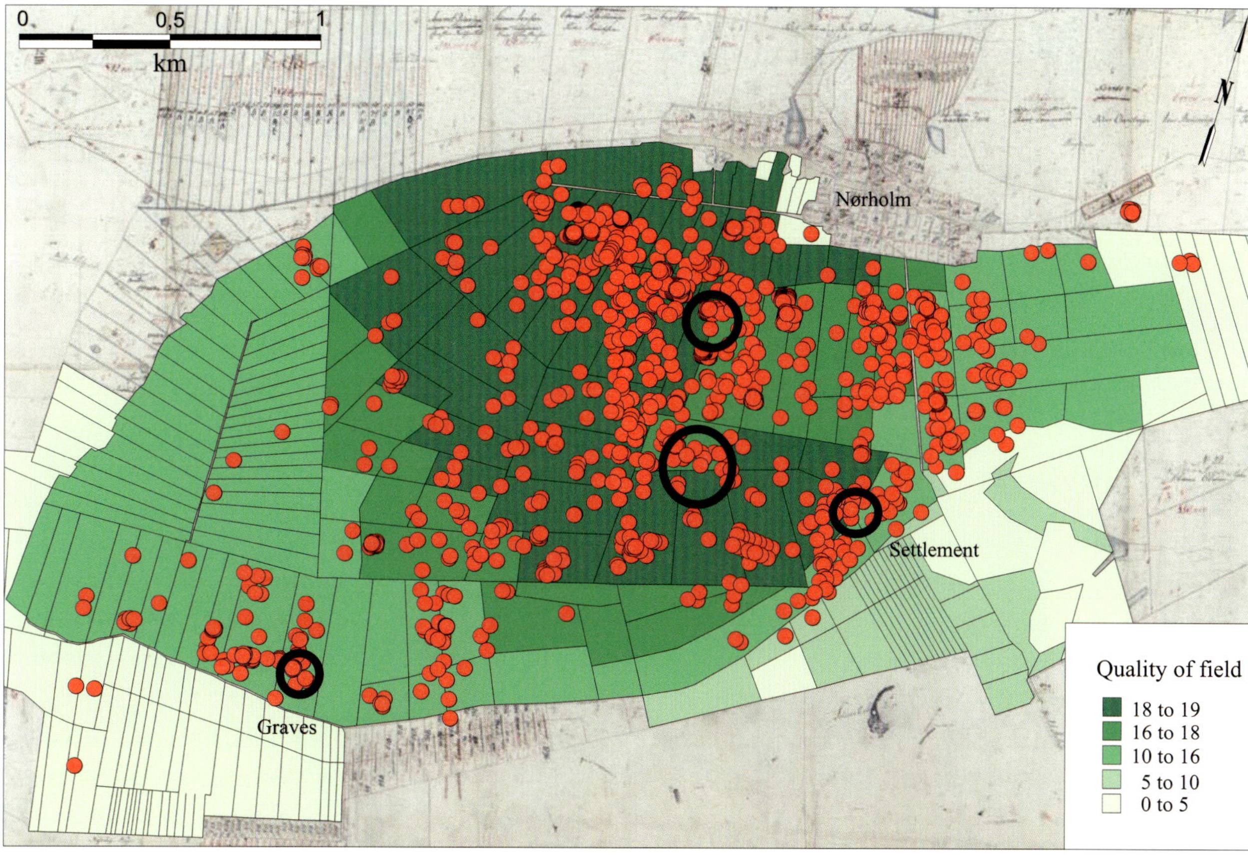

Fig. 11. | *Section of map showing the soil fertility of fields at Nørholm. All detector finds are marked in red. The black circles mark investigated areas.*

soil, several of the features contained chalk and chalk flecks, suggesting that chalk had been used in the floors of the longhouses – a familiar phenomenon seen at other Limfjord settlements. The presence of the chalk probably also explains the very well-preserved bone found in several features.

There was no opportunity to determine the extent of the settlement, but it was clearly associated with the sandy subsoil present at the foot of the hill, at the point where it flattens out towards the raised marine areas that separate Nørholm from Sønderholm, on the Himmerland 'mainland' a couple of kilometres further south.

The results of the 2009 trial excavation campaign are significant. Given the size of the hilltop, it is still much too early to discount the possibility that the remains of one or more settlements are yet to be found there. But at some of the topographically most obvious locations, which are also very rich in detector finds, actual settlement traces are completely absent. This phenomenon is also familiar from the thorough trial excavations at Bejsebakken (Christiansen 2008, 115).

Conversely, we have now demonstrated solid settlement traces at, in topographic terms, a rather divergent location – at the rear of the hill, near its foot, and away from the fjord, right down at a level of 9 m above mean sea level. The site is characterised by its sandy subsoil, in contrast to the chalk of the hilltop; perhaps this has contributed to the settlement remains not, as is commonly the case, resulting in higher soil fertility in the fields here, cf. the 'Original 1' cadastral maps of the area (fig. 11).

As the picture given by the finds appears at present, it seems likely that a major settlement 'wandered' around on the south side of Nørholm, very close to the foot of the hill. It began in the Early Iron Age with Mellemholm in the west then, during the Germanic Iron Age, it moved to the area just east of Østergård. In the Viking Age, the settlement lay just south of Nørholm, before finally ending its wanderings in the Middle Ages, where Nørholm lies today. Further investigations are essential, however, to answer questions concerning the significance of the many detector finds from the actual hilltop. The area immediately south of Nørholm School appears especially promising in this respect. There is a solid concentration of detector finds here and many fields show high soil fertility (fig. 11).

Other settlements in the region

Bejsebakken is not alone in having been subjected to actual archaeological excavations. As previously mentioned, extensive excavations have also been executed on Lindholm Høje and at Sebbersund. In recent years, Postgården has been subjected to systematic trial excavations and we now know that the settlement traces extend over c. 4.5 ha on the hilltop, including longhouses and probably also between 250 and 300 *Grubenhäuser*. A small part of the settlement to the north has also been excavated together with the final remains of an associated cemetery from the Germanic Iron Age. It is too early to say whether the relationship between the numbers of longhouses and *Grubenhäuser* is the same as that seen at Bejsebakken, as only 36 *Grubenhäuser* have been investigated so far. Postgården also differs from Bejsebakken in that remains were found of possible foundation ditches for fences that could at some point have enclosed the individual farmsteads on the hilltop. A point of similarity is, however, textile production, which also played a prominent role at Postgården. Ten of the excavated *Grubenhäuser* contained traces of textile production in the form of loom weights and/or spindle whorls.

Major excavation campaigns have also been executed on Lindholm Høje on several occasions (Ramskou 1953; 1955; 1957; 1976). The most well-known of these is the excavation of the cemetery with its c. 700 graves from the Germanic Iron Age and Viking Age; this took place during the 1950s. At the same time there was an investigation of the intensive settlement traces that lay partially over the cemetery, and on several occasions subsequently

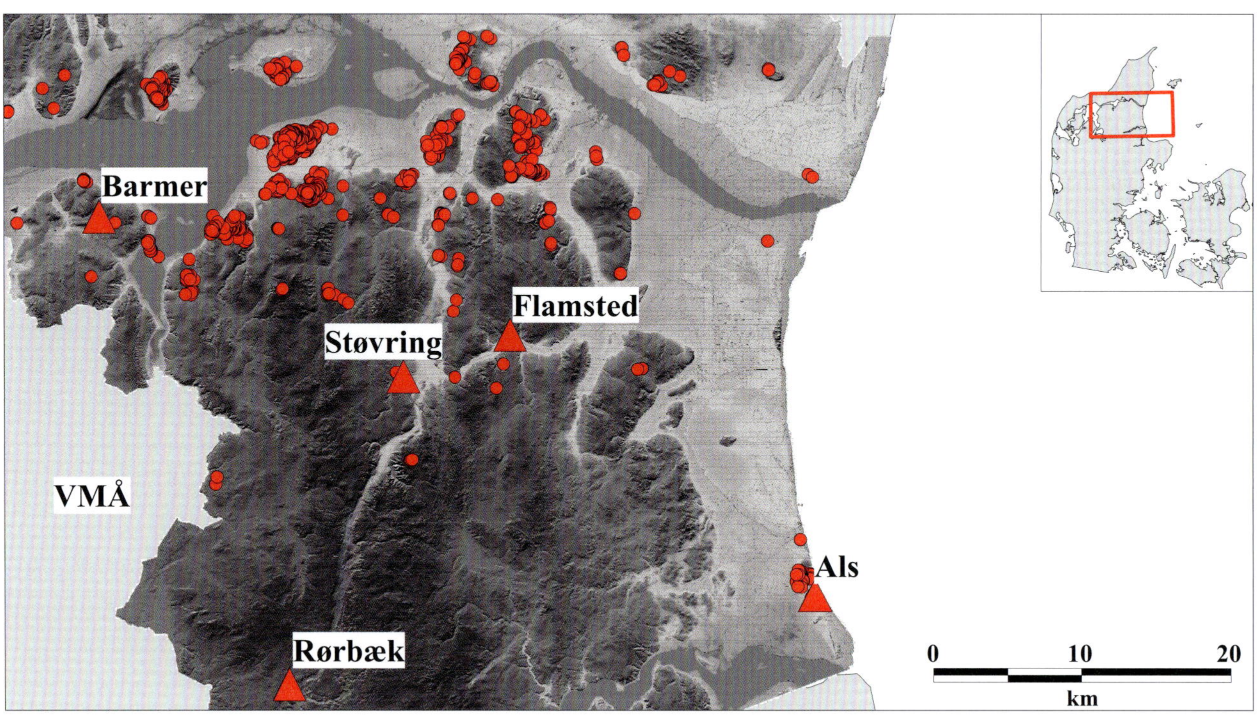

Fig. 12. | *Key map (lidar scan) showing the distribution of all metal-detector finds within Nordjyllands Historiske Museum's area of responsibility. The red triangles mark recently discovered sites mentioned in the text.*

investigations have been carried out of parts of the very large settlement on the hill. The latest of these was in 2006, in connection with the expansion of the Lindholm Høje Museum, in the course of which a further six *Grubenhäuser* were excavated. Despite these cumulatively very extensive excavations, we still do not know the original extent and structure of the settlement at Lindholm Høje. However, it clearly extended over several hectares and included a large number of *Grubenhäuser* (e.g. Johansen 1994; Ramskou 1953; 1955; 1957).

Sebbersund deviates in several ways from the other metal-rich sites in the region. Its topography is completely different, being situated on a low, narrow isthmus directly down by the fjord. Excavations here at the beginning of the 1990s revealed evidence of an extensive settlement, which the excavators interpreted as the remains of a craft and trading place with an associated church and cemetery (Birkedahl Christensen & Johansen 1992). During the investigations, a number of *Grubenhäuser* were excavated but no traces of actual longhouses were ever discovered. Only a small part of the settlement was investigated, but it is estimated to extend over c. 6.5 ha, and, on the basis of aerial photographs, it is calculated that there were as many as 300 *Grubenhäuser* on the site (Birkedahl & Johansen 2000, 28).

In order to acquire a more detailed understanding of the role of the major settlements in the whole settlement picture of the region, it is necessary to be familiar with the other settlements of the area. Unfortunately, in this respect the record is still incomplete. The settlements from the Late Iron Age and Viking Age have to a great extent been recognised due to detector finds of metal artefacts. Moving just a small distance away from the coasts of the Limfjord, detector finds are few and far between (fig. 12). Furthermore, when excavations have been carried out at inland sites, only small sections of the settlements have been investigated. In these inland areas there is a specific lack of exhaustive excavations producing finds that can securely be assigned to the Late Germanic Iron Age.

Fig. 13. | *Newly-submitted detector finds from Øland (A-D) and Als (E-F). A. Oval plate brooch. B. Fragment of mount or brooch. C. Bird brooch. D. Pendant. E. Conical brooch. F. Trefoil brooch. Scale 1:1. Photo: J. Slot-Carlsen.*

In recent years, however, slightly larger areas have been excavated in connection with new developments of building land at Rørbæk, northeast of Hobro, and at Støvring, resulting in the location of settlement traces from the Late Roman/ Early Germanic Iron Age (fig. 12). Both of these are very find-poor settlements merely comprising a few longhouses with one to three associated simple *Grubenhäuser*.

Finally, aerial survey has been able to supplement the finds picture with several new interesting sites[2] during the last couple of years (fig. 12). Near Barmer, c. 3 km west of Sebbersund, there is a site with more than 100 *Grubenhäuser*, and at Flamsted, which lies on the edge of the Lindenborg river valley, a settlement covering c. 2 ha with around 70 *Grubenhäuser* has been located. The museum has undertaken a minor preliminary excavation at Flamsted that confirmed the presence of settlement traces. Surprisingly, a detector survey yielded no prehistoric finds.

Of the newly discovered sites, mention should also be made of a new detector site at Als, near the mouth of Mariager Fjord (fig. 12). Here, on a distinctive hill on the Kattegat coast, numerous metal artefacts have been discovered from the Late Iron Age and Viking Age. These include a small circular conical brooch of northern Norwegian/Finnish origin (fig. 13e). Almost identical examples have been found at both Postgården and Bejsebakken.

Discussion

If an attempt is to be made, on the basis of the presently available evidence, to interpret the detector sites located along the eastern Limfjord and to draw an overarching picture of the settlement development and structure through the Late Iron Age and Viking Age, it will unavoidably rely very heavily on detector finds and the results of the excavations at Bejsebakken.

A number of the characteristics of Bejsebakken are also identifiable at the other metal-rich sites along the eastern Limfjord. All of them, with the exception of Sebbersund, are located on large distinctive hills alongside the fjord and are characterised by the presence of many metal artefacts with a very wide dating framework. Furthermore, the artefacts are distributed over large areas and, in the cases where actual excavations have been carried out at the sites, there are traces of major settlements including numerous *Grubenhäuser* (Christiansen 2008, 107-18).

The record of metal finds throughout the entire Iron Age and Viking Age is everywhere dominated by brooches of domestic, commonly occurring types and generally includes very few precious metals and luxury artefacts. At several of the sites there are, however, a few indications of trade in the form of parts of scales and weights. Similarly, almost all the assemblages include a minor component of imported metal artefacts that originate predominantly from Norway, Sweden, the British Isles and the northwestern part of Continental Europe (Christiansen 2008, 118-21).

The finds from Sebbersund have a slightly different chronological composition from those of the other sites, as no continuity is seen from the Early Iron Age to the Middle Ages. Conversely, its centre of gravity lies in the Viking Age and only limited activity is apparent from neighbouring periods. Relative to other sites, Sebbersund also deviates with respect to its location very close to the fjord, where there was apparently no association with an agrarian settlement. These deviations could very well reflect functional differences: Sebbersund apparently served, and was organised, as a dedicated trading and craft site, while the others presumably, as was the case at Bejsebakken, grew out of existing agrarian settlements.

Ultimately, we have to recognise that our knowledge concerning the majority of these settlements is, at the present time, too superficial to permit a more detailed interpretation of the role of these sites in the region's overall settlement structure. It is, however, a fact that the eastern Limfjord experienced an economic boom during the Late Iron Age and Viking Age, which left marked impressions on the settlement structure. On the hills alongside the fjord, greater and greater numbers of metal artefacts came into circulation. At Bejsebakken, we can see that this increased circulation is linked with a development from an ordinary rural settlement to a rural settlement with a specialised craft function and associated trade links. At Sebbersund, we perhaps see the next step in this development – a site exclusively based on trade and crafts.

Settlement development in the eastern Limfjord area during the Iron Age and Viking Age appears, unsurprisingly, to have moved towards increased specialisation and centralisation. This development was apparently most marked at settlements closest to the region's most important transport route – the Limfjord. Exactly how central the individual sites were with respect to the region is still very difficult to judge. The large number of detector finds at Bejsebakken and Nørholm indicate clearly, however, that there was greater activity here than at other sites, both along the fjord and inland. During certain periods, these sites could very well have performed various central functions relative to the hinterland and perhaps relative to the other sites alongside the fjord. The presence of a chieftain's farmstead at Bejsebakken during the Early Germanic Iron Age, which yielded finds of imported glass and at least 14 destroyed spearheads, some with barbs, similarly suggests a form of centralisation of power that may also have existed during the subsequent period. It is precisely these chieftain's farmsteads that must be perceived as a precondition for the flourishing and centralisation of trade and crafts during the subsequent periods. At Bejsebakken during the Late Germanic Iron Age, this is expressed by the fact that evidence of textile production lies far in excess of what an ordinary rural settlement would have produced. It is tempting to view this in connection with the increasing significance of the sailing ship. Increasing marine traffic and trade in the fjord area also provides an explanation for the many 'central places' which, if nothing else, indicate that the Limfjord area was a central region in respect of major transport and economic considerations.

It is with the presence of a royal power in the area in the Viking Age, made apparent by Aggersborg and the minting of coins in Aalborg, that the first clear evidence is seen of a marked centralisation of economic, political and military functions (e.g. Roesdahl 1980; Nielsen 1999). In several places, for example Nørholm, the level of activity, evaluated on the number of datable metal finds, appears to increase in the Viking Age and this heightened level of activity appears to continue into the Middle Ages. At Bejsebakken, however, development seems to stagnate, coincident with the appearance of early Aalborg, although development apparently continued at many of the other settlements in the Limfjord area.

Bibliography

Birkedahl, P. & E. Johansen 2000, The eastern Limfjord in the Germanic Iron Age and the Viking period. Internal structures and external relations. *Acta archaeologica* 71, 25-33.

Birkedahl Christensen, P. & E. Johansen 1992, En handelsplads fra yngre jernalder og vikingetid ved Sebbersund. *Aarbøger for Nordisk Oldkyndighed og Historie* 1991, 199-229.

Christiansen, T.T. 2008, Detektorfund og bebyggelse. Det østlige Limfjordsområde i yngre jernalder og vikingetid. *Kuml* 2008, 101-43.

Enevold, R. 2010, Pollenanalyse af en jordprøve fra en brøndkasse, ÅHM 3984, Bejsebakken. (FHM 4296/1). Rapport fra Moesgård Museums afdeling for konservering og naturvidenskab.

Hambro Mikkelsen, P. 2001, Makrofossilundersøgelser fra lokaliteten ÅHM 3984, Bejsebakken. NNU Rapport nr. 25.

Helgesson, B. 2004, Tributes to be spoken of. Sacrifice and warriors at Uppåkra. In: L. Larsson (ed.), *Continuity for Centuries. A ceremonial building and its context at Uppåkra, southern Sweden*. Stockholm. 223-39.

Herschend, F. 1995, Hus på Helgö. *Fornvännen* 90, 221-28.

Hårdh, B. 2003, Uppåkra i folkvandringstiden. In: B. Hårdh, (ed.), *Fler fynd i centrum. Materialstudier i och kring Uppåkra*. Stockholm. 41-80.

Jensen, S. 1982, Stengården, an east Jutland occupation site from the Early Germanic Iron Age. *Journal of Danish Archaeology* 1, 119-25.

Johansen, E. 1994, Lindholm Høje og Limfjorden. In: *Lindholm Høje. Gravplads og landsby*. Aalborg. 7-26.

Kivikoski, E. 1939, *Die Eisenzeit im Auraflussgebiet*. Helsinki.

Kristoffersen, S. 2006, *Kvinnedrakten fra Rogaland i folkevandringstid. Draktutstyr*. Stavanger.

Lehtosalo-Hilander, P.-L. 1982, *Luistari II. The Artefacts*. Helsinki.

Madsen, H.J. 1991, Vikingetidens keramik som historisk kilde. In: P. Mortensen & B.M. Rasmussen (eds.), *Fra stamme til stat i Danmark, 2: Høvdingesamfund og kongemagt*. Højbjerg. 217-34.

Meier, D. 1994, *Die wikingerzeitliche Siedlung von Kosel (Kosel-West), Kreis Rendsburg-Eckernförde*. Neumünster.

Nørbach, L.C. 2003, Bebyggelse og jernudvinding. In: L.C. Nørbach & P.H. Mikkelsen, *Drengsted. Bebyggelse, jernproduktion og agerbrug i yngre romersk og ældre germansk jernalder*. Højbjerg. 9-113.

Nielsen, J.N. 1999, Maritime influences on the foundation and early history of Aalborg, Denmark. In: J. Bill & B.L. Clausen (eds.), *Maritime Topography and the Medieval Town*. Copenhagen. 213-20.

Ohlsson, T. 1976, The Löddeköpinge Investigation I. The Settlement at Vikhögsvägen. *Meddelanden från Lunds universitets historiska museum* 1975-1976, 59-161.

Ramskou, T. 1953, Lindholm. Preliminary report of the 1952-1953 excavations of a late Iron Age cemetery and an Early Mediaeval settlement. *Acta Archaeologica* 24, 186-99.

Ramskou, T. 1955, Second preliminary report of the 1954-55 excavations. *Acta Archaeologica* 26, 177-85.

Ramskou, T. 1957, Lindholm Høje. Third preliminary report of the 1954-55 excavations. *Acta Archaeologica* 28, 193-203.

Ramskou, T. 1976, *Lindholm Høje gravpladsen*. København.

Roesdahl, E. 1980, *Danmarks Vikingetid*. Viborg.

Sarauw, T. 2006, *Bejsebakken. Late Neolithic houses and settlement structure*. Copenhagen.

Sarauw, T. 2008a, Early Late Neolithic dagger production in northern Jutland: marginalised production or the source of wealth? *Bericht der Römisch-Germanischen Kommission* 87 (2006), 215-72.

Sarauw, T. 2008b, On the outskirts of the European Bell Beaker phenomenon. The settlement of Bejsebakken and the social organisation of Late Neolithic societies. *Offa* 84, 83-125.

Sarauw, T. (forthcoming), Yngre jernalders bebyggelse på Bejsebakken.

Stoumann, I. 1980, A Viking Age village near Esbjerg. *Acta Archaeologica* 50 (1979), 95-118.

Strömberg, M. 1971, Grubenhäuser in Valleberga. *Meddelanden från Lunds universitets historiska museum* 1969-1970, 192-265.

Strömberg, M. 1978, *En kustby i Ystad – före stadens tillkomst*. Ystad.

Thomsen, L.G. 2009, Pit houses on Zealand in the Late Iron Age and the Viking period – a survey based on the material from the excavation at Tissø. In: U. von Freeden, H. Friesinger & E. Wamers (eds.), *Glaube, Kult und Herrschaft. Phänomene des Religiösen im 1. Jahrtausend n. Chr. in Mittel- und Nordeuropa. Akten des 59. Internationalen Sachsensymposions und der Grundprobleme der frühgeschichtlichen Entwicklung im Mitteldonauraum*. Bonn. 501-10.

Notes

1 There are four dates from *Grubenhäuser*. The dates lie within the given range with a probability of between 95.4 and 95.2 %.

2 Thanks to archaeologist Michael Vinter for information on these sites.

Metal-rich sites in Vendsyssel

A preliminary presentation

Sidsel Wåhlin

During the 1980s and 1990s, Vendsyssel Historiske Museum, working with a group of metal-detector enthusiasts, located a number of settlements that yielded metal finds from the topsoil. Three of these sites can now be described as metal-rich, with finds dating from the Late Roman Iron Age to the Medieval period: Stentinget, Ejstrup and Liver (fig. 1), though predominantly representing the Germanic Iron Age and Viking Age. The remaining sites have not yet been surveyed rigorously enough to justify the description metal-rich. Some finds, including pieces of scrap metal, do however indicate that several of these could, with further fieldwork, yield finds in sufficient numbers and of sufficient quality for them to deserve this label.

In this paper, I will introduce the three above-mentioned metal-rich sites and present a preliminary analysis of the finds.

Some general notes on sources and the landscape in Vendsyssel

In studies of Iron Age and Medieval central places, many non-archaeological sources are often drawn upon, such as historical maps, place names, analyses of topsoil chemistry, geological maps and surveys as well as metal-detector finds. However, in the case of Vendsyssel, landscape developments render many of these sources useless relative to a discussion of the landscape prior to the Renaissance. The oldest map with detailed topographical data was surveyed and drawn up in the 18th century by the Royal Danish Academy of Sciences and Letters and the oldest preserved land taxation survey was conducted in the 17th century (Christian 5's *Den store matrikel*, 1688). The problem in Vendsyssel is that continual sand drift has taken place since the 16th century, covering former arable land and, in some places, leaving it buried beneath sand dunes many metres deep, creating a desolate landscape. In the west, this sand drift is still ongoing, covering land that cannot therefore be subjected to topsoil analysis. On the positive side, the sand dunes protect sites from the destructive effects of modern agriculture. At Ejstrup, a cemetery dating from the Germanic Iron Age and Viking Age was covered with metres of shifting sand, resulting in the preservation of the only turf-built grave covering ever excavated in Denmark (fig. 2) (Nilsson 1994) and, directly to the north of Liver, sand dunes cover former arable land.

The coast has also changed radically and in some areas in the west it may have moved as much as a kilometre eastwards since the Viking Age, leaving all coastal sites from the period either submerged or washed away by the sea. The east coast has also changed – in this case as a result of land upheaval. These coastal changes, sand drift and modern agriculture have modified the watercourses, changing

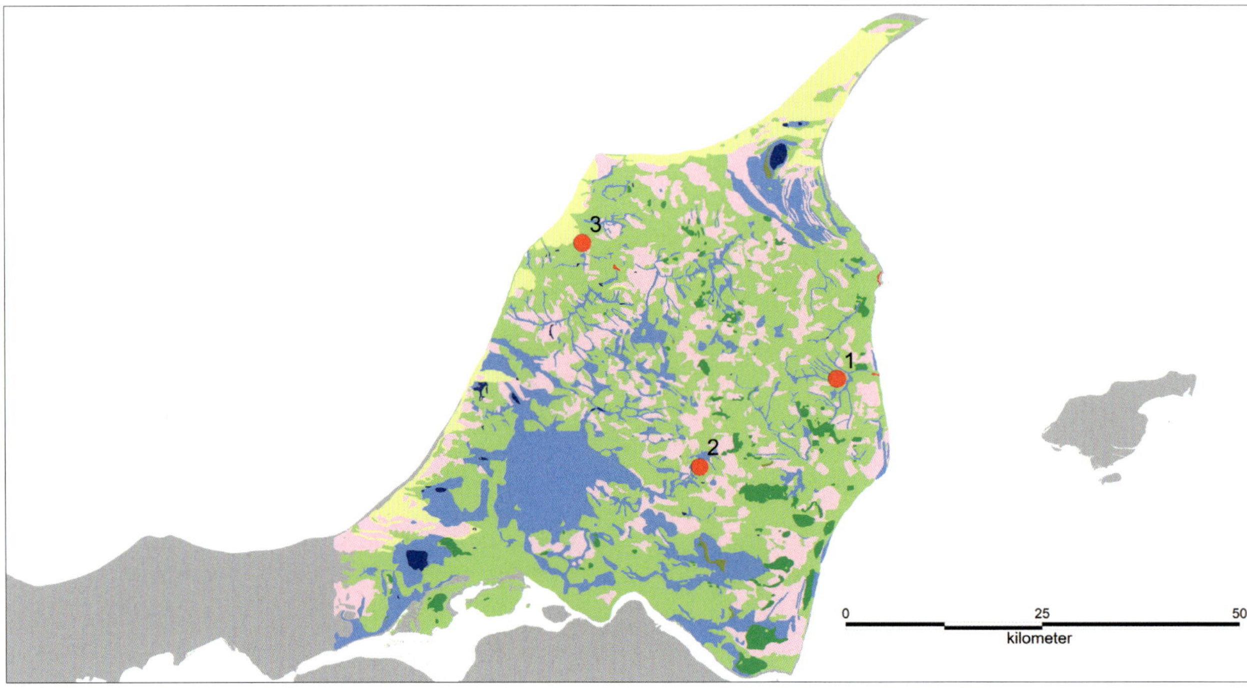

Fig. 1. | *Map of Vendsyssel showing the three sites: 1. Ejstrup, 2. Stentinget, 3. Liver. The landscape of Vendsyssel changed considerably between the Viking Age and the 18th century, when the Royal Danish Academy of Sciences and Letters produced the map used here. Nevertheless, it provides a better background than a modern map. Dark green: forest; pale pink: heath, inland sand dunes and non-arable land; light green: arable land; yellow: sandy beach and sand dunes; light blue: river valleys/wetland areas, bogs and meadows; dark blue: lakes; dark blue lines: rivers.*

their course and depth. Even so, as late as the early 20th century, farmers still travelled along the river Liver Å, a 19.5 km waterway, to Hjørring, some 9.5 km from the present-day coast.

Further to the problems caused by shifting sand, metal-detector surveys and conventional field-walking are not possible in the areas covered by heath. As a consequence, extensive, non-invasive survey techniques can only be used for the actual detection of remains and not to demonstrate the absence of settlements from particular areas or to determine settlement boundaries. Moreover, the very active landscape formation processes may bias any positive results obtained by favouring certain finds in some areas. On the positive side, the general condition of metal finds from the topsoil is excellent and many of the Early Medieval churches now lie isolated in open land, making it possible to conduct extensive field surveys on the areas around them.

Some general notes on the metal-detector surveys presented here

All three sites have only been surveyed for a limited number of years. Metal-detector surveys in the Ribe area indicate that at least ten years of survey are necessary in order to obtain representative data in terms of spatial distribution and find composition. This is of course only relevant if the fields are under cultivation. The settlement at Stentinget is at present partially protected through scheduling, which means that the ploughing is restricted to the top 10 cm of the topsoil. This has resulted in virtually no new finds since the late 1990s. However, the three sites discussed here are large, having yielded 1313, 578 and 172 finds, respectively, to date, and this makes it possible to conduct a number of analyses. Some areas can be identified as probable sites of craft activities, others as regular settlements. However, the settlement boundaries have not yet been located at any of the three sites –

Fig. 2. | *An inland dune overlying the turf cover of the grave (black and white). Taken during the excavation of the cemetery at Volstrup. The entire cemetery was covered by sand dunes; these had protected it from ploughing and from the roots of trees in the modern plantation.*

more systematic fieldwork is required before such conclusions can be reached.

At Liver, the metal-detector surveys were conducted by a number of amateur archaeologists working with archaeologist Torben Nilsson. Unfortunately, the finds were only recorded relative to three general areas and were not plotted on maps. Consequently, the present finds assemblage only permits a very general form of spatial analysis.

At Stentinget and Ejstrup, the metal-detector surveys were conducted by Verner Brath, an enthusiastic and methodical amateur detector archaeologist, again working with archaeologist Torben Nilsson. The finds were marked on a map, some individually and others as small circles that each contain a number of artefacts. As a result, it is possible to conduct a spatial analysis of these sites aimed at locating various functions and activities, living areas, craft areas and perhaps additional cemeteries, although the latter may be the most difficult to decipher (some of the finds from Stentinget have not been plotted due to missing data). It is not, however, possible to carry out micro-spatial analyses and to locate individual farmsteads or metalworking workshops, as more detailed survey procedures and recording are required to enable this. However, it is likely that such data would be obtainable should new, refined and perhaps modified field survey methods be applied, in combination with excavation.

Methodology

All finds recovered from the three sites have been allocated to some rather rough categories based on a methodology I developed for my master's thesis (Wåhlin 2004, 53-62; 2006). The aim is to produce a comprehensive overview of the finds and of the activities the assemblage, as a whole, appears to represent. There are several categories for finished items, such as ornaments and mounts/fittings, as well as one for workshop-related finds, such as scrap metal and weights (partially presented in table 1). In the research for my thesis, I found that only the finds in the workshop category showed a distinct spatial pattern. All other finds were distributed evenly over the settlement area, thereby defining merely the area of human activity. The present study attempts to discover whether it is possible to differentiate between the settlement and the cemetery, fully realising that the two may very well overlap. As a consequence, the spatial analysis focuses on Stentinget, where a trial excavation was carried out, and the results can provide a form of preliminary check for the methodology.

Ejstrup

The detector site of Ejstrup covers an area of 8 ha and forms part of a partially excavated settlement area known as Volstrup, located to the northeast of the solitary medieval parish church (fig. 3). A large cemetery dated to the Germanic Iron Age and Viking Age was excavated here in advance of motorway construction. A small part of the Germanic Iron Age settlement was investigated by excavation, with metal-detector surveys being conducted on non-excavated areas. The metal-detector finds included everything from scrap metal to some of the finest examples of metalwork yet found in Vendsyssel.

Of the 176 items located during the metal-detector surveys, 161 were of metal. Verner Brath occasionally also spotted pottery, glass and so on. In general, iron was neither recorded nor collected. The brooches recovered show an even distribution in date between the Germanic Iron Age (13) and the Viking Age/Medieval period (14), suggesting that the surveyed area was occupied over a long period. Workshop-related finds amount to 45.3 % of the total from Ejstrup, a far higher percentage than at the other sites. The finds show that metal-working in lead, copper alloy and silver took place at the site. It cannot be said at present whether metal crafts were of greater importance at Ejstrup than at Stentinget or Liver. The boundaries of this

Artefact group	Nørlev Østergård		Nørlev Søgård		Gårdestrup		Ejstrup		Stentinget	
	Sum	%	Sum	%	Sum	%	Sum	%	Sum	%
Total number of finds	583		617		113		172		578	
Lumps in total	113	19.4	114	18.5	9	8.0	43	25.0	150	26.0
Lumps of Bronze	47	8.1	26	4.2	2	1.8	12	7.0	73	12.6
Lumps of Tin	3	0.5	2	0.3						
Lumps of Lead	46	7.9	82	13.3	6	5.3	26	15.1	50	8.7
Lumps of Silver	2	0.3	3	0.5			4	2.3	22	3.8
Lumps of Amber	13	2.2	12	1.9	1	0.9			1	0.2
Lumps of Glass	2	0.3	1	0.2			1	0.6	3	0.5
Mould/model							2	1.2		
Casting crucible			1	0.2	1	0.9			1	0.2
Ingots/rods	14	2.4	9	1.5	1	0.9	3	1.7	3	0.5
Sheet metal	40	6.9	72	11.7	6	5.3	12	7.0	38	6.6
Weights	18	3.1	17	2.8	3	2.7	11	6.4	24	4.2
Hackgold			1	0.2						
Hacksilver/rods			1	0.2			7	4.1	3	0.5
Semi-precious stone			1	0.2						
Workshop, total	185	31.7	228	37.0	20	17.7	78	45.3	218	37.7
Coins	11	1.9	24	3.9	3	2.7	9	5.2	15	2.6
Mounts	54	9.3	58	9.4	17	15.0	9	5.2	75	13.0
Dress-accessories, total	166	28.5	169	27.4	39	34.5	41	23.8	148	25.6

Table 1. | *Ornaments and workshop-related finds from the three sites.*

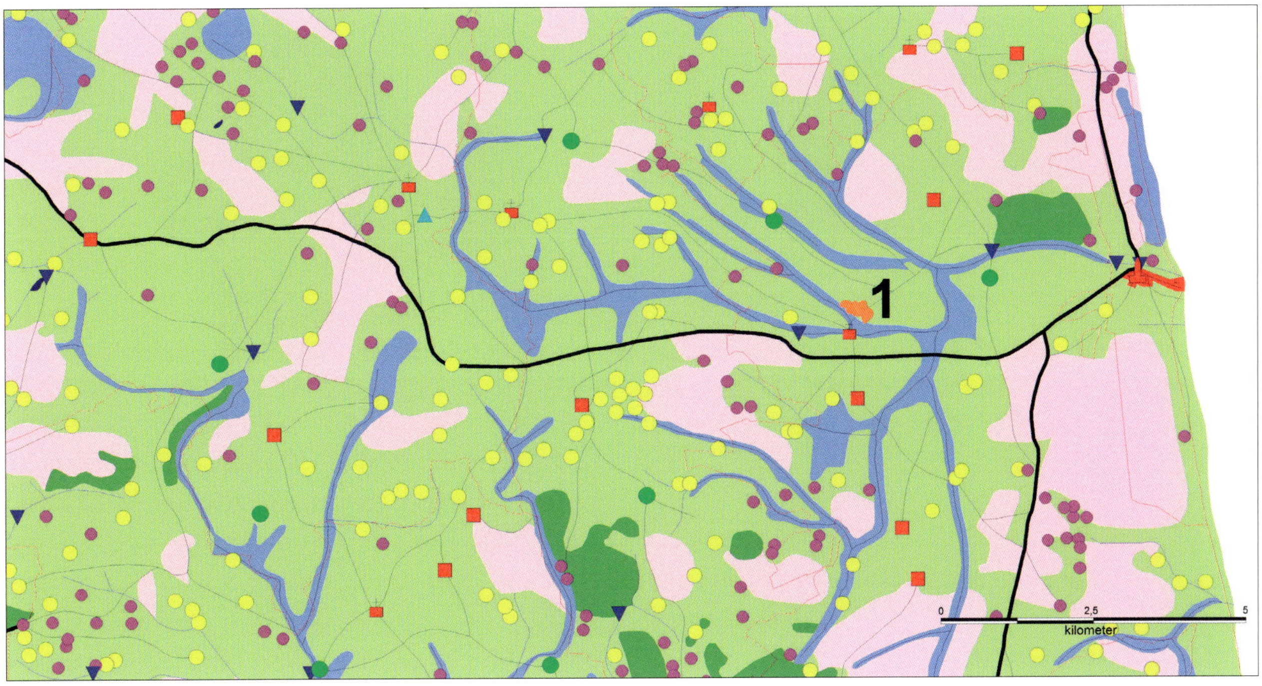

Fig. 3. | *The Ejstrup area (1). Map produced by the Royal Danish Academy of Sciences and Letters. Dark green: forest; pale pink: heath, inland sand dunes and non arable land; light green: arable land; yellow: sandy beach and sand dunes; light blue: river valleys/wetland areas, bogs and meadows; dark blue: lakes; dark blue lines: rivers; black lines: historical main roads; thin lines: minor roads; red areas: towns; red squares with a small cross: churches with or without a hamlet; coloured dots: farms and houses; blue triangles: water mills. Note that the site is situated on the opposite side of the river from the Medieval church. Metal-detector surveys around the church have not yielded any finds.*

vast settlement have not yet been properly located and, although the cemetery at Ejstrup has been excavated, it has not been subjected to metal-detector survey and the finds were not included in this analysis. The same applies to the minor settlement areas that have been excavated. Moreover, metal-detector surveys should not be used in isolation when analysing the economy of an archaeological site. Forms of metalworking that are revealed clearly in a metal-detector survey may very well have taken place on an agrarian settlement. The high percentage of workshop-related finds can presently only be explained in terms of surveys to date being mainly of craft-related areas. The presence of finished items, including household goods, indicates that the craft areas overlap with settlement areas.

Two high-quality items from the Germanic Iron Age stand out from the rest. One is a fragment of a silver-gilt rectangular mount with niello and garnet inlays (fig. 4), the other is a fragment of a gilt copper-alloy Anglo-Hiberno mount. The latter is most likely a harness mount reused as a brooch; it is dated to the beginning of the 9th century (fig. 5). Both pieces have been carefully smoothed and finished where they were broken or cut off, as if they were given a secondary function. It has been suggested that the small silver piece may have been used as a weight and this seems very likely.

Further investigation is, however, necessary, and this could include metal-detector surveys, combined with excavation and perhaps wet-sieving of samples of topsoil, aimed at recovering artefacts that can provide information about the site's internal structure and function and its relationship with other sites. Excavations have revealed an Early Roman Iron Age settlement in the area and the church bears witness to occupation in the 13th century. However, few post-Viking Age finds have been

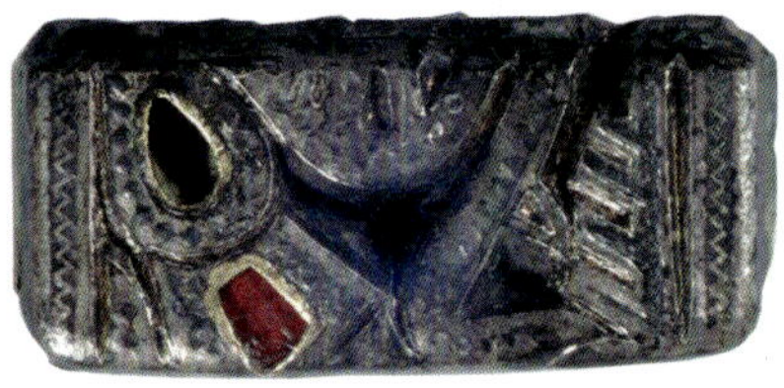

Fig. 4. | *Ejstrup. Part of a silver-gilt mount with niello and garnet inlay, probably part of a male belt fitting. The quality of the work is excellent. Scale 2:1.*

Fig. 5. | *Ejstrup. Part of gilt copper-alloy Anglo-Hiberno harness, later fitted with a pin and used as a brooch. Scale 1:1.*

recovered to date and it would be useful to locate the settlement from the 11th to the 13th century and determine whether it was still a production site.

Stentinget

The site lies furthest inland and is the most southerly of the three, being located 18 km north of the Limfjord and 18 km from the east coast of Vendsyssel (fig. 6). It is situated on the watershed between eastern and western Vendsyssel, and it has been argued that the site had no real access by water as the journey by way of the river Ry Å would be some 52 km, as opposed to 18 km by land (Nilsson 1993). This argument is incorrect for two reasons. When transporting heavy loads, a long river route may well have been preferable to a shorter one over land and there is also an alternative waterway. On maps produced by the Royal Danish Academy of Sciences and Letters in the late 18th century, it is apparent that the site lies only 5 km from a branch of the watercourse Voer Å, which was large enough to power two watermills in the 18th century. Voer Å offers a more direct route to the east coast of about 20 km in length. Stentinget also lies in close proximity to Vendsyssel's historical road network and, due to this relative proximity to both water and land traffic routes, the site can be said to have been well connected in regional terms. However, the proximity to waterways and the road network is perhaps of little relevance to a discussion of the location of these metal-rich sites, as the sea is never very far away in Vendsyssel, or the rest of southwestern Scandinavia for that matter. The site is presently known to cover about 60 ha and was discovered rather by chance by amateur archaeologist Verner Brath. It is interesting that the site is located mainly on the land belonging to one historical farm, Stentinget, from which the site has its name.

Stentinget has been subjected to metal-detector surveys, in addition to conventional field-walking, resulting in a total of 578 finds. Of these, 519 are of metal; most of the non-metal objects are Neolithic flints.

The numerous extraordinary finds and the fragmented state of many of them, showing recent fractures, indicated that the site was in danger of being ploughed out. Vendsyssel Historiske Museum therefore conducted a trial excavation, with trenches being opened up in the areas that had produced the most promising finds; the site has therefore not been subjected to systematic trial excavation.

Two small trenches were excavated: One was at the foot of a burial mound and it revealed five inhumation graves dated to the Germanic Iron Age and Viking Age, in addition to the remains of a Bronze Age house. Unfortunately, some possible cremation graves were not fully investigated because these were assumed to be cooking pits

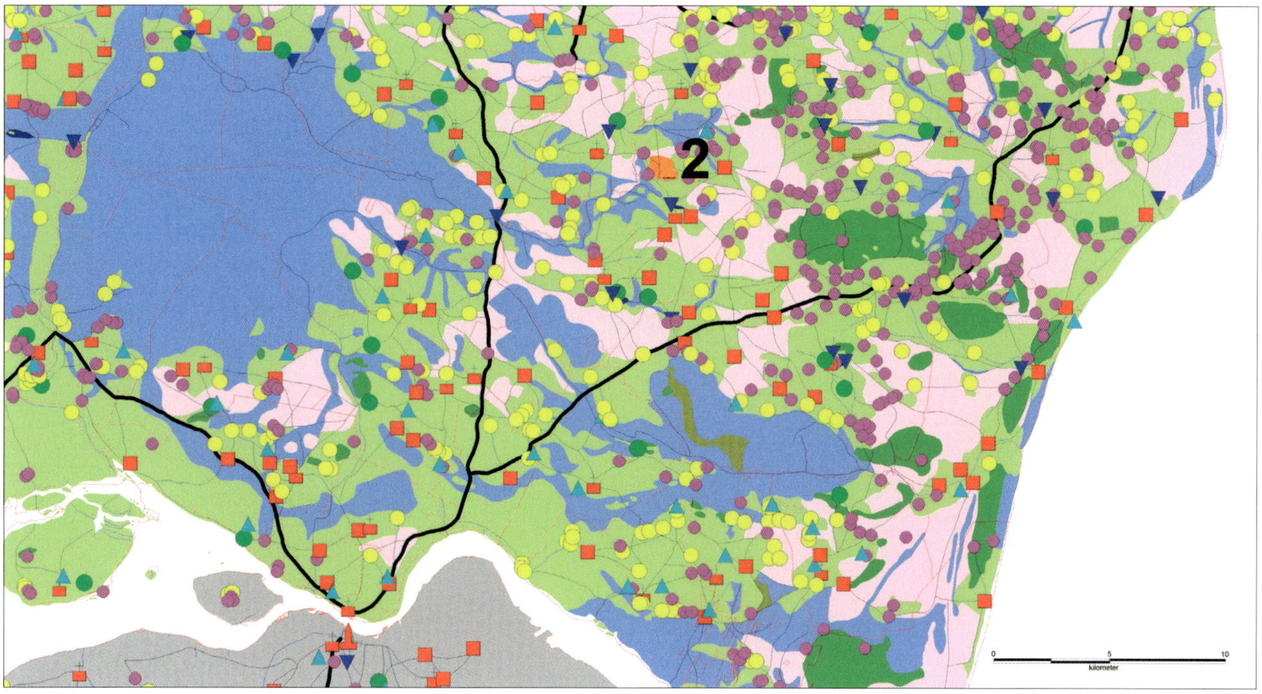

Fig. 6. | *The Stentinget area (2). Map produced by the Royal Danish Academy of Sciences and Letters. Dark green: forest; pale pink: heath, inland sand dunes and non arable land; light green: arable land; yellow: sandy beach and sand dunes; light blue: river valleys/wetland areas, bogs and meadows; dark blue: lakes; dark blue lines: rivers; black lines: historical main roads; thin lines: minor roads; red areas: towns; red squares with a small cross: churches with or without a hamlet; coloured dots: farms and houses; blue triangles: water mills. The formation of the heath to the north of the settlement is undated.*

associated with the Bronze Age house. The excavation was so small that the cemetery cannot be said to have been fully excavated. The trial trenches were too far apart for it to be possible to delimit the area over which the graves were distributed. There are definitely other burials at Stentinget: One grave situated north of the large workshop area and the Bronze Age barrow of Byrhøj was excavated when it appeared as a dark patch in the topsoil after ploughing, but no further investigations were carried out here.

Craft-related objects, such as metal lumps, drops and clippings and weights, moulds and bars account for 37.7 % of the finds and show a somewhat concentrated pattern of distribution (fig. 7). It is striking that almost no metal lumps were found in the area occupied by the five graves. This could be because there were no cremation graves in the cemetery or possibly because the metal finds represent craft activities rather than cremation graves. The large number of metal pieces found in areas yielding other objects indicative of metalworking tends to support the latter idea. There appear to be three areas with concentrations of workshop-related finds and the area north of Byrhøj yielded the greatest number. A trial excavation revealed the presence of *Grubenhäuser*, longhouses and fences here, located in close proximity. The *Grubenhäuser* may have been part of a designated workshop area, in which case the longhouses would be either earlier or later. The *Grubenhäuser* could also represent workshops associated with one particular farm that were rebuilt and replaced over time. More systematic trial excavations, perhaps combined with ground-penetrading radar surveys, are needed in order to resolve this. Discarded, failed metal castings show that metalworking took place during both the Germanic Iron Age and Viking Age.

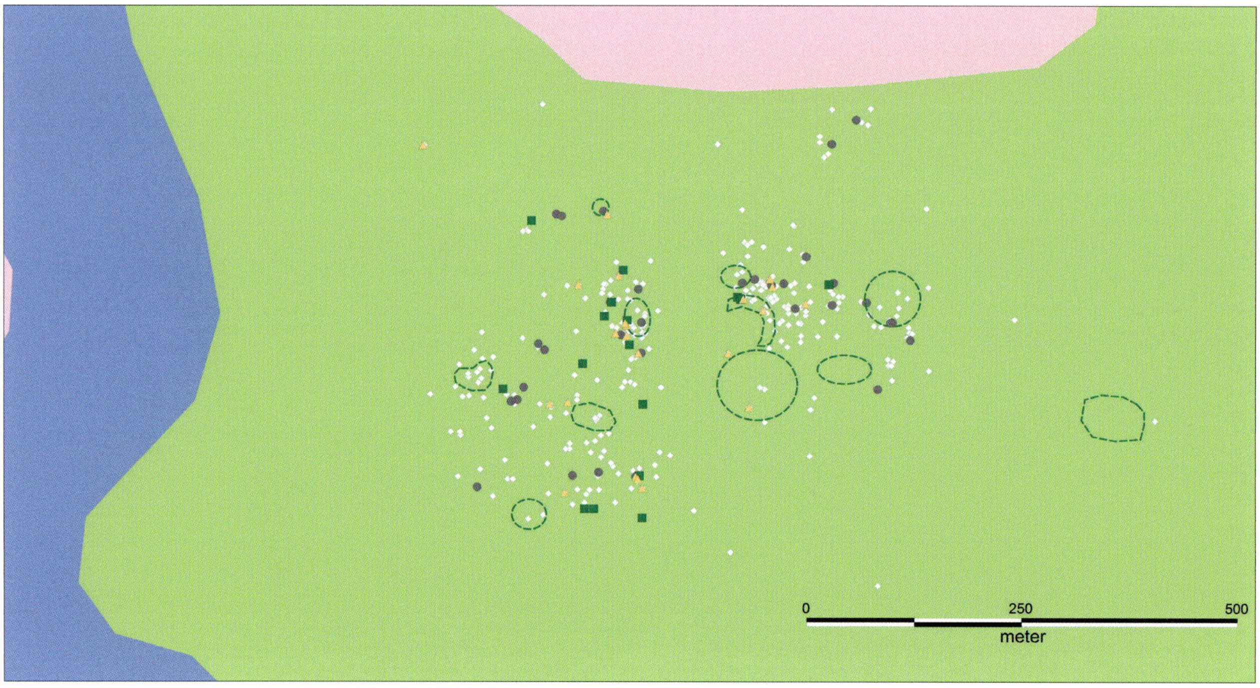

Fig. 7. | *Stentinget. Distribution of workshop-related finds. Weights (yellow triangles), sheet metal (green squares), lumps and drops of metal (grey dots).*

Ornaments account for 25.6 % of the finds. As expected, these do not show any particular overall pattern of distribution, indicating that much seems to have been dropped and lost as part of everyday life (fig. 8). Thirteen brooches date from the Roman Iron Age. A characteristic of southern Scandinavian metal-rich sites is that they yield few finds of Late Roman Iron Age date, often just 'everyday' objects. These do not indicate that production took place at that time, merely that the settlement dates from at least the Roman Iron Age. The finds show that the settlement at this time was primarily located west of Byrhøj. Ornaments from the Germanic Iron Age number 19, accounting 3.3 % of the dated finds, while Viking Age and later ornaments number 38 (6.6 %). Further study and a completed catalogue of the finds will no doubt result in these numbers increasing. The finds from the Germanic Iron Age were mostly located on the top of the hill and to the north and west of it. Viking Age finds were also located directly north of Byrhøj, as well as to the west and southwest. There seems to have been some movement of the settlement towards the southwest during this time, possibly as a result of settlement expansion.

Two items stand out in the finds assemblage – a Carolingian belt mount and a Valkyrie brooch – and not only just because they are on permanent display at the National Museum in Copenhagen (figs. 9 and 10). They indicate that Stentinget had contacts with other major Danish Viking Age sites, such as Tissø, and with the Frankish Empire.

Stentinget can presently be described as a large rural settlement of the Iron Age and Viking Age – a village. There is evidence of extensive metalworking in designated areas, but whether this took place on the farmsteads or in special workshop areas only future research can resolve. The limited excavations to date reveal that Stentinget provides a rare opportunity to excavate cemeteries, settlements and possible workshop areas that were in operation simultaneously. As there are two other major metal-rich sites in Vendsyssel, the idea of Stentinget being the seat of the regional magnate or the central settlement with complete control over metal distribution can now be dismissed. Nevertheless, it is clear that Stentinget was more than just a run

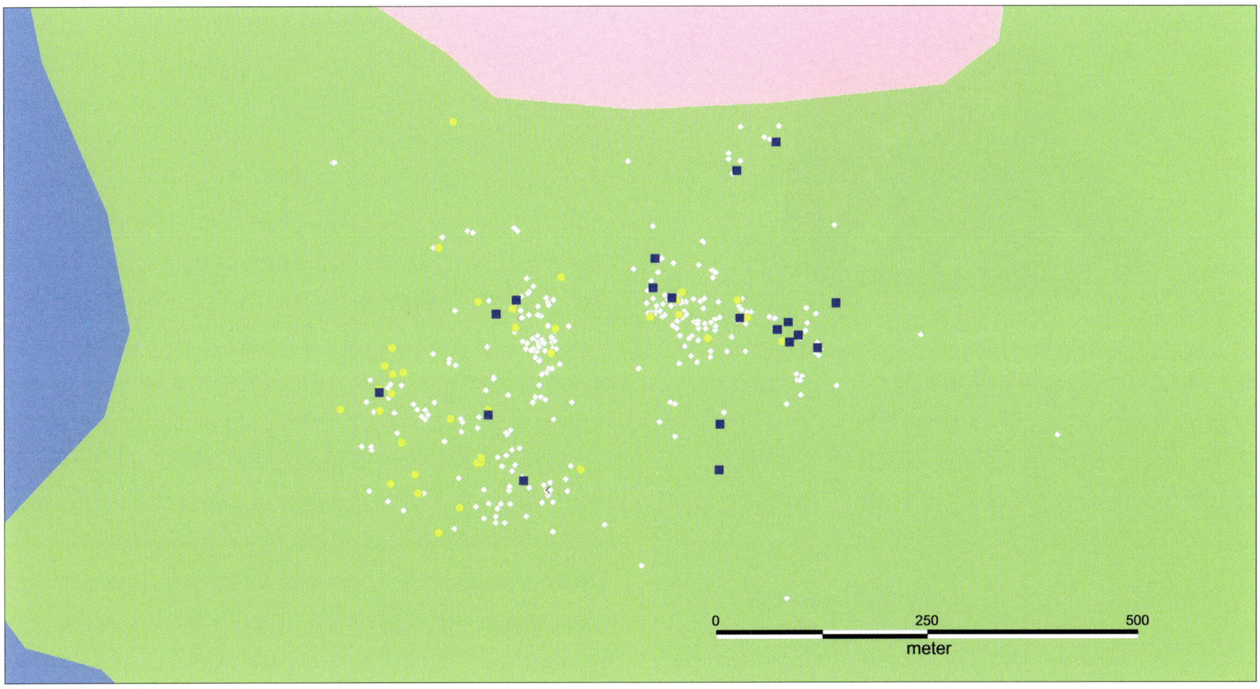

Fig. 8. | *Stentinget. Distribution of ornaments dated to the Germanic Iron Age (blue squares) and Viking Age (yellow dots). This map is only preliminary as further work will doubtless add to the number of securely dated objects.*

of the mill agricultural hamlet. By the 13th century, the situation may have changed, as the medieval church is situated furthe south, at the former village of Hellevad, today Klokkerholm. An investigation of the settlement Stentinget, including excavation, is therefore crucial to an understanding the spatial

Fig. 9. | *Stentinget. Carolingian belt fitting: gilt-silver with relief acanthus ornamentation on the front and niello acanthus ornamentation on the reverse. This find is by far the single most spectacular metal object found in Vendsyssel; probably part of a disturbed silver hoard. Scale 1:1.*

Fig. 10. | *Stentinget. Viking Age Valkyrie brooch in gilt copper alloy. This brooch is almost identical to ones found at Tissø and in Ribe; it is one of several finds indicating pre-Christian religious activity at Stentinget. Scale 3:2.*

structure of the area and its development over time. Was there a manorial farm with a workshop area and special buildings such as halls? The fact that ploughing depth has been restricted across the area could mean that the site is still in a state whereby such questions can be answered. The structure of the cemeteries is also of great interest and fortunately the restrictions placed on the area do not prohibit archaeological investigation.

Liver

The Liver complex is situated on both sides of a river, Liver Å, which flows into the North Sea (fig. 11). Today, the river marks the boundary between the parishes of Skallerup and Hjørring St. Oluf, located 5 km away. It seems likely that people travelled to the site by boat or barge as this river was navigable by the latter in historical times. The west coast of Jutland is an exposed, windy place and perhaps not the ideal location for a craft and trading site. Liver may have been the 'coastal site', even though the coast has moved considerably east since the Viking Age. The site was initially referred to as Nørlev, but this place name refers only to a settlement on the west bank of Liver Å. Furthermore, the place name Nørlev is not a *-lev* name, but refers to Liver Å, or a low marshy area near it, with a 'north' prefix. There is also a Sørlev – the southern settlement by Liver Å.

The Liver complex covers 31 ha and consists of three areas that were originally given separate names according to the farms on which they are situated: Nørlev Søgård and Nørlev Østergård in Skallerup parish, west of the river, and Gårestrup in St. Oluf's parish, east of the river. Gårestrup appears to have fewer metal finds, even though a 12 ha area has been surveyed. The finds from Gårestrup also differ somewhat from those at Østergaard and Søgård. There is very little scrap metal and metal lumps and droplets, i.e. the signature finds of metalworking. It could be argued that this is the result of the different collection policies adopted by the amateur archaeologists working in the field. However, Torben Nilsson was always keen to stress that all finds should be collected and recorded, and the low percentage of lead items, which are easily picked up by metal detectors, indicates that the area located slightly east of the river was mainly settlement.

There is also a difference in the ornaments found in the three areas. Brooches from the Germanic Iron Age are found primarily at Gårestrup, whereas the Viking ornaments occur in far greater numbers west of the river. Perhaps the settlement centre moved over time, from the east to the west bank of the river. Workshop-related items were mainly found in the areas yielding abundant Viking Age finds, but it does not follow that the workshops should be dated to the same period. The craft area may well have been situated to the west of the river during the Germanic Iron Age, and when this activity became less important the centre of settlement shifted from east to west. However, this is almost pure speculation – and further field surveys are needed to confirm this suggestion.

Interestingly, only the Liver complex has yielded a large number of small equal-armed brooches, indicating a peak in simple metal items during the early part of the Late Germanic Iron Age (fig. 12). Perhaps the surveys at Liver covered the settlement area more comprehensively than at the other sites, and future work at Stentinget and Ejstrup will yield similar finds. The large amount of amber is of note as this could have been involved in the metalworking or perhaps simply represents the presence of this raw material in its own right. A large num-

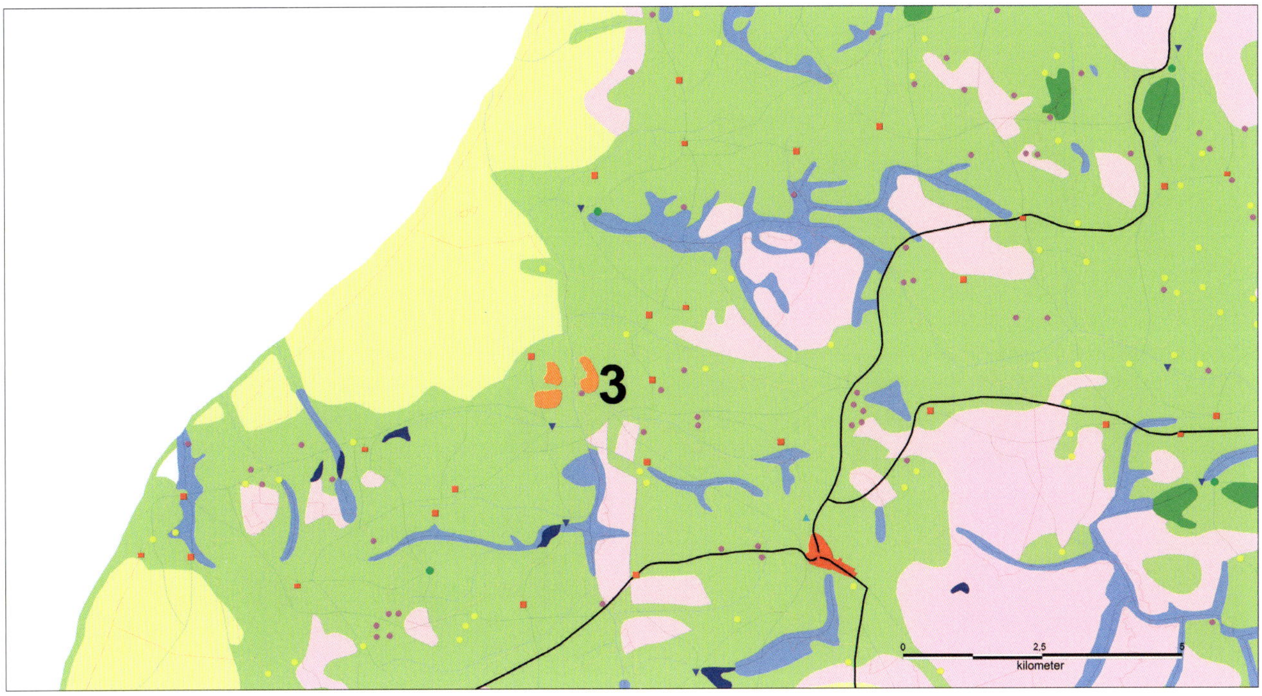

Fig. 11. | *The Liver area (3). Map produced by the Royal Danish Academy of Sciences and Letters. Dark green: forest; pale pink: heath, inland sand dunes and non-arable land; light green: arable land; yellow: sand beach and sand dunes; light blue: river valleys/wetland areas, bogs and meadows; dark blue: lakes; dark blue lines: rivers; black lines: historical main roads; thin lines: minor roads; red areas: towns; red squares with a small cross: churches with or without a hamlet; dots: farms and houses; blue triangles: water mills. Note the large area of sand dunes to the northwest of the site; these dunes are still visible today.*

ber of whetstones of Norwegian origin were also found at Liver, indicating links with a westerly trading network involving the exchange of 'everyday' goods. It is important to locate the boundaries of the site, but this might prove difficult to the north where sand dunes have covered the land. It will be necessary to carry out a trial excavation, perhaps combined with auger sampling for chemical analysis of the soil, together with systematic wet-sieving of topsoil samples.

At present, the finds reveal the existence of a large rural settlement with extensive evidence of metalworking, which apparently took place in designated areas within the settlement. More fieldwork is necessary if the internal structure of the site is to be analysed in more detail. Three *Grubenhäuser* were located in a small trial trench located in an area with a high concentration of scrap metal. However, no wet-sieving of the fills of these buildings was carried out during the excavation, so their specific functions have not been determined. Systematic trial excavations will be necessary to determine whether this was a designated workshop area with *Grubenhäuser* or simply a few buildings of this type located on a farm. A recent aerial photograph available on the Danish directory website www.degulesider.dk shows a line forming a right angle, together with some oval spots, which might indicate the former presence of a fence and some *Grubenhäuser* in the southwestern part of the settlement. However, the resolution of the image is too poor for this to be confirmed.

Concluding remarks

As stated above, much work involving data descriptions and various forms of analysis, together with more general research, is required before it is

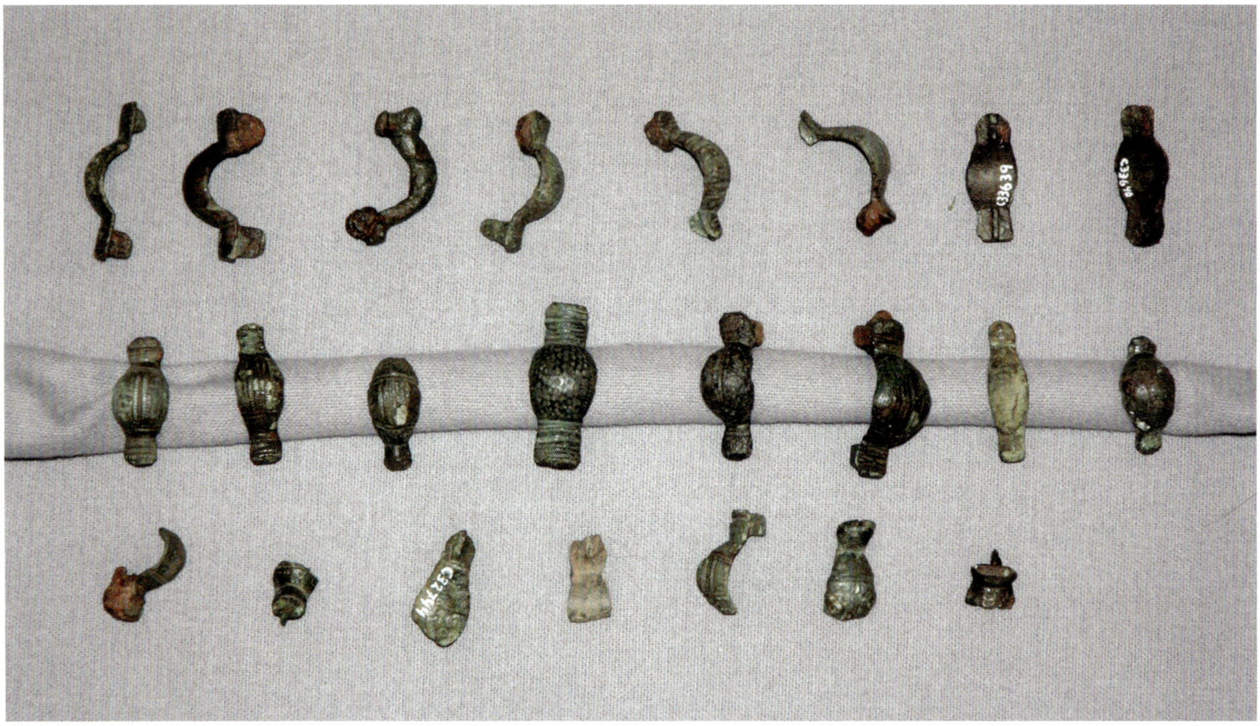

Fig. 12. | *Liver. A selection of the many small equal-armed brooches found at Liver. Scale 1:2.*

possible to reach an understanding of these three sites and Germanic Iron Age and Viking Age society in Vendsyssel. On the other hand this study, however preliminary, does outline the potential of these sites and provide clear evidence that Vendsyssel was connected to a wider trading network during this period, with the finds indicating relations with the Frankish Empire, the British Isles and Norway; they also reveal that many metal objects were produced locally. The three settlements have all yielded objects generally associated with the upper strata of society, but at present none of the three can be said to be more prominent than the others.

During this preliminary study of metal-detector finds held at Vendsyssel Historiske Museum it has become apparent that the original descriptions are rather unsystematic and occasionally incorrect. The museum therefore intends to catalogue all metal-detector finds and record their exact find spot as accurately as possible in a digital form in order for spatial analyses to be conducted, with the results being used in the planning of new field work.

Few metal-detector surveys are conducted in Vendsyssel today. This offers an opportunity to establish scientific rigor and to plan hypothesis-based fieldwork for the future, both on the three sites presented and those that have been located but not as yet investigated.

Each of the three sites presented warrants new fieldwork and research focussing on an individual metal-producing settlement site and its immediate environment. In combination, Stentinget, Ejstrup and Liver – situated within a naturally defined region – offer a remarkable opportunity to design a research project focussing on settlements, crafts and trade during the time from the Germanic Iron Age to the Medieval period.

This paper, and the work upon which it is based, have raised more questions than they have answered – but then again, answering questions was never the intention. The aim was to present three intriguing sites dating from the Germanic Iron Age and Viking Age that are important not only for an understanding of this period in Vendsyssel but also in southwestern Scandinavia in general. They are important not because they were particularly unique in their time, but because they have survived and have been located. They did not develop into towns or ecclesiastical, noble or royal manors and if they were once central sites, their functions did not prevail in the long term or were subsequently moved elsewhere.

Bibliography

Nilsson, T. 1993, Stentinget – en boplads med handel og håndværk fra germansk jernalder og vikingetid. *Vendsyssel Nu og Da* 1991-1993, 64-78.

Nilsson, T. 1994, Sjælens Hus. *Skalk* 1994:6, 3-7.

Wåhlin, S. 2004, Hviding – en kulturhistorisk analyse af et kystnært samfund 950-1250 AD. Unpublished mag.art. thesis. Aarhus University.

Wåhlin, S. 2006, Gården ved havet. *Arkæologi i Slesvig. Archäologie im Schleswig* 11, 127-36.

Early state formation in southern Scandinavia in the 1st-4th century AD

Per Ethelberg

Since the beginning of the 1970s, it has been common for archaeologists to define themselves in terms of their specialist subject. People are settlement archaeologists, cemetery archaeologists, war booty archaeologists and so on. It is against this background that researchers have attempted to understand and describe developments in society in prehistoric times. The question is, however, how tenable this approach is with respect to the Roman and Germanic Iron Ages? Reality at that time was more complex than this. Farmsteads, villages, trading places, cemeteries, offerings and defensive works were all coeval structures. The all-embracing common denominator was the society of which they were part and which consisted of the people who 'produced' them. If we are to attempt to understand the story told by the archaeological record, this is best done by considering it in context.

Schleswig in the Roman Iron Age

Geographically, Schleswig comprises more or less the area between the rivers Kongeå in the north and Eider in the south, the Wadden Sea to the west and the Baltic Sea to the east. Here lie some of the Iron Age's major war booty sites: Thorsbjerg, Nydam and Ejsbøl.

In the Early Roman Iron Age (50 BC-AD 200), Schleswig was divided into three culture groups: the Over Jerstal Group, the West Group and Angeln (fig. 1). The borders between these groups were fluid. In particular, it has proved difficult to define the boundary between the West Group and Angeln, begging the question as to whether these actually were two different groups. Perhaps the situation is a consequence of the Over Jerstal Group becoming

Fig. 1. | *Local groups in Schleswig in the Early Roman Iron Age. The boundaries are only approximate. There are unlikely to have been sharp lines of demarcation; more probably, there were zones of mixing between the individual groups. After Ethelberg 2003, 167, fig. 36.*

progressively smaller, while Angeln and the West Group became progressively larger.

Taking the Over Jerstal Group's hierarchical tribal society as a starting point, an attempt will now be made to illustrate, from a contextual point of view, the cultural developments that took place in Schleswig and the adjacent areas during the Roman Iron Age (50 BC-AD 350).

The Over Jerstal Group (50 BC-AD 200)

The Over Jerstal Group is more or less limited to North Schleswig, i.e. the area between the river Kongeå, the Vidå river system and Olgerdiget. The group was first defined by Plettke (1921), then by Tischler (1937) and subsequently by Neumann (1982) on the basis of the special form and ornamentation of the pottery: vessels with a faceted rim and vertical furrow ornamentation on the upper part. On larger vessels the lower part is often comb-ornamented. The reason it has proved difficult to define the group's geographic distribution could be because, as outline above, its area of distribution changed over time.

Burial practices and social layers

Burial customs are dominated by cremation, in the form of both urn burials and cremation patches. In addition to these is a smaller number of inhumation graves that are oriented either north-south or east-west. Weapon graves are common and are found evenly distributed across the entire area. Apparently, each farmstead and village had its own warriors. Weapons were perceived as personal property that accompanied the warrior to his grave. A small group of graves furnished with Roman imports, primarily in the form of bronze vessels, attracts particular attention.

Five social layers can be distinguished on the basis of the grave equipment found in male graves (fig. 2): peasant farmers, warriors, village heads, chieftains and princes (Ethelberg 1995). Slaves and serfs are excluded from this analysis.

Lowermost in the social pyramid we have the peasant farmers. They were buried with pots, knives, belt buckles, brooches and pins.

The warriors differ from the peasant farmers in that they were buried with their weapons – commonly javelins, thrusting spears and shields – and in a few cases also single-edged swords and spurs. These demonstrate that some of the warriors were mounted.

The village heads differ again in that they were buried with gold rings and often fine, black-burnished pottery. They never have weapons or spurs.

The chieftains are distinguished from the village heads and the warriors in that they were buried with silver-inlaid spurs, but never with weapons and gold rings. This does not mean, however, they had no access to gold. A characteristic feature of the furnishing of their wives' graves is pear-shaped gold pendants with filigree ornamentation.

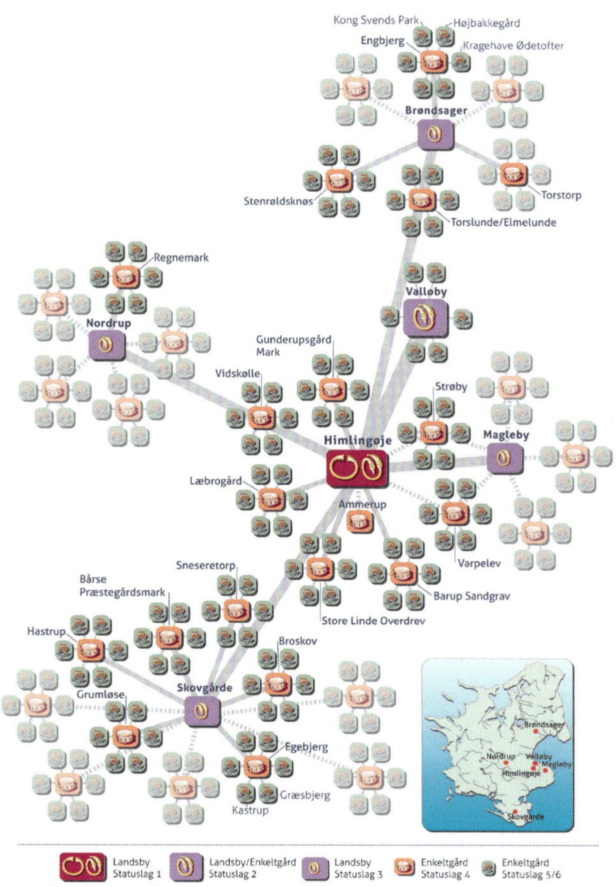

Fig. 2. | *Model of the social structure of the Over Jerstal Group during the Early Roman Iron Age. After Ethelberg 2003, 274, fig. 151.*

Uppermost in the social pyramid we find the prince. Roman imports constitute a particular characteristic of princely graves, usually in the form of bronze cauldrons, ladles, sieves and saucepans. In addition to these, a prince's grave may include all manner of additional furnishings, for example gold rings, weapons, and silver-inlaid spurs.

It has become apparent that the earthwork Olgerdiget (see below) constitutes the southern boundary for the distribution both of inhumation graves and princely graves. Furthermore, the continuity of use of the princely cemeteries apparently increases in duration with distance north of Olgerdiget. A good example of this is seen at Kastrup, located between Haderslev and Gram (Jensen 2007).

Farm and village

Traces of the Over Jerstal Group's settlements are found everywhere in North Schleswig. Nowhere have they been so fully investigated, however, as at Galsted near Agerskov in the heart of the area. This settlement complex includes a village, single farms and contemporaneous cemeteries (Ethelberg 2003).

The earliest village, which dates from the 1st century AD, comprised 13 farms surrounded by a common fence. The village fence enclosed an area of about 70 x 100 m. The farms were positioned along the fence such that an open space was left in the middle of the village. Each farm consisted of a single house with its own entrance in the common fence, which was always located opposite the main entrance to the farm. The farms were separated from one another by small side fences running between the house and the common fence. Together with the houses, the side fences enclosed crofts of up to 300 m².

None of the farms stood out as being larger than the others, but four were smaller. The typical farm was a three-aisled longhouse with six pairs of roof-bearing posts – three on each side of the entrance. This has proved to be the 'type house' for the Over Jerstal Group (fig. 3). The deep palisade trench, the side fences and the lack of traces of wall posts show that the walls must have been built on sills.

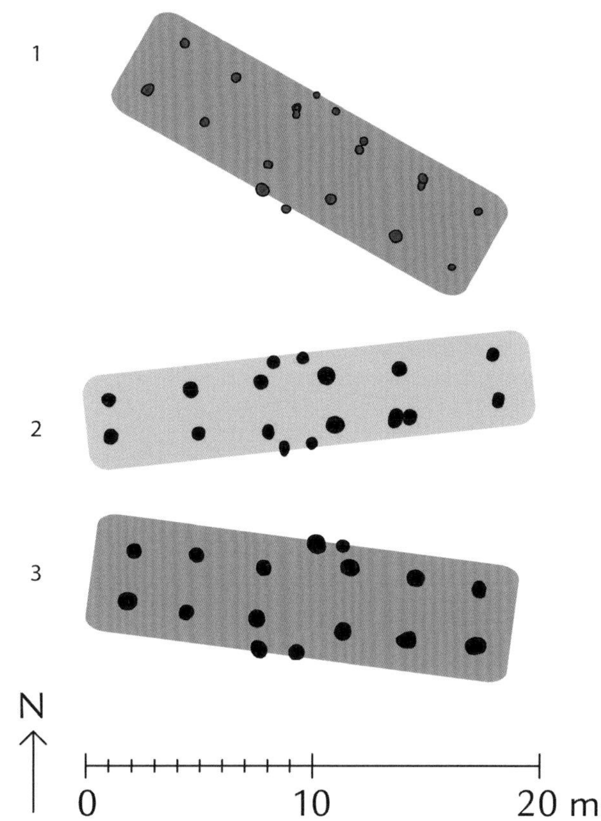

Fig. 3. | *Typical houses from the Over Jerstal Group. 1: Galsted (B1). 2: Hammelev Nørremark (B2). 3: Stepping Mølle (B2).*

The above village type was replaced by a so-called linear settlement, in which each farm had its own fenced area – precisely as described by the contemporary Roman historian Tacitus (Tacitus 16.1). Seven farms of greatly varying size stood in a row (fig. 4a). Each croft could cover as much as 1500 m² and there could be several buildings on each farm. The largest were as much as 30 m in length and oriented either north-south or east-west.

Directly east of the village lay a cemetery used for burials of both warriors and peasant farmers (fig. 4b).

Separate from the village, located about 50 m to the south, was a single farmstead. This did not differ from the village farms either in the extent of its croft or the size and number of its buildings, but it did have its own cemetery which lay to the west of the farm. This included both urn graves

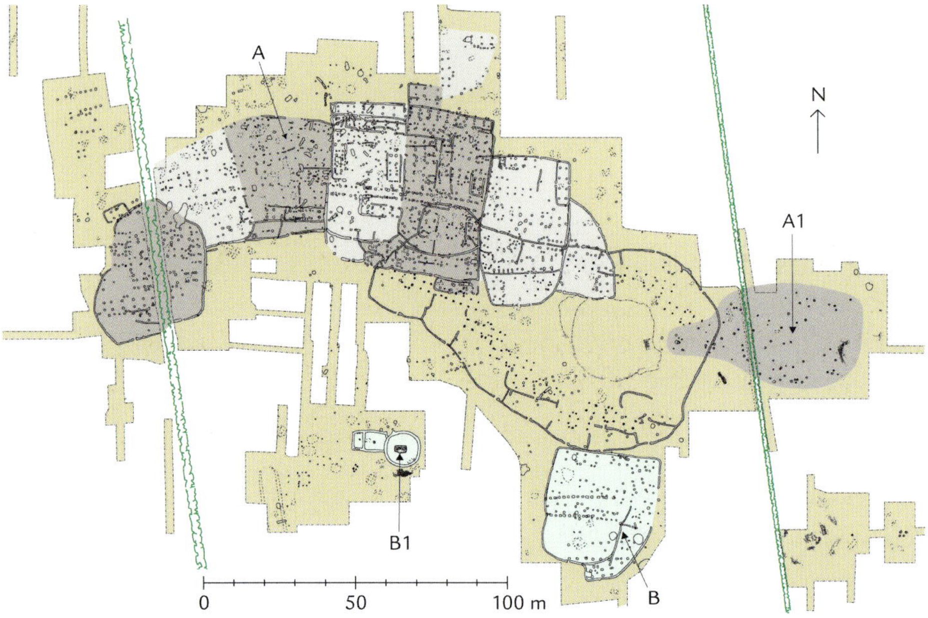

Fig. 4a. | *Site plan of the latest village at Galsted (B2). The individual farmsteads are hatched without taking account of the way in which they developed. A: Village; A1: cemetery for peasant farmers and warriors; B: Village head's farmstead; B1: village head's cemetery. After Ethelberg 2003, 201, fig. 72.*

Fig. 4b. | *The latest village at Galsted (B2) – reconstruction. After Ethelberg 2002, fig. 73 and 2003.*

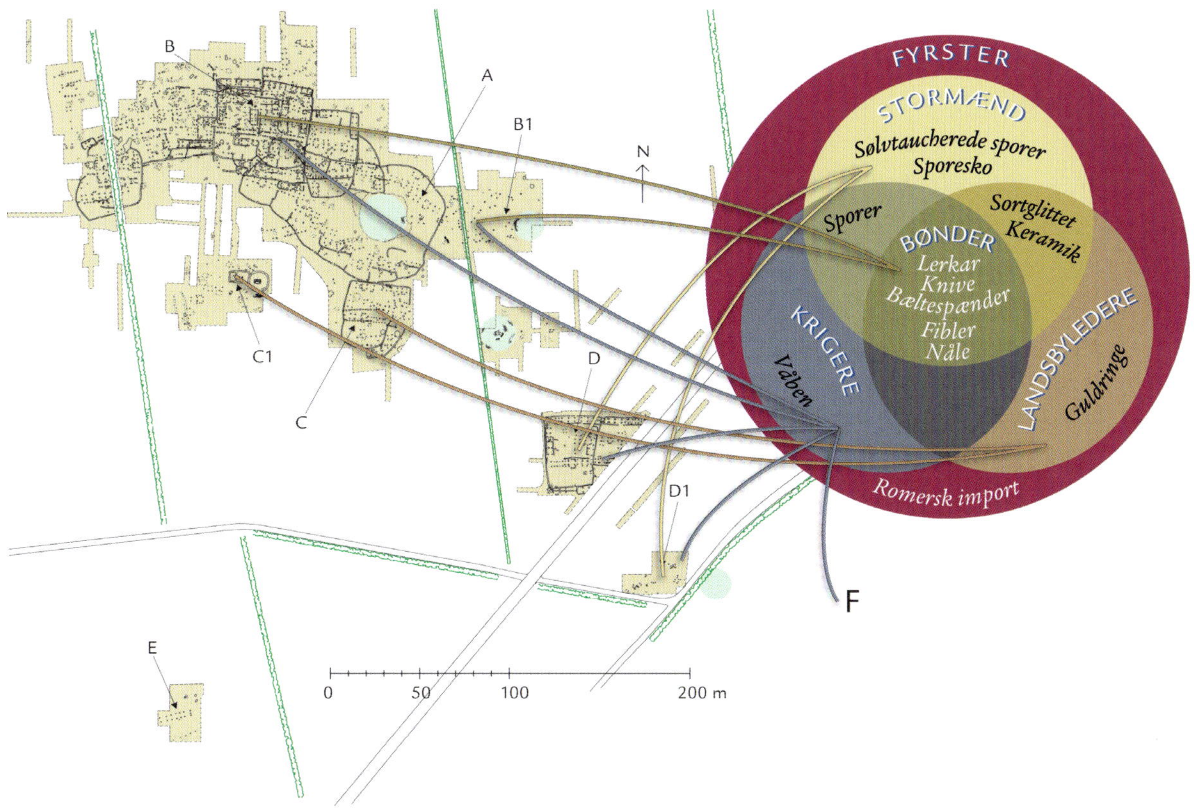

Fig. 4c. | *Galsted. Settlement structure related to social structure (cf. fig. 2).*

and inhumation graves. The latter were, according to Roman example, surrounded by circular and rectangular ditch systems, or burial gardens. The grave furnishings included black-burnished pottery and one of the urns contained a gold ring. There were no weapons. Presumably, this was the home of the village head (fig. 4c).

Just less than 90 m east of the village head's farmstead was a further settlement. At first glance, this appeared to be a double farm. However, on closer examination it became clear that there were probably three farms of different sizes, although none of them differs in terms of size from those seen in the village complex. It is worth noting, however, that in the largest farm the byre function became detached from the main dwelling house with time and was removed to an independent building. To the south of the settlement lay the contemporary cemetery, where three family clusters can be identified, corresponding to the three farms. In one of these clusters, a woman's grave was found containing a gold pear-shaped pendant. This identifies the cluster as that of the chieftain's family. There were no traces of the chieftain himself, but to the east of the cemetery there is a ploughed-over burial mound, which has not yet been investigated. Perhaps this is not Bronze Age in date, as has previously been assumed.

In another family cluster there were two weapon graves but otherwise nothing remarkable. The third grave cluster contained only ordinary furnishings and no weapons.

As yet, we do not know how princes lived within the Over Jerstal Group, but a recently excavated settlement – albeit located outside the Over Jerstal Group – near Herning in central Jutland suggests that the prince's residence comprised a large farm within which several smaller farms were integrated (Møller 2006; Olesen & Rostholm 2004). Settlements such as these are impossible to distinguish from ordinary villages if the accompanying cemetery cannot be located. This did, however, prove to be possible at Herning, and some of the graves were found to be furnished with Roman imports.

The distribution of weapons and weapon graves suggests that, at this early point in time, social elites had already established entourages of various sizes according to their economic abilities. Apparently, it was more important to demonstrate one's position by establishing dependence, rather than via prestige building in the form of large houses or large farms.

The Over Jerstal Group constituted a local tribal area divided up into at least seven loosely-structured power centres. At the head of each centre, covering an area of about 1000 km^2, stood a prince. There was no army. Security was built on the entourages of the village heads, chieftains and princes, and the alliances into which they entered.

Angeln and the West Group (50 BC-AD 450)

South Schleswig constituted the core area for Angeln and the West Group. The area is delimited to the north by the Vidå river system and in the south by the river Eider; to the west is the Wadden Sea, and to the east are Kiel Fjord and the Baltic Sea. The central areas are Angeln, Schwansen and the Wadden Sea region, but the northernmost parts of present-day Holstein also belong to this area. Although circumstances are considerably less clear than in North Schleswig, a number of factors indicate that quite a different power structure prevailed here.

Burial practices

In contrast to North Schleswig, cremation was the universal burial custom here from the decades around the birth of Christ until the beginning of the 3rd century AD. It continued to dominate until the middle of the 5th century AD. In the first decades AD, a significant number of very large cemeteries were established which subsequently saw continuity of use until the end of the Late Roman Iron Age or the beginning of the Migration period.

Occasionally, graves contain Roman imports but there are no princely graves like those seen in North Schleswig. They do not appear again until south of the river Elbe. During the first century AD the number of weapon graves was considerably reduced, suggesting that control of weapon circulation had become centralised. This can be taken as an expression of the establishment of an army of professional warriors, as was the case in the Roman Empire.

The Bornstein cemetery at Neudorf-Bornstein, northwest of Kiel, is as yet unique (Schäfer 1968). Large areas containing exceptionally rich inhumation graves have been excavated here. The graves can best be compared with those at Himlingøje on the Stevns peninsula on Zealand (Lund Hansen 1995) or the Haßleben-Leuna graves at Thüringen in Sachsen-Anhalt (Schulz 1933; 1953), which can mostly be dated to the 3rd century AD.

Farm and village

During the 1980s, several farmsteads dating from the beginning of the Early Roman Iron Age were excavated at the small village of Osterrönfeld near Rendsburg in northernmost Holstein (Jöns 1993). The main house on one of the farms represents a very special building tradition that appears to be specific to South Schleswig (fig. 5) and is, to date, the oldest known example of this tradition. Such houses are therefore termed Osterrönfeld houses. They were three-aisled longhouses, divided up into three rooms: living quarters to the west, byre in the middle and barn to the east. A characteristic of the roof-bearing posts in the dwelling end is that they were erected in two rectangular, north-south oriented modules, each of which consisted of two pairs of roof-bearing posts. The byre is distinguished by the roof-bearing posts standing closer together.

The settlement pattern in South Schleswig is generally poorly studied and no such village complex can be confidently said to have been excavated in full. The best studied examples are Kosel West, located south of Schlei Fjord (Meier 1986) and Joldelund (Jöns 1997). Kosel West, in particular, suggests that there was the same continuity in the villages as is seen in the cemeteries. The earliest buildings at Kosel West have proved to be houses of Osterrönfeld type.

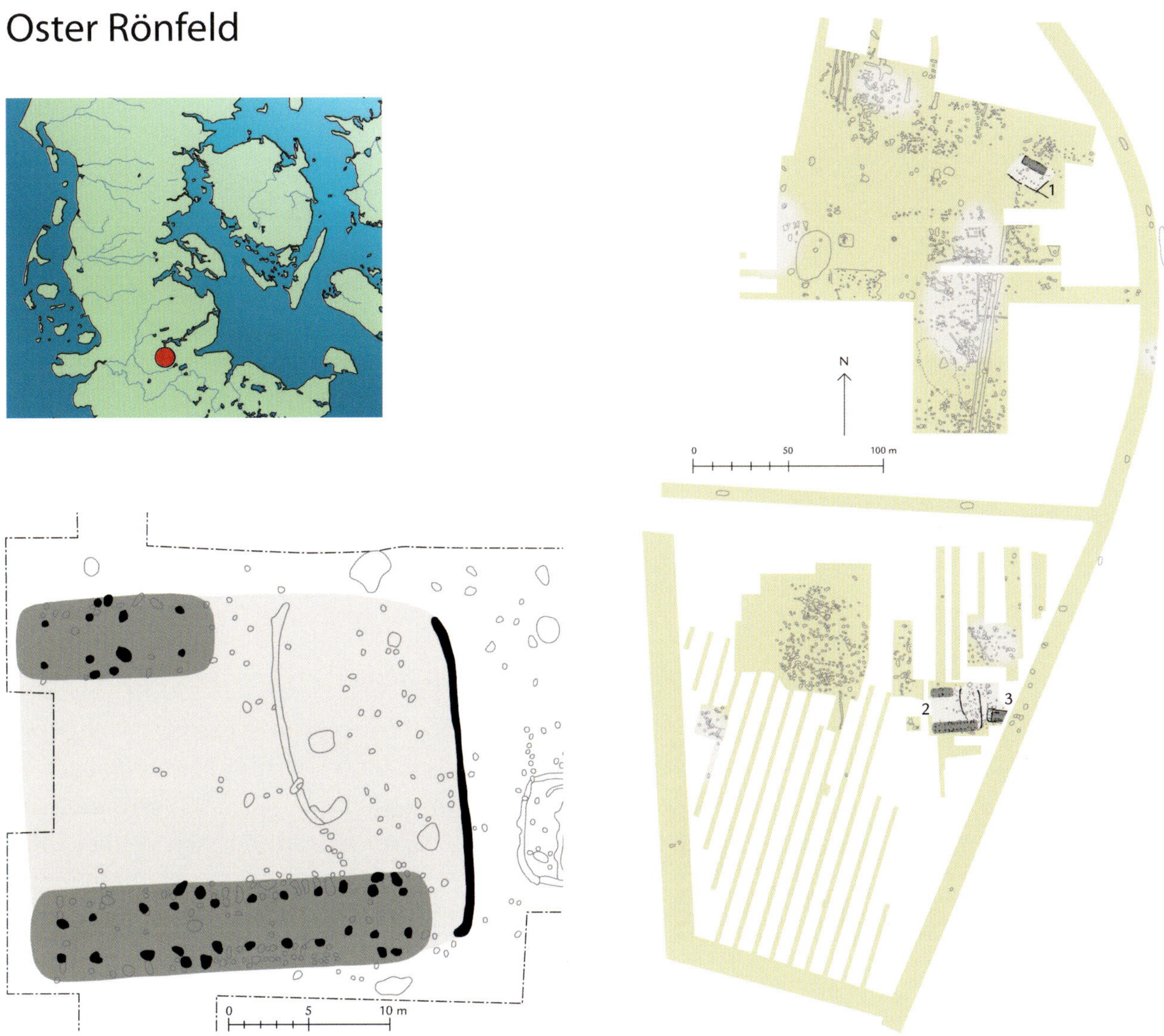

Fig. 5. | *The farmstead at Osterrönfeld, Kreis Rendsburg-Eckernförde, Schleswig-Holstein, with the prototypical Osterrönfeld house. After Ethelberg 2007, 146, Abb. 1.*

War booty sites and defensive works

The first major war booty deposits took place in a bog called Thorsbjerg Mose and large, communal defensive works were built on the periphery of the area. To the west, in the Wadden Sea area, Archsumburg and Trælbanke were constructed (Harck 1990); these were two strategically well-situated ring fortresses[1] that afforded control of navigation into the Vidå river system. Excavations carried out at these sites suggest that the fortresses were built during the course of the 1st century AD. To the north, between Tinglev and Aabenraa, Olgerdiget was constructed – a defensive structure, comprising palisade, ditch and bank, which extends for more than 12 km (Neumann 1982).

It was previously thought that Olgerdiget was built at the beginning of the 3rd century AD, modelled on the Roman Limes. However, new excavations at Uge, northeast of Tinglev, have revealed (fig. 6) that it has at least three construction phases (Christensen 2006; Ethelberg 2007) and these have now been dated dendrochronologically. The earliest phase is dated to AD 31, the second to AD 51 and the third to AD 90/91.[2] After AD 150, the function of Olgerdiget was overtaken by Æ Vold (Andersen 1990), located c. 4 km north of Kloster-

Olgerdiget

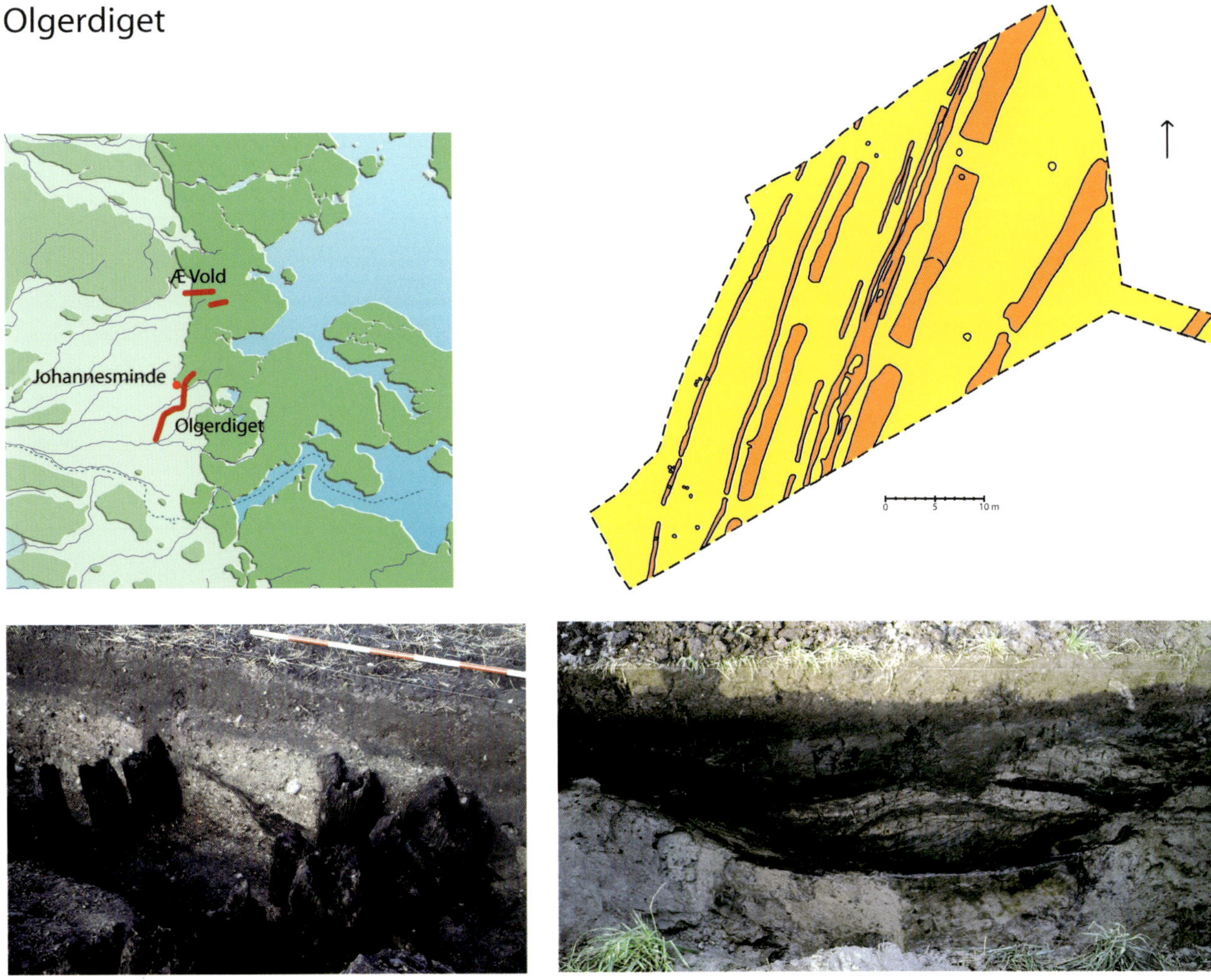

Fig. 6. | *Olgerdiget at Ligård near Uge – the 2003 excavation. After Ethelberg 2007, 148, Abb. 2.*

bakken in Rødekro (see below). Consequently, the line of defence moved northwards towards the bay Genner Bugt. Æ Vold very closely resembles Olgerdiget, both in construction and appearance. However, it has only a single phase, comprising a palisade, a ditch and a bank. Wood from the palisade has been dated dendrochronologically to after AD 150 (Ethelberg 2007).

Formation of territorial polities or early states?

As mentioned above, a completely different power structure appears to have prevailed in South Schleswig relative to that in North Schleswig. But what form did this take? It can be described as a structure that was able to:

1. Centralise weapon circulation and presumably establish a professional army for communal protection.
2. Build and maintain large communal defensive works such as Olgerdiget and the ring fortresses in the Wadden Sea area.
3. Centralise religious practice through major communal offering activities.
4. Ensure continual use of villages and burial grounds through many generations.
5. Monopolise Roman imports such that, with time, these were only found in the very richest graves.

On the face of it, an early state formation or kingdom appears to be the political structure that best matches the evidence provided by the archaeological record. It is difficult, however, to find clear and unequivocal definitions of the terms 'king' and 'kingdom'. Lexically, a king is a life-long leader of a delimited area, a kingdom. From time to time, various researchers have attempted to flesh out these terms. There seems to be fairly general agreement that execution of power should be of a dynastic nature (Schneider 2001, 103). That is, power is passed down from father to son through several generations. In connection with the project *Fra Stamme til Stat* (From Tribe to State), Olaf Olsen is cited as holding the view that 'A judiciary is one of the old functions of the monarchy ... Executive power is a prerequisite for a monarchy. When this power is exercised centrally from within a more or less well-defined territory, we speak of a kingdom' (cited from Fenger 1991, 294). Peter Sawyer is of the view that execution of power depends on officials: 'These could ... be people who supported him and in recompense were given some of the newly conquered areas of land' (Sawyer 1991, 280). For Ulf Näsman, the term kingdom means 'governance', 'power', first of all over people, and figuratively the term is used about the territory they occupy, i.e. 'country', 'state'. He goes on to state that 'In the Iron Age society I regard a regional central administration or governance as equal to a chiefdom or a petty kingdom, whereas an over-regional central administration or governance equates with an oligarchy or a kingdom' (Näsman 1996, 50). The qualities highlighted – kingdom, dynastic character, execution of power, clearly defined territory and an entourage of trusted men – in my opinion constitute the foundations for the characterisation of a society as a kingdom or an early state.[3] These are qualities that are evident in the archaeological record for South Schleswig and parts of North Schleswig from as early as the first half of the 1st century AD, and for Zealand from the second half of the 2nd century AD.

The Over Jerstal Group and the Kingdom of Angeln

If an early state formation process took place in South Schleswig around the time of the birth of Christ, with Angeln as its core area and political territory, one would expect this to be evident in the form of territorial expansion. The fact that this actually was the case can be seen from the distribution of Osterrönfeld houses (fig. 7) to the north of the present-day Danish/German border (Ethelberg 2001; 2007; Ethelberg & Kruse 2013). Prior to 2008, Osterrönfeld houses had been found at 11 sites here. Eight of these sites lie between Aabenraa Fjord and Flensburg Fjord and on Als. One is located as far north as Christiansfeld.

At Vestergård, west of Bov, a house was found that was almost identical to the Osterrönfeld house. The distance between the two settlements is c. 70 km, but the similarity is so striking that it cannot be attributed to mere coincidence (fig. 8). The Osterrönfeld house is dated to the first half of the 1st century AD, while that at Vestergård is probably a little later. As both houses have peripheral location relative to the main settlements in South

Fig. 7. | *Distribution map of houses of Osterrönfeld type – last updated 2008. After Ethelberg 2009a, 176, Abb. 7.*

Schleswig, one would expect to find houses of the same type distributed between the two locations, but slightly earlier in date.

At Hjøhøj, similarly situated near Bov, a site has been located with many Osterrönfeld houses. These are in general very long, i.e. around 30 m or more in length, and often laterally reversed, i.e. the byre was to the west and the living quarters to the east. This suggests that, as also seen at Kosel West, there was settlement continuity around the transition between the Early and Late Iron Age (Ethelberg 2003).

At Klosterbakken, immediately west of Rødekro, there was intensive settlement during the Early Roman Iron Age. Two of the farmsteads here are of particular interest because they almost overlap (fig. 9) and are therefore unlikely to have existed at the same time. The main building in one farmstead is an Over Jerstal house, whereas in the other it is of Osterrönfeld type. The Over Jerstal house burnt down; the Osterrönfeld house did not. Both houses have been radiocarbon dated to AD 70-140. Perhaps we see here a snapshot of the meeting between an expanding territorial polity and a local peasant farming society. Just such an encounter is described by Tacitus (33.1-2). He reports how the Bructeri were completely exterminated by the Chamavi and the Angrivarii, after the latter had migrated to the former's tribal area. Ethnic cleansing is apparently no new concept in European history.

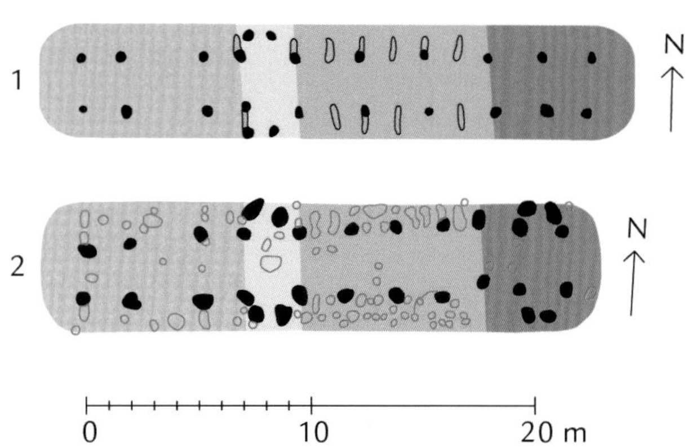

Fig. 8. | *Examples of modular longhouses of Osterrönfeld type with three main rooms (living quarters, byre and barn). 1: Vestergård near Padborg. 2: Osterrönfeld near Rendsburg.*

An entire village of Osterrönfeld houses has been excavated at Johannesminde, east of Tinglev, less than 1 km from Olgerdiget. Potsherds from the houses are of the same type as those known from the Early Roman Iron Age in South Schleswig, though not from the Over Jerstal Group. Several intentional breaches in Olgerdiget have been demonstrated here, supporting the conclusion that Olgerdiget was constructed by people from South Schleswig, with the Angles being the most obvious possibility. Prior to the construction of Danfoss Universe on the northern tip of Als, a large settlement was discovered dating from the Early Roman Iron Age. Farm 2 had two phases: the main building in the first phase can best be characterised as an Over Jerstal house, whereas the main building in the second phase is clearly of Osterrönfeld type. The latter has been radiocarbon dated to AD 135-235. The Osterrönfeld house at the 'Sportspladsen' site in Christiansfeld appears to be one of the latest houses of this type. It forms part of a farmstead that is partially enclosed by a fence, a so-called *sadeltagshegn* (i.e. the farmyard area alongside the fence is covered by a pitched roof). This fence type dates from the 3rd century AD or later.

There appears then to be a horizontal stratigraphy in the distribution of houses of Osterrönfeld type, progressing to the north and east. It is intriguing that the distribution of Osterrönfeld houses and that of princely graves of the Over Jerstal Group appear to respect one another, i.e. princely graves area absent when the Osterrönfeld houses appear. At Tombølgård on Arnkiløre, northwest of Sønderborg, there are two princely graves, both of which can be dated to the Early Roman Iron Age phase B1 (Norling Christensen 1960), i.e. the first half of the 1st century AD. There are no other examples of princely graves on Als from this or any other period.

To the northeast of Rødekro are two princely graves: Genner, dated to phase B2, and Bodummark, which is a little later (Norling Christensen 1960). Bodummark presumably replaced Genner

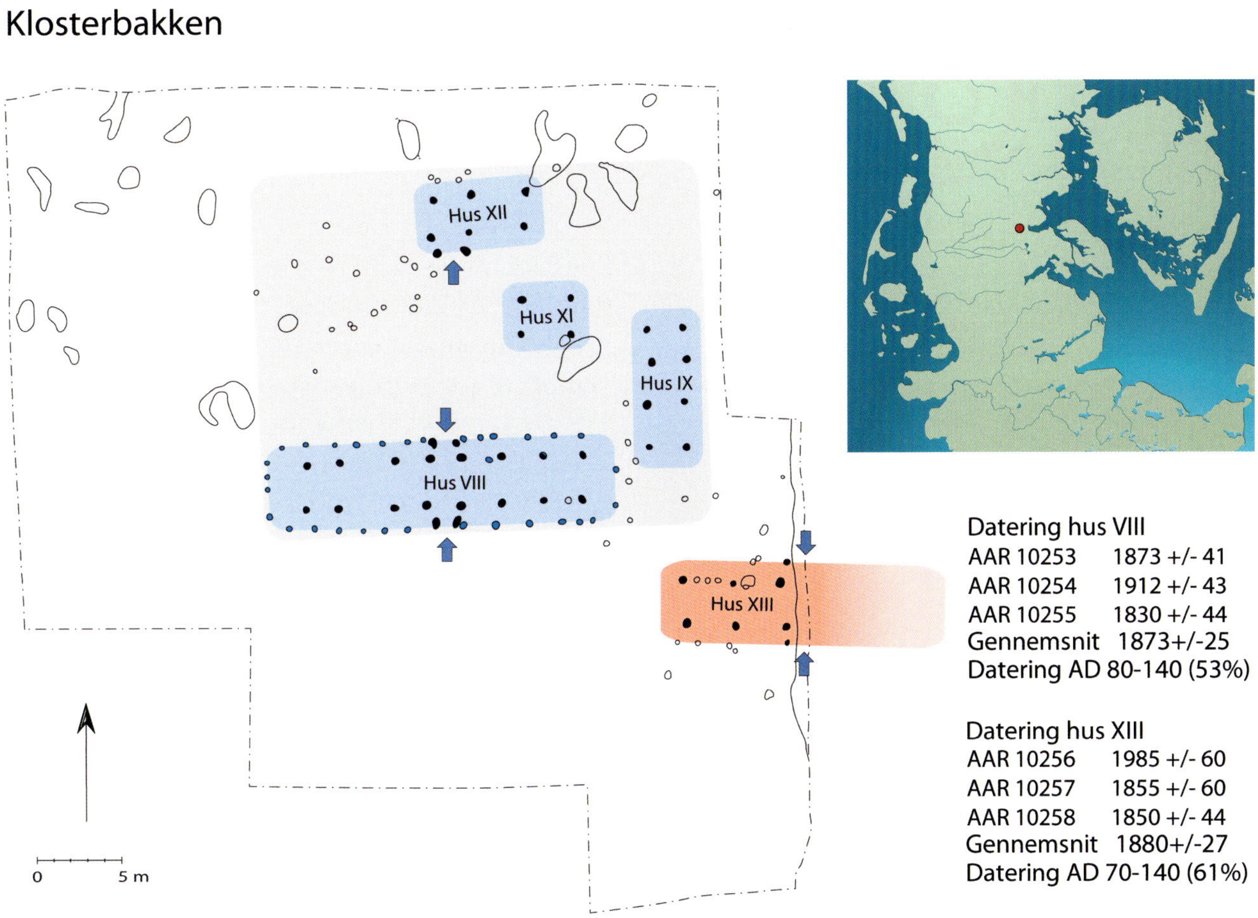

Fig. 9. | *Klosterbakken with floor plans of houses VIII, IX and XI, XII and XIII. After Ethelberg 2007, 150, Abb. 3.*

as the princely seat and lies directly south of Æ Vold, assuming that this continued in the same direction towards Genner Bugt. The princely seat at Bodummark was apparently abandoned when Æ Vold was built.

The princely cemeteries of Kastrup (Jensen 2007; Neumann 1957) and Brokær (Rasmussen 1995), both located in the central and northwestern part of the Over Jerstal Group's area of distribution, were used through a greater number of generations than for example Tombølgård. This suggests that there was a gradual reduction in the Over Jerstal Group to the south and east as a consequence of an expansion from South Schleswig towards the north and northeast.

If this development is seen in conjunction with the war booty deposits at Thorsbjerg (Engelhardt 1863), Nydam (Engelhardt 1865) and Ejsbøl (Ørsnes 1988) there appears to be a remarkable degree of consistency with the process outlined above (fig. 10). All three were bogs that had had a sacred function since at least the Pre-Roman Iron Age. The war booty deposits were not, therefore, carried out in 'virgin' mires. The first extensive deposits took place at Thorsbjerg in phase B2 (1st/2nd century AD) (Ilkjær 1990), at Nydam in sub-phase C1b (first half of the 3rd century AD) and at Ejsbøl in phase C2 (middle of the 3rd century AD). There is therefore a clear horizontal stratigraphy running from south to north, concurrent with both the distribution of Osterrönfeld houses and the establishment of Olgerdiget and Æ Vold. At the same time, the practice of princely graves appears to have ceased in these areas.

A series of finds, sites and lines of evidence has been outlined above suggesting that an early state

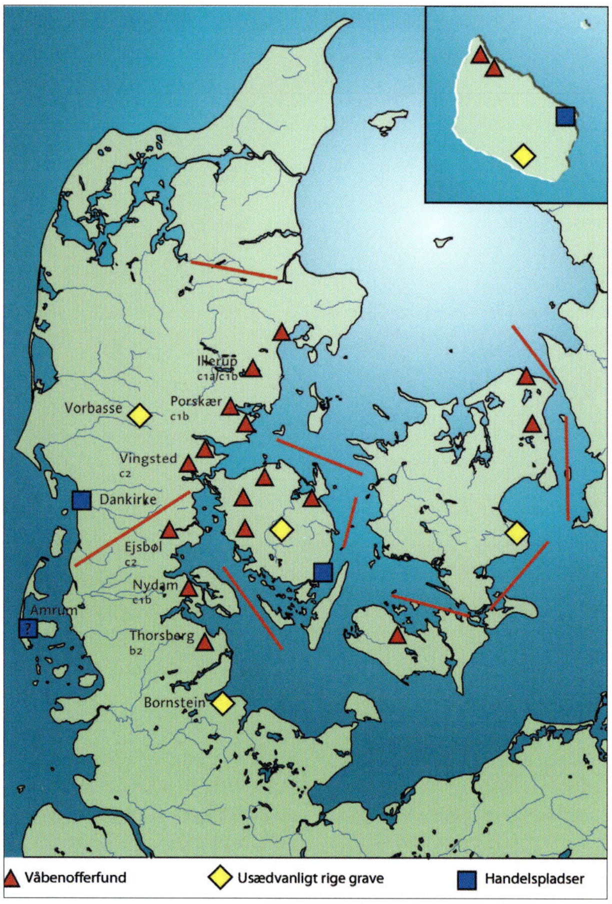

Fig. 10. | *Locations of Jutish and northern German war booty deposits, trading places and high status graves (*rex *level) seen in relation to the presumably very labile boundaries between possible early state formations during the Late Roman Iron Age from C1b to C2. After Ethelberg 2007, 152, Abb. 5.*

formation and the expansion of a territorial polity took place in the eastern parts of South Schleswig during the decades around the birth of Christ. As the development appears to have its origin around Angeln and Schwansen, it seems obvious to ascribe it to the Angles. Is it possible that the magnificent cauldron grave at Husby (Raddatz 1974), located c. 10 km east of Flensburg, which dates from this very period, should be considered as the founder grave? The territorial polity came quickly to include the whole of South Schleswig and continued to expand towards the north and east. The intention here could have been to create a kingdom comprising all of the western part of the Baltic area and Als. This would also explain the great similarities seen between Angeln and Funen during these centuries.

The Over Jerstal Group and the Jutish South Group

The Over Jerstal Group was not only under pressure from the south, from the expanding Kingdom of Angeln, but also from another early state formation or territorial polity in the north (Ethelberg 1990; 1992), which can be assumed to have had its origin in central Jutland – perhaps modelled on the Kingdom of Angeln. At least, these events appear first to have taken place during the second half of the 2nd century AD (fig. 11).

Over the course of a few short decades, the Over Jerstal Group was wiped off the map. This was one of the most striking upheavals in all of North Schleswig's prehistory. Society changed fundamentally in all aspects. Burial practices shifted from cremation to inhumation. The material culture changed completely: Brooches with a spring cover were replaced by brooches with a high catch plate; Over Jerstal pottery was replaced by thin-walled, elegantly ornamented handled vessels; necklaces with beads of glass and amber became common; new weapon types replaced old. Over Jerstal houses disappeared, and house walls were no longer built on sills but using earth-fast posts. The old villages, with 100 inhabitants or more corresponding to 8-10 farms, were replaced by single farms. Some of the latter, for example Hjemsted at Skærbæk near Rømø, rapidly developed into villages, while others disappeared. Many of the new settlements were located close to present-day villages with names ending in *-sted* (-place) or *-lev* (-inheritance). The first syllable in the village name is often a man's name (Hedeager 1990, 186), so Hjemsted means 'Hemir's place (farm)' and Hammelev means 'Hamis's inheritance (farm)'. A characteristic of these new settlements was that the farmsteads were totally or partially enclosed within a special type of fence, a *sadeltagshegn* (see above). The upheaval was so complete it can be feared that the Over Jerstal Group suffered a fate comparable to that which befell the Bructeri.

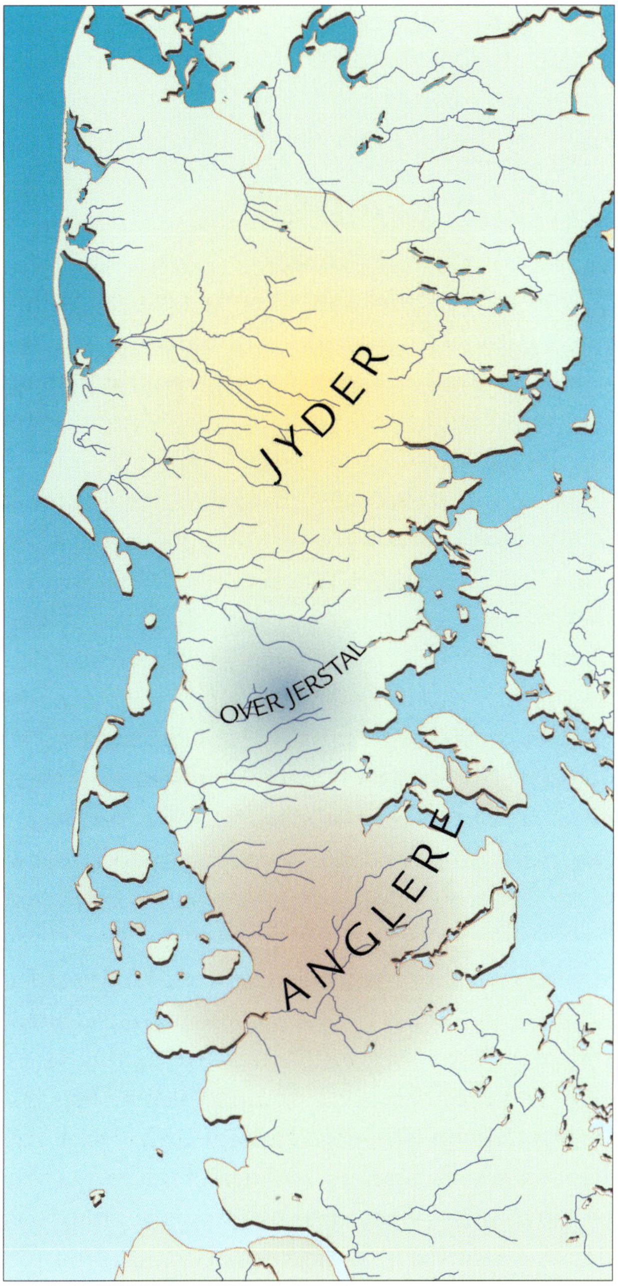

Fig. 11a. | *The relationship between the Kingdom of Angeln, the Over Jerstal Group and the Jutish South Group in the middle of the 2nd century AD. After Ethelberg 2003, 223, fig. 91:1.*

Fig. 11b. | *The relationship between the Kingdom of Angeln, the Over Jerstal Group and the Jutish South Group at the transition from the 2nd to the 3rd century AD. After Ethelberg 2003, 223, fig. 91:3.*

As regards the distribution of war booty sites in central Jutland (Ilkjær 1990), a horizontal stratigraphy can be identified corresponding completely to that observed in Schleswig, but in the opposite direction – from north to south (fig. 10). The earliest site is Illerup, where the main offerings took place during the Late Roman Iron Age at the transition between sub-phases C1a and C1b (c. AD 200). Next is Porskær, in sub-phase C1b (the first half of the 3rd century AD), and then Vingsted in phase C2 (the mid-3rd century AD).

With time, the 'Jutish South Group' expanded

to cover an area extending from Randers Fjord and Agger Tange in the north to the Kingdom of Angeln in the south. Within this area, it is possible to identify a development corresponding completely to that seen in Schleswig. Weapon circulation was centralised. At the centre of the area lay the largest and most remarkable settlement of all: Vorbasse (Hvass 1979), the only site within the South Group so far known to have rich weapon graves, graves containing Roman imports and graves containing magnificent female ornaments. Vorbasse was to the South Group what Bornstein Neudorf was to the Kingdom of Anglen, and what Himlingøje was to Zealand. As such, the South Group can be characterised as an early state formation and due to its origin in central Jutland, it seems obvious to ascribe this to the Jutes.

Early state formation in Scandinavia

An argument has been presented above for the emergence of a territorial polity in the eastern parts of South Schleswig (Angeln and Schwansen). A corresponding development can be demonstrated in central Jutland, but not until the second half of the 2nd century AD. The question now is whether this represented a unique developmental pattern limited to the Jutland peninsula, or whether it applied across larger parts of southern Scandinavia.

Zealand/Himlingøje 1st-3rd centuries AD

Until the decades just prior to the birth of Christ, cremation was the dominant burial practice on Zealand. Around, or shortly after, the birth of Christ, the practice of inhumation was introduced and quickly became universal (Liversage 1980). At the same time, people began to make use of Roman-produced metal vessels as grave furnishings; these were both rare and exquisite. Towards the middle of the 2nd century AD, the number of graves containing imports progressively increased, but Roman imports never became everyday objects. Graves containing imported furnishings are found fairly evenly distributed across most of the island, though they are commoner towards the north and east than towards the south and west. No area – not even Stevns – stands out at the expense of others. On the face of it, the picture appears to correspond roughly to that outlined above for the Over Jerstal Group.

The graves containing imports are presumably a reflection of the society's elite and they demonstrate that Zealand –like Jutland – was divided up into autonomous principalities of equal status during the Early Roman Iron Age.

It is generally accepted that a significant number of warriors from Zealand took part in the Marcomannic Wars (AD 166-180), either as Roman mercenaries or as allies in Germanic tribal alliances (Lund Hansen 1987, 222; Jensen 2003, 483ff). This is also true of warriors from the two princely families on Stevns. When they returned home, they brought new ideas with them. Whether these ideas originated from direct contact with the central authorities of the Roman Empire or from contact with fellow Germanic tribes – for example the Angles – cannot be said. On returning home, one family settled at Himlingøje (Lund Hansen 1987; 1995) on the north side of Stevns, while the other settled at Spjellerup Præstegårdsmark on the south side (Lund Hansen 1987). As a completely new, and for Zealand unique, development at that time, the founder graves in the second half of the 2nd century AD took the form of cremations furnished with both weapons and Roman imports. Large burial mounds were raised over the graves. However, this new burial practice never found general application and inhumation remained the dominant practice throughout the 3rd century AD. From time to time, a small number of particularly important people were honoured with a burial mound.

The two families presumably battled for control of Stevns. The Himlingøje family was ultimately victorious: Their cemetery continued to be used until the end of the 3rd century AD, whereas that at Spjellerup Præstegårdsmark ceased before the end of the 2nd century.[4]

With this development, a new territorial polity saw the light of day, with Himlingøje at its centre.

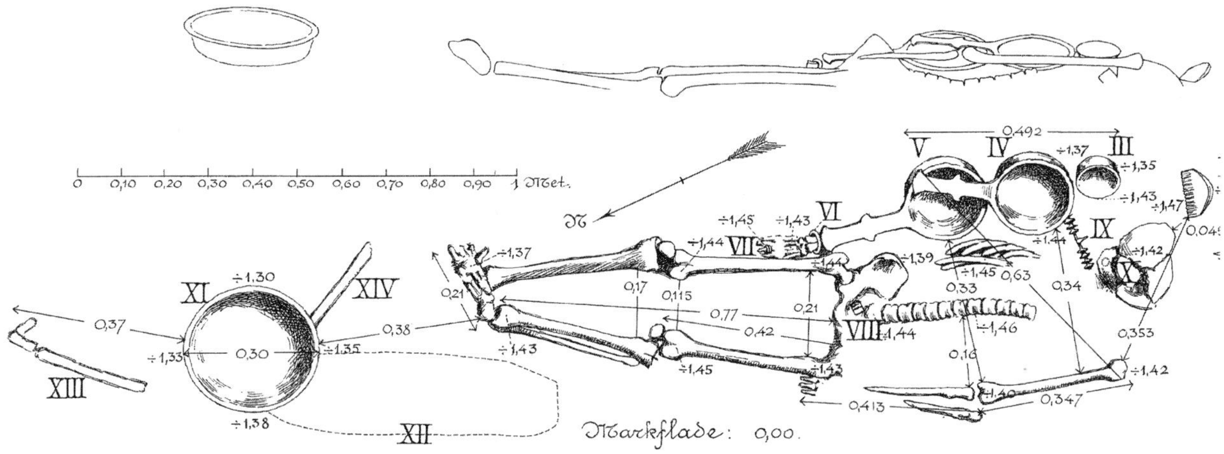

Fig. 12a. | *Grave 1894-1 of the Himlingøje dynasty's cemetery on the Stevns peninsula. Drawing of the presumed rex-level grave. After Lund Hansen 1995, 103, fig. 3:46.*

The contemporaneous farmsteads and villages are yet to be located, but it was here at Himlingøje that the dead were buried – often beneath impressive burial mounds (fig. 12a and b).

After winning control over Stevns, the new kingdom expanded first to the west, then to the south and subsequently also to the north. Finally, i.e. from the middle of the 3rd century AD,

Fig. 12b. | *The grave's location in the cemetery. Photo: M.S. Jørgensen; after Lund Hansen 1995, 95.*

Himlingøje exerted control over all of Zealand. But how can we be sure of this? The truth is we cannot, but an analysis of grave sites on Zealand does support the scenario outlined above (Ethelberg 2000).[5]

On the basis of the grave finds, six social layers can be identified (Ethelberg 2000, 162ff; 2009a; 2011a; Boye et al. 2009, 255ff) (fig. 13). Uppermost we have *rex/reges* (the king(s)). The royal family's insignias were heavy gold arm rings such as *Kolben* and snake's head arm rings. Immediately below rex we find *dux* (the army commander), but this rank will not be discussed further here because, whereas the rank of rex is hereditary – as demonstrated by the dynastic character of the Himlingøje cemetery – the dux was chosen from those considered most able.

Then comes *principes* (the lords); for the moment we must be content to characterise these as proto-nobility. We know that the rank of princeps was hereditary, but we do not know whether it was associated with judicial privileges. As a sign of their rank, the heads of the princeps families wore gold finger rings that are faithful imitations of the snake's head arm rings. The snake's head finger rings are the key to an understanding of early formation of a territorial polity in Zealand (Boye et al. 2009).

The princeps surrounded himself with *comitatus* (the retinue), comprised of *comites* (the companions), who displayed their rank partly via simpler gold rings and partly via Roman imports. Of course, the rex also had a retinue, but we do not know how these people were recruited.

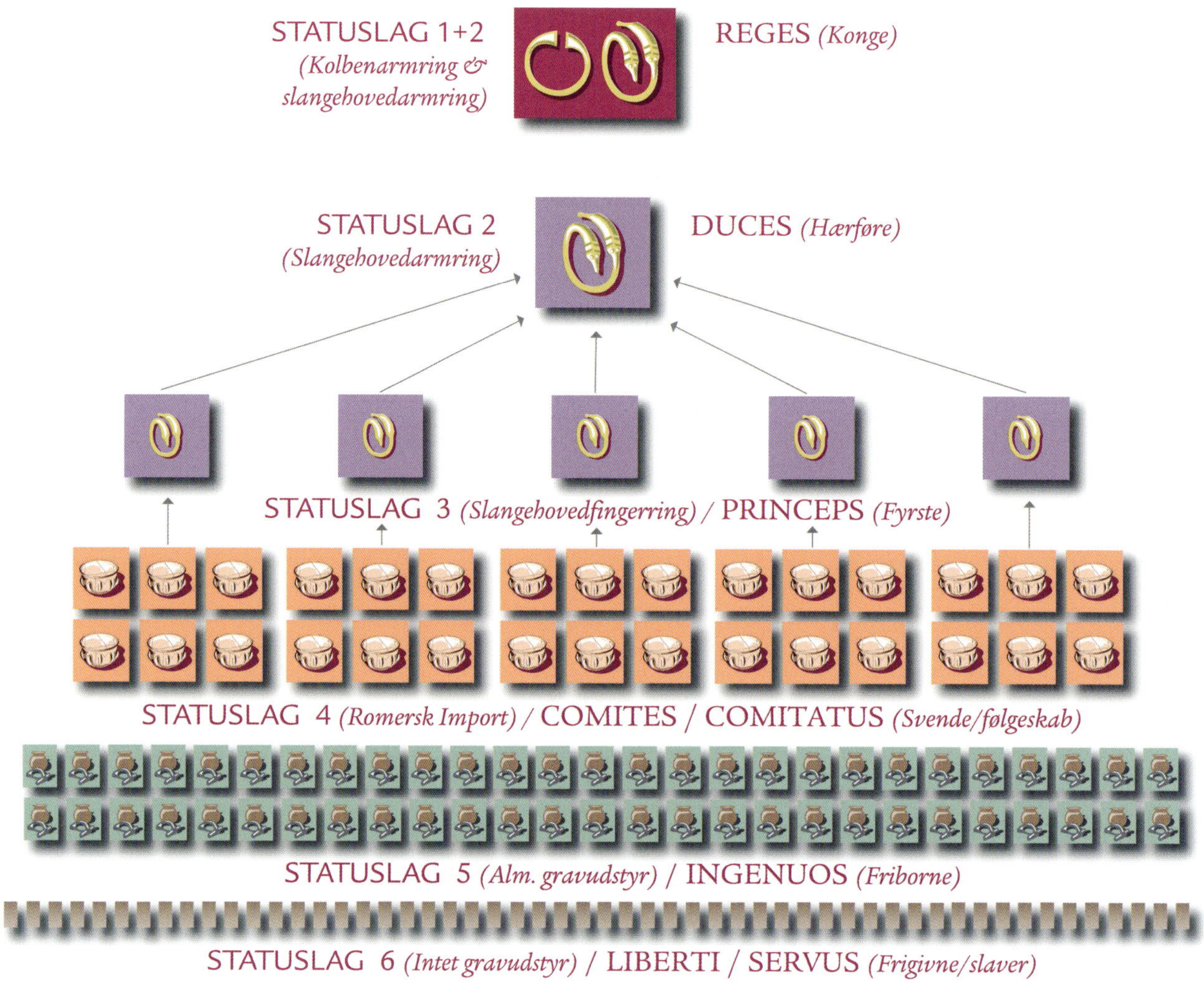

Fig. 13. | *The social hierarchy on Zealand during the Late Roman Iron Age. After Ethelberg 2003, 273, fig. 150.*

Beneath princeps and comitatus were *ingenui* (the freemen). Their grave furnishings include pottery vessels, combs, brooches and sometimes glass and amber beads. Lowermost in the social pyramid were *liberti* and *servi* (the freedmen and the slaves). They were often considered unworthy of a burial and certainly never had grave furnishings.

The snake's head finger rings, as a type, show very great variation, and attention here will primarily be focused on the finger rings of Beckmann's type 39 (Beckmann 1969), because all the evidence suggests that its area of provenance is around Himlingøje on Zealand (Ethelberg 2000; Raddatz 1957).

It is possible to distinguish three types: a, b and c. Type a has two turns, type b has three and in type c the turns are fused together to form a continuous plate. The three types represent a chronological/typological development with type a being the earliest and type c the latest (Raddatz 1957). This development covers the period from c. AD 200 to c. AD 275.

The earliest rings of types a and b are found primarily on the Stevns peninsula, central Zealand (Nordrup) and southern Zealand (Skovgårde), while the latest rings of type c are found on the periphery of this area. Type c has so far not been recorded from northernmost and northwesternmost Zealand.

Distributed around Zealand are numerous examples of weapon graves and stray finds of weapons that presumably originate from damaged graves (Lund Hansen 1995). If both a snake's head finger ring of type 39 and a weapon grave are found within the same area, the ring is thought to be latest in date. Outside Himlingøje, there are no contemporary weapon graves in the areas with finds of snake's head finger rings. In other words, where snake's head finger rings turn up, weapons disappear. This can only mean that the people who manufactured, distributed and wore snake's head finger rings were also those who controlled weapon circulation.

While the polity on Stevns consolidated and expanded its territory, there were small principalities distributed around Zealand that functioned autonomously relative to Himlingøje. Some perhaps lived according to the norms of the Early Roman Iron Age, whereas others possibly attempted to imitate Himlingøje. A good example of the latter is a grave at Kirkebakkegård in northeastern Zealand (Thrane 1967). It is one of the richest graves from Zealand outside Himlingøje. Its furnishings include a snake's head finger ring. However, this is a primitive, rough imitation of the Himlingøje rings, revealing it to be a local product that definitely did not originate from Himlingøje. The grave can be dated to slightly before the middle of the 3rd century AD (C1b). Not far from Kirkebakkegård, a snake's head finger ring of type 39c (AD 250/275) was found at Kirke Værløse. Unfortunately, this was a stray find but it undoubtedly originates from a damaged grave. The ring indicates that the Himlingøje dynasty took over control of this area a generation at the most after the Kirkebakkegård prince was laid to rest.

It is therefore possible to talk of a two-speed development on Zealand. One represents the expanding monarchy, the other the old tribal society.

By following the distribution of objects definitively produced in the workshops of the Himlingøje family, it is possible to gain an impression of the size and extent of the network that the new polity attempted to establish (fig. 14). The objects in question are primarily snake's head finger rings and magnificent ornaments such as rosette and swastika brooches. These objects are found in Jutland, Norway, Sweden and northern and central Germany, in areas where there was also substantial iron production extending far and above the needs of local consumption. Iron was apparently in short supply on Zealand during the 3rd century AD. In some instances, attempts were made to ensure external supplies via alliances, while in others military force was employed. Evidence of the latter is provided in particular by the war booty deposits at Thorsbjerg, which include several fragments of snake's head rings that could only have been manufactured on Zealand. As already outlined above, Thorsbjerg is located in the area with the earliest documented territorial polity in southern Scandinavia to date.

The final burials at the Himlingøje cemetery took place during the second half of C2. A re-ex-

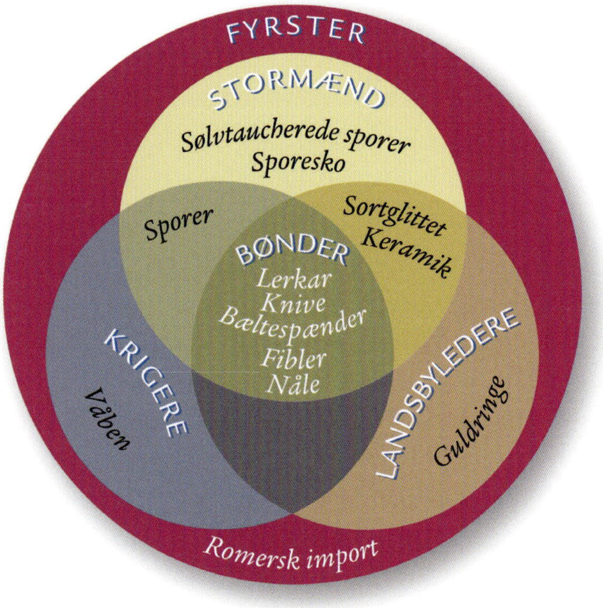

Fig. 14. | *Simplified model of the settlement structure in eastern and southern Zealand as reflected in the political network. After Ethelberg 2003, 287, fig. 159.*

amination of a representative selection of Zealandic graves dating from the Late Roman and Early Germanic Iron Ages, in conjunction with the publication of the rich grave finds from Copenhagen's West District, has strongly suggested that there is discontinuity between C2 and C3 on Zealand (Ethelberg 2009b; 2011b; 114). Over time, a significant number of graves have been found with combination finds of brooches from C1b and C2 and from C3 and D1. However, there have been no combination finds to date of brooches from C2 and C3.

This could suggest that the first kingdom on Zealand had played out its role by the end of C2. The key to an understanding of what actually happened is perhaps to be found in the nearby cemetery at Varpelev (Engelhardt 1877; Lund Hansen 1995). It is apparent that this cemetery was established in C1b and that burials continued after the cemetery at Himlingøje had gone out of use, but they did not continue into C3.

The contents of grave α at Varpelev include a snake's head finger ring of Beckmann's type 39c and a four-armed swastika brooch. This shows, on the one hand, that the grave can be dated to C2 and, on the other, that the deceased had the status of princeps and was subordinate to the Himlingøje dynasty.

Grave a is slightly later and much richer. Even so, it has no snake's head finger ring of Beckmann's type 39. However, it does contain a solid gold snake's head arm ring, although it is not formed like the Himlingøje rings and must be classified as an example of Beckmann's type 40. It has been demonstrated that rings of this type are Swedish and were probably produced in the Mälar area (Ethelberg 2000).

The Varpelev cemetery can perhaps be ascribed a completely new significance on the basis of this evidence. A plausible scenario is that the Varpelev family rebelled against the Himlingøje dynasty and captured the kingdom. The solid gold arm ring suggests that the Varpelev family enjoyed close relations with society's highest echelons on the opposite side of the Øresund. It is unlikely to be a coincidence that this was precisely the time when the central place at Uppåkra became established in earnest, demonstrating the emergence of a new regional power on the eastern side of the Øresund (Larsson & Hårdh 1997; 1998).

It is difficult to imagine that Uppåkra and Himlingøje could live in peaceful co-existence without one wanting to exert dominance over the other. The central power responsible for Uppåkra appears to have existed uninterrupted from the Late Roman Iron Age until well into the Germanic Iron Age. Accordingly, Uppåkra was the victor in this power struggle, possibly with Varpelev as vassal. While Uppåkra retained its position through many generations, Varpelev lost its position prior to the end of the 3rd century AD. Perhaps it is these episodes that are referred to in Classical sources with respect to the Danes' immigration (Hedeager 1988, 212).

Conclusion

Employing the analogy of Zealand, the case has been put for the whole of southern Scandinavia having been involved in an early state formation process during the course of the 2nd and 3rd cen-

Social level	Zealand	South Group
Reges	Himlingøje	Vorbasse
Principes	Brøndsager, Nordrup, Skovgårde	Hjartbro, Jens Kuskvej, Lærkenfeldt
Comites	Engbjerg, Egebjerg, Torslunde	Hjemsted, Bakkegården, Enderupskov
Ingenui	Kong Svends Park, Kastrup	Østergård, Bolderslev

turies AD, resulting in a number of territorial polities. The object types and the object combinations that most readily reflect these territorial polities vary from area to area. On Zealand, developments are best seen through the chronology and distribution pattern of snake's head finger rings, whereas in the case of the Jutish South Group it is the distribution pattern of fully furnished weapon graves that is crucial. The table below attempts a status comparison between Zealand and the South Group.

The table classifies cemeteries according to the social level of their richest graves. At cemeteries with *reges* graves, those of *principes*, *comites* and *ingenui* are as a rule also represented. Correspondingly, *comites* and *ingenui* are usually represented at *princeps/principes* cemeteries, and so on.[6]

By the second half of the 3rd century AD there was hardly anywhere in the central and western Baltic area that was not subordinate to one of the territorial polities. To date, it has been possible to identify at least five early state formations in the area: Angeln-Holstein-Schleswig, central and southern Jutland, Funen, Zealand and Bornholm. On further, more detailed examination of the archaeological record, it will probably also prove possible to document early state formations in northern Jutland and southern Sweden, as well as on Lolland and Falster.

Within each of the five aforementioned territorial polities, a striking uniformity is apparent in the distribution of the characteristic site categories: the war booty deposits, the richest graves and the earliest trading places. It is a general feature that the richest graves are usually found at a central location within the territory. This applies to Bornstein for Holstein/North Schleswig, Vorbasse for southern and central Jutland, Haagerup, Årslev and Sanderumgård for Funen, Himlingøje for Zealand and Slusegård for Bornholm. In southern and central Jutland, on Funen and on Bornholm, early trading places have been identified, respectively at Dankirke, Lundeborg and Sorte Muld. It is striking that these are all located at a distance from the areas with the richest graves, i.e. they are detached from the political centre. A trading place that was active during the 5th and 6th centuries AD has been demonstrated at Amrum, which lies diametrically opposed to Bornstein (Segschneider 2002). However, only a very small part of the site has been uncovered. It is possible that future excavations will demonstrate that it began functioning as early as the 3rd century AD, or even earlier. It definitely has the 'correct' location. Finally, there are the war booty sites in bogs; these all seem to be located diametrically opposite the trading places, on the periphery of the aforementioned territorial polities. It is almost as if they were oriented towards neighbouring areas as territorial markers.

In early state formations, the king is very unlikely to have had a permanent residence. There is more likely to have been a structure resembling that of the travelling kings of the Middle Ages. The king was obliged to travel around his kingdom in order to enforce his power. This means that there had to be settlements distributed across the kingdom where the king could reside with his entourage for shorter or longer periods. Perhaps it was in these settlements that the princeps lived, in which case the distribution on Zealand of for example snake's head finger rings of Beckmann's type 39 marks the approximate location of these settlements. In this respect, it is interesting that the distance between the find sites for these rings appears to be in the region of 20-30 km, which in the Iron Age corresponded to a day's journey on horseback.[7]

If this line of argument is accepted, a sixth criterion can be added to the diagnostic characteristics for early state formation and the development of territorial polities, i.e. the development of an infrastructure. This is precisely what can be observed on Zealand; the clearest example is the establishment of the Broskov roads at Præstø (Kunwald 1962).

With time, as the borders of these territorial polities began to brush against one another, the early state formation process was replaced by a process of unification of the territorial polities. The conflicts that arose as a consequence are presumably reflected in the repeated war booty offerings seen in bogs. The best way of communicating to a defeated enemy that the battle has been lost is to usurp their sacred places and re-use them. Seen in this light, the war booty deposits, like the centralised weapon distribution, the establishment of centralised defensive works, the distribution of the richest graves, the location of the first trading places and the distribution of the Osterrönfeld houses, have to be an important factor in our understanding of the formation of early state and territorial polities. On the basis of the current *Stand der Forschung*, South Schleswig must be considered as an innovative area as regards early state formation in southern Scandinavia.

Bibliography

Andersen, S.W. 1990, "Æ Vold" ved Øster Løgum – et gammelt fortidsminde i en ny belysning. *Sønderjysk Månedsskrift* 1990:1, 7-15.

Beckmann, C. 1969, Metallfingerringe der römischen Kaiserzeit im Freien Germanien. *Saalburg-Jahrbuch. Bericht des Saalburg Museum* 26, 5-106.

Boye, L. & U. Lund Hansen 2009 (eds.), *Wealth and prestige. An analysis of rich graves from Late Roman Iron Age on eastern Zealand, Denmark.* Tåstrup.

Boye, L., P. Ethelberg & U. Lund Hansen 2009, Conclusion. In: L. Boye & U. Lund Hansen (eds.), *Wealth and prestige. An analysis of rich graves from Late Roman Iron Age on eastern Zealand, Denmark.* Tåstrup. 255-62.

Christensen, L. 2006, Nye undersøgelser af Olgerdiget – en langvold fra jernalderen. *Sønderjysk Månedsskrift* 2006:1, 3-10.

Cohen, R. and E. Service (eds.) 1978, *Origins of the State: the Anthropology of Political Evolution.* Philadelphia.

Engelhardt, C. 1863, *Thorsbjerg Mosefund.* København.

Engelhardt, C. 1865, *Nydam Mosefund.* København.

Engelhardt, C. 1877, Skeletgrave på Sjælland og i det østlige Danmark. *Aarbøger for Nordisk Oldkyndighed og Historie* 1877, 347-402.

Ethelberg, P. 1990, *Hjemsted 2 – tre gravpladser fra 3. & 4. årh. e. Kr.* Haderslev.

Ethelberg, P. 1992, Hjartbro – et våbengravsfund fra 3. århundrede fra Sønderjylland. *Aarbøger for Nordisk Oldkyndighed og Historie* 1991, 111-22.

Ethelberg, P. 1995, The chieftains' farms of the Over Jerstal Group. *Journal of Danish Archaeology* 11 (1992-93), 111-36.

Ethelberg, P. 2000, *Skovgårde. Ein Bestattungsplatz mit reichen Frauengräbern des 3. Jhs. n. Chr. auf Seeland.* København.

Ethelberg, P. 2001, Haus und Siedlung der älteren Römischen Kaiserzeit im ehemaligen Herzogtum Schleswig. *Probleme der Küstenforschung im südlichen Nordseegebiet* 27, 57-73.

Ethelberg, P. 2003, Gården og landsbyen i jernalder og vikingetid (500 f. Kr. – 1050 e. Kr.). In: P. Ethelberg, N. Hardt, B. Poulsen & A.B. Sørensen, *Det Sønderjyske Landbrugs Historie. Jernalder, vikingetid og middelalder.* Haderslev. 123-371.

Ethelberg, P. 2007, Verteidigungsanlagen und Haustypen der älteren römischen Kaiserzeit im ehemaligen Herzogtum Schleswig-Holstein. In: C. Grünewald & T. Capelle (eds.), *Inneren Strukturen von Siedlungen und Gräberfeldern als Spiegel gesellschaftlicher Wirklichkeit? Akten des 57. Internationalen Sachsensymposions vom 26. bis. 30. August 2006.* Münster. 145-55.

Ethelberg, P. 2009a, Frühe Königreiche. Machtkonzentrationen in Südskandinavien im 1.-4. Jahrhundert n. Chr. In: S. Burmeister & H. Derks (eds.), *2000 Jahre Varusschlacht: Konflikt.* Stuttgart. 170-83.

Ethelberg, P. 2009b, Die Fibeln. In: L. Boye & U. Lund Hansen (eds.), *Wealth and prestige. An analysis of rich graves from Late Roman Iron Age on eastern Zealand, Denmark.* Tåstrup. 15-36.

Ethelberg P. 2011a, Early state formation in southern Scandinavia – a proposal for a hierarchical terminology. In: L. Boye (ed.), *The Iron Age on Zealand. Status and perspectives.* Copenhagen. 67-73.

Ethelberg, P. 2011b, Zealand and the Roman Empire – a comment on Thomas Grane's article. In: L. Boye (ed.), *The Iron Age on Zealand. Status and perspectives.* Copenhagen. 113-16.

Ethelberg, P. (forthcoming), Schleswig as Borderland in the 1st and 2nd centuries AD. *Neue Studien zur Sachsenforschung.*

Ethelberg, P. & P. Kruse 2013, Das Osterrönfeld-haus. Status nach 10-jähriger Untersuchung. *Archäeologie in Schleswig/Arkæologi i Slesvig* 14, 103-30.

Fenger, O. 1991, Fra stammeret til statsbegreb. In: P. Mortensen & B.M. Rasmussen (eds.), *Fra stamme til stat i Danmark 2: Høvdingesamfund og kongemagt.* Højbjerg. 289-96.

Harck, O. 1990, *Archsum auf Sylt. Teil 3: Die Ausgrabungen in den römerzeitlichen Erdwerken Archsumburg, Tinnumburg und Trælbanken an der Westküste Schleswigs.* Mainz.

Hedeager, L. 1988, *Gyldendal og Politikens Danmarkshistorie. Bind 2: Danernes land. Fra ca. 200 f. Kr. – ca. 700 e. Kr.* København.

Hedeager, L. 1990, *Danmarks jernalder. Mellem stamme og stat.* Århus.

Hedeager, L. 1992, *Iron-age societies. From tribe to state in northern Europe, 500 BC to AD 700.* Oxford.

Hvass, S. 1979, Die völkerwanderungszeitliche Siedlung Vorbasse, Mitteljütland. *Acta Archaeologica* 49 (1978), 61-111.

Ilkjær J. 1990, *Illerup Ådal 1. Die Lanzen und Speere.* Højbjerg.

Jensen, J. 2003, *Danmarks Oldtid, Ældre Jernalder 500 f. Kr. – 400 e. Kr.* København.

Jensen, M.L. 2007, Kastrup-fundet – de ukendte fyrsters grave. Unpublished MA thesis. Saxo-Instituttet, Københavns Universitet 2007.

Jöns, H. 1993, *Ausgrabungen in Osterrönfeld. Ein Fundplatz der Stein-, Bronze-und Eisenzeit im Kreis Rendsburg-Eckernförde.* Bonn.

Jöns, H. 1997, *Frühe Eisengewinnung in Joldelund, Kr. Nordfriesland. Ein Beitrag zur Siedlungs und Technikgeschichte Schleswig-Holsteins.* Vol. 1. Bonn.

Kunwald, G. 1962, Broskov-vejene. *Nationalmuseets Arbejdsmark* 1962. 149-67.

Larsson, L. & B. Hårdh 1997, Uppåkra – et hövdinga- eller kungasäta. *Fornvännen* 1997, 139-54.

Larsson, L. & B. Hårdh (eds.) 1998, *Centrala platser – centrala frågor. Samhällsstrukturen under järnålderen: en vänbok till Berta Stjernquist.* Stockholm.

Liversage, D. 1980, *Material and interpretation. The archaeology of Sjælland in the Early Roman Iron Age.* København.

Lund Hansen, U. 1987, *Römischer Import im Norden. Warenaustausch zwischen dem Römischen Reich und dem freien Germanien.* København.

Lund Hansen, U. 1995, *Himlingøje – Seeland – Europa. Ein Gräberfeld der jüngeren römischen Kaiserzeit auf Seeland, seine Bedeutung und internationalen Beziehungen.* København.

Meier, D. 1986, Ausgrabungen frühgeschichtlicher Siedlungen in Kosel. *Jahrbuch Heimatgemeinschaft Eckernförde* 44, 169-184.

Møller, E. 2006, Bonde, Høvding, Fyrste. Økonomiske, sociale og samfundsmæssige forhold på Skovbjerg Bakkeø i ældre jernalder. Belyst ved to lokaliteter beliggende ved Rosenholmvej, Tjørring og Stenbjerg, Snejbjerg. Unpublished MA thesis. Aarhus University 2006.

Näsman, U. 1996, Från *region* till *rike* – från *stam* till *stat*: Om danernas etnogenes och om den danska riksbildningen. In: J.F. Krøger (ed.), *Rikssamlingen. Høvdingmakt og kongemakt. Karmøyseminaret 1996.* Stavanger. 46-65.

Neumann, H. 1957, Kastrup, en hedensk offerplads. *Sønderjyske Årbøger* 1957, 237-52.

Neumann, H. 1982, *Olgerdiget – et bidrag til Danmarks tidligste historie.* Haderslev.

Norling-Christensen, H. 1960, Romerske industriprodukter i Sønderjylland. In: H. Krogh (ed.), *Jens Raben 14. marts 1880, 18. februar 1960. Et mindeskrift.* Sønderborg. 129-45.

Olesen, M.W. & H. Rostholm 2004, Guld fra Tjørring. *FRAM* 2004, 9-27.

Plettke, A. 1921, *Ursprung und Ausbreitung der Angeln und Sachsen. Beiträge zur Siedlungsarchäologie der Ingväonen.* Hildesheim & Leipzig.

Raddatz, K. 1957, *Der Thorsberger Moorfund. Gürtelteile und Körperschmuck.* Kiel.

Raddatz, K. 1974, *Husby. Ein Gräberfeld der Eisenzeit in Schleswig.* Kiel.

Rasmussen, B.M. 1995, Brokær. Ein Reichtumszentrum der römischen Kaiserzeit in Südwestjütland. *Acta Archaeologica* 66, 39-111.

Sawyer, P. 1991, Konger og kongemagt. In: P. Mortensen & B.M. Rasmussen (eds.), *Fra stamme til stat i Danmark 2: Høvdingesamfund og Kongemagt.* Højbjerg. 282-88.

Schneider, R. 2001, König und Königtum. In: *Reallexikon der germanischen Altertumskunde* 17. Founded by Johannes Hoops. 2nd ed. Berlin/New York.

Schulz, W. 1933, *Das Fürstengrab von Haßleben.* Berlin & Leipzig.

Schulz, W. 1953, *Leuna. Ein germanischer Bestattungsplatz der spätrömischen Kaiserzeit.* Berlin.

Schäfer, G. 1968, Bericht über die Auffindung und Untersuchung von Fürstengräbern der jüngeren römischen Kaiserzeit bei Bornstein, Kreis Eckernförde. *Jahrbuch der Heimatgemeinschaft des Kreises Eckernförde* 26, 41-59.

Segschneider, M. 2002, Fränkisches Glas im Dünensand – ein Strandmarkt des 5. Jahrhunderts auf der nordfriesischen Insel Amrum und die völkerwanderungszeitliche Handelsroute zwischen Rhein und Limfjord. *Archäologisches Korrespondenzblatt* 32, 117-36.

Service, E. 1975, *Origins of the State and Civilization: The Process of Cultural Evolution.* New York.

Tacitus, P.C., De origine et situ germanorum liber. Oversat af: N.W. Bruun og A.A. Lund: Germanernes historie og befolkning. Vol. I & II. Wormianum 1974. Århus.

Tischler, F. 1937, *Fuhlsbüttel, ein Beitrag zur Sachsenfrage.* Neumünster.

Thrane, H. 1967, Fornemme fund fra en jernaldergrav i Uggeløse. *Nationalmuseets Arbejdsmark* 1967, 67-79.

Ørsnes, M. 1988, *Ejsbøl I. Waffenopferfunde des 4.-5. Jahrh.* København.

Notes

1 There are a further two known ring fortresses in the area: Lembeckburg and Tinnumburg. However, it is not possible to document securely whether these were established in this form as early as the Early Roman Iron Age or whether they represent more ordinary settlements.

2 The dendrochronological analyses were carried out by Kjeld Christensen, Wormianum. For a more detailed discussion of the results see Ethelberg forthcoming.

3 The use of the terms 'early state' and 'state formation' have caused some problems: 'Finding an appropriate terminology to be used in discussing and describing political structures and relationships in long-past periods such as the early centuries AD in southern Jutland is a great challenge in any language. In an Anglophone context, the term "state" may be justified, at least in light of the acceptance of a reference scale "from tribe to state" in the influential American anthropology/archaeology of the 1960s and 1970s and the relevant concept of the "early" (or "proto-") state therein (Cohen & Service 1978; Hedeager 1992, 83-7; Service 1975). Unfortunately, the Danish and German terms *stat* and *Staat* have considerably more anachronistic connotations. The English term "realm" has been proposed for use in this context, but there are comparable problems with this word. It is not in widespread use in modern English. It derives from a medieval French word meaning "kingdom", but the Oxford English Dictionary shows that since the 19th century its use has been primarily rhetorical or poetical, while in modern English it tends to be used mostly to refer to some "sphere" or "domain", often abstract. In many cases words such as "polity", "political", "political territory" or "territorial polity" could represent the appropriate concept without presupposing a particular relationship to the nation-state of modern history.' (Pers. comm. John Hines).

4 To be fair, it should be pointed out that the area around Spjellerup Præstegårdsmark has never been subjected to such an intensive series of investigations as was the case at Himlingøje.

5 The presentation of the grave sites from Copenhagen's West District has provided significant further support for this assumption (Boye & Lund Hansen 2009).

6 In the classification, no account has been taken of whether the graves are male or female.

7 These ideas are explained in more detail in Boye & Lund Hansen (2009).

Warrior aristocracy and village community

Two fundamental forms of social organisation in the Late Iron Age and Viking Age

Mads Kähler Holst

The Late Iron Age and Viking Age in southern Scandinavia is characterised by extensive social and ideological upheaval. These changes can be traced everywhere, from the individual farmstead up to the overall settlement pattern; they are evident in agrarian production, weaponry and military installations, ritual practices and the expression of power as well as in trade and crafts. In the course of these developments, a number of fundamental institutions must have been redefined, within the household, judicial principles and religion, as well as in the political and military organisations.

With such extensive changes occurring in a number of central social institutions, it is obvious that tensions and inconsistencies could arise. These developing institutions were not necessarily consolidated and adjusted relative to one another. It was therefore possible for different organisational forms to emerge in different regions and within different social domains. As a basic premise, therefore, we must expect Late Iron Age society to have been characterised by conflicting tendencies and parallel developmental sequences.

The intensive rescue excavations carried out in recent decades provide an increasingly clear picture of diversity and this is particularly obvious with respect to villages and the central places. The development of the village from the Iron Age to the Middle Ages was seen previously as having followed a unilinear course (Hvass 1988; Mikkelsen 1999), but now its history appears to be much more complex: There was apparently parallel occurrence of a range of diverse settlement types: some well-organised, with parcelled-out plots, others scattered and spatially unstructured settlements; some long-term and stable with clear farmstead continuity, others very labile with single-phased farmsteads; some consisting of uniformly-sized farmsteads, other demonstrating clear size and architectonic differentiation.

Diversity is also a feature of the so-called 'central places'. Starting with the hierarchical classification of these sites, as proposed by for example Charlotte Fabech and Jytte Ringtved (Fabech & Ringtved 1995), and the suggestion of a uniform spatial and functional organisation (Brink 1996; 1997; 1999), 'central place' has to an increasing extent become a catch-all term for a group of archaeological sites which, to a varying degree and in various combinations, are thought to be linked with the manifestation or execution of power, trade, crafts, communication and religion.

Instead of assuming the existence of a uniform social organisation that developed unilinearly through the course of the Late Iron Age and Viking Age, it seems therefore obvious to investigate the possibility of a differentiated and dynamic social structure within which different forms of organisation and interaction saw expression in different situations.

In the following, I will focus on two forms of social organisation generally considered to be of central significance in the Late Iron Age and Viking Age. The first is often summarised under the term 'village community', while the other relates to the military and aristocracy. Both forms have been highlighted previously in numerous contexts as being fundamental to an understanding of Iron Age society. The subject was dealt with explicitly by Lotte Hedeager in 1990 and, more recently, Chris Wickham has employed a distinction between a peasant and a feudal mode of organisation in order to characterise major developments in northern and western Europe and in the Mediterranean area between AD 400 and AD 800 (Wickham 2005).

There are, however, reasons for reconsidering the relationship between village communities and military-aristocratic organisations. In previous studies the tendency has been to see these two organisational forms from a hierarchical and evolutionary perspective; the agrarian peasant society of the Late Iron Age thereby represented an earlier organisational form that came under pressure from an established central or feudal power. In practice, this means that agrarian communities are ascribed very little influence on the overall historical development of societies. This point of view is prevalent throughout the various tribe-to-state projects and also features markedly in Wickham's work, in which his peasant mode of organisation is portrayed almost as a kind of historical dead end that, after AD 800, survived in the form of scattered relics in politically and economically isolated refugia (Mortensen & Rasmussen 1988; 1991; Wickham 2005). Such interpretations describe a very clear hierarchical relationship that anticipates a feudal structure.

This scenario can be questioned, particularly with respect to the northern European lowlands extending from Drenthe in the Netherlands to Jutland. Here, the village appears to have been well developed at an early stage in the Early Iron Age and also to have been of a size and a complexity suggesting it could have played a more dominant role in the development of society than in other parts of western and northern Europe. The Iron Age village society was therefore not necessarily just a prelude to the politically and socially marginalised agrarian Medieval settlement. For one thing, it is possible to question the degree to which agrarian societies actually did become marginalised in the Middle Ages. For another, it seems likely that the organisational structures of the villages were transferred to many other aspects of Medieval society.

Another aspect evident from an archaeological assessment of the relationship between the agrarian society and the emerging elite is the sharp distinction made between the two. It is clearly seen as being possible to assign settlements, artefact types and graves to either one or the other of these two environments. In terms of interpretation, this results in a clear spatial and person-related division. This is, of course, a product of our archaeological methodology, but it seems important to highlight that this classificatory approach does not necessarily provide a true picture of past realities. In fact, the difficulties of maintaining the classificatory boundaries are also apparent from the increasingly complex and variable picture that continues to emerge from the ever-growing archaeological record. It could, therefore, be an advantage to our discussion to push the perception of agrarian communities and military-aristocratic organisations as actual places and people into the background for a while. Instead, we might focus on them as two abstract organisational principles, each bound up with its own norms and practices. This makes it much easier to see them as contingent on certain situations, such that they can potentially also occur outside their most obvious environments in, respectively, a village and a central place. The following discussion takes this as its starting point.

The argument that will be presented here is that agrarian communities and the military-aristocratic apparatus must be perceived as having been fundamentally equal. To a very great extent they were based on opposing organisational principles, but in practice there were many situations where these two organisational forms coincided and where, as a consequence, ambiguity could arise concerning the principles that should apply. This ambiguity provided certain opportunities and must have been central to the social dynamic of the relevant period.

It could for example have been a significant reason for the emergence in southern Scandinavia of a striking regional difference between the landscape of Jutland, where the principles of agrarian communities dominated, and the islands to the east, where aristocratic principles carried most weight.

Two organisational forms

The division between agrarian communities and military-aristocratic organisations is essentially an analytical construct. There is nothing whatsoever to suggest that either of these was well-delimited and well-defined in the Late Iron Age and Viking Age. Rather, they were two complexes comprised of material culture, norms and practices that often occurred together in concrete and tangible situations. They had some place-related fix-points and some individuals who were clearly their representatives, but neither people nor places can define these two organisational forms clearly. There was presumably an overlap in personnel as well as an overlapping set of rules, meaning that the village community influenced the military-aristocratic organisation and vice versa (Hedeager 1990, 136-138; Näsman 1988; 2006; Ramquist 1991). Despite this, the overall patterns in organisational principles suggest that village community and military aristocracy can justifiably be perceived as two relatively clear domains which, in their organisational principles, contained a number of conflicting tendencies and which were each bound up with their own institutions.

The military and aristocratic organisation appears to have been linked with the development of strongly hierarchical structures with associated social roles and formalised administrative divisions of larger regions. The village and the agrarian communities consisted of basic family units that were responsible for primary production and that followed their own organisational principles, not least as regards rules pertaining to private ownership. Both domains have, on the one hand, deep roots in the preceding centuries and must therefore be presumed to contain well-established and fixed norms; on the other hand, they both changed markedly in the course of the Late Iron Age and Viking Age.

The deep roots and the long coexistence of the two organisational forms make it necessary to consider developments from a long-term perspective. Processes of change appear in several instances to extend over the course of centuries, and in temporally more constrained studies this long-term dynamic is rarely caught. The nature of the archaeological record is such that it is often difficult to identify the time at which crucial organisational changes took place. Seen from a long-term perspective it is, however, possible to identify some general trends relating to change even without, in the first instance, being able to date these precisely. In the following, questions concerning the interplay between the military aristocracy and the village organisation will be addressed within a time frame extending from the transition between the Early and Late Roman Iron Age until the end of the Viking Age, i.e. from AD 200 to AD 1000.

The military-aristocratic organisation

It is open to discussion whether the military organisation can, and should, be separated from the aristocratic element in an analysis of Late Iron Age and Viking Age society. By all accounts the aristocracy had a number of functions that were not directly linked with the military organisation. This applies of course to religion and law, and an understanding of the role of women in the aristocracy requires that the military aspect should not be thought of as overly dominant. In a similar way, the military organisation extended beyond individuals who were members of the aristocracy. In this respect, the argument can be made for perceiving the military and the aristocracy as two different forms of organisation. To date, however, the archaeological evidence related to military organisation and aristocratic structures is so interwoven that it is almost impossible to make such a clear distinction. This is the case both with respect to individuals and functions. On this basis, the military and the aristocratic organisations are in the following assumed to constitute a coherent and integrated complex.

Military organisation appears to undergo significant developments in the course of the Late

Iron Age. Weapon types and their combinations change, as does the degree of standardisation, and this presumably reflects differences in the army's recruiting principles, organisation and combat techniques. Military facilities and the definitions of borders vary in chronological and geographic foci and also in extent, and this is presumed to reflect strategic displacements (Hedeager 1990; Ringtved 1999). The precise significance of these various changes is, however, uncertain. The relationship between standing militias in the form of house-carls or other retainers and an institutionally recruited army remains unresolved, and existing interpretations appear to be based on very slight evidence (Reuter 1997). A similar situation also prevails with respect to the size of the army. Some war booty sites perhaps provide relatively reliable indications of the scale of conflict, but it is uncertain whether these data are representative. Accordingly, the degree of integration of the military organisation into the population, and the settlement in general, also remains an open question.

It is possible to distinguish between two forms of military organisation in the Iron Age and Viking Age. One of these relates to offensive raiding tactics which are very clearly evident as plundering activities, not least during the Viking Age, but which probably had much earlier roots. This form of military organisation can potentially operate independently of the village community and appears therefore to presuppose a standing entourage of house-carls (*hird*) or army. The other form of military organisation is primarily defensive and is bound up with organised (domestic) defence, defensive structures and fortifications. This can be assumed to have been much more integrated into the village organisation. Its emergence and character are, however, the subject of much debate. Historians have had a tendency to perceive defensive military organisation as a very late phenomenon (e.g. Lund 1996), but there are clear indications that an institutionalised warning and defence organisation, in some form or other, had its roots in the Iron Age, at least within some of the Germanic areas. Such indications are apparent in place-name evidence, in early documentary sources relating to the Germanic peoples, in archaeologically demonstrated defensive works and fortifications and at war booty sites. Analyses of the latter have demonstrated an advanced level of organisation in the armies represented at these sites (Dobat 2008; Jørgensen 1988; Näsman 1997; Ringtved 1999).

Any understanding of the aristocracy of the Late Iron Age and Viking Age builds first and foremost on the evidence provided by graves and so-called central places. These sources, like the military record, undergo a significant development during the course of the period in question. However, developments seen in the evidence from graves appear to a very great extent to reflect changes in the general norms for the inclusion of grave goods, and this complicates any interpretation of the social development based on this source group alone. Its usefulness accordingly lies primarily in synchronous analyses within the individual periods. By the time in question, the central places comprised an extensive and complex group of sites with major significance for the interpretation of organisational forms. It is also clear, however, that there are still many unresolved questions associated with them. As yet for example we have no explanation for the breadth of variation seen within this group of sites and no answer to the question of how unequivocally each individual site can be linked to an aristocratic level in the society. As a consequence, the term 'central place' is only used in the following with respect to sites that, on the basis of excavation data and metal-detector finds, display clear indications of having occupied an actual role as a centre and having been associated with an elite. In southern Scandinavia this applies to places such as Gudme-Lundeborg, Sorte Muld, Uppåkra, Tissø, Lejre, Toftegård and presumably also Neble-Boeslunde. These are included as part of a wider category of metal-rich sites where functions and organisation remain as yet unresolved. The interpretation of the metal-rich sites will be discussed in more detail in a later section.

There are, accordingly, a number of uncertainties with respect to the interpretation of the military and aristocratic organisation in the Iron Age and Viking Age. Even so, the archaeological record reveals a number of clear tendencies, and it is possible to argue the case for the existence of a number of fundamental structures:

1. Hierarchical structure

The military organisation appears to have been built up hierarchically. The variously armed groups that can be identified in war booty deposits and graves suggest a well-defined organisational structure with differentiated levels of military leaders and warriors (Bemmann & Bemmann 1998, 357-363; Carnap-Bornheim & Ilkjær 1996, 483-485; Mikkelsen 1990; Nørgård Jørgensen 1996; 1999). This is also in accordance with historical-ethnographic sources (Myhre 1987; Ramquist 1991). At a more general level, the grave record displays both a qualitative and a quantitative differentiation, especially during the Roman Iron Age. This differentiation is often interpreted as an indication of a hierarchical social structure that applied more generally; the military hierarchy is not perceived as conflicting with, but rather as an extension of this social hierarchy (e.g. Ethelberg 2000; 2003, 272-300; Lund Hansen 1995). It is debatable how well-defined a hierarchy it is possible to identify on the basis of the grave data. Significant developments in burial practices and great regional diversity suggest some caution is necessary with respect to the often very direct interpretations that have been proposed (Henriksen 2009, 324-334; Rasmussen 1995).

2. Institutionalised roles and functional specialisation

As a consequence of its hierarchical structure and many specialised functions, the military organisation is assumed to have been characterised by its members having specialised roles and entering into relationships of mutual dependence. There was a close association between positions in the military organisation and titled political and social leadership functions (e.g. the king, i.e. royal power), as evident from written documentary sources relating to the Germanic peoples of central and western Europe. This relationship appears to reflect a fusion of political and military leadership, with better defined and perhaps more institutional roles in the military organisation than in other parts of the social organisation. This situation culminated in the coupling of military organisation with the kingship and the nobility in the High Middle Ages. There was greater variation in the degree of specialisation in aristocratic functions lying outside the military organisation, for example in religious, judicial and production-related roles. In analyses of the grave data there has been a tendency among archaeologists for the individual artefact types to acquire emblemic status as indicators of very specific roles (e.g. Ethelberg 2000; 2003, 272-300; Lund Hansen 1995). These interpretations build on a prior assumption that Tacitus, in his general descriptions of the form of Germanic society, also applied to southern Scandinavia in the Roman Iron Age. The validity of this assumption, however, is very much open to debate (Henriksen 2009, 324-334).

3. Patrilinear heredity

The military organisation was exclusively male dominated, and there are good arguments, both in written sources relating to the Germanic peoples and in archaeological interpretations of weapon graves in southern Scandinavia during the Roman and Germanic Iron Ages, for the positions within it being hereditary to some degree (Hedeager 1990; Jørgensen 1988; 1991). The earliest and clearest example of a hereditary position is seen in connection with the kingship; the king is always a member of a particular family (*stirps regia*) (Tacitus 7.1; Wenskus 1961). It is also apparent in a number of other leading positions in the Germanic military, and is evident in the Middle Ages among the nobility. Another tendency is the apparent favouring of one particular heir or successor with respect to particular roles and distribution of land. Although partial inheritance was maintained in principle, in these cases there was manipulated partiality.

4. Latent and periodic structures

The military organisation was not necessarily present everywhere equally at all times in society. Military roles were probably well defined and clearly linked with specific individuals, but activation of these roles would to varying degrees have been situation dependent, and often prompted by specific conflicts. This is of course most clearly seen in the defensive structure of a local militia. As mentioned above, the relationship between a recruited army and a standing army remains unresolved. However, even in the standing army roles would have been reconfigured in response to a conflict, just as the military leadership's sovereignty relative to the rest of society would be accepted more easily in a conflict situation. As such, the military organisation in some respects represented a latent structure that could be activated when necessary (cf. Wolfram 1988). The documentary sources also reveal that the military organisation had a latent structure – a perception underlined by the developments in, and character of, the military fortifications, where there was a late transition to more continual maintenance (Dobat 2008, 57-59).

5. Individual- and alliance-based prestige economy

In both archaeological and historical research, the uppermost level of the military organisation in particular is often associated with individual- and alliance-based political strategies (Hedeager 1990; Steuer 1982, 128; 1992). Examples of this seen in the documentary sources are retinues of house-carls (*hird*) or retainers and alliances sealed by marriage. In addition, the rich metal finds from archaeologically recognised central places are often linked with the giving of gifts and other kinds of 'conspicuous consumption'; these are similarly mentioned in the written sources as central elements in the social strategies of the elite and of course the king.

Village community

The village and its community is perceived here as comprising the complex of social norms and rules together with its architectonic manifestations that from the beginning of the Iron Age onwards developed via an interplay between independent but closely coexisting farmsteads. With regard to population, the village constituted the most extensive and complex settlement type throughout the course of the Iron Age and as such it became central to the development of obligations and rights relating to co-residence.

Although there was continuity in many aspects of the organisation of villages from the Late Iron Age and Viking Age through to the historically known villages of the Middle Ages (after AD 1000/1100), it is important to keep in mind that the village community was to a very great extent a dynamic entity that underwent major changes during the course of the period, with significant regional variation. The villages of the Iron Age and those of the Middle Ages were not necessarily the same as regards institutions, the character of the community and its regulatory principles. The term 'village' must therefore be seen as covering many different forms of organisation within these periods.

Throughout the Late Iron Age and Viking Age, the village community appears to manifest itself most strongly in Jutland, especially in the north and west, beyond the Weichsel moraines. The settlements here have the largest number of farmsteads and the most constrained spatial structures are evident, reflecting the most extensive regulation of the community apparent in the archaeological record. Differences in conditions for preservation could have reinforced this impression of regional differences; however, in the light of data now available from a very large number of rescue excavations in eastern Denmark, it appears that there are actual regional differences in the settlement pattern. It is the Jutish village studies first and foremost that form the basis for the following characterisation of the Iron Age village community:

1. Farmstead autonomy, role parallelism and equality

In connection with studies of the villages' organisational principles there has been intense focus over the years on the identification of large farms in Iron Age settlements. This has been motivated by a more or less explicit assumption that these large farms represented a special primus motor in the village communities – in other words, villages had a fundamentally hierarchical social organisation

(Ethelberg 2003, 197-222; Haarnagel 1979, 316-322; Hvass 1985, 175-182). It is true that there is an unquestionable differentiation in farmstead sizes. There are, however, a number of other features evident in the archaeological record that appear to undermine the idea of a fundamental hierarchical organisation in the villages.

First, there is the farmstead's architectonically defined autonomy. A recurrent feature of Jutish settlements from the Roman Iron Age onwards is that farmsteads are individually fenced and each contains all the necessary elements for independent operation: living quarters, byre, storage buildings and fenced (i.e. enclosed) farmyard.

On closer examination, the farmsteads are in general also remarkably uniform both in size and layout. There is clearly variation, but this occurs within certain definite limits, which are most obvious in the accumulated fence structures seen at large settlements such as Vorbasse[1] and Nørre Snede (fig. 1) (Egeberg Hansen 1988; Holst 2010; Hvass 1986). A picture emerges here of a comprehensive division of the area into uniformly-sized plots. All the fences making up this structure represent boundary enclosures. Consequently, the fence of each plot only functioned for a short period of time within the collective lifetime of the system of plot division. This is due to the fact that the plot divisions reflect an underlying field system made up of uniform plots, the boundaries of which were in the main respected throughout the centuries in the establishment and development of farmsteads. Even variations in size during the individual farmstead phases consistently take place within the boundaries of a plot until sometime in the Early Germanic Iron Age. From the Early Germanic Iron Age onwards, farmsteads incorporating two plots begin to appear, and it is probably a continuation of this trend that leads to the formation of the very large farmsteads of the Viking Age (Holst 2010).

Fig. 1. | *The cumulative fence structures at Vorbasse and Nørre Snede constitute a coherent site structure that was maintained throughout the settlements' 500 year history despite several significant settlement restructurings. After Hvass 2003 (Vorbasse) and Holst 2010 (Nørre Snede).*

The system of plot division also defines the size limits of the farms. The layout of the farmsteads within these limits is composed from a limited repertoire of building types and respects fixed norms about the positioning of these buildings within the plot and relative to one another. A degree of specialisation on the farmsteads is evident with respect to a few functions, for example ironsmithing. Otherwise, the general picture is one of pronounced parallelism in the functions executed on

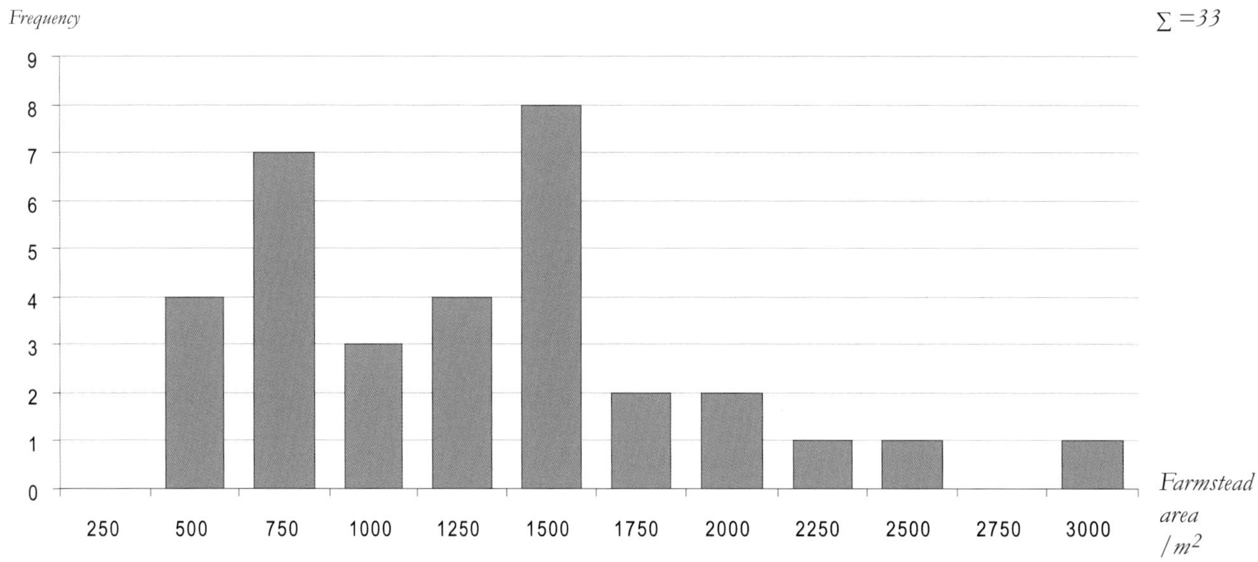

Fig. 2. | *Frequency distribution of farmstead sizes in a section of the Nørre Snede settlement dated to the 2nd to 6th century AD. After Holst 2010.*

the farmsteads. It can also be presumed, therefore, that there was a great degree of parallelism in social roles from farm to farm.

The uniformity in farmstead function and architecture and the limits defined by the system of plot division creates an image of a fundamental egalitarian structure. The layout of the farmsteads expresses a form of normative conformity rather than an architectonic striving to demonstrate power and wealth. In other words, it was more important to comply with the ideals of good housekeeping within a framework of mutual respect than to enter into antagonistic and competitive demonstrations of one's resources.

2. Institutionalised rights and duties

It is possible that evidence of further regulation lies hidden in the villages' fences. A study of the sizes of the fenced farmstead areas in the part of the Nørre Snede settlement dated to the Late Roman and Early Germanic Iron Age shows a tendency towards a bimodal distribution with peaks at 750 m^2 and double that area at around 1500 m^2 (fig. 2). This suggests a differentiation of the farmsteads into two groups. Moreover, the dichotomy does not simply reflect a distinction between longhouses with fenced farmyard areas on one or both sides of the building. A bipartite division relative to size can also be recognised at Viking Age Vorbasse in the best elucidated of the phases (phase 5), where the width of the crofts on the individual farms clearly falls into one of two categories: a single and a double dimension (Holst 2010).

This tendency towards a bipartite distribution can be seen as an expression of a modulated perception of the value and significance of the farmsteads, and it seems obvious to link this to Early Medieval valuations of farmsteads and land in Scandinavia, such as the number of *bol* (probably a form of farmstead count) in Denmark (Ulsig & Sørensen 1985) and the *marketal* (mark-value assessments) of the Faroe Islands (Bjørk 1957; Brandt 1996). It has been suggested that these measures originally reflected a form of basic value of a farmstead and its owners' consequent degree of influence in decisions within in the village community; furthermore, this value could initially only be subdivided to a limited extent. This view seems to fit very well with the system of plot division at Nørre Snede and Vorbasse.

The bipartite division of farmsteads according to size seen at Nørre Snede from the Late Roman Iron Age onwards can accordingly be interpreted as an indication that formalised differentiation of farmsteads has deep roots. Modulation of farms in this respect therefore occurs long before any suggestion of the buying and selling of farms and land (Iversen & Myking 2005). The division of farms into two size categories should not, therefore, be seen as a monetary valuation but rather as a modulation of their owners' obligations and rights within the village community, with a distinction being made between full and half rights. If this interpretation is correct, a very well-developed and strongly institutionalised organisational principle based on a form of distributional number existed in Jutish village society as early as the Late Roman Iron Age. The relations between households were accordingly not based solely on individual alliances and negotiations, but also to a great degree on formalised rules.

3. Bilateral kinship and partial inheritance

Kinship obviously constituted an important type of relationship within the village. The principles associated with the transfer of property in connection with marriage and inheritance can be assumed to have been some of the most important regulators of change in the villages through time, in that they influence both the establishment and the closing down of farms and any consequent redistribution of rights.

Kinship structures can be difficult to identify, and the Germanic legal texts (*leges barbarorum*) from the 6th to the 9th century AD show very significant variation. Even so, these legal texts provide a general picture. A strong bilateral element was a recurrent feature among the various peoples, although in matters of inheritance and especially the transfer of landed property it was often weighted towards the male line. In contrast, the female line is weighted in connection with the transfer of movable property on marriage (Murray 1983; Wenskus 1961). The bilateral element also emerges clearly in the Scandinavian landscape laws of the Early Middle Ages and possibly also in the runic inscriptions of the Late Viking Age and the Early Middle Ages, but it is of a very variable character geographically (Fenger 1971; Sawyer 2000; Sjöholm 1988). At the same time, there is also a clear ideal as regards the partial distribution of estates, i.e. equal distribution of the inheritance among those of each sex entitled to inherit. This applies to both *leges barbarorum* and the landscape laws.

The dynamic apparent in Iron Age settlements – with the progressive establishment and closing down of farms at new locations – in the landscape can be interpreted as a reflection of these principles. New farms were founded on entry into marriage and changed ownership following deaths on parents' farms (Holst 2010). Consequently, the toft divisions that can be recognised at several large farms of the Viking Age and the Early Middle Ages, first and foremost at Vorbasse[2] and Østergård, can be related to divisions and consolidations taking place as a consequence of inheritance and marriage (Sørensen 2000; 2011).

Interaction

When the fundamental organisational principles of the military-aristocratic domains and the village community are directly compared, a picture emerges of two very different – almost antagonistic – structures (fig. 3). This is of course in part a product of the division between the two domains being analytically constrained and focused on the main organisational principles. In practice, there is unlikely to have been such a clear distinction. There was, as previously underlined, frequent interplay and probably also considerable overlap with regard to individuals. We must therefore expect that situations frequently arose when the question of which organisational principles should be applied remained unresolved. The characteristics underlined here should accordingly be seen as optimum features – and as extremes at either end of a spectrum of organisational forms existing in parallel.

One important purpose for this dichotomy is that it can help re-evaluate social and settlement organisation during the Late Iron Age and Viking Age. Since the emergence of metal-rich sites, there has been a tendency to see the village community as a part of the military-aristocratic organisation. The villages and their farms have been perceived

Village and ownership communities	Military/aristocratic organisation
Egalitarian ideal	
Decentralized farmstead autonomy	Centralized person bound hierarchical organisation
Modularized differentiation	
Permanent organisation	Partly latent organisation
Normative conformity	Prestige economy
Parallel roles	Specialized roles
Institutionalized rights and obligations	Institutionalized roles
Bilateral emphasis	Patrilineal emphasis
True partial inheritance	Manipulated partial inheritance

Fig. 3. | *Schematic summary of the diagnostic characteristics of the two organisational forms.*

as one level – and a relatively low one – in a hierarchical political-economic structure. This looks like a backward projection of the village's politically peripheral role in historic times, when towns and manors had achieved a clear central position (e.g. Randsborg 1980). Such a view can be questioned on several grounds:

1. There is no geographic coincidence between well-developed villages and sites with spectacular aristocratic features in the form of great halls and exclusive prestige artefacts from the Late Roman Iron Age to the Viking Age.

2. The degree to which the apparent wealth of centres could actually be realised as assets in the villages is questionable. In societies without a well-developed coin-based market economy, barter and exchange of similar items and commodities – perishable foodstuffs for perishable foodstuffs, rights to land for rights to land, etc. – tend to be common. The actual value of prestige artefacts often lies in the fact that they remain within a prestige sphere, clearly isolated from the rest of the economy (Kopytoff 1986). Gold is therefore not necessarily a good measure of potential power and influence in everyday trade and activities in the villages; it was primarily a material reserved for symbolic expressions, not least within the environment of the hall (cf. Zachrisson 1998, 29-32).

3. The character of the exchange taking place between villages and the central places remains unresolved. Metal production at the western Jutish iron-smelting sites is suggestive of exchange on a relatively large scale (Nørbach 1999), and there are suspicions that no agrarian production took place at some of the central places. At the central residence in Gudme, this was perhaps the case as early as the Late Roman Iron Age (Callmer 2001; Jørgensen 1995). However, how the exchange was organised and the magnitude of the distances over which it took place are both very unclear.

Consequently, the village communities were – during periods without major, extended wars or conflicts – not necessarily particularly integrated into the military-aristocratic organisation. In the light of this, the theory proposed here is that the village community is better perceived in its own right, functioning according to different principles and to a great extent independently.

Another important point with respect to the division between the two organisational forms is that it underlines a strong internal tension between two different perceptions of what is right and fair. New explanations of the social developments that took place during the course of the Late Iron Age and Viking Age thereby become available. Social organisation did not arise exclusively via an evolutionary development consequent on a continuing battle between various competing petty kings of more or less equal standing, with a consequent gradual accumulation of greater areas under sovereignty and an ever increasing hierarchy (Näsman 2006). Social structures also unfolded via an interplay – both positive and negative – between the two different organisational forms. Their parallel existence would have lead to many situations where there was some ambiguity in past references and therefore an increased openness with regard to the development of hybrids. The theoretical consequence would be that many, often conflicting, organisational principles arose that were contingent on specific situations and also historically specific.

In the light of the above theory, episodes in which the two organisational forms collide attain a particular importance. This applies first and foremost with respect to long-term armed conflicts, during which the military organisation achieves a greater permanence and the agricultural communities in the villages are required to accommodate military activities. In these situations, a transfer of organisational principles from one domain to the other is to be expected, and this would probably be primarily from the military organisation to the villages. The defence-oriented military organisation, as exemplified by militias, can be seen as a product of this transfer – as a form of negotiated and institutionalised compromise – though the transfer is unlikely to have been stable.

In his analysis of the social organisation of the Visigoths in the Black Sea region during the 4th century AD, Ulf Näsman highlights the bipartite structure of Visigothic society. He then suggests a similar interpretation of contemporary Scandinavian society, with reference to the similarities in material culture and the possibility of cultural connections between the two (Näsman 1988). The Visigoths had a form of semidemocratic village council that was responsible for decisions within the individual settlement communities, alongside a tribal community led by a form of aristocratic council with a *reiks* – a chieftain or king – as its head.

Näsman follows the line adopted by historical research and suggests that there were two chronological layers: The tribal community and aristocratic council represent a later layer about to impose its power relative to the village communities. This perception of a chronological difference between the two phenomena builds on Tacitus' early identification of a form of settlement democracy amongst the Germans, but Tacitus also makes reference to a military organisation, centred on a *rex* (Tacitus 7.1).

As an alternative to the chronological segregation of village community and aristocratic council, the two organisational forms should instead be considered as having developed in parallel, each associated with its own domain and with old inherent conflicts, but adapted partially in response to one another, with a mutual dependent power structure, in which the dominance of the two institutions alternated through time.

It is debatable how directly and to what extent these Gothic organisational forms can be transferred to an interpretation of south Scandinavian society. Nevertheless, the description does capture some of the tensions that are apparently reflected in the archaeological record of southern Scandinavia.

Regionality

As more and more finds see the light of day, it becomes increasingly clear that significant regionality existed in the southern Scandinavian landscape during the Late Iron Age and Viking Age (Fabech & Ringtved 1991; 1995; Helgesson 2008; Ringtved 1988; Sindbæk 2008; Svanberg 2003a; 2003b); a regionality was to a very great degree associated with the division between village community and military-aristocratic organisation.

Some form of village community existed in the eastern part of the region, but constrained regulated structures appear not to occur to the same extent as seen in the west. Similarly, the size of the villages and the number of farms within them seem generally not to reach the levels apparent in Jutland. This picture is evidently also reinforced by the differing degrees of preservation. However, given the increasing amount of evidence that has nevertheless been unearthed on Zealand in recent years, the problem of representativity seems unable, in isolation, to explain the observed picture (Christensen & Tornbjerg 2009). This suggests that egalitarian and cooperative functions were better developed in the west. Conversely, expressions of aristocracy are much more conspicuous in the east. Prestige artefacts are clearly concentrated in the east and the hall phenomenon also manifests itself here, particularly from the Late Germanic Iron Age onwards, in a more striking way than in the west with earlier and a larger number of architecturally more conspicuous buildings (Jessen & Holst 2008; Jørgensen 2009). Dankirke, once described as a Jutish counterpart to eastern centres such as Gudme, Uppåkra and Sorte Muld, now appears to have been much smaller than the eastern Danish sites – in terms of both settlement size and finds – and more on a par with other Jutish sites such as Dejbjerg (Jarl Hansen 1990; Egeberg Hansen 1996). The sites in Jutland appear to form a relatively dense scatter along the coast, and they most likely represent farmsteads integrated in a trade network or magnate residences rather than large settlement complexes with centralised religious and political functions.

These regional differences appear to have had deep roots. If evidence from graves is taken into consideration, the eastern dominance of prestige artefacts can be traced back to at least the Late Roman Iron Age, whereas the Early Roman Iron Age perhaps had a more geographically even distribution of prestige display. From the Late Roman Iron Age onwards both the settlement and the graves at Gudme also appear as early representatives of a number of the features which later became dominant in the eastern organisational form. The well-organised village structure in Jutland can be said to have had its roots way back in the village-formation process, which took place at the beginning of the Pre-Roman Iron Age. At present, the village societies in Jutland during the Pre-Roman Iron Age appear to have been significantly more striking both in terms of size and indications of community. The latter is reflected in the local and periodic occurrence of common fencing (i.e. enclosures) around settlements and more extensive collective divisions of the landscape, involving field systems and landscape barriers in the form of so-called pit zone barriers being laid out at the same time (Mauritsen 2010). A little later, ditches and banks also made an appearance. The western Danish field systems are accordingly often characterised by distinctive continuous lines and suggest a larger-scale collective laying out of the land, whereas the corresponding eastern Danish examples have a much more natural character adjusted to the features of the landscape and with indications of gradual growth (Hatt 1949; Nielsen 2000). However, it was in the Early Roman Iron Age that rigidly organised villages with uniform parcelling out of the settlement first began to appear in large numbers (in the first instance concentrated in northern Jutland). With the transition from the Early to Late Iron Age, this parcelling out of land also seems to have encompassed field systems, for example at Nørre Snede and Vorbasse (Holst 2010).

These regional differences within Denmark are clearly also associated with some patterns on an even greater geographic scale. The eastern focus on halls and a prestige economy can be traced across into Sweden and to Bornholm, where Järrestad, Gamla Uppsala, Uppåkra and Slöinge all appear to underline the same set of values and the same employment of material culture (Jørgensen 2009). Conversely, the Jutish villages show great morphological, and thereby probably also organisational, similarities with northwest German and Dutch village settlements (Hamerow 2002, 52-80). This applies to the standardizised farmstead layout, the occurrence of large village communities and the plot organisation of settlements. As in Jutland, the NW German and Dutch area have revealed indicative glimpses in both graves and settlements of the same aristocratic expression that stands out so clearly in eastern Scandinavia; examples include finds from Wijnaldum, Sievern and the graves at Brokær, as well as the gold horns found at Gallehus (Besteman 1999; Rasmussen 1995; Zimmermann 2005). In general, though, such features are much less prominent here than in eastern Scandinavia, and they are also of significantly shorter duration at the individual sites.

These regional differences should not be interpreted as evidence that the military-aristocratic organisation existed solely in the east and the village community solely in the west. The individual organisational forms would surely, to a great extent, have existed in parallel in both regions, but there is little doubt that they were weighted differently in each. In conflicts between these organisational principles there was accordingly a regional difference with respect to which rule set was most often implemented and therefore came to feature most prominently in the archaeological record.

With regard to the military organisation, there is a particularly obvious and remarkable discrepancy between the relatively modest occurrence of prestige objects in Jutland and the marked dominance of actual physical traces of warfare in the form of war booty deposits in this area during the very period when the two organisational forms begin to crystallise out, i.e. from the Late Roman Iron Age onwards (Ringtved 1999). Many explanations are conceivable for this contrast, but one of the most convincing is that the duties of agrarian societies relative to the military organisation had already become institutionalised in these well-ordered villages, even at this early stage. Consequently, it would have been less necessary for the military organisation to manifest itself in Jutland and also for it to draw on personal alliances. Jutland's very rigid institutionalisation can be traced throughout the entire Germanic Iron Age and up into the Viking Age, at which time Klavs Randsborg has argued that the rigid structures may have constituted part of the foundation for the growth of the Jelling dynasty (Randsborg 1980).

A greater degree of domain separation is thereby suggested for Jutland; its military organisation was decentralised and rule-bound, as opposed to the eastern version, which was very much based on individuals. The eastern military organisation was apparently also tangibly confined to a specific site and heavily dependent on prestige and economically-based personal alliances. We are dealing therefore with two very different cultural regions which potentially had different kinship structures, different decision-making processes, varying degrees of institutionalisation, different forms of military organisation and different norms with respect to what was right and fair.

Metal-rich sites

In recent years, rapid growth in the number of known metal-rich sites dating from the Late Iron Age and Viking Age has made a crucial contribution to our perception of the society of this period and its spatial social organisation. Moreover, the very considerable degree of variation within this category of metal-rich sites is also becoming increasingly clear. This variation encompasses artefact types, categories of crafts represented at the sites, the character of the trading elements, spatial organisation in the landscape, links with other settlements, dates and duration and the seasonality or permanence of the sites. There were large settlement complexes probably comprised of numerous farmsteads that had an early beginning in the Late Roman Iron Age. Examples include Gudme, Uppåkra and Sorte Muld, all of which reveal striking expressions of wealth, religious functions and extensive crafts. Though the breadth of function was maintained, they were essentially different from a number of the sites dating from the Early Germanic Iron Age and Viking Age, which appear to have been built up around a single large farm with clear aristocratic architectonic expressions; examples of this include Lejre, Tissø and Järrestad (Christensen 1993; 2007; Jørgensen 2009). Other sites dating from the Germanic Iron Age onwards were completely dominated by *Grubenhäuser*, for example Sebbersund (Birkedahl Christensen & Johansen 1992), while yet other sites had a settlement element encompassing longhouses and other indications of farmsteads associated with trade and craft activities, for example at Stavnsager (Høilund Nielsen 2009; Høilund Nielsen & Loveluck 2007). Some of the sites appear to have had clear central functions and are markedly different from the other settlements in the hinterland, for example Tissø (Jørgensen 2002; Jørgensen & Pedersen 1996). Still other sites are grouped in a region with many similar sites of equal status, often located within a belt running along the coast as has been documented in the Aalborg area (Birkedahl & Johansen 2000; Christiansen 2008; Ulriksen 1989). In this way, we begin to see a differentiation of these metal-rich sites, suggesting other dimensions of variation than that accommodated within the hierarchies first used to classify them (Fabech & Ringtved 1995).

The hierarchical model of the metal-rich sites and the previously dominant category of the 'central places' are excellent examples of a tendency to interpret such sites as being associated with different levels within the aristocratic environment. This situation has arisen partly on research-historical grounds; the study of metal-rich sites has been borne by very spectacular sites, for example Gudme-Lundeborg and Sorte Muld, which encompassed clear aristocratic elements such as prestige artefacts and obvious central-place functions (Jensen & Watt 1993). Another explanation for this interpretative emphasize on the military-aristocratic organisational form may be found in the prevailing investigative methods. Metal-detector surveys quite naturally focus on the artefacts and these are easily used to compare sites and to find links and similarities between them (Høilund Nielsen & Vang Petersen 1993). This has led to a focus on the unique and spectacular objects, which are interpretatively linked to the aristocratic level of society.

These regional variations lead us to consider whether the metal-rich sites were also integrated into two very different broader forms of organisation – with a consequent difference in the weighting of functions in individual parts of the south Scandinavia. Prestige-economic, symbol-laden exchange is generally less striking in the archaeological record from Jutland; the spatial distribution of settlements here suggests a decentralised structure of closely-spaced sites linked via a new form of trade, which was also accompanied by an increase in certain forms of craft activity (Birkedahl & Johansen 2000; Christiansen 2008). The term 'central place' can only be applied in a very general sense to this type of site. There is nothing to suggest that these sites had a well-defined hinterland, with settlements that were unequivocally linked to specific trading or landing places. Such sites are also present in the east (Ulriksen 1989, 226f), but here they are accompanied by another kind of metal-rich site yielding high-prestige artefacts and, where these have been excavated, showing architectonic traces of the presence of an elite. This latter kind of site is more easily termed a central place. Furthermore, several of them also show marked traces of trade and craft activity. The coupling of trade and crafts with aristocratic environments may signal the beginning of controlled centralisation of the trade-based exchange network in the eastern parts of southern Scandinavia.

As a working hypothesis, we might assume that the robust village organisation of western Denmark, with its emphasis on the autonomy of individual farmsteads, undermined the development of actual central places, at least with respect to a classical centre-periphery model whereby the units of the periphery are unequivocally linked to a specific centre. This does not exclude the possibility of the sites differing significantly in terms of size, which in the absence of controlled centralisation could be the result of location in relation to main communication structures, trade networks and the interests of the members of these networks. The early emporia can perhaps be seen as extreme examples of this (Sindbæk 2007).

Consequently, metal-rich sites can be understood to belong to one of two regionally distinct organisational forms. The social preconditions for and the development of these sites were therefore very different, even when they yield relatively similar finds assemblages and even though they contributed to a common exchange network.

Parallel development

The idea that two or more forms of social organisation coexisted in Iron Age and Viking Age society is, as mentioned in this chapter's introduction, not a new one. The contrast between a (military) elite and an agrarian community was a central theme in a number of tribe-to-state studies carried out in the 1980s and 1990s (Hedeager 1990; Mortensen

& Rasmussen 1988; 1991). The understanding of the interplay and significance of the two domains has been heavily influenced, however, by a marked social evolutionism, which sees the village as a representative of a tribal society that was gradually superseded, following a time of upheaval and unrest, by a more developed early state formation represented by the military-aristocratic organisation. A form of paradigm-shift model has thereby arisen for developments occurring throughout the Iron Age.

A fundamental problem associated with this explanatory model was determining precisely when this shift took place. It has been associated with the appearance of the first elites in the Pre-Roman Iron Age (Madsen 1995); the marked reorganisation of the settlement, the massive military manifestations and the rich eastern Danish graves apparent at the beginning of the Late Roman Iron Age (Hedeager 1990); the appearance of aristocratic sites in the Germanic Iron Age (Høilund Nielsen 2005); and the extensive restructuring of the Late Viking Age (Randsborg 1980). All these cases assume the introduction of a form of centralised control or government of village societies and thereby implicitly a cessation of the self-regulating village community.

On the basis of the observations outlined above, it is obvious that many of the suggested dates for the shift from village organisation to central power result from an incorrect premise, i.e. the paradigm model in which there are two mutually exclusive, universal organisational forms, one of which gradually supersedes the other. There is another possible interpretation of the conflicts that occurred between village organisation and military aristocracy during the course of the Iron Age and Viking Age: That is, these structures continued to develop in parallel and under mutual influence, involving both conflict and cooperation, in a way that prevented either achieving secure dominance throughout the entire 1st millennium AD. As such, organisational forms were developed that were domain- and situation-specific. The increasing degree of variation that is becoming steadily more apparent in the archaeological record for the Late Iron Age and Viking Age also defies the idea of a successional development of organisational forms, instead implying a parallel development offering many opportunities for cross-communication.

Village organisation at the beginning of the Viking Age represented the continuation of a long tradition. However, it had undergone comprehensive changes since the Pre-Roman Iron Age and was therefore completely different from village organisation in the Early Iron Age. This process took place in parallel with developments in the military-aristocratic organisation, which must have been extensive over the course of the 1st millennium AD. It is therefore impossible to view village organisation as an archaic Iron Age feature about to be superseded by a new Medieval, feudal military-aristocratic organisational form. These were two fundamentally equal and parallel organisational forms – each probably more dominant in some regions than others, but generally able to maintain some kind of balance throughout the entire 1st millennium AD.

In the above discussion, boundaries and contrasts between the two organisational forms are thrown into sharp relief; further organisational forms and regional variations will probably be identified in the future, adding detail and subtlety to the picture. Nevertheless, village community and military aristocracy can be seen as the two dominant organisational types throughout the Iron Age and Viking Age. The interplay between them – in the contexts of both fierce opposition and more harmonious fusion and transfer – must be seen as a decisive factor in the dynamic of Iron Age and Viking Age society.

Acknowledgements

I would like to thank Charlotte Fabech, Andreas Dobat, Mads Dengsø Jessen, Ulf Näsman and Karen Høilund Nielsen for valuable discussions on Iron Age and Viking Age society as well as their comments on an earlier version of this manuscript.

Bibliography

Bemmann, G. & J. Bemmann 1998, *Der Opferplatz von Nydam. Die Funde aus den älteren Grabungen: Nydam-I und Nydam-II. Band 1: Text.* Neumünster.

Besteman, J.C. 1999, *The excavations at Wijnaldum: reports on Frisia in Roman and Medieval times.* Rotterdam.

Birkedahl, P. & Johansen, E. 2000, The eastern Limfjord in the Germanic Iron Age and the Viking Age. Internal structures and external relations. *Acta Archaeologica* 71, 25-33.

Birkedahl Christensen, P. & E. Johansen 1992, En handelsplads fra yngre jernalder og vikingetid ved Sebbersund. *Aarbøger for Nordisk Oldkyndighed og Historie* 1991, 199-229.

Bjørk, E.A. 1957, *Færøsk bygderet. 1ste del: Husdyrbruget m.v. Fotografisk genoptryk af stencileret udgave.* Matrikulstovan, Torshavn.

Brandt, J. 1996, Den færøske bygd i ældre tid. In: R. Guttesen (ed.), *Topografisk Atlas Færøerne.* København. 80-81.

Brink, S. 1996, Political and social structures in early Scandinavia. A settlement-historical pre-study of the central place. *Tor* 28, 235-81.

Brink, S. 1997, Political and social structures in early Scandinavia II. Aspects of space and territoriality – the settlement district. *Tor* 29, 389-437.

Brink, S. 1999, Social order in the early Scandinavian landscape. In: C. Fabech & J. Ringtved (eds.), *Settlement and landscape. Proceedings of a conference in Århus, Denmark May 4-7 1998.* Højbjerg, 423-39.

Callmer, J. 2001, Extinguished solar systems and black holes: traces of estates in the Scandinavian Late Iron Age. In: B. Hårdh (ed.), *Uppåkra. Centrum och sammanhang.* Stockholm. 109-38.

Carnap-Bornheim, C.v. & J. Ilkjær 1996, *Illerup Ådal. 5. Die Prachtausrüstungen.* Højbjerg.

Christensen, T. 1993, Lejre beyond the myth. *Journal of Danish Archaeology* 10, 163-85.

Christensen, T. 2007, A new round of excavations at Lejre (to 2005). In: J.D. Niles (ed.), *Beowulf and Lejre.* Tempe, Arizona. 109-26.

Christensen, T. & S.Å. Tornbjerg 2009, Jernalderbosættelsen i det gamle Roskilde Amt. In: J.-C. Eisen (ed.), *Mellem fjord og bugt.* Roskilde. 25-86.

Christiansen, T.T. 2008, Detektorfund og bebyggelse. Det østlige Limfjordsområde i yngre jernalder og vikingetid. *Kuml* 2008, 101-43.

Dobat, A.S. 2008, Danevirke revisited: an investigation into military and socio-political organisation in south Scandinavia (c. AD 700 to 1100). *Medieval Archaeology* 52, 27-67.

Egeberg Hansen, T. 1988, Die eisenzeitliche Siedlung bei Nørre Snede, Mitteljütland. Vorläufiger Bericht. *Acta Archaeologica* 58, 171-200.

Egeberg Hansen, T. 1996, Et jernalderhus med drikkeglas i Dejbjerg, Vestjylland. *Kuml*, 1993-94, 211-36.

Ethelberg, P. 2000, *Skovgårde. Ein Bestattungsplatz mit reichen Frauengräber des 3. Jhs. n. Chr. auf Seeland.* København.

Ethelberg, P. 2003, Gården og landsbyen i jernalder og vikingetid (500 f. Kr. – 1000 e. Kr.). In: P. Ethelberg, N. Hardt, B. Poulsen & A.B. Sørensen, *Det sønderjyske landbrugs historie. Jernalder, vikingetid og middelalder.* Haderslev. 123-373.

Fabech, C. & J. Ringtved (eds.) 1991, *Samfundsorganisation og regional variation. Norden i romersk jernalder og folkevandringstid. Beretning fra 1. nordiske jernaldersymposium på Sandbjerg slot 11.-15. april 1989.* Højbjerg.

Fabech, C. & J. Ringtved 1995, Magtens geografi i Sydskandinavien – om kulturlandskab, produktion og bebyggelsesmønster. In: H.G. Resi (ed.), *Produksjon og samfunn: om erverv, spesialisering og bosetning i Norden i 1. årtusen e. Kr.: Beretning fra 2. nordiske jernaldersymposium på Granavolden Gjæstgiveri 7.-10. mai 1992.* Oslo. 11-37.

Fenger, O. 1971, *Fejde og mandebod. Studier over slægtsansvaret i germansk og gammeldansk ret.* København.

Haarnagel, W. 1979, *Die Grabung Feddersen Wierde. Methode, Hausbau, Siedlungs- und Wirtschaftsformen sowie Sozialstruktur.* Wiesbaden.

Hamerow, H. 2002, *Early Medieval Settlements: The Archaeology of Rural Communities in North-West Europe 400-900.* Oxford.

Hatt, G. 1949, *Oldtidsagre.* København.

Hedeager, L. 1990, *Danmarks jernalder. Mellem stamme og stat.* Aarhus.

Helgesson, B. 2008, Kan regionalitet påvisas genom arkeologiskt fundmaterial? Några metodiska och källkritiska närmanden. *Hikuin* 35, 49-62.

Henriksen, M.B. 2009, *Brudager Mark – En romertidsgravplads nær Gudme på Sydøstfyn*. Vol. I. Odense.

Høilund Nielsen, K. 2005, "...the sun was darkened by day and the moon by night ... there was distress among men ..." – on social and political development in 5th- to 7th-century southern Scandinavia. *Studien zur Sachsenforschung* 15, 247-85.

Høilund Nielsen, K. 2009, Stavnsager 400-1100: Weiler, Zentralort, Herrenhof. In: S. Brather, D. Geuenich & C. Huth (eds.), *Historia archaeologica: Festschrift für Heiko Steuer zum 70. Geburtstag*. Berlin. 415-33.

Høilund Nielsen, K. & C.P. Loveluck 2007, Fortid og fremtid på Stavnsager – om de britiske undersøgelser august 2005 og de foreløbige resultater. *Kulturhistorisk Museum Randers Årbog* 2006, 63-79.

Høilund Nielsen, K. & P. Vang Petersen 1993, Detector finds. In: S. Hvass & B. Storgaard (eds.), *Digging into the past: 25 years of archaeology in Denmark*. Copenhagen/Højbjerg. 223-27.

Holst, M.K. 2010, Inconstancy and stability: large and small farmsteads in the village of Nørre Snede (central Jutland) in the first millennium AD. *Siedlungs- und Küstenforschung im südlichen Nordseegebiet* 33, 155-79.

Hvass, S. 1985, *Hodde. Et vestjysk landsbysamfund fra ældre jernalder*. København.

Hvass, S. 1986, Vorbasse. Eine Dorfsiedlung während des 1. Jahrtausends n. Chr. in Mitteljütland, Dänemark. *Bericht der römisch-germanischen Kommission* 67, 529-42.

Hvass, S. 1988, Jernalderens bebyggelse. In: P. Mortensen & B.M. Rasmussen (eds.), *Fra Stamme til Stat i Danmark. 1. Jernalderens stammesamfund*. Højbjerg. 53-92.

Iversen, T. & J.R. Myking (eds.) 2005, *Land, lords and peasants: peasents' rights to control land in the Middle Ages and the Early Modern Period – Norway, Scandinavia and the Alpine Region*. Trondheim.

Jarl Hansen, H. 1990, Dankirke. Jernalderboplads og rigdomscenter. Oversigt over udgravningerne 1965-1970. *Kuml* 1988-89, 201-47.

Jensen, S. & M. Watt 1993, Trading sites and central places. In: S. Hvass & B. Storgaard (eds.), *Digging into the past: 25 years of archaeology in Denmark*. Copenhagen/Højbjerg. 195-201.

Jessen, M.D. & M.K. Holst 2008, Om huse og slægtskab. *Jordens Folk – Etnografisk Revy* 43:3, 44-51.

Jørgensen, L. 1988, Family burial practices and inheritance systems. The development of an Iron Age society from 500 BC to AD 1000 on Bornholm, Denmark. *Acta Archaeologica* 58, 17-53.

Jørgensen, L. 1991, Våbengrave og krigeraristokrati. Etableringen af en centralmagt på Bornholm i 6.-8. årh. In: P. Mortensen & B.M. Rasmussen (eds.), *Fra Stamme til Stat i Danmark 2. Høvdingesamfund og Kongemagt*. Højbjerg. 109-25.

Jørgensen, L. 1995, The warrior aristocracy of Gudme: The emergence of landed aristocracy in Late Iron Age Denmark? In: H.G. Resi (ed.), *Produksjon og samfunn. Om erverv, spesialisering og bosetning i Norden i 1. årtusen e. Kr.* Oslo. 205-20.

Jørgensen, L. 2002, Kongsgård – kultsted – marked. Overvejelser omkring Tissøkompleksets struktur og funktion. In: K. Jennbert, A. Andrén, & C. Raudvere (eds.), *Plats och praxis. Studier av nordisk förkristen ritual*. Lund. 215-47.

Jørgensen, L. 2009, Pre-Christian cult at aristocratic residences and settlement complexes in southern Scandinavia in the 3rd to 10th centuries AD. In: U.v. Freeden, H. Friesinger & E. Wamers (eds.), *Glaube, Kult und Herrschaft. Phänomene des Religiösen im 1. Jahrtausend n. Chr. in Mittel- und Nordeuropa*. Bonn. 329-54.

Jørgensen, L. & L. Pedersen 1996, Vikinger ved Tissø. Gamle og nye fund fra et handels- og håndværkscenter. *Nationalmuseets Arbejdsmark* 1996, 22-36.

Jørgensen, M.S. 1988, Vej, vejstrøg og vejspærring. Jernalderens landfærdsel. In: P. Mortensen & B.M. Rasmussen (eds.), *Fra Stamme til Stat i Danmark 1. Jernalderens stammesamfund*. Højbjerg. 101-16.

Kopytoff, I. 1986, The cultural biography of things. In: A. Appadurai (ed.), *The social life of things: commodities in cultural perspective*. Cambridge. 64-91.

Lund, N. 1996, *Lið, leding og landeværn. Hær og samfund i Danmark i ældre middelalder*. Roskilde.

Lund Hansen, U. 1995, *Himlingøje – Seeland – Europa. Ein Gräberfeld der jüngeren römischen Kaiserzeit auf Seeland, seine Bedeutung und internationalen Beziehungen*. København.

Madsen, O. 1995, Produktion, bebyggelse og samfundsorganisation i sen førromersk og ældre romersk jernalder. Et midtjysk eksempel. In: H.G. Resi (ed.), *Produksjon og samfunn. Om erverv, specialisering og bosetning i Norden i 1. årtusen e. Kr.* Oslo. 183-203.

Mauritsen, E.S. 2010, Brændgaards Hede. A settlement surrounded by pit zone fortification from the early Pre-Roman Iron Age in Denmark. In: M. Meyer (ed.), *Haus – Gehöft – Weiler – Dorf: Siedlungen der vorrömischen Eisenzeit im nördlichen Mitteleuropa. Internationale Tagung an der Freien Universität Berlin vom 20.-23. März 2009.* Rahden/Westf. 262-80.

Mikkelsen, D.K. 1990, To ryttergrave fra ældre romersk jernalder – den ene med tilhørende bebyggelse. *Kuml* 1988-89, 143-99.

Mikkelsen, D.K. 1999, Single farm or village? Reflections on the settlement structure of the Iron Age and the Viking period. In: C. Fabech & J. Ringtved (eds.), *Settlement and landscape. Proceedings of a conference in Århus, Denmark, May 4-7 1998.* Højbjerg. 177-93.

Mortensen, P. & B.M. Rasmussen (eds.) 1988, *Fra stamme til stat i Danmark. 1. Jernalderens stammesamfund.* Højbjerg.

Mortensen, P. & B.M. Rasmussen (eds.) 1991, *Fra Stamme til Stat i Danmark, 2. Høvdingesamfund og Kongemagt.* Højbjerg.

Murray, A.C. 1983, *Germanic kinship structures. Studies in law and society in Antiquity and the Early Middle Ages.* Toronto.

Myhre, B. 1987, Chieftains' graves and chiefdom territories in south Norway in the Migration period. *Studien zur Sachsenforschung* 6, 169-87.

Näsman, U. 1988, Analogislutning i nordisk jernalderarkæologi. In: P. Mortensen & B.M. Rasmussen (eds.), *Fra stamme til stat i Danmark 1. Jernalderens stammesamfund.* Højbjerg. 123-40.

Näsman, U. 1997, Strategies and tactics in Migration period defence. In: A.N. Jørgensen & B.L. Clausen (eds.), *Military aspects of Scandinavian society in a European perspective AD 1-1300.* København. 146-55.

Näsman, U. 2006, Danerne og det danske kongeriges opkomst. Om forskningsprogrammet "Fra stamme til stat i Danmark". *Kuml* 2006, 205-41.

Nielsen, V. 2000, *Oldtidsagre i Danmark. Bornholm.* Højbjerg.

Nørbach, L. 1999, Organising iron production and settlement in northwestern Europe during the Iron Age. In: C. Fabech & J. Ringtved (eds.), *Settlement and landscape. Proceedings of a conference in Århus, Denmark, May 4-7 1998.* Højbjerg. 237-47.

Nørgård Jørgensen, A. 1996, Kriger og hird i germansk jernalder. *Nationalmuseets Arbejdsmark* 1996, 84-98.

Nørgård Jørgensen, A. 1999, *Waffen und Gräber. Typologische und chronologische Studien zu skandinavischen Waffengräber 520/30 bis 900 n. Chr.* København.

Ramqvist, P.H. 1991, Perspektiv på regional variation och samhälle i Nordens folkevandringstid. In: C. Fabech & J. Ringtved (eds.), *Samfundsorganisation og regional Variation. Norden i romersk jernalder og folkevandringstid. Beretning fra 1. nordiske jernaldersymposium på Sandbjerg Slot 11-15 april 1989.* Højbjerg. 305-18.

Randsborg, K. 1980, *The Viking Age in Denmark: The formation of a state.* London.

Rasmussen, B.M. 1995, Brokær. Ein Reichtumszentrum der römischen Kaiserzeit in Südwestjütland. *Acta Archaeologica* 66, 39-109.

Reuter, T. 1997, The recruitment of armies in the Early Middle Ages: what can we know? In: A.N. Jørgensen & B.L. Clausen (eds.), *Military aspects of Scandinavian society in a European perspective, AD 1-1300.* Copenhagen, 32-37.

Ringtved, J. 1988, Jyske gravfund fra yngre romertid og ældre germanertid. Tendenser i samfundsudviklingen. *Kuml* 1986, 95-231.

Ringtved, J. 1999, Settlement organisation in a time of war and conflict. In: C. Fabech & J. Ringtved (eds.), *Settlement and landscape. Proceedings of a conference in Århus, Denmark, May 4-7 1998.* Højbjerg. 361-81.

Sawyer, B. 2000, *The Viking-age rune-stones: custom and commemoration in Early Medieval Scandinavia.* Oxford.

Sindbæk, S. 2007, Networks and nodal points: the emergence of towns in early Viking Age Scandinavia. *Antiquity* 81:311, 119-32.

Sindbæk, S.M. 2008, Kulturelle forskelle, sociale netværk og regionalitet i vikingetidens arkæologi. *Hikuin* 35, 63-84.

Sjöholm, E. 1988, *Sveriges medeltidslagar. Europeisk rättstradition i politisk omvandling.* Lund.

Steuer, H. 1982, *Frühgeschichtliche Sozialstrukturen in Mitteleuropa.* Göttingen.

Steuer, H. 1992, Interpretationsmöglichkeiten archäologischer Quellen zum Gefolgschaftsproblem. In: G. Neumann & H. Seemann (eds.), *Beiträge zum Verständnis der Germania des Tacitus* 2. Göttingen. 203-57.

Sørensen, A.B. 2000, Østergård. A medieval settlement in southern Jutland through time, emphasising the period 1000-ca. 1200. In: J. Klápště (ed.), *Ruralia III: conference Ruralia III, Maynooth, 3rd – 9th September 1999*. Praha. 156-67.

Sørensen, A.B. 2011, *Østergård – vikingetid og middelalder*. Haderslev.

Svanberg, F. 2003a, *Decolonizing the Viking Age*. Stockholm.

Svanberg, F. 2003b, *Death rituals in south-east Scandinavia AD 800-1000. Decolonizing the Viking Age 2*. Stockholm.

Tacitus, C., *Germania*. Translated with introduction and commentary by J.B. Rives. Oxford 1999.

Ulriksen, J. 1989, *Anløbspladser. Besejling og bebyggelse i Danmark mellem 200 og 1100 e. Kr. En studie af søfartens pladser på baggrund af undersøgelser i Roskilde Fjord*. Roskilde.

Ulsig, E. & A.K. Sørensen 1985, Om begrebet bol. *Historisk tidsskrift* 85:1, 110-16.

Wenskus, R. 1961, *Stammesbildung und Verfassung. Das Werden der frühmittelalterlichen Gentes*. Köln.

Wickham, C. 2005, *Framing the Early Middle Ages. Europe and the Mediterranean 400-800*. Oxford.

Wolfram, H. 1988, *History of the Goths*. Berkeley.

Zachrisson, T. 1998, *Gård, gräns, gravfält. Sammanhang mellan ädelmetalldepåer och runestenar från vikingatid og tidig medeltid i Uppland och Gästrikland*. Stockholm.

Zimmermann, W.H. 2005, Sievern. § 1 Archäologisch. In: *Reallexikon der germanischen Altertumskunde* 28. Founded by Johannes Hoops. 2nd ed. Berlin/New York. 368-74.

Notes

1 For details, see Hvass, *Vorbasse, en landsby gennem 2000 år*, available at http://udgravningsarkiver.ancher.kulturhotel.dk/vorbasse.htm (accessed 5.7.2003). Unfortunately, this home page is no longer accessible.

2 See note 1.

Find-rich settlements from the Late Iron Age and the Viking Age and their external contacts

Jens Ulriksen

In recent decades, the metal detector has completely transformed the archaeological record for the Iron Age, Viking Age and Middle Ages and our perception of the period between the birth of Christ and the Renaissance has correspondingly been subject to revision. Twenty-five years ago, the recovery of a few bronze brooches and fittings could attract significant attention; today, such finds are commonplace. The number of detector sites has increased markedly, as has the variation in artefact types recovered from these locations. The waste products from for example bronze casting and ironworking now form assemblages with ornaments, parts of weapons, weights and coins. Some of these sites are even designated as 'find-rich' without necessarily providing any definition of this term.

The extensive and diverse artefact assemblages seen at some sites are challenging when attempting to decode their function, status and position in the social order. Terms such as 'magnate's residence', 'centre of wealth' and 'trading place' are nevertheless commonly used with reference to detector sites. Artefacts of foreign origin in particular attract considerable attention. In the following, focus will be directed towards the indications of trade and external contacts that can be deduced from the archaeological artefact record.

Detector sites as study objects

'The mother of all detector sites' is Gudme on Funen (Jørgensen 1994; Østergaard Sørensen 2000; Thrane 1992). Southeast Funen has for many years been famous for its numerous hoards dating from the Iron Age, but the special archaeological status achieved by Gudme is a direct consequence of the introduction of the metal detector towards the end of the 1970s (Thrane 1994). By the early 1980s, metal artefacts began to be submitted to Odense Bys Museer and to the National Museum in Copenhagen in increasing numbers (fig. 1). Since then, the fields to the east of the village have been intensively investigated, not just by metal detector but also through excavation campaigns extending over many years (Østergaard Sørensen 1994).

The Gudme investigations are a textbook example of how detector surveys and excavation can complement one another. Excavations of find sites of hoards discovered by metal detector revealed that these typically lay in association with houses or fences. The abundance of detector finds of ornaments, fittings and weapons, combined with waste products and metal scrap, raised excavators' awareness with respect to fills in features and patches of cultural deposits in low-lying areas (Kromann Balling & Vang Petersen 1985). Through detector survey and sieving operations, it became apparent that finds could also be recovered from features beneath the plough soil (Vang Petersen 1994).

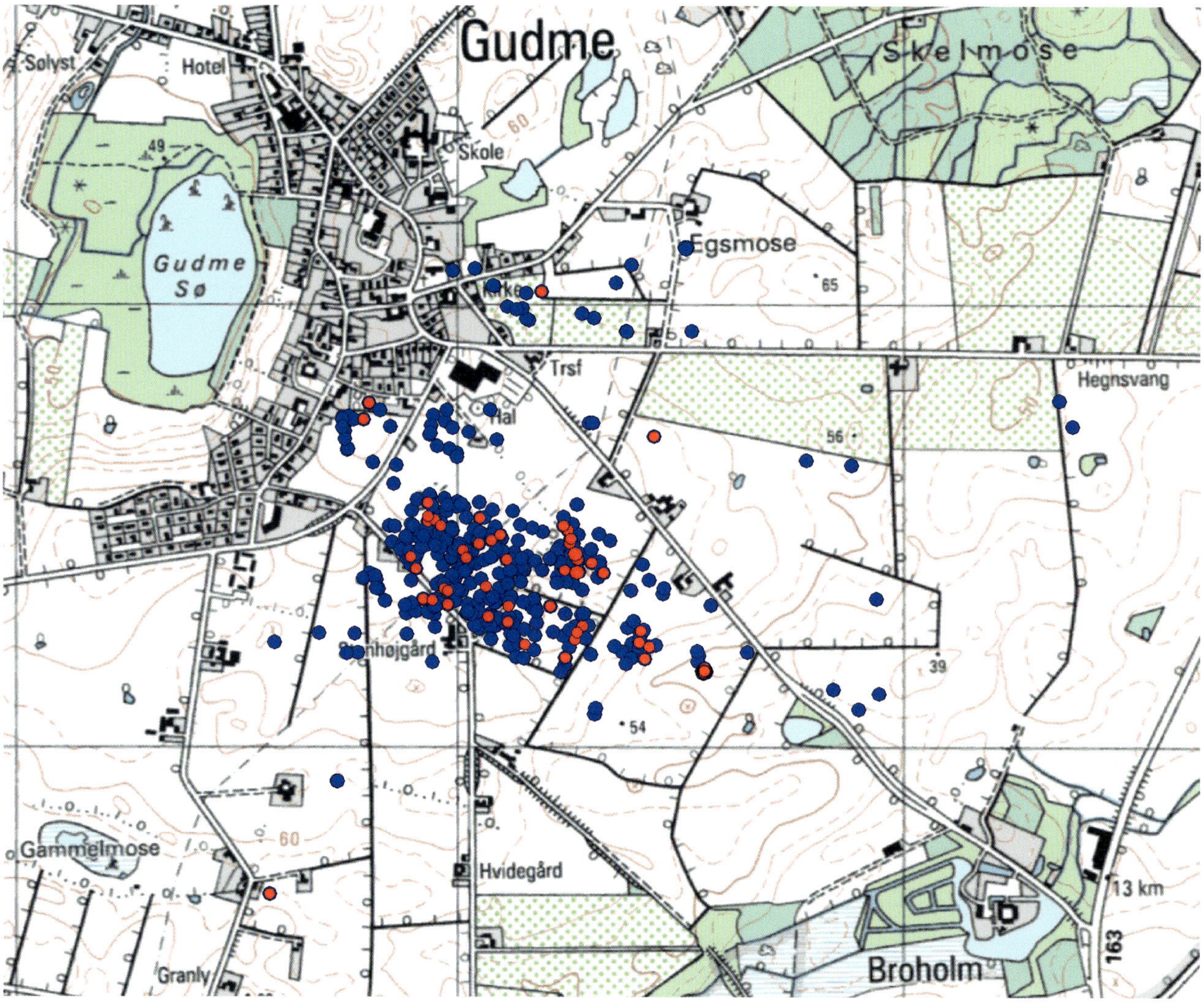

Fig. 1. | *Gudme. Distribution of detector finds from the 6th to the 11th century AD. Foreign artefacts are shown in red. J. Ulriksen.*

Since Gudme – and in parallel with the work carried out there – other sites have been discovered. A well-known example is the Tissø complex in western Zealand where, after a rather slow start following the discovery of a gold neck ring weighing 1.8 kg in 1977, research gathered momentum at the beginning of the 1990s. By 1995, the lands west of the lake, i.e. Tissø, had yielded such numbers of metal artefacts from the Germanic Iron Age and Viking Age that it prompted the National Museum and Kalundborg Museum to follow up the preliminary trial excavation of 1989 (Jørgensen & Pedersen 1996).[1] Extensive archaeological investigations and systematic detector surveys subsequently revealed an extensive finds assemblage originating from a chieftain's residence, complete with *Grubenhäuser*, workshops and what may have been a marketplace, in use from the 6th to the 11th century (Jørgensen 1998; 2000; 2003).

Gudme and Tissø are two of the most find-rich archaeological sites known in Denmark. Both have yielded numerous detector finds and attention has inevitably been focused on those artefacts that were manufactured outside Denmark. External contacts and their significance for these sites are prominent elements in the archaeological debate.

The excavations at Gudme and by Tissø have, over the years, been supplemented by numerous other investigations of Iron Age settlements of varying size that have yielded metal-detector finds.

Some sites were discovered by metal detector, others by traditional reconnaissance and excavation. A common feature is, however, that the fundamental dating and interpretational framework of Iron Age sites, based on evidence from the excavated house structures, fences and refuse pits, can always be profitably supplemented by a systematic detector survey. In many cases, such surveys have expanded and qualified our knowledge of Iron Age, Viking Age or Medieval settlements. Finds of metal artefacts often provide a better basis for dating, and detectors frequently locate artefacts associated with functions and contacts other than those indicated by the usual spectrum of finds, but which only rarely end up in refuse pits and postholes.

An example is a site at Kirke Hyllinge on Zealand, discovered by metal detector survey, where the stray finds were restricted to an area of 500 x 600 m. In a subsequent excavation, 17 *Grubenhäuser* were found distributed within an area of c. 220 x 300 m and, slightly off-centre relative to the detector finds and the *Grubenhäuser*, a longhouse and some three-aisled ancillary buildings (fig. 2).

The *Grubenhäuser* and the three-aisled buildings could be assigned to the Late Germanic Iron Age and the Viking Age. This dating is partly typological and partly based on the fairly ambiguous pottery evidence, but the *Grubenhäuser* and the cultural layers also yielded a couple of silver coins, a sheath suspension fitting, a strap-end and a trefoil brooch that could be dated to the Viking Age (Ulriksen 1999).

The detector finds contributed manyfold to the total finds assemblage. From the Late Germanic Iron Age and Viking Age alone, there are 170 artefacts, including 47 brooches, 30 balance weights and 26 silver coins, of which almost half are dirhems, with the remainder originating from England, the Frankish Empire, Germany and Denmark. The detector finds contributed a further facet to the site: While the building remains and the artefacts they contained were from the Late Iron Age, the plough layer contained no less than 180 metal artefacts from the Middle Ages. In particular, these comprised coins ranging in date from Erik Menved (1286-1319) to Christian I (1448-1481), but there were also lead spindle whorls, various fittings, belt buckles and so on.

The brooches from Kirke Hyllinge also included several types of Carolingian-Ottonian enamel

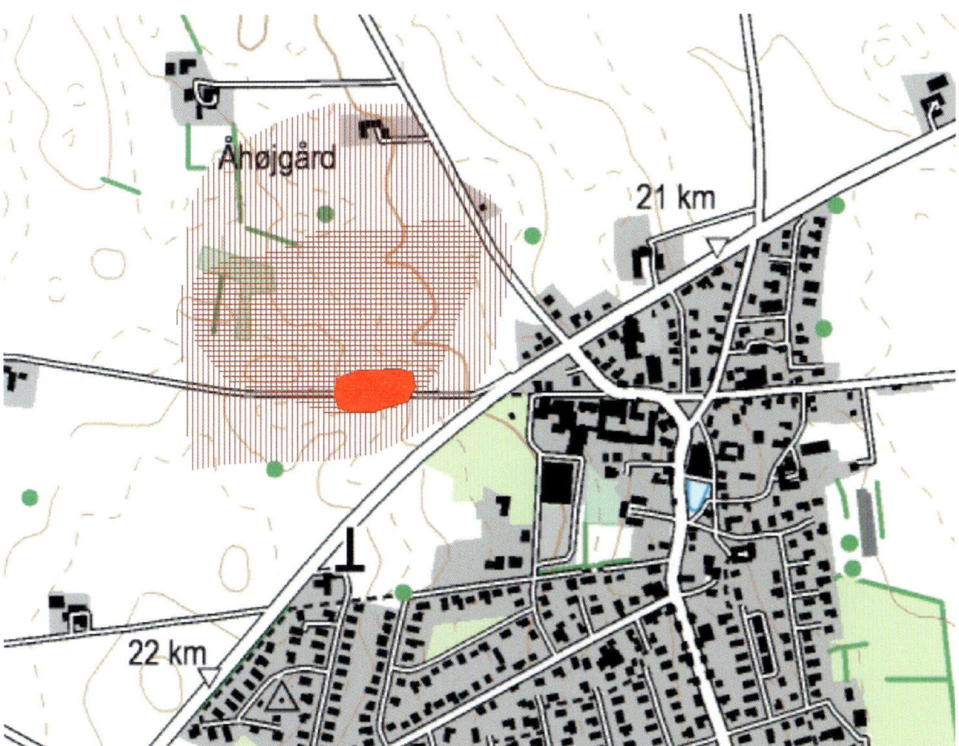

Fig. 2. | *Kirke Hyllinge. Distribution of detector finds from the Late Germanic Iron Age and the Viking Age (vertical hatching),* Grubenhäuser *(horizontal hatching) and longhouses (red). J. Ulriksen.*

brooches with cross motif, which were not commonly found in Denmark when the excavation took place in the late 1990s (Ulriksen 2000). The subsequent increase in the number of finds of these brooches demonstrates clearly the extent and speed of the changes to the archaeological record brought about by the metal detector. Ten years ago, there were about 30 examples from the whole of Denmark; by 2007 the total had risen to 47 (Baastrup 2009; Ulriksen 2005), and in 2009 it increased further with major contributions from the Ribe area, around Thisted and in the district of Hornsherred.

Enamel brooches with cross motif are just one of several find groups from western Europe that have become more frequent among detector finds in recent years. Another example is bronze stirrup-strap fittings dating from the end of the Viking Age; these were either imported from England or had found their inspiration there (Pedersen 1999). The small hooked tags with a triangular or circular plate bearing circle-dot decoration provide a similar example of an object turning up in steadily increasing numbers (fig. 3).

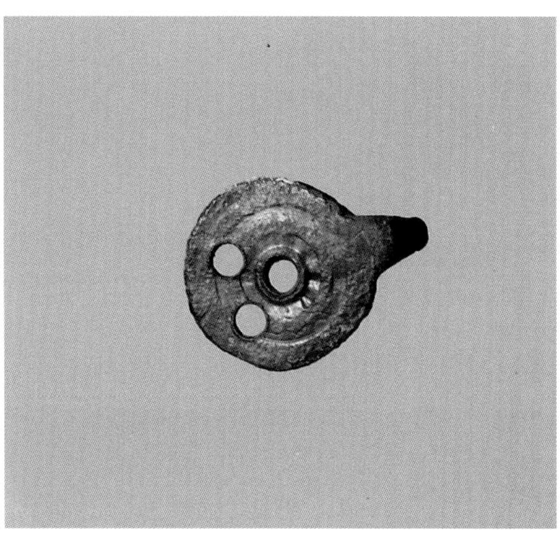

Fig. 3. | *Bronze hooked tags found at Kirke Hyllinge. Scale 2:1. Photo: F.G. Rasmussen.*

Exotica, imports and external contacts

There is inevitably a special interest in foreign artefacts, i.e. artefacts that were not manufactured in the area corresponding to present-day Denmark. How each individual artefact arrived here, and ultimately ended up in the soil, is rarely easy to determine with certainty. There are several ways in which external connections could have been established: through trade, plunder or the giving of gifts. Whatever the reason for their journey, artefacts did not necessarily travel directly from their place of origin to where they were found. Their journey may have been long, both in terms of time and distance, and objects may have passed through many hands en route: The same artefact could, in principle, have been traded, stolen or given away before it ended up in what is now Danish soil.

In order to evaluate the extent and significance of these external connections, it is essential to be fully aware of what, in a given context, is local and what is foreign. Imported items can be identified as foreign either because of the materials from which they are made or because their form deviates from that typically seen at the find site. It is important to remember that 'external contacts' do not necessarily correspond with places beyond modern Danish borders; connections between Bornholm and Jutland for example may have been perceived on a par with contacts with Vestfold in Norway, northern Germany or Gotland in Sweden. In principle, a connection between a tortoise-brooch workshop in Ribe, Jutland, and settlements on Funen and Zealand could count as an external contact. The matter is wholly dependent on where one chooses to draw the line between domestic and foreign.

In the context of the present article, it is understood that present-day Denmark, Scania in present-day Sweden and Schleswig in present-day Germany together constituted a culturally and stylistically coherent region at the time. Anything produced outside this area is deemed as foreign.

In Denmark, where raw materials such as metals and minerals have a very limited natural occurrence, these materials had to be imported to meet demand. All the gold, silver, copper, tin and lead in Denmark present during prehistory and the Middle Ages was obtained externally and artefacts made from these materials consequently represent a history of imports. This view is, however, much too simplistic. Though bronze could not have been made from raw materials available naturally in Denmark, people at that time were unlikely to have thought of a beak brooch or a tortoise brooch as an imported item. Moreover, metallurgical analyses indicate that Roman bronzes were extensively melted down and the material used repeatedly throughout the major part of the Late Iron Age and Viking Age. Following the collapse of the West Roman Empire, copper extraction suffered a marked decline and it was only in the 9th and 10th centuries that copper ore began to be mined again in the Frankish Empire (Jouttijärvi 2002, 37). Consequently, it was, to a very great extent, antiquated ornaments and fittings that were melted down in order to produce new versions of the same items. There was not, therefore, an immediate primary import for every piece that was manufactured. In order for a bronze ornament to be identified as an import, its form and style must be foreign.

It was possible to make iron from local deposits of bog iron ore. This took place during the Iron Age, Viking Age and presumably a large part of the Middle Ages (e.g. Voss 1991; Lyngstrøm 2008). In parallel with this domestic extraction, iron was also imported into the region, for example in the form of ingots and weapons. Other imported materials included slate for whetstones, soapstone for making vessels etc., and basalt and mica schist for quern stones. Glass, in the form of drinking glasses, raw glass and tesserae for bead production, similarly came from foreign parts and there are also records of imported pottery. It is easy to identify the Roman Iron Age's terra sigillata and the Viking period's Tating, Badorf and Pingsdorf wares as foreign. In other cases, the situation is less straightforward, such as with the apparently imported wheel-thrown pottery found in Ribe and Okholm; this has subsequently proved to be made of local clay (Feveile et al. 1998). The same is true of the glazed, red-fired ceramics from the 11th century, found for example in Lund and at Lejre. These are English in form and style but they were not made using English clay (Christensen et al. 1994). Some Baltic Ware pottery was undoubtedly imported but it seems likely that it was imitated at a very early stage in southern Scandinavia, though it is not known when exactly this development took place. Baltic Ware pottery is not categorised as being foreign in the present context.

There is a widespread perception that there was a difference between the importing of so-called consumer goods, for example iron ingots, quern stones and whetstones, relative to the situation for prestige or luxury items, such as drinking glasses or ornaments displaying a high level of craftsmanship and originating, for example, from Frankish or Anglo-Irish workshops. This perception is founded on the signals and symbols assigned to individual artefact types.

It is important to bear in mind that archaeologists' understandings of the value of prehistoric artefacts are unavoidably coloured by modern conventions. It is probably correct to think that gold and silver were also rated very highly in the Iron Age, but the lower prestige that archaeologists associate with consumer goods could very well obscure the fact that iron of high quality, well-chosen ship or building timbers or a barrel of Frankish wine could also have been prestigious and valuable gifts or commodities.

Table 1 presents an attempt at classifying the contexts to which artefacts of foreign origin may be assigned. This is a subjective evaluation, but it does seem likely that the borders between the various spheres were very fluid. Conversely, particular artefacts or materials – some perhaps considered as taboo – may have been linked to discrete groups in society.

Prestige level 1 comprises leaders – kings or chieftains – who had personal alliances outside the regional area as well as what would be referred to in modern terms as 'diplomatic links'. Prestige level 2 comprises people linked to the kings or chieftains in prestige level 1 through personal associations. One can well imagine the giving of gifts from level 1 to level 2, including the category of the marriage

	Raw material	Utilitarian object	Prestige level 1	Prestige level 2	Diplomacy	Plunder	Dowry
Iron	x		x	x	x		
Tin	x						
Lead	x						
Copper	x						
Gold	x		x		x	x	x
Silver	x		x		x	x	x
Slate	x						
Timber	x						
Whetstone (slate)		x					
Soapstone		x		x			
Basalt		x		x			
Slate with garnets		x		x			
Pottery		x	x	x	x		(x)
Barrels		x	(x)	(x)	(x)	(x)	
Jewellery		x	x	x	x	x	x
Weaponry		x	x	x	x	x	
Mounts		x	x	x	x	x	x
Riding gear		x	x	x	x	x	
Clothing		x	x	x	x	x	x

Table 1. | *Imported artefacts and raw materials according to their usage.*

gift/dowry; weddings would have resulted in the transfer between the parties and their families of the rights to use land or other resources, as well as of valuable objects. Similarly, the bride would have brought her trousseau into her new household. The upper echelons of society could have seen marriages between people from different regions, and this is sometimes evident in the archaeological record, for example from ornaments (Lund Hansen 1995, 213). Some foreign objects may well have arrived in the form of plunder or booty and this category would have involved the same types of object as are seen in the prestige spheres.

An important aspect in understanding external contacts involves interpreting the character of such contacts. If 'imports' were not the result of robbery, then something else must have been given in exchange. They could represent payment by a foreign prince for personal service, or they may have been gifts exchanged in the forging or maintenance of an alliance, or they may simply have been bought and paid for in a modern sense with silver or gold, though other means of value and bartering would also have been employed. The latter could have taken the form of a surplus from agricultural production (hides, meat, live cattle, sheep or horses etc.), fishing or hunting; textiles, tools and ornaments would also have been bartered, as well as refined raw materials in the form of semi-finished goods. Neither should the trade in thralls be forgotten. If we are to believe Gregor of Tours's description of a Danish attack in Gaul, this was already part of the system in the 6th century; prisoners are mentioned on a par with other booty (Gregor of Tours/I.P. Jacobsen 1911-13, 159).

Agricultural wares are difficult or completely impossible to detect archaeologically. Conversely, the refuse resulting from various craft activities seen at many find-rich sites may indicate commodities being produced for trade. For example, there is evidence of textile production: Local raw

	Late Germanic Iron Age/Viking Age Number	Imports	Coins	Weights	Find area in hectares
Hjulby N = 457	101	2%	1%	3%	29
Veddelevgård N = 61	26	-	24%	8%	7
Øm-Gammeltoft N = 116	37	9%	8%	8%	12
Glim N = 139	43	2%	9%	14%	19
Kr. Hyllinge-Stensgård N = 396	150	4%	17%	20%	20
Kunderslev N = 331	78	4%	9%	15%	18
Hennings Mark, Græse N = 138	32	3%	34%	22%	6
Lejre N = 393	345	4%	0.5%	8%	16
Vester Egesborg N = 492	357	1%	11%	6%	6.2
Selsø-Vestby N = 194	32	6%	6%	19%	4
Sønderø N = 44	29	3%	3%	21%	2.5
Gudme N = 2269	301	2%	17%	6%	152

Table 2. | *Detector finds from the 6th to the 11th century according to imports, coins and weights.*

materials such as wool or flax could have been processed for the purpose of being sold on. Bog iron ore was another local resource that may have been exploited for trade, and waste from iron refining support this conclusion. A number of the find-rich sites may well prove to be craft or production sites rather than 'magnate's residences', 'centres of wealth' or 'trading places'.

Foreign artefacts attract attention when they turn up in a Danish context, but their actual number is relatively small when compared with that of domestic artefacts from the same sites.

A selection of detector sites on Zealand and Funen serves to illustrate this situation (table 2).[2] One should be aware that when the total number of finds is less than 100, the addition or subtraction of a single artefact makes a relatively large difference to the percentages. Moreover, it is important that the recording methods are fairly uniform across the excavated sites involved. For example, there are museums that record all the potsherds from a feature under the same finds number, while others separate the recovered pottery into rim sherds, side sherds, ornamented side sherds and base sherds. This results in a significant difference between the total finds numbers obtained and obviously has consequences when percentages are calculated on the basis of finds numbers. Despite these problems, the table clearly shows the tendency for the proportion of imported artefacts to be relatively limited, i.e. less than 5 %. This applies also to Gudme, when the very extensive finds assemblages from the Roman Iron Age and Early Germanic Iron Age are excluded.

	Vessel glass	Slate	Basalt	Slate with garnets	Soapstone	Percentage of total
Kirke Hyllinge-Stensgård N = 591	0	5	2	0	3	1.7%
Lejre N = 3100	1	8	0	4	14	0.9%
Næs N = 1071	1	10	0	0	12	2.1%
Vester Egesborg N = 3305	11	45	10	0	23	2.7%
Selsø-Vestby N = 4616	3	-	4	2	8	0.4%
Strandby-Gammeltoft N = 2848	(1)	10	39	0	1	1.8%
Sønderø N = 215	0	0	0	0	0	0%

Table 3. | *Foreign artefacts from the 6th to the 11th century from excavated features.*

In the case of detector sites that have also been excavated, it transpires that the proportion of foreign artefacts is either roughly equal to or less than that outlined above, but never greater (table 3). This also applies to sites as special and significant as Lundeborg, where 550 foreign artefacts were recorded out of a total of 12 000 finds. This corresponds to 4.5 %.[3] Overall, foreign artefacts are rare.

Another aspect that becomes apparent when the data are studied in detail is the development in the number and diversity of foreign artefacts that took place in Denmark during the course of the 1st millennium AD.

Between the 1st and the 5th century, the number of foreign artefacts is limited and mostly comprised of luxury or prestige objects such as drinking glasses, weapons and tableware. In addition to these there are glass beads, coins and a small proportion of ornaments, fittings and so on. Apart from the coins and a small number of the brooches, most of the foreign artefacts were found in graves and bog offerings. There are also finds from a handful of special settlements such as Gudme, Sorte Muld (Adamsen et al. 2009), Dejbjerg (Egeberg Hansen 1996), Dankirke (Jarl Hansen 1990) and Østervang near Køge (Tornbjerg & Woller 2000).

Artefacts from the 6th and 7th centuries are frequent among the detector finds. They come from settlements and what might be damaged graves, and they provide a broad impression of contemporary forms and styles. Consequently, when foreign artefacts only occur in very small numbers in these assemblages, such finds can be seen as representative of the general situation. This does not mean, however, that contacts were not developed at this time, but only that they were not expressed in the form of foreign artefacts, as was the case during the Roman Iron Age and the Early Germanic Iron Age.

During the 8th century the picture changes, and during the 9th and 10th centuries the transformation becomes still clearer. It was not just luxury and prestige objects that were entering the country; there were also imports of semi-finished goods and raw materials intended for further manufacture, including glass, slate, soapstone, basalt and iron. This change was revealed both through the use of metal detectors and in the excavation of settlements.

Specialised landing places as 'transit sites'

Due to Denmark's geography, more distant external connections required people to travel by sea. The hubs for sea transport during the Late Germanic Iron Age and Viking Age could well have been specialised landing places. As long as people have sailed, they have needed places to land; but it is at the beginning of the Late Germanic Iron Age that this special type of site first manifests itself archaeologically. The exception that proves the rule is Lundeborg, which flourished as Gudme's landing place during the Late Roman Iron Age and Early Germanic Iron Age (Thomsen 1994). As a consequence, traces of craft activities, foreign artefacts and weapons ended up in the sand over the beach ridge on which the site was located. It is true that a few brooches dating from the Roman or Early Germanic Iron Age have been found at other specialised landing places, such as Lynæs and Vester Egesborg (Ulriksen 1998; 2006), but there are no complementary finds of structures, pottery or other more general settlement evidence (fig. 4).[4] These do, however, exist for the 6th and 7th centuries, and there are often ornaments, production waste, pottery and animal bones preserved in the features. Sites from this latter period are not numerous, but they do occur at several places around the country (fig. 5), and all of these continued to be occupied into the Viking Age. To some extent, this period can be considered as the heyday of specialised landing places, the function of which ceased during the course of the 11th century (fig. 6). With the advent of the Viking Age, soapstone and basalt begin to appear on Danish settlement sites. There is an obvious connection between the increased numbers of both specialised landing places and imports of consumer wares, though it is unlikely that imports occurred in large enough quantities for us to speak of trade in modern terms.

The frequency of foreign artefacts is no greater at the specialised landing places than seen elsewhere (table 4), doubtless because there was no conspicuous consumption of imported items where the ships landed. Almost all of the landing places are presumed to have been transit sites, where wastage and loss would have been limited.

Exceptions to this are Lundeborg, Ribe and Haithabu and, despite the difference in date, Lun-

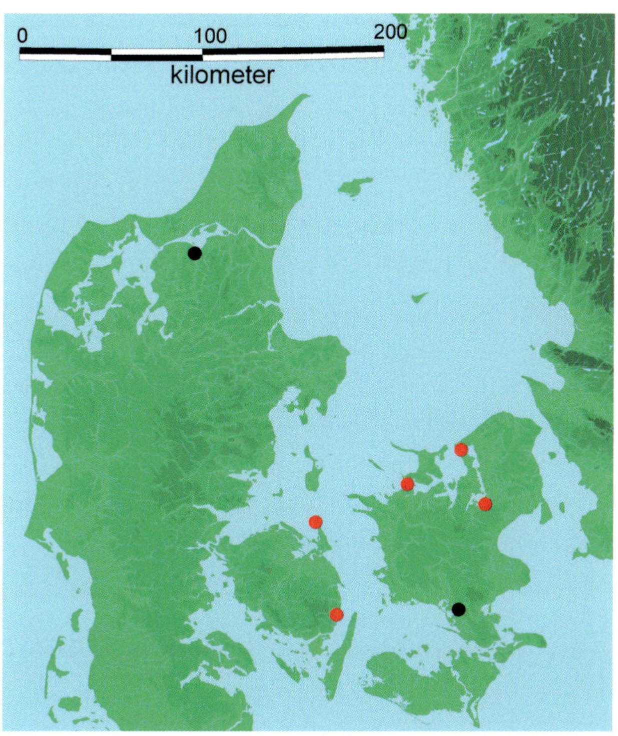

Fig. 4. | *Specialised landing place from the 6th to the 11th century, with single finds from the Roman Iron Age (red) and Early Germanic Iron Age (black). J. Ulriksen.*

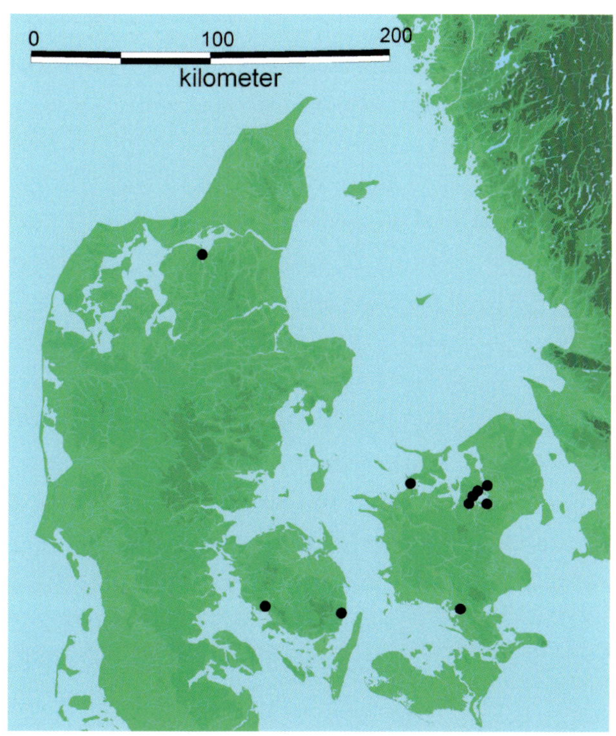

Fig. 5. | *Specialised landing places from the Late Germanic Iron Age. J. Ulriksen.*

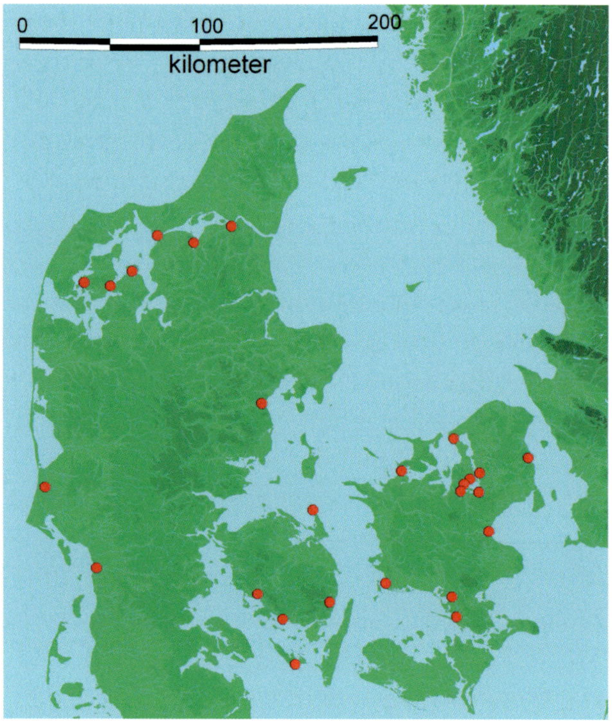

Fig. 6. | *Specialised landing places from the Viking Age. J. Ulriksen.*

deborg between the 3th and 5th century is reminiscent of Viking Age trading and production sites such as Ribe and Haithabu with regard to its activities and the quantities of finds. Lundeborg's mother site, Gudme, also looks towards later times with its magnificent hall complex.

During the Late Germanic Iron Age and the Viking Age there were monumental hall buildings at Tissø and Lejre – as early as the beginning of the 6th century in the latter case. Tissø can boast an artefact assemblage and a level of activity comparable with that of Gudme. However, we still lack a 'Lundeborg' both at Tissø and in the vicinity of Lejre, as well as at the third of the 'major' sites from the Late Viking Age on Zealand: Strøby-Toftegård on the Stevns peninsula (Tornbjerg 1998). The question is whether we should expect these important sites to have been associated with find-rich landing places during the 6th to the 10th century.

With reference to Lejre, no traces have yet been found of a particularly rich landing place either on Isefjord or Roskilde Fjord. Several sites have been considered as being particularly associated with Lejre, including Selsø-Vestby in the inner part of Roskilde Fjord (Ulriksen 1998, 42ff) and Gevninge, which lies a couple of kilometres inland on the river Lejre Å (Ulriksen 2008). These two sites have in common the fact that their finds and traces of craft activities do not stand out in type or quantity from the general occurrence.

In the case of Tissø, the river Halleby Å is thought to have been the main access route to the settlement; the workshop area in the southern part of the site, close to the river, is reminiscent in many ways of a specialised landing place. Traffic to and from the site by way of Halleby Å can neither be confirmed nor discounted. However, the river was not necessarily navigable for vessels larger than barges. Its fall is so slight that the current has difficulty in carrying the sediment, which is deposited on the riverbed; in time, this results in reduced water flow and difficult conditions for navigation. In the middle of the 18th century, Halleby Å is recorded as being 4-5 m wide, strongly meandering and overgrown with reeds, grasses and rushes, which frequently caused the river to shift its course. It also had sand banks and small islands which in places alternated with deep holes (Hansen 1998, 122).

One alternative access route may have been via a landing place on the Great Belt. The actual mouth

	Foreign objects as detector-finds (%)	Foreign objects from excavated contexts (%)
Næs	0	2.1
Vester Egesborg	1	2.7
Selsø-Vestby	6	0.4
Strandby-Gammeltoft	0	1.8
Sønderø	3	0

Table 4. | *Foreign artefacts at specialised landing places.*

of the river has been the focus of attention, but the area at Dalby Hals, south of the causeway leading to Reersø, is also a possibility. In recent years, several detector finds from the Late Germanic Iron Age have turned up here, but it is still too early to say anything about the character or active period of the site.[5]

The last of the three sites on Zealand with large hall buildings, Strøby-Toftegård, is not located in the immediate vicinity of a watercourse or on the coast. It lies 2 km from the river Tryggevælde Å and the same distance from the shore at the Strøby Ladeplads. It has been suggested that a nearby detector site, Kastaniehøj, functioned as the marketplace for Strøby-Toftegård, but the site has yet to be investigated in detail (Sørensen 2005, 32f). On Tryggevælde Å, there are indications of two landing places: one on the west bank at Vallø-Toftegård and the other, Prambroen, close to the river mouth (Rasmussen 2008, 99). None of these sites has, as yet, produced finds indicating the existence of an extensive and diverse finds assemblage, either with regard to artefacts or traces of craft activities.

Many kilometres of coast and riverbank have yet to be surveyed before it is possible to discount the presence of find-rich landing places in connection with the Viking Age's most important sites. As has been suggested for Tissø, landing places could have been located very close to habitation areas. Another possibility is that large, organised trading and craft places, such as Ribe and Haithabu, constituted remote 'transit sites' for settlements of this very special character and therefore had little need for their own landing sites.

Conclusion

Settlements yielding a large and diverse finds assemblage – in other words find-rich sites – are known from the entire 1st millennium AD. The external contacts of these settlements – expressed in artefacts – changed in character and extent several times during the course of this period.

During the Roman Iron Age and Early Germanic Iron Age these contacts primarily took the form of imports of luxury and prestige objects from the Roman Empire and the western part of the Black Sea area. The artefacts are typically found as grave furnishings, hoards and offerings, as well as at a limited number of settlements.[6]

During the Late Germanic Iron Age, the finds, in themselves, do not reflect the same interest in western and central European artefacts. Foreign artefacts are rare and contacts are evident to a greater extent in the inspiration craftsmen took from lands located to the south and west of Denmark. Paradoxically, detector-located bronze brooches and fittings, the raw material for which was initially imported, are much more frequent and widely distributed during the 6th and 7th centuries than previously. It is also interesting that it was during this phase that special settlements such as Tissø and Lejre became consolidated and specialised landing places emerged as a distinct type of site.

From the beginning of the 8th century, the foundation of Ribe demonstrated a targeted interest in trade dealings with Franks, Anglo-Saxons and Frisians. At the same time, the number of specialised landing places increased along the coasts. It was not just luxury items that were brought into the country; raw materials for the local production of ornaments, weapons and tools were also important. Similarly, imported articles for everyday use, such as quern stones, soapstone vessels and whetstones, appear in the archaeological record from the 9th century onwards. Even so, the quantity of foreign artefacts in the settlement assemblages is always limited, regardless of settlement type.

External contacts during the Late Iron Age and the Viking Age took the form of imports and exports of artefacts and raw materials as well as ideological influences that were interpreted and transformed so they fitted into the southern Scandinavian perception of the world. The finds from the detector sites and settlements appear not to reflect a situation where there was extensive and frequent trade with a large number merchants who travelled far and wide in order to sell their wares in the villages and farmsteads they passed on their way. Only in the 10th century do we begin to find signs that controlled trade came under pressure and was gradually replaced by a commercial economy commensurate with that in Christian western Europe, into which Denmark eventually became integrated.

Bibliography

Adamsen, C., U. Lund Hansen, F.O. Nielsen & M. Watt (eds.) 2008, *Sorte Muld*. Rønne.

Arkæologiske udgravninger i Danmark 1989. Det Arkæologiske Nævn 1990.

Baastrup, M.P. 2009, Småfibler af karolingiske og ottonske typer i Danmark. *Aarbøger for Nordisk Oldkyndighed og Historie* 2005, 209-55.

Christensen, T., A.-C. Larsen, S. Larsson & A. Vince 1994, Early glazed ware from Medieval Denmark. *Medieval Ceramics* 18, 67-76.

Egeberg Hansen, T. 1996, Et jernalderhus med drikkeglas i Dejbjerg, Vestjylland. *Kuml* 1993-94, 211-37.

Feveile, C., S. Jensen & K. Lund Rasmussen 1998, Produktion af drejet keramik i Ribeområdet i sen yngre germansk jernalder. *Kuml* 1997-98, 143-60.

Gregor af Tours, *Frankerkrøniken. 1.-5. Bog*. Bind I. Ved J.P. Jacobsen. Udg. af Selskabet for historiske Kildeskrifters oversættelse. København 1911-1913.

Hansen, P. 1998, *Bidrag til det danske landbrugs historie. Jordfællesskabet og Landvæsenskommissionen af 1757*. Fotografisk genoptryk af 1. udgave (1889). Ebeltoft.

Henriksen, M.B. 1994, Vikinger på Fyns Hoved. *Fynske Minder* 1994, 181-91.

Jarl Hansen, H. 1990, Dankirke. Jernalderboplads og rigdomscenter. Oversigt over udgravningerne 1965-1970. *Kuml* 1988-89, 201-47.

Jouttijärvi, A. 2002, Kobberlegeringer i jernalder og vikingetid. In: M.B. Henriksen (ed.), *Metalhåndværk og håndværkspladser fra yngre germanske jernalder, vikingetid og tidlig middelalder. Rapport fra seminar om håndværksspor på bopladser fra yngre jernalder*. Odense. 27-40.

Jørgensen, L. 1994, The find material from the settlement of Gudme II – composition and interpretation. In: P.O. Nielsen, K. Randsborg & H. Thrane (eds.), *The archaeology of Gudme and Lundeborg. Papers presented at a conference at Svendborg, October 1991*. Copenhagen. 53-63.

Jørgensen, L. 1998, En storgård fra vikingetid ved Tissø, Sjælland – en foreløbig præsentation. In: L. Larsson & B. Hårdh (eds.), *Centrala platser, centrala frågor. Samhällsstrukturen under järnåldern: en vänbok till Berta Stjernquist*. Stockholm. 243-48.

Jørgensen, L. 2000, Storgården ved Tissø. Tolkning af aktivitetsområder og anlæg på grundlag af detektorfundene fra pløjelaget. In: M.B. Henriksen (ed.), *Detektorfund – hvad skal vi med dem? Dokumentation og registrering af bopladser med detektorfund fra jernalder og middelalder. Rapport fra et bebyggelseshistorisk seminar på Hollufgård den 26. oktober 1998*. Odense. 61-68.

Jørgensen, L. 2003, Manor and market at Lake Tissø in the sixth to eleventh centuries: the Danish 'productive' sites. In: T. Pestell & K. Ulmschneider (eds.), *Markets in Early Medieval Europe: trading and productive sites, 650-850*. Macclesfield. 175-207.

Jørgensen, L. & L. Pedersen 1996: Vikinger ved Tissø. Gamle og nye fund fra et handels- og håndværkscenter. *Nationalmuseets Arbejdsmark* 1996, 22-36.

Kromann Balling, A. & P. Vang Petersen 1985, Romerske mønter, skattefund og jernalderhuse. Fra et rigdomscenter på Sydfyn. *Nationalmuseets Arbejdsmark* 1985, 194-206.

Lund Hansen, U. 1995, Analysen von Grabausstattungen mit Ausgangspunkt im Fundmaterial des Gräberfeldes von Himlingøje. In: U. Lund Hansen (ed.), *Himlingøje – Seeland – Europa. Ein Gräberfeld der jüngeren römischen Kaiserzeit auf Seeland, seine Bedeutung und internationalen Beziehungen*. København. 203-41.

Lyngstrøm, H.S. 2008, *Dansk jern. En kulturhistorisk analyse af fremstilling, fordeling og forbrug*. København.

Østergaard Sørensen, P. 1994, Houses, farmsteads and the settlement pattern in the Gudme area. In: P.O. Nielsen, K. Randsborg & H. Thrane (eds.), *The archaeology of Gudme and Lundeborg. Papers presented at a conference at Svendborg, October 1991*. Copenhagen. 41-47.

Østergaard Sørensen, P. 2000, Detektorfundene fra Gudme og den digitale arkæologi. In: M.B. Henriksen (ed.), *Detektorfund – hvad skal vi med dem? Dokumentation og registrering af bopladser med detektorfund fra jernalder og middelalder. En rapport fra et bebyggelseshistorisk seminar på Hollufgård den 26. oktober 1998*. Odense. 69-78.

Pedersen, A. 1999, Riding gear from Late Viking Age Denmark. *Journal of Danish Archaeology* 13 (1996-97), 133-60.

Rasmussen, U.F. 2008, Anløbspladser ved Køge Bugt – fra vikingetid og middelalder. *Årbog for Historisk Samfund for Roskilde Amt* 2008, 93-110.

Sørensen, A.C. 2005, Centralpladser og detektorlokaliteter fra jernalder og vikingetid på Køge egnen. *Årbog for Køge Museum* 2004-05, 19-38.

Thomsen, L.G. 2007, Grubehuse på Sjælland i yngre jernalder og vikingetid – med udgangspunkt i materialet fra Tissø-udgravningerne. In: H. Lyngstrøm et al. (eds.), *Specialer i forhistorisk arkæologi 2004-2005*. SAXO-Instituttet. København. 81-95.

Thomsen, P.O. 1994, Lundeborg – an early port of trade in south-east Funen. In: P.O. Nielsen, K. Randsborg & H. Thrane (eds.), *The archaeology of Gudme and Lundeborg. Papers presented at a conference at Svendborg, October 1991*. Copenhagen. 23-29.

Thrane, H. 1992, Das Reichstumszentrum Gudme in der Völkerwanderungszeit Fünens. In: K. Hauck (ed.), *Der historische Horizont der Götterbild-Amulette aus der Übergangsepoche von der Spätantike zum Frühmittelalter: Bericht über das Colloquium vom 28.11.-1.12. 1988 in der Werner-Reimers-Stiftung, Bad Homburg*. Göttingen. 299-380.

Thrane, H. 1994, Gudme – a focus of archaeological research 1833-1987. In: P.O. Nielsen, K. Randsborg & H. Thrane (eds.), *The archaeology of Gudme and Lundeborg. Papers presented at a conference at Svendborg, October 1991*. Copenhagen. 9-15.

Tornbjerg, S.Å. 1998, Toftegård – en fundrig gård fra sen jernalder og vikingetid. In: L. Larsson & B. Hårdh (eds.), *Centrala platser, centrala frågor. Samhällsstrukturen under järnåldern: en vänbok till Berta Stjernquist*. Stockholm. 217-32.

Tornbjerg, S.Å. & T. Woller 2000, Østervang – en jernalderbebyggelse med håndværk og handel. *Årbog for Køge Museum* 1999, 15-30.

Ulriksen, J. 1998, *Anløbspladser. Besejling og bebyggelse i Danmark mellem 200 og 1100 e. Kr. En studie af søfartens pladser på baggrund af undersøgelser i Roskilde Fjord*. Roskilde.

Ulriksen, J. 1999, En ejendommelig sag. *ROMU* 1998, 7-28.

Ulriksen, J. 2000, Vikingetidige korsemaljefibler fra Roskildeegnen. *ROMU* 1999, 11-30.

Ulriksen, J. 2005, Scheibenförmige Kreuzemailfibeln der Wikingerzeit und des Mittelalter in Altdänemark. *Offa* 59/60 (2002/03), 145-65.

Ulriksen, J. 2006, Vester Egesborg – a coastal settlement from the Late Iron Age on Zealand. *Journal of Danish Archaeology* 14, 187-99.

Ulriksen, J. 2008, Gevninge – leddet til Lejre. *Kuml* 2008, 145-85.

Vang Petersen, P. 1994, Excavations at sites of treasure trove finds at Gudme. In: P.O. Nielsen, K. Randsborg & H. Thrane (eds.), *The archaeology of Gudme and Lundeborg. Papers presented at a conference at Svendborg, October 1991*. Copenhagen. 30-40.

Voss, O. 1991, Jernproduktion i Danmark i perioden 0-550 e. Kr. In: C. Fabech & J. Ringtved (eds.), *Samfundsorganisation og regional Variation. Norden i romersk jernalder og folkevandringstid. Beretning 1. nordiske jernaldersymposium på Sandbjerg Slot 11. – 15. april 1989*. Højbjerg. 171-84.

Notes

1 *Arkæologiske udgravninger i Danmark* (AUD) 1989, entry no. 60.

2 Data from Hjulby and Strandby Gammeltoft kindly provided by museum curator Mogens Bo Henriksen, Odense Bys Museer. Data from Kunderslev and Hennings Mark kindly provided by museum curator Søren A. Sørensen, Museet Færgegården. Data from Næs kindly provided by museum director Keld Møller Hansen, Vordingborg Museum/Danmarks Borgcenter. Data from Lejre kindly provided by museum curator Tom Christensen, Roskilde Museum. Data from Gudme kindly provided by museum curator Palle Østergaard Sørensen, Museet Færgegården.

3 Data from Lundeborg kindly provided by museum curator Per O. Thomsen, Svendborg og Omegns Museum.

4 An exception is Fyns Hoved, where pottery was found (see Henriksen 1994).

5 Thanks to museum curator Lars Jørgensen, the National Museum, Copenhagen, for information on Dalby Hals.

6 Roman coins are, however, found with a wider distribution.

From hamlets to central places

Integrated survey and excavation strategies for the social analysis of settlements in northern Europe c. AD 400-1100

Christopher Loveluck and Kristian Strutt, with Philip Clogg

This chapter will explore a range of archaeological approaches to the social analysis of rural settlements in northern Europe, dating predominantly from the 1st millennium AD, through the intensive use of integrated and superimposed archaeological survey and targeted excavation strategies. The overall aim is to show how superimposed survey techniques (geophysical, geochemical and surface collection) can be applied to landscapes to define the character of different land-use zones within and beyond settlements. These, in turn, allow the targeting of specific areas for excavation, post-excavation analysis and ground penetrating radar (GPR) survey for the purposes of confirming the character of remains and the chronology of occupation, as well as deposit modelling. In this volume, a specific discussion of the application of radar is presented by Yossi Salmon; here, reference will only be made to the context of the use of GPR within integrated methodologies. The collective data from survey, excavation and post-excavation phases of research can then be combined within a contextualised interpretation of settlement morphology, discard strategies and preservation conditions to produce holistic social analyses of lifestyles and settlement biographies through time.

The discussion below is framed mainly around case-study evidence from Stavnsager, eastern Jutland (Denmark), Wilskerke-Haerdepollemswal, West Flanders (Belgium) and Breamore, Hampshire (England), although references are also made to other settlement studies from England to illustrate specific points (fig. 1). Within the different settlement and landscape contexts, the application of a range of superimposed archaeological survey and excavation strategies is explored in relation to specific questions posed by the individual projects. Several different types of settlement and associated landscapes are examined, from a harbour central place and linked settlements (Stavnsager), to an estate centre, nucleated settlement and associated hamlets (Breamore), and a landscape of dispersed hamlets and farms (Wilskerke). All are located in different topographical situations, all have different underlying geological conditions and all have been subjected to different geo-morphological influences. The landscapes of all the case studies, however, have been significantly altered by human action, including agriculture, land drainage and the alteration of the topography through the dumping of archaeological deposits.

This chapter begins with an overview of the different archaeological approaches and survey techniques, and the stages at which they have been applied during the analysis of the settlements and landscapes discussed. These commence with a discussion of the landscape-wide application of fluxgate gradiometer and electrical resistivity surveys at Breamore in Hampshire, followed by an account of the nature of minor element analysis and the scales of its application, and a succinct summary of the more often utilised intensive methods of

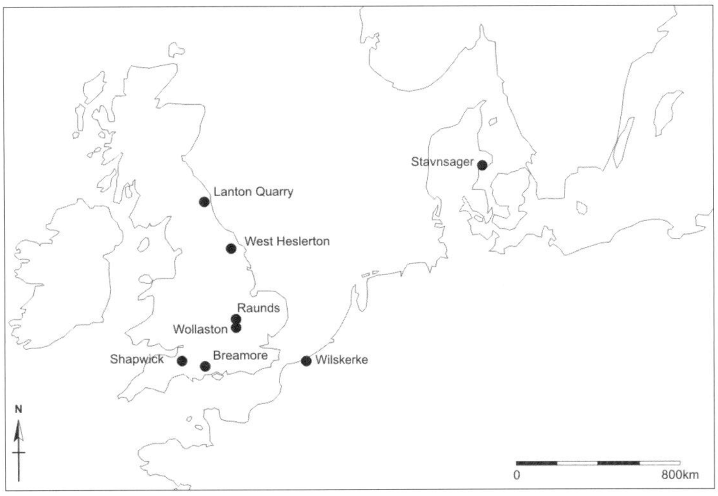

Fig. 1. | *Location of places discussed in the text. K. Strutt.*

surface collection. A review is then provided of methods for linking or 'calibrating' the results of different archaeological survey methods with archaeological features and deposits cut into and lying upon the natural subsoil. Two detailed case studies of research at Wilskerke-Haerdepollemswal and Stavnsager-Hørning are then presented to illustrate how superimposed and staged surveys and excavations can investigate different aspects of settlement dynamics and social change.

Overview of the superimposed survey techniques

The different intensive survey methods discussed below have different aims and purposes. Geophysical survey methods, using magnetometry and electrical resistivity techniques, have been widely applied in the last forty years. No claim is made here for the application of these techniques, in themselves, as new. Rather, it is the scale of their use and their combined utilisation with other images of human action that is innovative in the context of this paper. Magnetometry and resistivity techniques tend to identify structural features usually relating to buildings, trackways, ditches and pits. As such, they can provide guides for studies of settlement morphology. In most cases, aerial photographic evidence is also used as a survey tool prior to more intensive investigation by geophysical and other means. Aerial photographic and multi-spectral analyses are not discussed here, however, as they are the subject of another contribution to this volume, and they do not provide base-line data of uniform quality due to the impact of different soil conditions on aerial survey results.

In contrast to geophysical methods, geochemical survey techniques have usually been employed to provide indications of the use of space within and adjacent to settlements, relating especially to intensity of human and animal occupation and differentiation of industrial and cemetery zones. Since the 1940s, analysis of phosphate/phosphorous distributions has been conducted in Scandinavia and northern Europe in relation to the use of space in and around excavated buildings, as it is today (Zimmermann 1992, 104-38). Here, however, an expanded range of minor elements is discussed for the indications they can give of human activity, in relation to analysis by energy-dispersive X-ray fluorescence. Key to the application of these geophysical and geochemical techniques is their integrated application, if feasible, on the scale of hectares, to place settlements in their landscape and social contexts.

In the field, strategies are designed to affiliate all of the geophysical survey techniques to the same grid system, which is also used for geochemical soil sampling and surface collection. Surveys are normally based on an arbitrary grid coordinate system, tied into a national or international coordinate system, or to a series of physical markers on the ground corresponding to points on a map. A set of 30 m grids is then laid out to provide the background for magnetometry, resistivity, and other survey techniques that will complement the results of field-walking and geochemical sampling, for instance.

Surface collection survey, i.e. the retrieval of archaeological remains (especially pottery) from the surface of the plough soil by field-walking, is considered to a lesser extent below. In Scandinavia, the view has been held that ceramics from the mid and later 1st millennium AD rarely survive in the plough soil, due to their poorly fired nature, and when they do are likely to be unrepresentative reflections of settlement remains lying upon and cut into the subsoil (Jensen 1985).The plotting of metal artefacts recovered from plough soil by metal detector, however, has been widely practised since the late 1980s, and the results are abundantly illustrated in this volume. In England since the 1980s there has also been much debate over the representativity of Anglo-Saxon pottery recovered from the plough soil, due to the poor survival of much of the handmade pottery, especially that dating from the 5th to the 8th century, and also significant regional variation in the use and survival of pottery. In specific regions, such as East Anglia and the East Midlands, the locations of settlements from the end of the 7th to the early 8th century AD could be identified on the basis of the presence and survival of Ipswich and Maxey-type wares in the plough soil, and by the mid to late 9th century, a range of wheel-thrown wares allowed the identification of settlements across eastern England. Sites dating from the 5th to the 7th century in this area may be indicated by one or more sherds; in western England, however, Anglo-Saxon pottery in the plough soil was almost non-existent. It was also noted that Anglo-Saxon pottery on the surface tended to cluster in refuse zones on the peripheries of settlement areas (Schofield 1989). More intensive grid-based surface collection since the late 1980s, in the context of the Raunds Area Project in Northamptonshire, for example, has demonstrated the value of plotting small quantities of 5th to 9th century pottery distributions from the plough soil, in conjunction with aerial photography and geophysical surveys (Parry 2006).

Finally, methods for testing what the different archaeological survey results can actually tell us are explored. Understanding their representativity is critical for planning excavations to investigate different settlement zones, in order to interpret the nature of settlements through time in terms of the lifestyles of their inhabitants, their networks and, potentially, their worldview. Excavation and post-excavation research strategies have to be applied on a sufficiently large and detailed scale to enable social analysis.

Integrated geophysical surveys: Magnetometry and resistivity

The geophysical survey techniques of magnetometry and resistivity represent two of the key methods of survey utilised in archaeology for the mapping of sub-surface archaeological features (Clark 1996; Gaffney & Gater 2003; Scollar et al. 1990). Magnetometry, and especially the use of the fluxgate gradiometer, has been integral to the development and ongoing success of geophysical prospecting in the United Kingdom and elsewhere in Europe. The survey technique is rapid and effective on shallow archaeological deposits, especially in modern rural areas under arable use and pasture, and has thus been applied on a landscape scale in an increasing number of locations, for instance at West Heslerton in Yorkshire (Lyall & Powlesland 1996; Powlesland 2000), and in surveys of large, former urban sites around the Mediterranean, such as Portus, Rome, and in the United Kingdom, at Wroxeter (Buteux et al. 2000; Gaffney et al. 1998, 148-154; Keay et al. 2005; 2008; 2009; Strutt & Keay 2008). The technique has also been applied across perimarine landscapes in the Low Countries to assess the nature of archaeological and geomorphological features (Kattenberg & Aalbersberg 2004). Resistivity surveys, though regularly conducted at archaeological sites in the United Kingdom, have received less attention from archaeologists elsewhere in Europe, particularly in the Mediterranean, where soil aridity can affect the usefulness of the technique. The time-consuming nature of resistivity surveying restricts to a certain degree

A

B

c

Fig. 2. | *The different landscapes of Breamore parish: a. the 10th century church on the summit of a chalk plateau (Down); b. sloping gravel terrace; c. the alluvial water meadows. C. Loveluck.*

its widespread application. It has proven to be extremely useful, however, for investigating specific areas of sites and landscapes (Barker et al. 2005; Keay et al. 2005; Prevosti et al. forthcoming; Strutt et al. 2004). The integrated use of the different geophysical survey techniques is best illustrated using the example of a landscape survey conducted by the authors together with Prof. David Hinton and Mr Dominic Barker (University of Southampton) at Breamore, Hampshire, on the northern edge of the New Forest in southern England. The aims of the project were to investigate the history of land-use and settlement within the parish of Breamore, in the valley of the River Avon. This built upon the results of the 'Middle Avon' extensive surface collection survey (Light et al. 1994), and more recently discovered evidence housed in the Hampshire County records (The Historic Environment Record – HER).

The modern village of Breamore is situated on the valley floor and gravel terraces of the River Avon in Hampshire (fig. 2). The discoveries made during the Middle Avon valley survey provided extensive evidence of activity from the Mesolithic to the post-Medieval period (Light et al. 1994). The scatters of surface material comprised lithics, pottery and metalwork, and surviving earthworks and monuments are protected as scheduled sites or within registered 'historic parkland'. The evidence from the plough soil and earthworks is augmented by some exceptional standing remains, including a large Late Saxon church, probably dating from the late 10th century (Rodwell & Rouse 1984); the remains of the Augustinian priory of St

Michael, which was founded in the 12th century; and Breamore House, built in the 1580s, amongst other post-Medieval buildings in the vicinity. Furthermore, in the early years of this century, discoveries by metal-detector users indicated 5th to 7th[th] century Anglo-Saxon remains in the parish, including cemetery and settlement zones (Brooks 2001; Gifford 1997).

Documentary evidence concerning Breamore and its nearby hamlets begins with the Domesday survey. In 1066, Breamore was a royal estate of Edward the Confessor, linked with Rockbourne to the west. Other nearby hamlets are also mentioned as the foci of smaller estates held by Edward; the whole area appears to have been royal land in 1066. As a directly administered royal estate, Rockbourne-Breamore was not assessed for taxation like the surrounding smaller estates, creating an intriguing documentary void upon which only archaeological investigation might shed light. The place name Breamore is Old English for 'broom-marsh' (Coates 1989, 40), and the Domesday Book also makes clear the different ecological resources available in the locality, namely well-drained chalk land in the north, arable land on the river gravel terrace, marshy heath land on the river alluvium and woodland to the south (Munby 1982, ref. 39b). Further extant documentation relates to the Augustinian priory, dedicated to St Michael and founded in the early 1130s, and Medieval manorial accounts. Recent historical and morphological studies of Medieval settlements in the Avon valley and other parts of Hampshire have also emphasised the unusually dispersed nature of the settlement pattern, with only very limited nucleation until the post-Medieval period (Lewis 1997, 81; Roberts & Wrathmell 2000).

The survey of Breamore and its environs was conducted to answer two principal research questions:

- What was the pattern of long-term settlement development and landscape management at Breamore from prehistory to the present?
- Is the present pattern of apparently dispersed settlement within the parish/estate a phenomenon of long duration?

In order to answer these questions, topographic and geophysical surveys were undertaken across a 40 ha transect in the eastern part of the parish, adjacent to the River Avon. The principal sites within the transect were located in three different topographical and geological situations. The Late Saxon nucleus around the 10th century church at Breamore was located just below the chalk upland (Downs), incorporating the manorial centre and settlement (Strutt 2004a). To the southeast, the gravel terraces of the Avon contained evidence of Bronze Age burial complexes and Iron Age, Roman and Anglo-Saxon settlements, as well as a more dispersed Medieval and post-Medieval settlement pattern. Finally, a spur of gravel and alluvium next to the Avon included the site of St Michael's priory, founded in the 1130s (Strutt 2004b).

The integrated results of the geophysical surveys at Breamore were crucial to the mapping and interpretation of the archaeological landscape. In particular, the combination of magnetometry and resistivity provided detailed information on the distribution, form and extent of archaeological features. This was augmented by limited surface collection and test pitting before trial excavations were conducted to evaluate the results (see below).

The magnetometry and resistivity (fig. 3) surveys indicated complicated phases of settlement at Breamore. To the west and north of Breamore Church two parallel linear anomalies enclose the church and the area of a likely settlement core, probably the 10th to 13th century manorial centre. The area of Breamore Park to the south of Breamore House is dominated by a series of linear features aligned with the front of the manor, representing two garden terraces with a number of features, possibly ponds or fountains, extending to the south. These results were complemented by targeted resistivity over areas in the vicinity of the church and gravel terrace to the east. The resistivity indicated some phasing of the settlement around Breamore Church. The line of the enclosure ditch was also well-defined, curving around to the west of the church. It appears to have cut through the high resistance plan of a house platform and walls and some further high resistance features to the north, suggesting other house platforms across the area. A possible structure and another possible building are located within the ditch. A range of anomalies also suggested the possibility of *Grubenhäuser* (sunken-featured buildings), large pits and wells in this settlement zone. The survey results also showed a number of trackways cutting across the landscape, emanating from the manorial settlement focus and church.

Moving from the upper valley terrace to the flat gravels adjacent to the river alluvium, a complex range of archaeological features were evident, reflecting human activity from the Late Neolithic/ Early Bronze Age to the Medieval period. In a large field known as the Bullcroft, which runs along the north-south axis of the modern road (A36), a major settlement agglomeration was evident with a barrow cemetery to its north (fig. 4). The circular barrows, ranging between 15 and 25 m in diameter, were located on the former levees of a palaeochannel of the River Avon (Strutt 2004a; 2005). The reflections of the settlement comprised a system of boundary features, mostly ditches marking plots within a large roadside settlement dating from the Romano-British period. Surface finds also suggested significant Iron Age and Anglo-Saxon settlement activity within the same area as the Roman nucleated settlement (Strutt 2004a). The modern A36 road seems to be a north-south route down the Avon valley of considerable antiquity.

Results of the magnetometry and resistivity surveys also provided comprehensive data from the alluvial water meadow and gravel promontory/ island zone. On the gravel promontory known as 'the Shallows' (fig. 5), a barrow in the northeast of the field formed a focal point for a 5th to 7th century Anglo-Saxon cemetery, with a number of low resistance pit or grave features in the vicinity. In addition, the line of a track is plainly visible in the results, together with a more substantial trackway. The background responses to the resistivity survey also appear to indicate a boundary to the gravel ridge, and what may be the cemetery (Strutt 2002). The results from St Michael's Priory (fig. 6), also in the alluvial zone, showed that an incredibly rich and complicated range of deposits survive at the site. The priory cloister, surrounded by buildings, is prominent in the centre of the results. To the west, a structure, some 40 m in length from north to south and 10 m in width, demarcates the side of the cloister. A larger structure is located along the south side of the cloister measuring some 50 m in length and 35 m in width. A smaller structure is visible to the north of the cloister, consisting of a small chamber and a longer building. The structures comprising the monastic complex ended abruptly to the east, close to the channel of the River Avon.

Overall, the results of the landscape-wide magnetometry and more targeted resistivity surveys have revolutionised our understanding of the development of the settlement pattern in Breamore parish, especially from the Roman to the post-Medieval periods. Following use of the lower gravel terrace for Bronze Age barrow cemeteries, an Iron Age settlement was developed in the Roman period to become a large nucleated roadside settlement (in the modern Bullcroft field), sited on a north-south axis along a trackway that has since become a modern road, the A36. Between the 5th and the 7th century, several foci of settlement and cemetery activity are visible in the surveys, but the largest Anglo-Saxon settlement agglomeration still seems to have been located on or immediately adjacent to the former Roman nucleated settlement. The largest Anglo-Saxon cemetery between the 5th and the 7th century was also located near to the agglomeration in the Bullcroft field, to its southeast on the gravel promontory at 'the Shallows'. At an unknown date between the 7th and the 10th century, the Anglo-Saxon settlement pattern appears to have become more dispersed, forming the royal estate centre and hamlets recorded in the Domesday Book. Settlement activity around the 10th century church seems to reflect the estate centre or what became the royal manor, and the resistivity survey in particular identified stratigraphic relationships illustrating the development of the settlement core and its enclosure. By the mid 12th century, there were two principal nucleated settlement cores in the parish, at the manorial centre and at the Augustinian priory of St Michael, in addition to the several dispersed hamlets.

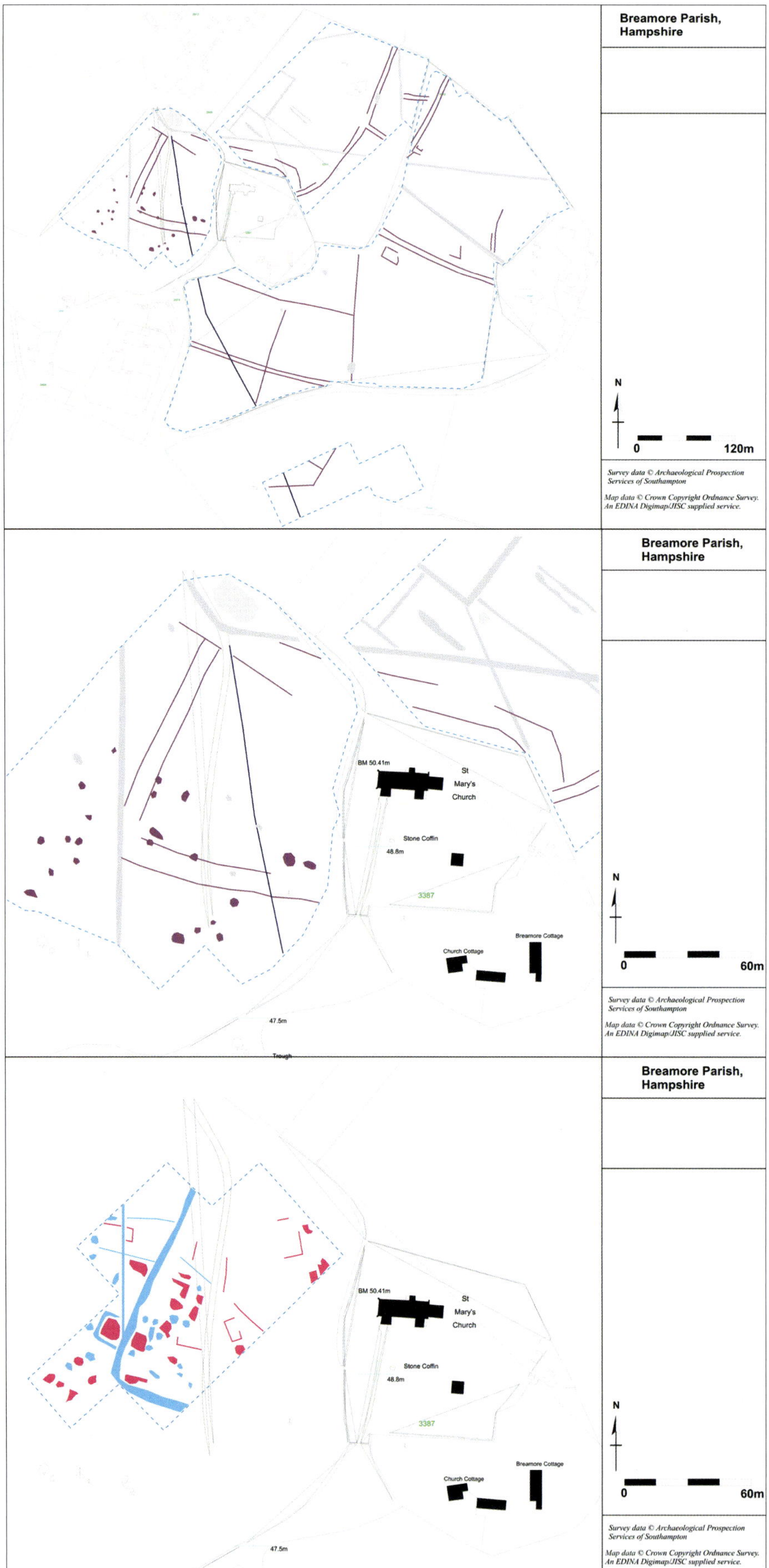

Fig. 3. | *The 10th to 13th century manorial centre and associated settlements: a. large-scale magnetometer plot (schematic); b. magnetometry, close-up of enclosure (schematic); resistivity – close-up of enclosure and buildings. After Strutt 2002 and 2004a.*

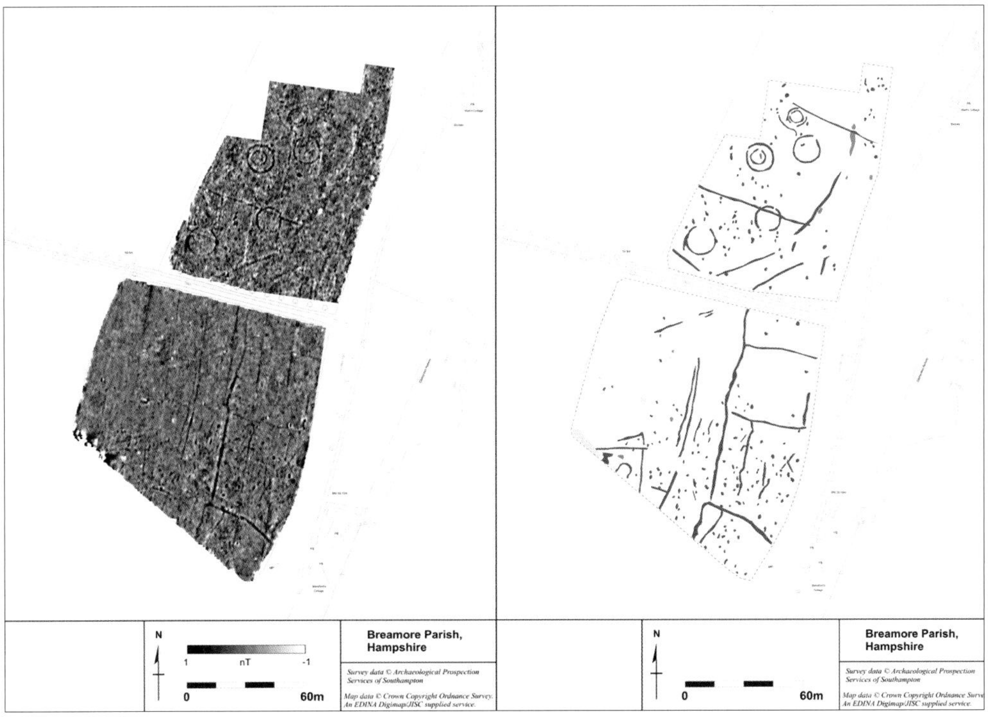

Fig. 4. | *Bronze Age barrows and Iron Age, Roman, Anglo-Saxon and Anglo-Norman nucleated settlement on the lower gravel terrace (Bullcroft): a. magnetometry – greyscale; b. magnetometry (schematic). After Strutt 2004a and 2005.*

Fig. 5. | *Early Anglo-Saxon cemetery and Bronze Age features on a gravel promontory ('The Shallows') in the river alluvium: a. magnetometry; b. resistivity. After Strutt 2002 and 2004a.*

The period between the 16th and the 18th century appears to have been the most disruptive, creating the impression that there were no significant nucleated settlements in the parish. During the building of a new manor house in c. 1580 – the present Breamore House – and the laying out of formal gardens, the former manorial enclosure was probably removed, along with any remnant of nucleated settlement in the area. There is evidence of massive garden terraces to the south of the facade of Breamore House, probably dating from the late 16th to the 17th century, and these gardens were probably replaced, in turn, by open parkland in the 18th century.

Fig. 6. | *Plan of the Augustinian priory, founded in the 1130s, on a gravel island next to the River Avon: a. resistivity – greyscale; b. resistivity (schematic). After Strutt 2004b.*

The geophysical survey results proved beyond doubt that the dispersed settlement pattern that currently exists at Breamore is not a 'historical fossil' from the Early Medieval period, as previously suggested (Lewis 1997). Instead, there have been complex cycles of settlement nucleation and dispersion, including a Roman and Early Anglo-Saxon phase with a principal large agglomeration, Middle and Later Anglo-Saxon settlement dispersion, two nucleated Medieval settlement cores, and then post-Medieval dispersion, following the dissolution of the priory and the creation of formal gardens and parkland around the post-Medieval manor house, during the 16th century.

Geochemical surveys

Geochemical prospection in archaeology is concerned with investigating the spatial variation in the chemical composition of deposits across the archaeological landscape. It is based on the assumption that human activity will influence and alter the natural chemical balance of deposits. When this influence can be detected, the analysis has the potential to provide information on land-use and intensity of use, to define the location and limit of site boundaries and to aid in the interpretation of settlement features.

In order for an element or compound to be of use for archaeological diagnostic purposes, it must fulfil the following three criteria as defined by Entwistle et al. (1998): Human action must alter the natural concentrations across a defined site, the influence must be readily apparent in comparison to background levels, and any alteration needs to be fixed in a persistent form to ensure a lasting record.

The most consistently useful element that fits these criteria is phosphorus. This is due to its high concentration in many different types of human waste material and its ability to become fixed in a mineral form within the soil matrix. Phosphate surveys on archaeological sites, therefore, are the most studied and reported of geochemical surveys (Craddock et al. 1985; Crowther 1997; Walker 1992). Recently, however, with the growing availability and use of analytical techniques such as inductively coupled mass spectrometry (ICPMS), gas chromatography mass spectrometry (GCMS) and energy-dispersive X-ray fluorescence (EDXRF), research areas have broadened and a number of additional groups of elements and compounds are being studied. These include:

- *Macro- and micro- nutrients*: the minor elements calcium, magnesium, potassium, phosphorus, sulphur, manganese and iron (Clogg & Taylor 2001).
- *Heavy metals*: typically the elements copper, zinc, lead, cadmium, cobalt and nickel (Rippon et al. 2001).
- *Trace and rare earth elements*: those that appear to be indicators of human activity include caesium, barium, thorium and rubidium (Entwistle et al. 1998).
- *Organic compounds*: lipid biomarkers, of which the most important are considered to be those with 5b stanol components.

The multi-element analysis of soil macro- and micro-nutrients as indicators of human activity in the past forms the focus of this discussion. The method utilises energy-dispersive X-ray fluorescence (EDXRF) to provide a rapid quantitative multi-element analysis of soils from archaeological and potential archaeological deposits. It allows for the simultaneous accurate analysis of all the major and minor elements present within a given sample, thus providing a detailed geochemical characterisation of the deposit. A range of elements can be chosen for analysis, including phosphorous, sodium, magnesium, aluminium, silicon, sulphur, potassium, calcium, titanium, manganese, iron and strontium. Analysis is undertaken using a Links Systems XR200 EDXRF spectrometer, employing a rhodium anode X-ray tube running at 10kV. All analyses are carried out in a vacuum to allow detection of the low atomic number elements, and the spectra are collected for a live time of 100 seconds. The results are then calibrated using an intensity-based correction model derived from the analysis of a suite of eight international soil standards. The results, measured as weight percent distributions, are then transferred to appropriate computer software for statistical analysis and mapping.

High concentrations of certain elements can indicate different human uses of space, as well as different intensities of use. For example, a high concentration of phosphorous can indicate intensive settlement activity and discard of human and animal waste, though levels can also be influenced by the nature of the diet (Craddock et al. 1985). It can also indicate a high concentration of osseous material (bones), especially in conjunction with calcium. Manganese concentrations tend to indicate two general phenomena: Very strong discrete concentrations often indicate intense human activity, while a general rise in manganese levels often seems to indicate peripheral human activity or the edge of sites. Strong calcium concentrations can reflect the presence of osseous materials, either the disposal of animal bones or human cemetery zones, and strong iron (and also copper) concentrations can reflect metalworking areas. Care has to be taken, however, with different geological and soil conditions. For example, levels of calcium may be meaningless on a chalk- or limestone-based geology. The same would be true for silica levels on sand geology.

An alternative to minor element analysis of soil micro- and macro-nutrients is the analysis of levels of heavy metals, which are consumed by humans in food and water; settlements provide concentrated zones for their excretion. Within the context of a specific settlement, notably the Shapwick project, Somerset, Andrew Jackson analysed a range of heavy metal distributions, including lead, cadmium, chromium, cobalt, copper, molybdenum, nickel and zinc, in conjunction with levels of phosphorous, manganese and magnetic susceptibility. Soil samples were generally taken from the topsoil, between 0.05 and 0.20 m in depth, along transects and within grids of varying sizes. At different settlement nuclei within the parish of Shapwick, he was able to identify core areas of settlement linked to specific metal and element concentrations. High concentrations of lead, zinc, phosphorous, and cadmium were found most consistently within settlement foci indicated by aerial photography and gradiometer surveys; higher general levels of manganese, nickel, cobalt and chromium seemed to identify the edges of intensively occupied settlement areas (Jackson 2007, 183-200).

Analysis of the minor element and heavy metal components of soils has been applied on a range of scales. The heavy metal distributions at the Shapwick settlements were used primarily for macro-scale analysis, to identify cores of human activity and their edges. Similarly, analysis of multiple minor elements has been used to help define core activity areas and settlement peripheries at a macro-level, as at Wilskerke-Haerdepollemswal and Stavnsager-Hørning (see below). Unlike soil sampling for heavy metals, however, the samples for multi-element analysis at the latter settlements were taken at intervals of 10 m, within a larger network of 30 m grids that acted as a base for the geophysical surveys. The samples were collected by soil auger from just below the base of the modern plough soil, at an approximate depth of 0.75 m. This ensured a minimal contamination risk from the modern topsoil/plough soil. At both settlements, the minor element analysis also indicated different uses of space within the former settlement areas, including a farmyard zone at Wilskerke (fig. 13, below), geochemical 'fingerprints' of former buildings with calcium-based mortar (fig. 13, below), and cemetery and industrial zones at Stavnsager (fig. 16, below).

Minor element analysis has also been applied at the micro-scale by Philip Clogg, in order to give context to excavated settlement and cemetery remains dating from the mid 1st millennium AD, in England. For example, following the discovery during the course of development of a late 7th century 'pioneer' helmet, in a grave at Wollaston, Northamptonshire, in the 1990s, minor element surveys were conducted in an attempt to give con-

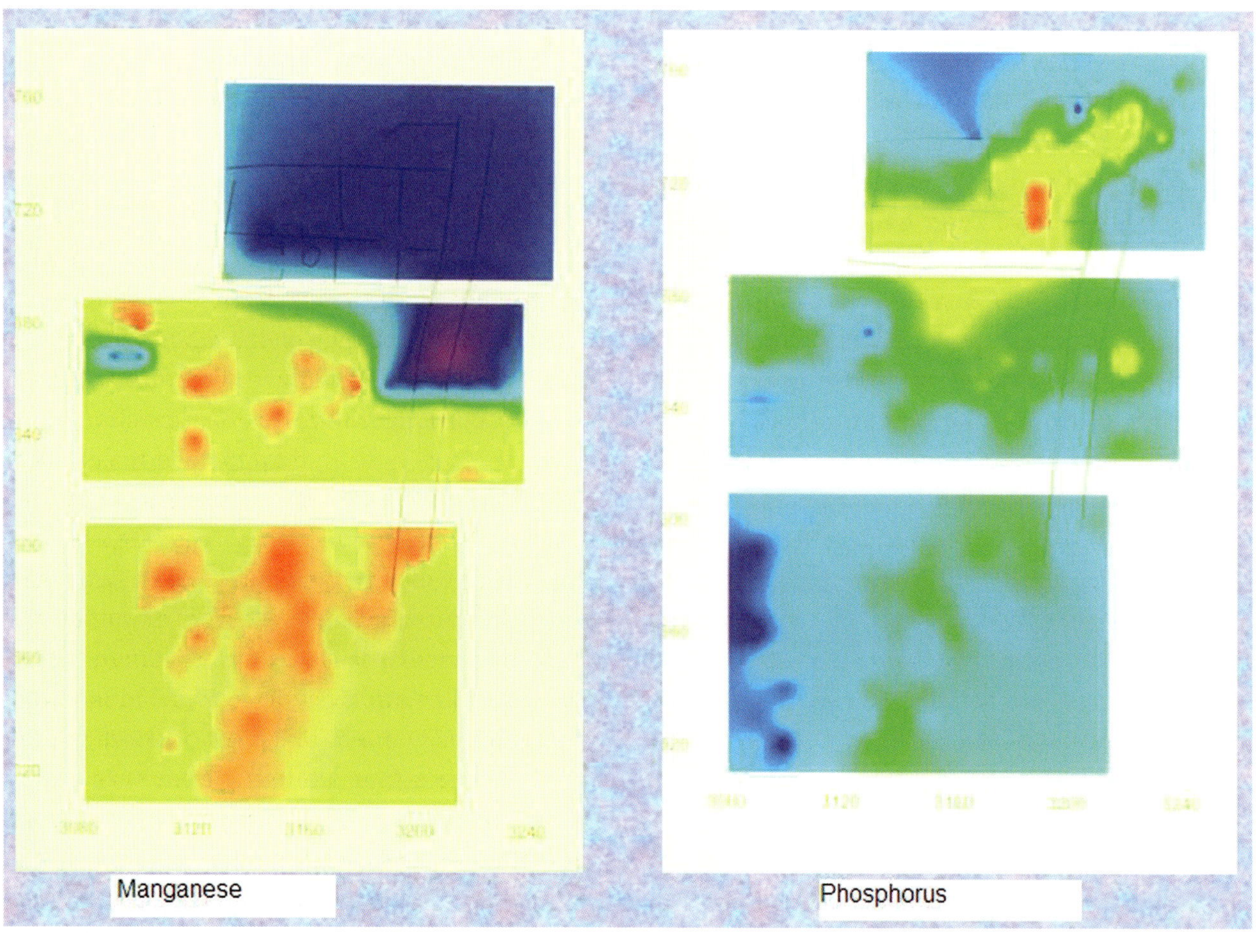

Fig. 7. | *Relative distributions of phosphorous and manganese in relation to the grave containing the late 7th century 'pioneer' helmet, from Wollaston, Northamptonshire, England. The manganese distribution is presented on the left, the phosphorous on the right. Higher concentrations of the elements are shown in orange and yellow. The orange elongated feature in the phosphorous distribution is the 'pioneer' helmet grave. P. Clogg.*

text to the apparently isolated grave. A differential relationship was discovered in relation to levels of phosphorous and manganese. At a relative scale, high levels of phosphorous occurred within and in the vicinity of the grave, while a general rise in levels of manganese on the periphery of the grave and possible cemetery area marked the edge of intensive human use (fig. 7).

At Lanton Quarry, Northumberland, in the northeast of England, a detailed elemental analysis was undertaken in conjunction with magnetic susceptibility surveys to investigate the possible functional use of five *Grubenhäuser* (sunken-featured buildings/SFBs). A total of 784 samples were analysed from the areas of features SFBs 2, 3, 4, 5 and 6. Each area was sampled at a 0.5 m interval, over an area of approximately 45 m². The results were complex but a number of general observations could be made in relation to phosphorous and manganese distributions.

The phosphorous distribution across SFB 4 showed a very marked delineation of high phosphorus values within the confines of the structure, with some zoning of these higher values across the middle and to its eastern end (fig. 8). This distribution pattern would be expected from structures that have been used for a reasonable length of time, with specific tasks being undertaken in specific areas – particularly if there was no regular cleaning regime. The opposite pattern would be expected if the structure had been continually cleaned and the debris/waste deposited away from the working area; there is some suggestion of this in the distribution for SFB 5 (fig. 8). All manganese distribution plots showed remarkably similar patterns with high values across the features and clearly defined areas of very high concentrations around the inner perimeter of the structures (fig. 8). The measured concentration range of manganese was wide, with the highest concentrations over twice the value

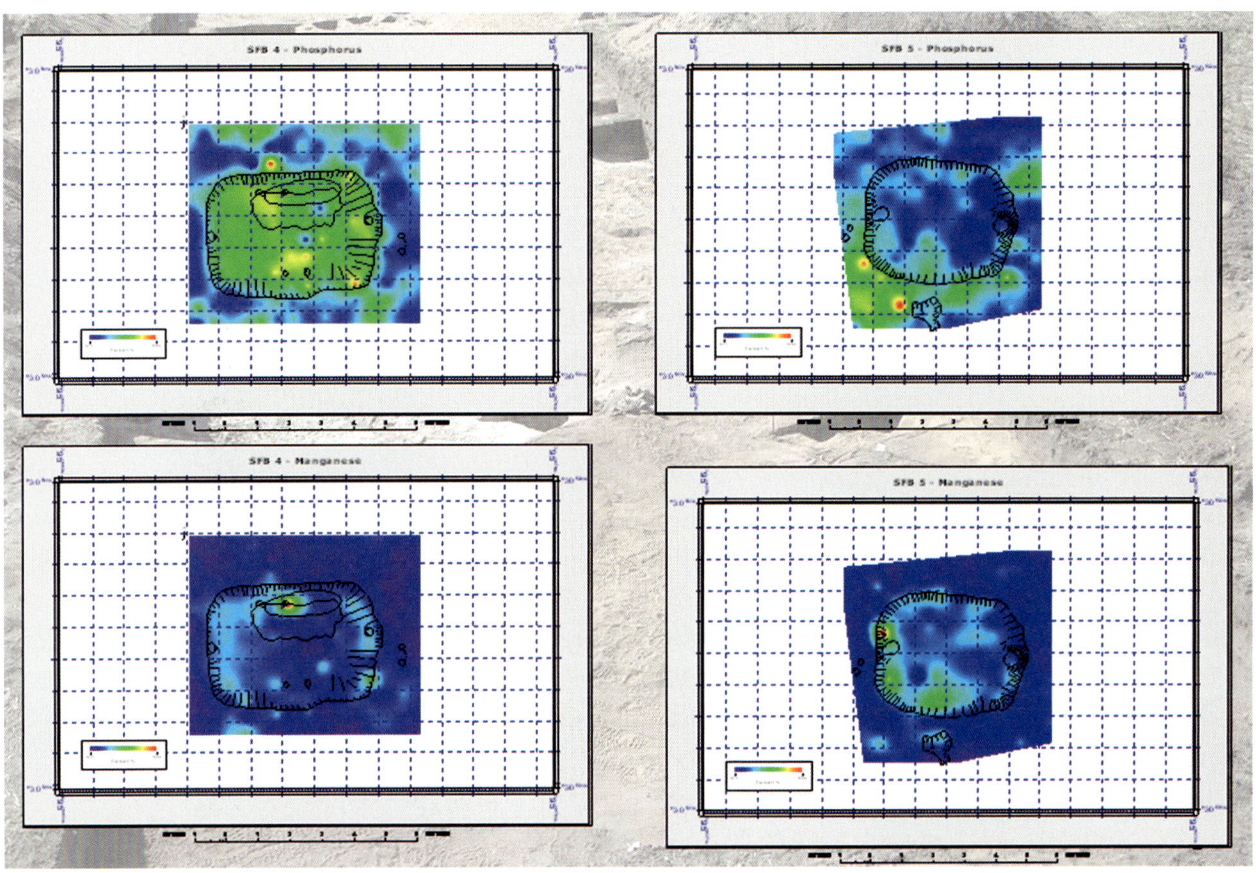

Fig. 8. | *Relative distributions of phosphorous and manganese in* Grubenhäuser*/SFBs 4 and 5, at Lanton Quarry, Northumberland, England. P. Clogg.*

of what could be considered 'normal background' levels. Build-up of manganese within intensively used areas, or structures, has been associated with compaction leading to 'gleying' within deposits. This could be the case here, since the sunken edges of the features were compacted and supported by some form of wooden structure.

Intensive surface collection surveys

Surface collection surveys by field-walking have been carried out extensively across the Mediterranean since the late 1940s, beginning with the South Etruria survey in Italy by Ward Perkins and others (Potter 1979). Extensive transect-walking techniques to identify settlements and grid-based techniques to differentiate settlement character are routinely used today, alongside increasing critique of what plough soil assemblages might represent (Bintliff et al. 2000; Franovich et al. 2000; Schofield 1991;). In northern Europe there have also been large-scale regional surveys, using both transect-based surface collection and some intensive grid-based walking. Examples include the Fenland Survey in eastern England (Hayes & Lane 1992; Lane, with Hayes 1993; Silvester 1988) and the Middle Avon valley survey in southern England (Light et al. 1994). These regional-scale surveys showed that settlement sites from the Early Middle Ages could be identified in some areas using this method – certainly in eastern England, and to a lesser extent in central southern and western England.

It was only with the application of intensive grid-based surface collection at the level of individual settlements, however, that surface collection became a key tool in reconstructing settlement chronologies and uses of space, usually in conjunction with aerial photography and/or geophysical evidence and excavation. Such settlement-focused studies have been undertaken on the scale of individual parishes and groups of parishes, as at Barton Bendish, Norfolk (Rogerson et al. 1997); Raunds, Northamptonshire (Parry 2006); Shapwick, Somerset (Gerrard, with Aston 2007); and Whittlewood, Buckinghamshire/Northamptonshire (Jones & Page 2006). They have also been used alongside targeted geophysical surveys to elucidate the nature of settlements detected by extensive regional surveys, as in the northern Fenland of Lincolnshire (Crowson et al. 2005).

Results from the Raunds and Shapwick projects have been fully published, and their comparison is informative due to their locations in eastern and western England, respectively. In the settlements of the Raunds area, for example, at Thorpe End and at Mallows Cotton, the recovered ceramics demonstrated a stable settlement pattern of hamlets from the Iron Age through to the Later Middle Ages. Such a conclusion could be reached because of the relatively large-scale survival of Anglo-Saxon pottery (over 800 sherds at Thorpe End), and their being discarded within and immediately adjacent to enclosures, which were identified by magnetometer/gradiometer survey (Parry 2006, 177-81, 234-36). Unfortunately, however, follow-up excavations for the survey results were generally limited, with trenches only 2 m in width designed to confirm the survey results – although large excavated settlements, such as Raunds-West Cotton, existed nearby (Parry 2006). At Shapwick, Somerset, in the southwest of England, surface collection rarely recovered diagnostic 5th to 10th century pottery sherds. Indeed, datable material culture from this period was generally sparse, despite the long-term settlement occupation suggested by aerial photography and geophysical and geochemical evidence (Gerrard, with Aston 2007). The situation in the southwest of England seems similar to that in Denmark, in terms of the visibility of pottery dating from c. AD 400 to 1000 within the plough soil.

The case studies of the integrated surveys at Wilskerke and Stavnsager discussed below highlight situations where surface collection should and should not be applied as a representative technique for intensive settlement analysis, based on preliminary feasibility studies.

Understanding and testing survey results: What do they represent?

Survey results have to be tested to see whether they are representative of human action in the past.

Magnetometers and resistivity meters generally measure changes in the earth's magnetic field or in electrical resistivity to depths of between 0.5 and 0.8 m below the modern ground surface. If landscapes have been subject to significant alluviation, colluviation or deliberate topographical change by man, deposits may exist below the range of normal geophysical instruments, other than ground-penetrating radar. Alluviation, colluviation and intentional topographic change by human action also have a very significant impact on the reliability of surface collection data in terms of reconstructing past settlement patterns and landscape management.

For example, in the landscape of Breamore parish in Hampshire, discussed above, very clear representations of the 10th to 13th century manorial core of the royal estate, its enclosure and internal space were reflected in the superimposed gradiometer and resistivity surveys. This estate centre core is located just below the summit of a chalk plateau, overlooking the valley of the River Avon. Today, the topography slopes gently from the chalk plateau downwards on to a gravel terrace; the terrace flattens out for its final 200 m, eventually meeting river alluvium, occasional gravel islands, and the river channel itself. On the flat gravel terrace and islands, the gradiometer and resistivity surveys again produced exceptional results, identifying the Iron Age, Roman and Anglo-Saxon nucleated settlement, the plan of the 12th century priory, and Bronze Age and Anglo-Saxon cemeteries. The gently sloping area between the plateau and the flat lower terrace was suspiciously empty, however. A similar difference was also initially evident following grid-based surface collection on the lower terrace, on the site of the nucleated settlement, and on the slopes of the valley side.

The flat terrace yielded prehistoric flints, Iron Age pottery, Romano-British pottery, a 6th to 7th century Anglo-Saxon bead, as well as Medieval and post-Medieval pottery during a provisional examination. In contrast, only sporadic flints and post-Medieval pottery were represented on the surface of the valley slopes. A series of 2 x 2 m test pits were excavated at intersections of grids to investigate the extent to which geomorphological processes had influenced the results of the geophysical and surface collection surveys. It was found that very significant colluviation had taken place, giving the modern valley slope a much gentler gradient than its predecessor had during the Medieval period. Medieval ditches and cobbled hardstanding from a yard or structure were found stratified below the colluvium, containing Medieval pottery (fig. 9). In one test pit, Late Neolithic flints were found stratified below 1.5 m of colluvium (fig. 9). It was thus established that there was no relationship between surface data taken from the modern plough soil or geophysical results taken from the surface of the valley slopes, and archaeological features sealed under the layers of colluvium.

If a comprehensive understanding of settlements and their interrelationships is to be achieved, then intensive survey results need to be 'calibrated' with assessment studies linked to archaeological excavation and post-excavation analysis on an appropriate scale. Three such predictive assessment strategies are discussed below, in relation to the research at Stavnsager-Hørning. Firstly, close-interval gradiometer and resistivity surveys were taken after the plough soil had been removed from an excavation trench, in order to assess the difference between results taken from the surfaces of the plough soil and subsoil, respectively. Such an exercise might, superficially, be viewed as a waste of resources, if it were not for the fact that the geophysical instruments identified a small number of additional anthropogenic features that were not visible to the human eye (see below). Secondly, ground-penetrating radar (GPR) and excavation were used together for the assessment of gradiometer and geochemical survey results, and for predictive deposit-modelling (Loveluck & Salmon 2011; Salmon this volume). And thirdly, detailed analysis of excavated deposits at the micro-scale was conducted in order to investigate the relationship between minor element distributions obtained from a depth of c. 0.75 m and those from discrete excavated deposits, again to enhance predictive targeting for excavation. This micro-analysis was achieved using a scanning electron microprobe at

A

B

the University of Nottingham (Faber forthcoming).

The remainder of this paper is given over to the detailed presentation and discussion of the settlement research conducted at Wilskerke-Haerdepollemswal in West Flanders, and at Stavnsager-Hørning in eastern Jutland, as these two case studies illustrate the potential of the integrated and superimposed application of survey and excavation strategies for understanding the social biographies of settlements in the second half of the 1st millennium AD.

Wilskerke-Haerdepollemswal – a hamlet in the coastal plain of West Flanders, AD 500-1600

The analysis of the location, morphology, chronology of occupation and networks of the settlement at Haedepollemswal, at the hamlet of Wilskerke in West Flanders, provides an excellent case study of the limits of inference from superimposed gradiometer, resistivity, grid-based surface collection, micro-topography and minor element surveys. These surveys were conducted as part of the Leffinge Area Pilot Project in September 2002, a collaborative research project between the University of Southampton and the Free University of Brussels (VUB), funded primarily by the British Academy and the University of Southampton (Loveluck & Tys 2002). It was undertaken within the context of radically changing ideas about the nature of the clay, peat and sand island geology of the coastal plain of West Flanders during the Early Middle Ages. Cecile Baeteman had conducted a very intensive coring campaign to analyse the sediments in the coastal plain linked to high-resolution radiocarbon dates, which suggested that between c. AD 400 and 800 the coastal marshes were not uninhabitable due to a marine transgression (Dunkirk II), but were instead stable raised marshes, with cultivatable areas (Baeteman 1999; Baeteman et al. 2002).

The early research undertaken by Dries Tys in the late 1990s during his doctorate also encountered chance finds of Early Medieval pottery and other artefacts, and this was enhanced by some additional transect surface collection (Tys 2003). There seemed to be a particular concentration of finds and also possible enclosed hamlets around a larger communal terp mound at Leffinge, West Flanders (Loveluck & Tys 2006). The principal aim of the Leffinge Area Pilot Project was to evaluate whether the Early Medieval pottery finds, recovered within a single enclosure or ring-dike at Wilskerke-Haerdepollemswal, represented a permanent settlement or seasonal, temporary activity. If the settlement proved to be permanent, then that would support Baeteman's view that there was no marine transgression in the coastal plain between the 5th and the 9th century.

The defined surface area for analysis covered 5.2 ha of clay soils. There were two forms of land-use within the study area. These comprised a northern field of 2.9 ha, currently being used for arable agriculture, and a southern field of 2.3 ha, used as arable pasture (fig. 10). It was likely that the pasture area had also been ploughed in the past. The different areas of land-use obviously conditioned the application of a range of superimposed survey techniques. On the ploughed element of the study area, micro-topography, gradiometer, resistivity, grid-based surface collection and minor element analysis were applied. The same range of techniques was used on the pasture, with the exception of surface collection. While the full 5.2 ha were covered by geophysical and geochemical survey, therefore, only 2.9 ha were subjected to surface collection. A detailed micro-topographical survey was conducted using a total-station theodolite as a preliminary base for the other superimposed techniques.

The geophysical surveys were conducted in September 2002 by Kristian Strutt of the APSS,

Fig. 9. | *Test pits at Breamore showing the extent of colluviation and the unrepresentative nature of the data collected at the surface, during field-walking: a. Medieval ditch sealed below colluvium; b. Neolithic land surface sealed below 1.5 m of colluviums. Photo: C. Loveluck.*

Fig. 10. | *Photographs showing the nature of modern land-use on the Haerdepollemswal settlement: a. deep-ploughed clay used for arable, potato and sugar beet cultivation; b. pasture, with the field boundary seemingly following the line of the former D-shaped enclosure. Photo: C. Loveluck.*

University of Southampton, within the overall survey directed by Christopher Loveluck. At the time, significant solar storms caused difficulty in balancing the FM36 Geoscan Fluxgate gradiometer, which was utilised alongside the RM15 Geoscan resistance meter in a twin electron probe formation. The magnetometer/gradiometer and resistivity surveys were conducted by dividing the 5.2 ha study area into grids of 30 x 30 m. Within the 30 m grids, readings were taken at intervals of 1 m for both surveys (Strutt & Hay 2003).

A series of positive magnetic anomalies was identified in the western part of the survey area (in both the ploughed and pasture zones). These anomalies are thought to indicate the bank of a D-shaped enclosure. Running along the outside of the positive anomalies was a band of negative anomalies, which probably represent a ditch outside the bank (fig. 11). The D-shaped modern field structure seems to have developed around this previous enclosure, which according to the geophysical surveys had an internal surface area of approximately 70 x 40 m. In the northwest corner of the D-shaped enclosure the resistivity survey identified a smaller circular enclosure, approximately 20 m in diameter, with an entrance in its eastern sector and indications of possible structures within it (fig. 12).

To the northeast and east of the D-shaped enclosure, magnetic and resistance anomalies suggest the levées of a paleochannel or a tidal inlet. Since the geophysical surveys were conducted in 2002, recent satellite images of the D-shaped enclosure and its environs have confirmed the possibility of the proximity of a tidal creek. The satellite images show a complex and meandering tidal creek system, immediately adjacent to the enclosure on its northeastern side. This creek system drains into a major tidal channel which would have given direct access to the sea during the Early Middle Ages (Davies et al. forthcoming; Loveluck & Tys 2006).

Directly to the east of the D-shaped enclosure and to the south of the tidal creek system, a series of approximately north-south aligned linear boundaries was identified. They probably represent the remains of open fields for arable cultivation, of unknown original date; a number of the field boundaries are identifiable in the micro-topographical survey as well as the geophysical surveys. These field boundaries appeared on the detailed cadastral maps compiled in the early 19th century, and they probably existed until the reorganisation of the field system around 1970.

For the minor element survey, samples were taken with a soil auger from just below the base of the plough soil (at a depth of between 0.75 and

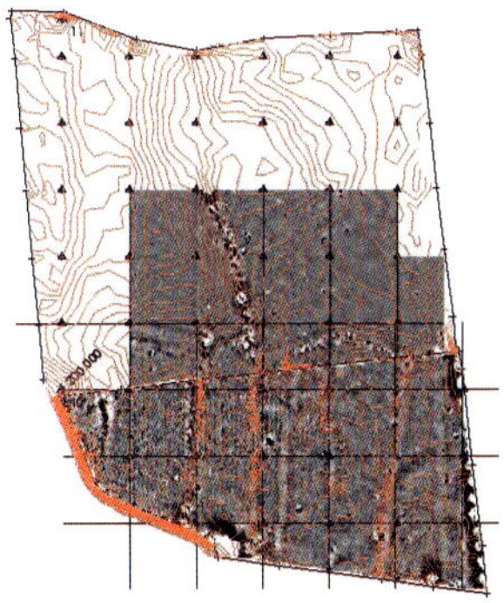

Fig. 11. | *Magenetometry/gradiometer survey results showing aspects of the morphology at Haerdepollemswal. After Strutt & Hay 2003.*

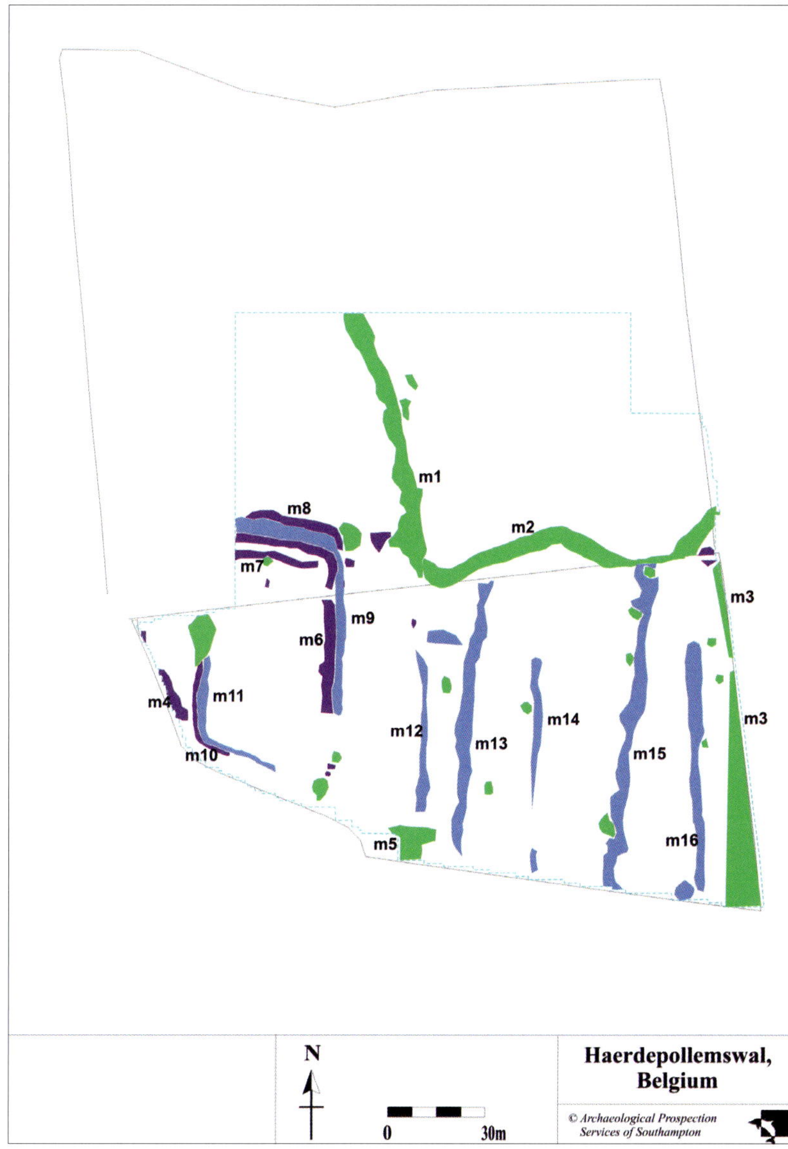

0.85 m). Samples were also taken from the same depth from the field now under pasture. The sample interval was 10 m over the entire 5.2 ha study area, and the sample points were located within the network of grids laid out for the geophysical and other surveys. Distinct patterns were evident among the minor element distributions, suggesting the use of space within the D-shaped enclosure and the field system to its east, and there were also some patterns relating to the tidal creek, which seems to have terminated immediately to the north of the settlement.

The value of superimposing geophysical and geochemical survey methods on the same grid for understanding use of space is emphatically demonstrated in the enclosure area. All the figures illustrating the minor element distributions from Haerdepollemswal are superimposed with a schematic representation of the resistivity survey results. The distributions of phosphorous, calcium and magnesium have distinct concentrations within the area defined by the enclosure, identified in the geophysical surveys (and not visible on the surface). Indeed, the distribution of phosphorus around the edges of the open space within the enclosure gives the distinct impression of a farmyard, with areas of midden/animal waste (fig. 13), while calcium and magnesium concentrations seem to locate the positions of buildings. A long calcium concentration runs on a north-south alignment down the interior of the eastern bank of the enclosure, and a further concentration exists in the southeast corner – the

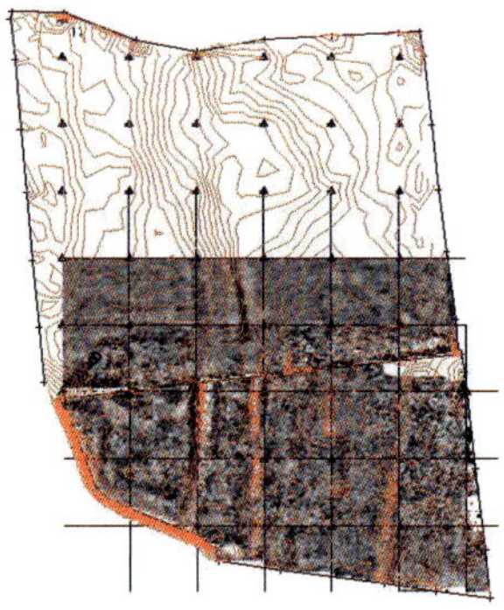

Fig. 12. | *Resistivity survey showing the morphology of the settlement at Haerdepollemswal. After Strutt & Hay 2003.*

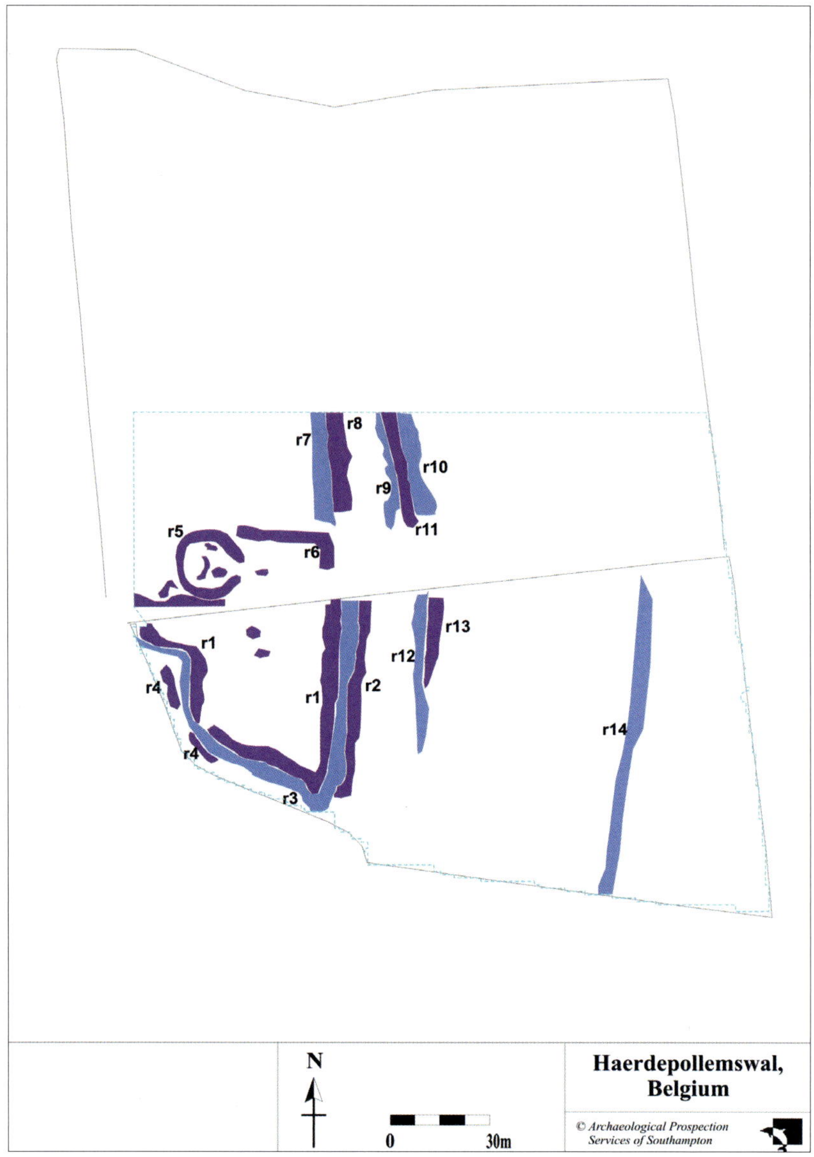

latter also mirrored by a magnesium concentration (fig. 13). All are likely to reflect the geochemical fingerprints of former stone footings, either of limestone (calcium carbonate) or, more likely, the remnants of masonry footings bonded with lime mortar (calcium hydroxide). The long, north-south concentration probably marks the position of a longhouse from the 12th century or later (although the enclosure space was occupied from the 6th or 7th century, on the basis of ceramics).

There were also distinct concentrations of minor elements outside the enclosure, to the east, within the area of the north-south linear strips of an open field system. Particularly high concentrations of potassium and aluminium were found within the fields, and there was also a significant rise in the quantity of iron measured (fig. 14). The potassium and aluminium concentrations mark the development of an enhanced agricultural soil within the fields, in contrast to the internal settlement space of the enclosure. Distributions of calcium and magnesium seem to demarcate the channels of the tidal creek to the north of the enclosure and field system. A higher calcium concentration could reflect the deposition of marine mollusc shells in the channel, with calcium ions leached out over time (fig. 13). Above all, however, the minor element distributions reflect a very stable, indeed static use of space within the enclosure, with phosphorous and calcium concentra-

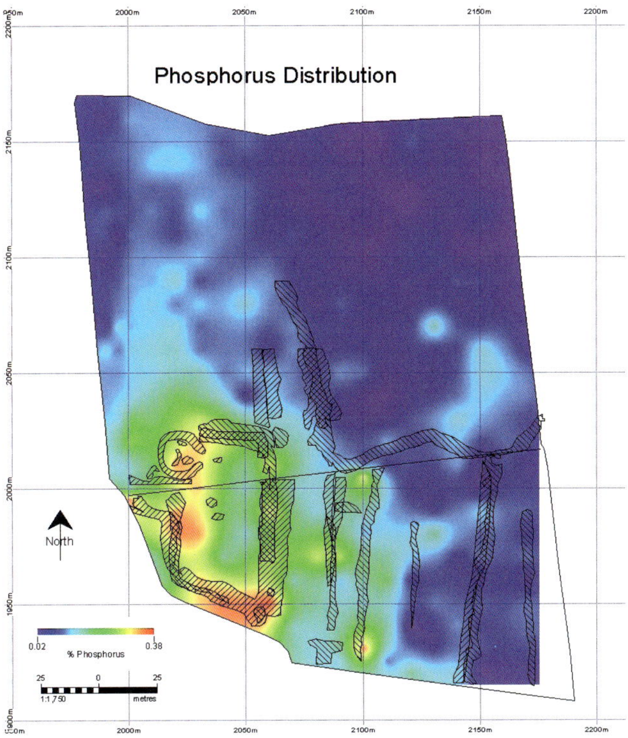

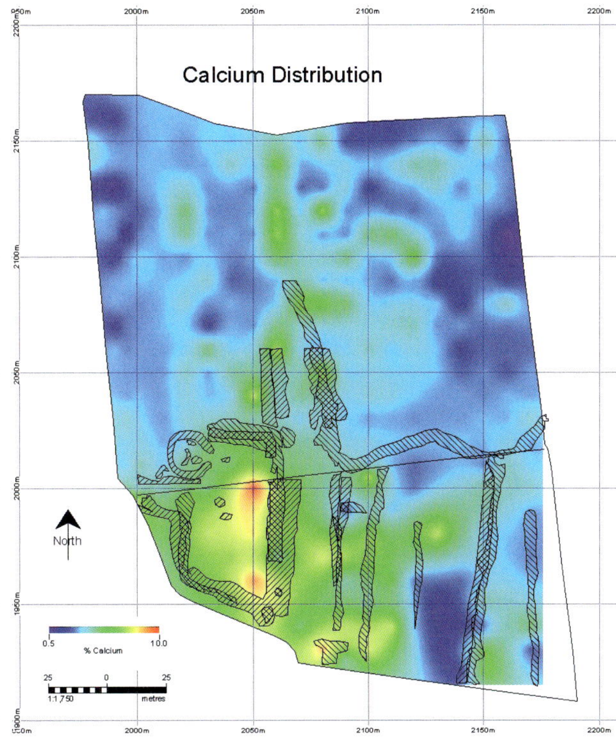

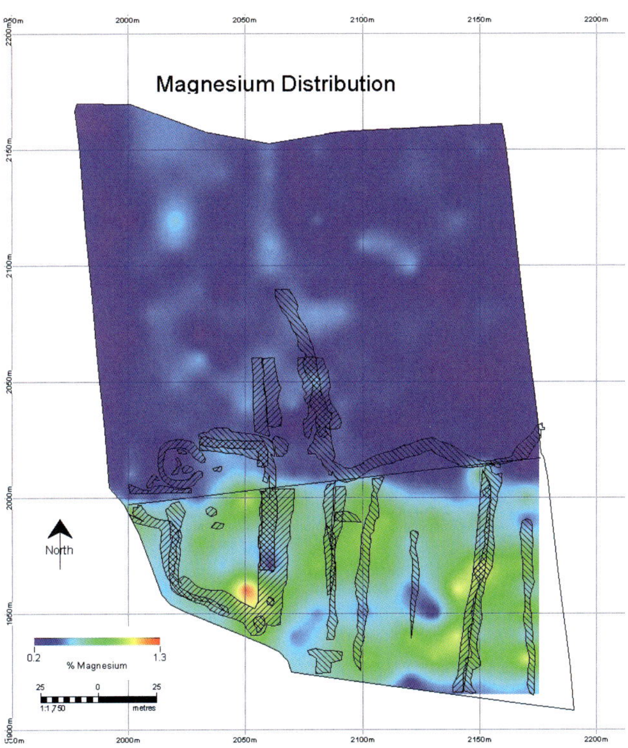

Fig. 13. | *Use of space within the D-shaped enclosure at Haerdepollemswal: distributions of a. phosphorous, b. calcium and c. magnesium. High concentrations of elements are represented in orange and yellow. P. Clogg.*

tions only building up in this area; the settlement did not wander.

The picture of stable settlement occupation indicated by the geophysical and minor element surveys was also reflected in the grid-based surface collection results. Several thousand sherds of pottery were recovered from the surface, dating from approximately AD 300 onwards, without a break in discard until c. AD 1600 (Davies et al. forthcoming). A Spanish army besieged the town of Oostende, to the northeast of Wilskerke, between 1601 and 1604; the provisioning and billeting of the Spanish army is likely to have caused considerable disruption to the nearby rural population. For the Medieval settlement, however, it is possible to conclude that it was occupied continually from the 6th/7th to the late 16th century, with the distribution of pottery dating from between AD 300 and 1100 being identical to that from 1100 to 1600. The pottery, the stable settlement morphology and the stable use of space within the enclosure all suggest a permanent, static hamlet, which existed throughout and beyond the period of any 'Dunkirk II' transgression (c. AD 400 and 800), suggested in the past. Recent sediment studies and

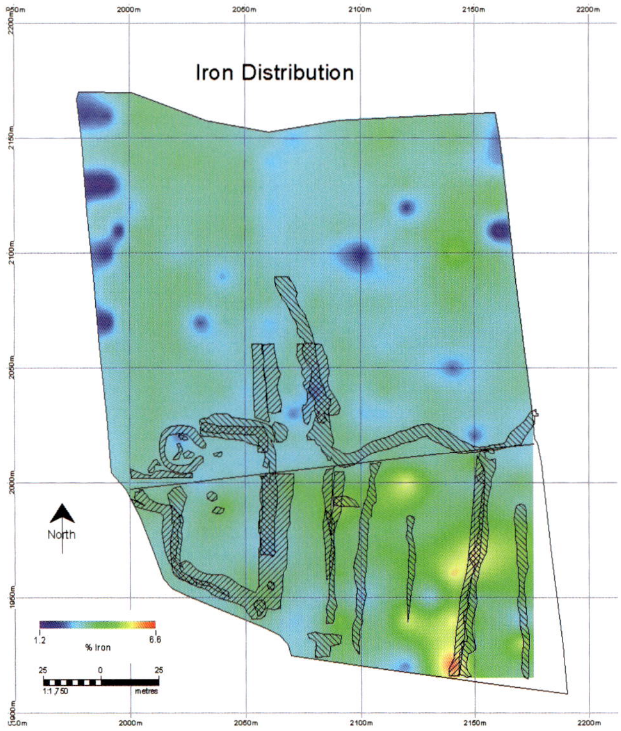

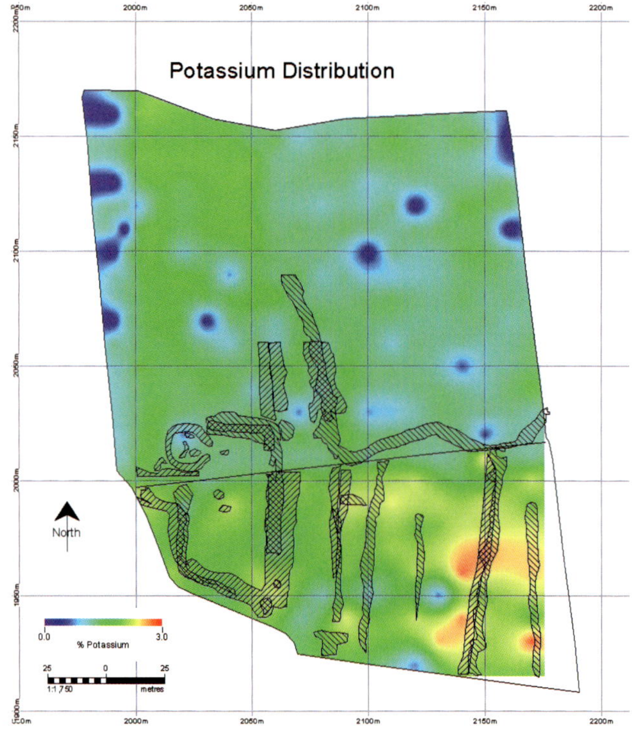

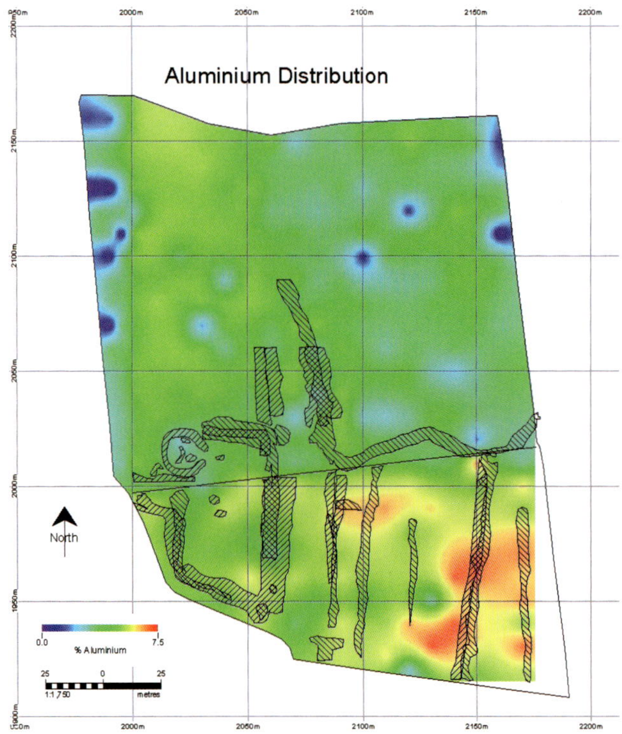

Fig. 14. | *Use of space outside the enclosure at Haerdepollemswal: distributions of a. iron, b. potassium and c. aluminium. High concentrations of elements are represented in orange and yellow. P. Clogg.*

archaeological studies both suggest, therefore, that in the coastal plain of West Flanders any sea-level rise was compensated for by the coastal ecological system, and did not result in the absence of permanent settlements (Davies et al. forthcoming; Loveluck & Tys 2006).

Towards a 'biography' of the settlement at Stavnsager-Hørning, eastern Jutland, AD 400-1100: integrated surveys and excavations, 2005-2009

Stavnsager is located in eastern Jutland, near the Medieval and modern town of Randers, and in close proximity to the strait of Kattegat – the 'bottle-neck' maritime corridor linking the Baltic and North Seas. Today, it is situated on the southern periphery of a wetland area, bisected by the watercourse known as the Oksenbæk. The Oksenbæk joins the river Alling Å, which runs into the fjord system of Kolindsund and Grund Fjord, which opens into the Kattegat (see Høilund Nielsen and Fiedel this volume). The settlement at Stavnsager and a potentially linked site at Hørning, to its southwest, are situated on a plateau and slope overlooking what would have been a navigable waterway between AD 400 and 1000. A dendrochronological date of 1106 from a raised wooden trackway that crossed the watercourse, travelling in a northwest direction from Stavnsager, suggests that the waterway had silted up significantly by the 12th century (Fiedel et al. 2011).

The settlement at Stavnsager was discovered as a result of chance finds during ploughing and metal detecting, and through exploratory excavations by Reno Fiedel and his colleagues from the Kulturhistorisk Museum Randers in the mid 1990s. Karen Høilund Nielsen has shown that the range of artefacts currently being discovered at Stavnsager is directly analogous to those from the settlements at Gudme on Funen, Tissø on Zealand, and Sorte Muld on Bornholm (Høilund Nielsen 2009). The Stavnsager concentration of finds indicates continuous activity from c. AD 400 until the early 1100s. To date, the finds demonstrate links with contemporary societies around the Baltic, North Sea, English Channel and, at times, Irish Sea coasts, at different periods within the activity sequence. The character of the artefacts, typified by aristocratic dress jewellery, weapons, riding gear, bullion in the form of 'hack gold/silver', and a gold foil plaque (*guldgubbe*) also attest to the high social standing of a proportion of the inhabitants. Furthermore, weights for bullion-related exchange, silver coinage, fine metalworking and ironworking debris as well as other artisan activity also point to the regional and interregional importance of this centre at different times in its history. Overlooking Stavnsager, to the southwest of the finds concentration, is the site of the mid to late 11th century stave church at Hørning, built directly on top of a levelled-out, late 10th century barrow and chamber grave, which had sealed graves from an earlier Viking Age cemetery (Krogh & Voss 1961). To the north, on the opposite side of the wetland, Stavnsager is also overlooked by another early church at Virring.

Since 2005, the settlement area has been the subject of systematic study in a collaborative research venture undertaken by Kulturhistorisk Museum Randers, Karen Høilund Nielsen, now of the University of Southern Denmark (Odense), the University of Nottingham, with the Universities of Southampton (APSS) and Durham contracted to it, and the University of Haifa. This systematic research involved the spatial plotting of all chance and metal-detected finds using GIS techniques, alongside preliminary rescue excavation data, to establish that the probable area of human activity covered at least 100 ha. The second part of the pilot project involved a superimposed and multiscaled survey programme, followed by targeted excavations, in order to fulfil two principal objectives: firstly, to begin to identify the morphology and spatial organisation of the settlement, and secondly, to investigate its chronological development.

The Feasibility Project, 2005: Testing the applicability of different superimposed survey techniques

In 2005, a feasibility project was undertaken to test the applicability of different survey techniques on the sand and gravel 'young moraine' geology at Stavnsager (Jakobsen & Hermansen 2007). This involved the superimposed use of a fluxgate gradiometer and RM 15 resistivity meter over 6 ha, and soil sampling for geochemical survey over 3 ha, with samples taken every 10 m, below the base of the modern plough soil, at a depth of approximately 0.75 m. All the surveys were geo-referenced within the same network of 30 x 30 m grids. The soil samples were then analysed by energy-dispersive X-ray fluorescence for a range of minor elements (Clogg & Taylor 2001). The aim of the integrated use of the geophysical and multi-element techniques was to investigate both structural features (reflected by geophysics) and potential refuse or other zones of land-use more susceptible to geochemical detection, such as industrial areas and cemeteries.

The superimposed surveys identified anomalies that seemed to reflect occupation and human use of space throughout the areas sampled. The magnetometer survey, in particular, picked out positive and negative anomalies that seemed to equate with a trackway traversing the settlement from east to west, terminating in a possible slipway or harbour facility (fig. 15), *Grubenhäuser* in large numbers, and anomalies suggesting high-temperature industrial activities (Strutt 2006). The minor element distribution of iron also suggested specific areas of ironworking, associated with major geophysical anomalies, and an intense concentration of phosphorous and calcium suggested a cemetery area (Clogg in Høilund Nielsen & Loveluck 2006, 66f, fig. 16). A series of the 30 x 30 m grids were also the subject of surface collection, comprising 10 transects running east to west at 3 m intervals. Grids with and without identified geophysical anomalies were selected. Several sherds dating from the 1st millennium AD were the only finds, and given the extent of the activity suggested by the other surveys and the evaluation excavations (discussed below), surface collection was not deemed a representative method for establishing past settlement activity in this instance.

Two small evaluation trenches were excavated to test the predictive use of the superimposed survey techniques and the spatial plotting of the metal-detector finds for evaluating archaeological features cut into and deposited upon the natural subsoil, or suspended within the plough soil. One of the trenches (trench 2), which was focused on high magnetic anomalies and a high iron concentration, uncovered a four-phase occupation sequence dating from the 6th to the 12th century AD, on the basis of the artefacts and stratigraphic sequence. Parts of at least two longhouses, three *Grubenhäuser*, and large external stone hearths were revealed. There was a very close correlation between expectations established by the survey results and the data from the excavations. The external hearths dated from between the 6th and the 9th century and may have been used for metalworking (casting sprue and models are among the metal-detector finds from the area). By the Viking Age (from the 9th to the 11th century) a large smithy had been constructed and one of the partly in-filled *Grubenhaus* pits had also been reused for ironsmithing. A small hammer for ironsmithing, spindle whorls and a large fragment of an imported steatite vessel were also recovered from the Viking Age structures.

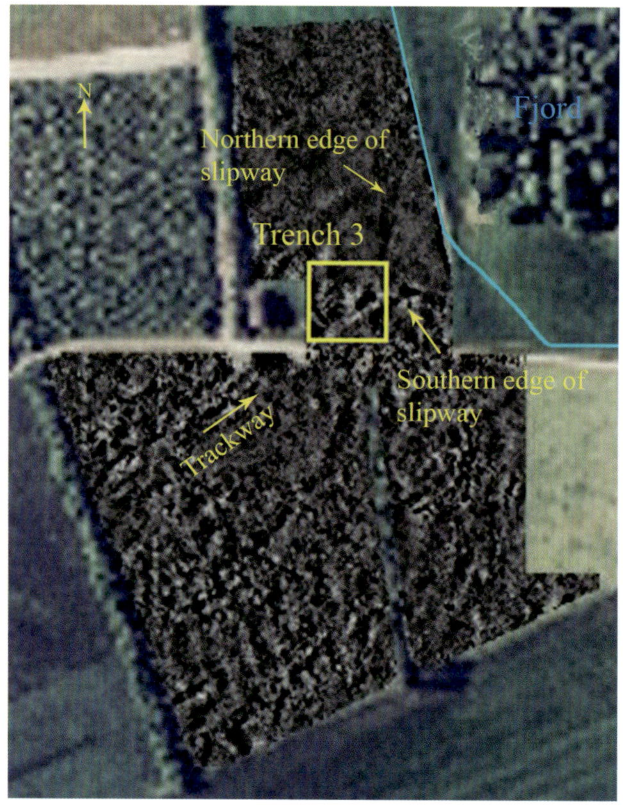

Fig. 15. | *Annotated greyscale image of the trackway and 'slipway' of heat-shattered granite from the magnetometry/gradiometer survey in 2005, subsequently confirmed by excavation in 2008. R. Fiedel, K. Strutt, D. Taylor and C. Loveluck.*

The character of the excavated deposits from trench 2, and their relationship to the survey results, was further clarified by their micro-analysis in a scanning electron microprobe at the University of Nottingham. The correlation between the high iron distribution from the minor element analysis and the ironsmithy was further reinforced by the identification of different types of hammerscale and heat-shattered granite from the hearths and smithy (Faber forthcoming). Phosphatic nodules were also identified using the microprobe, which could reflect fused ash and correlates with a discrete phosphorous peak over and adjacent to the smithy (Macphail & Cruise 2001, 258f). Close interval (0.5 m) magnetometry and resistivity surveys were also conducted at the surface of the subsoil in trench 2 once the plough soil had been removed, in order to investigate differences from measurements taken

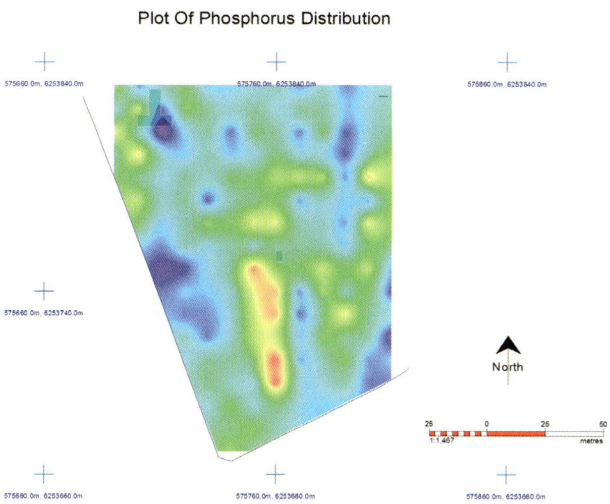

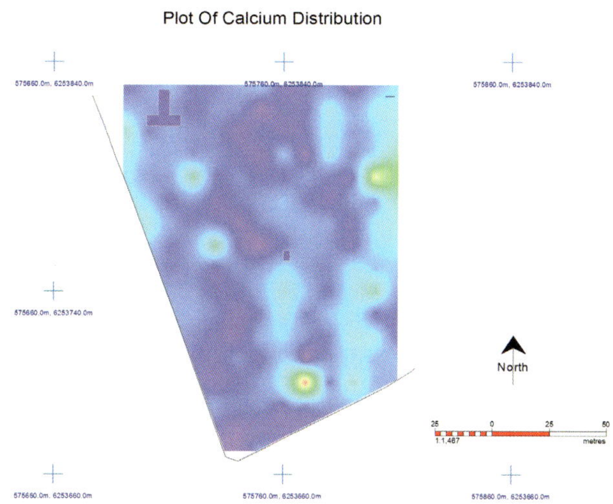

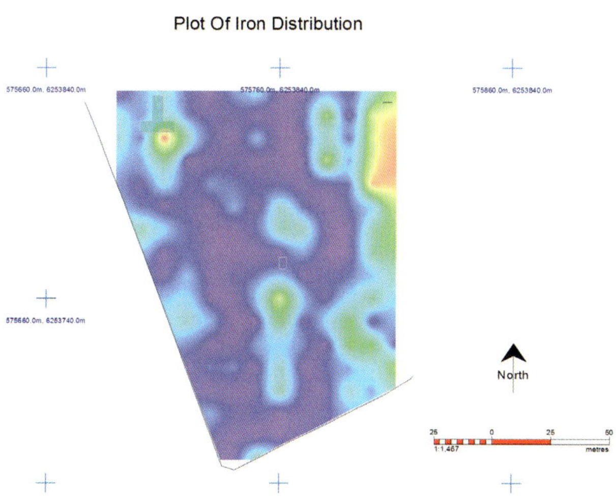

Fig. 16. | *Distributions of phosphorous, calcium and iron suggesting a cemetery focus and sites of ironworking, from the feasibility study of 2005. High concentrations of elements are shown in orange and yellow. P. Clogg.*

from the surface, and hence the reliability of the geophysical survey results. The combined close-interval results demonstrated a very similar pattern of features in the excavation plan to that suggested by the surface survey. The *Grubenhäuser* were visible in the results, together with three sub-circular features of high magnetism in the south of the trench, which were not visible during the excavations. The general alignment of the longhouse walls in the trench is represented in two linear trends in the survey results, together with the line of the gulley from a Medieval open field system (fig. 17).

The second trench (trench 1) did not demonstrate such a close correlation between surveys and archaeological features cut into or lying upon the natural subsoil, due to the extent of destruction by modern ploughing. Trench 1 was located on geophysical anomalies thought to represent *Grubenhäuser* and other pits on the northern extremity of what is thought to have been a cemetery, judging by the very high phosphorous and calcium concentrations in the area. A *Grubenhaus* and pit were located as predicted but the location, on the brow of a hill, and centuries of ploughing had rendered the plough soil less than 10 cm deep, with abundant evidence of the ploughing out of the underlying sand geology. The extensive degradation of the natural sand and acid leaching seem to have destroyed any obvious signs of graves; however, a concentration of dress accessories dating from the 5th to the 7th century, down the hill slope, in the direction of modern ploughing, together with the phosphorous and calcium concentrations suggest that clues to past use of this space could be gained

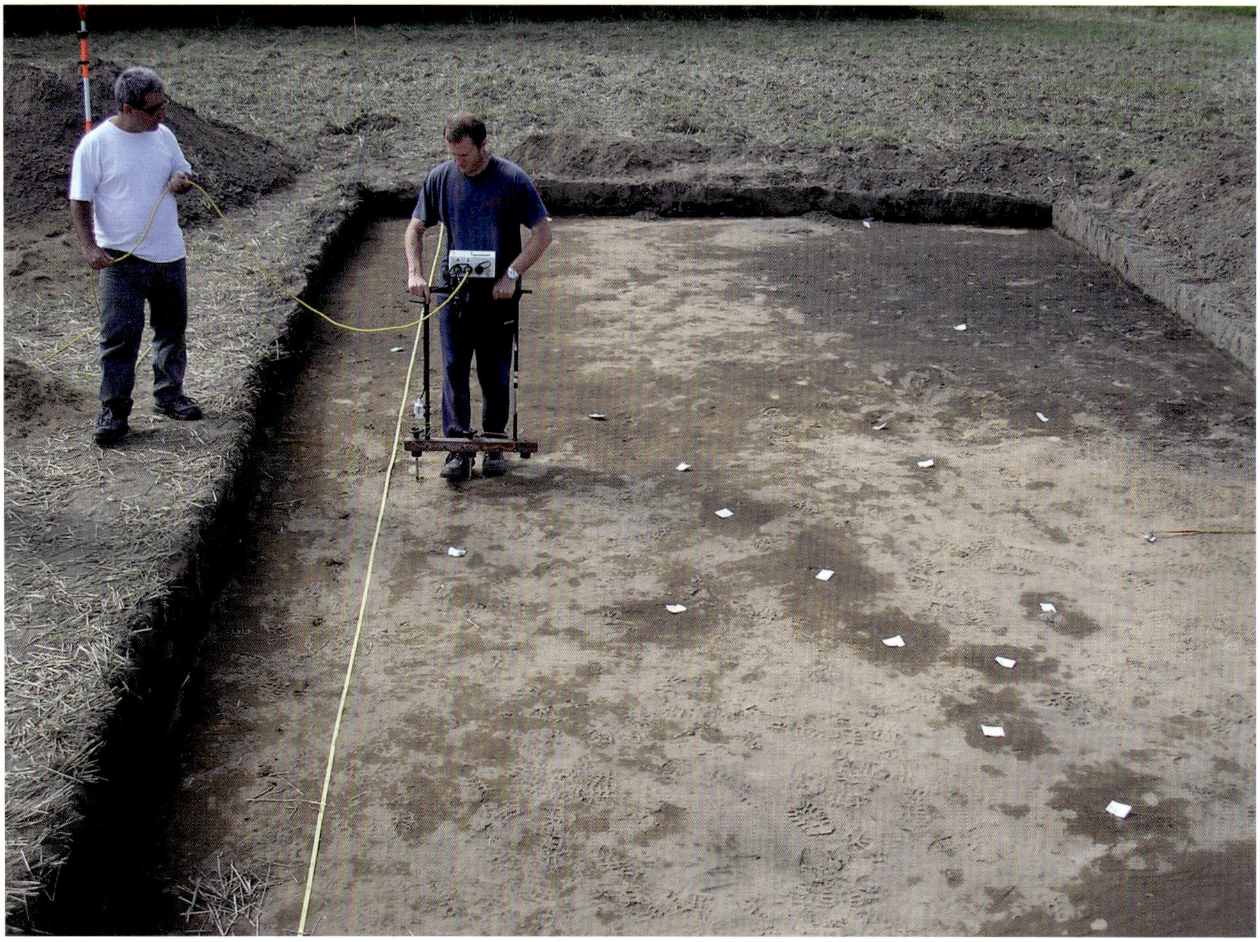

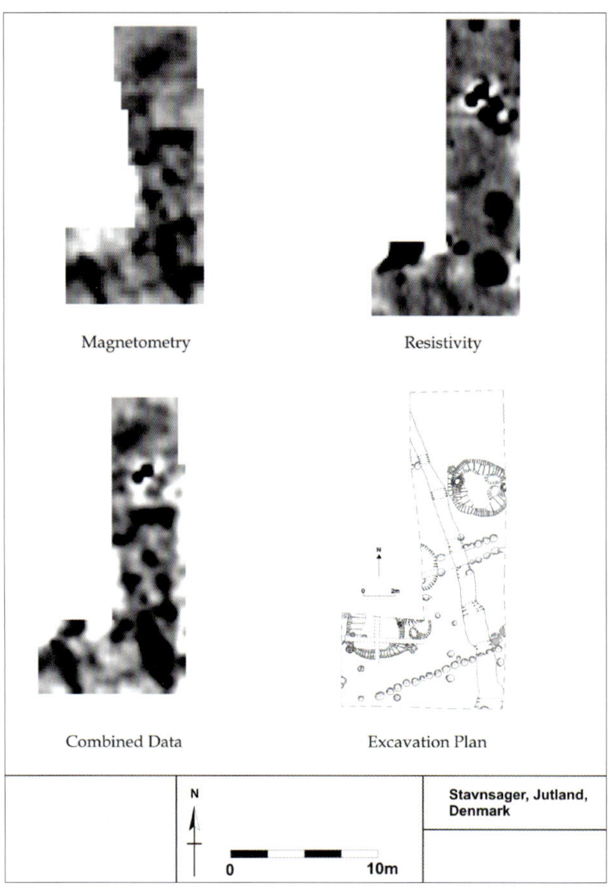

Fig. 17. | *Comparing the geophysical results from the surface of the plough soil and at the surface of the subsoil at Stavnsager, 2005: a. close-interval resistivity survey in progress; b. schematic of close-interval resistivity and magnetometry results compared with excavated features in trench 2. C. Loveluck and K. Strutt.*

from unstratified metal-detector finds allied to the geochemical 'fingerprint'. In this case the archaeological and geochemical evidence that remained was largely suspended within the modern plough soil, and the potential importance of the evidence would not have been recognised if evaluation by excavation had been the sole method of investigation.

The Expanded Pilot Project, 2007-2009

Following the evaluation of the survey strategy for identifying settlement zones, a further 20 ha

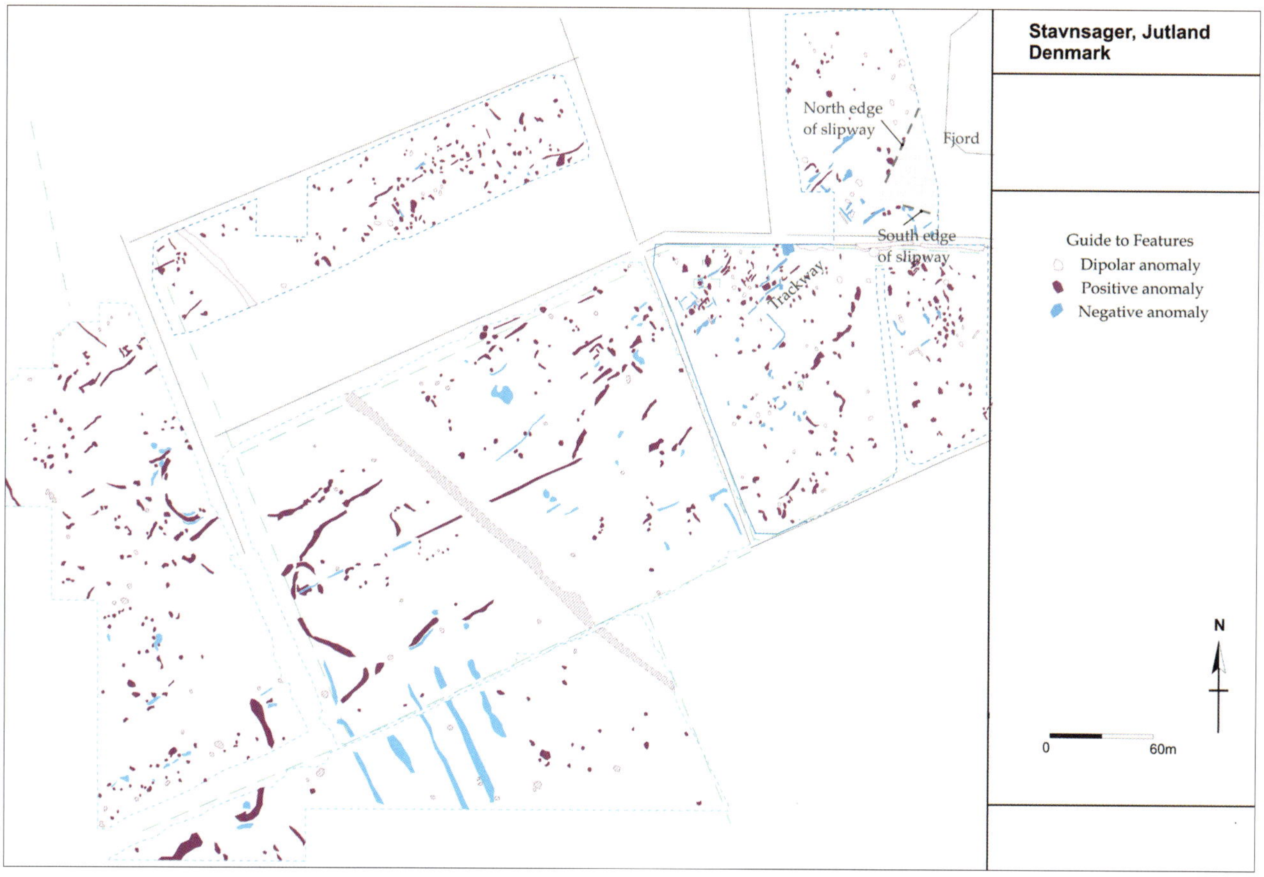

Fig. 18. | *Schematic representation of the results of the gradiometer surveys at Stavnsager, 2005-2007. After Strutt 2006 and 2007.*

of gradiometer survey was conducted in 2007, in several 'landscape blocks' within the area of the 100 ha artefact scatter (fig. 18) (Strutt 2007). A further 16 ha were also sampled for multi-element analysis, superimposed on the same geo-referenced grid. A 4 ha area immediately east of Hørning Church was included for magnetometer and minor element survey, to begin to explore the potential contemporary use of a settlement or cemetery zone in this location, overlooking the fjord-edge settlement at Stavnsager. On the basis of the survey results and availability, three areas were chosen for evaluation by excavation in 2008, with each trench measuring 30 x 30 m.

The aim was to sample three different zones within the settlement through excavation: firstly, an area in the former harbour zone close to the Early Medieval waterway that also coincided with the eastern terminus of the trackway/slipway identified in 2005 – trench 3 (fig. 15); secondly, a zone of habitation with geophysical anomalies suggesting *Grubenhäuser*, and a phosphorous concentration suggesting intensive occupation – trench 4 (fig. 19); and thirdly, a peripheral zone of the settlement, with a view to finding the 'edge' of the occupation area – trench 5 (fig. 19). The aim was to examine different structural and artefact 'signatures' in areas likely to have had different discard and preservation circumstances. On removal of the topsoil within these three trenches, calibration exercises were also undertaken with ground-penetrating radar (GPR) by colleagues from the University of Haifa, with a view to establishing the appropriate velocity of radar needed to identify earth-cut features and archaeological deposits from the surface, without excavation (Loveluck & Salmon 2011; Salmon this volume).

Trench 3 was located immediately to the landward side of one arm of the navigable waterway.

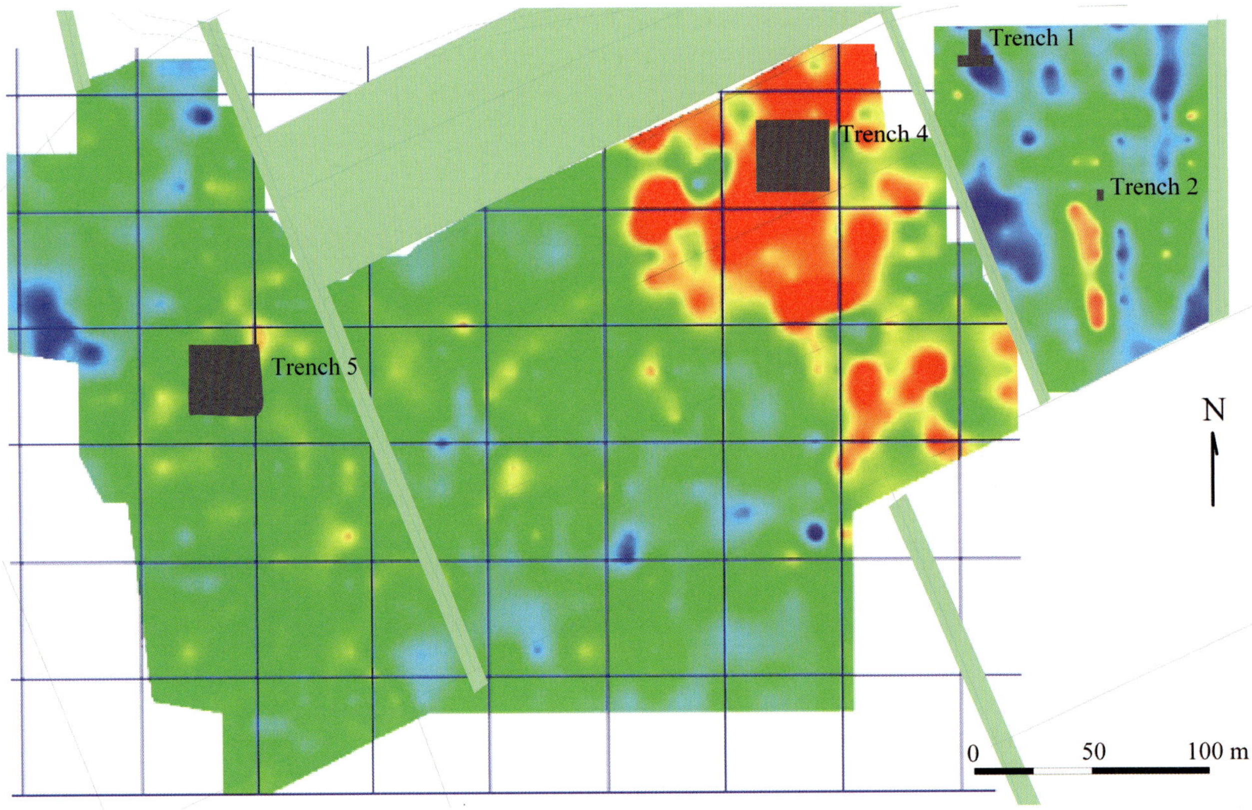

Fig. 19. | *Locations of trenches 4 and 5 from 2008, and trenches 1 and 2 from 2005, superimposed on to a distribution of phosphorous across the areas sampled. R. Stidsing and P. Clogg.*

An activity sequence extending from the 6th/7th century to the 11th century was uncovered, dated on the basis of artefact spot dates and dendrochronological data. A north-south aligned sand spur extended out into the water, with posthole foundations of small storage or workshop buildings on the summit. Several superimposed phases are evident in relation to one of the small buildings on the summit. Originally, the watercourse seems to have been located at the foot of the eastern slope of the spur, and a possible retting pit was excavated near the water's edge. Sometime in the early Viking Age, however – probably during the later 8th or early 9th century – huge deposits of fire-shattered granite and charcoal were dumped to reclaim and create a raised land surface, extending eastwards from the spur summit. This preceded the laying (and subsequent maintenance) of a metalled track of fire-shattered granite, expanding towards an apparent metalled slipway or harbour facility, as indicated by the gradiometer (fig. 20).

This area of stone metalling is likely to have been linked to a 700 m earth and fire-shattered granite embankment, still evident in the landscape, which lined the southern edge of the waterway (now the wetland area). Subsequently, a smaller metalled pathway led off from the main track to a well, and a *Grubenhaus* and other structures were cut into, and through, a general 'dark earth' that developed over the reclaimed area, reflecting intensive use of space throughout the 10th and 11th centuries (fig. 20). The earliest Viking Age well, cut through the dumped deposits, possessed an oak plank in its initial timber lining that is dated to AD 746 by dendrochronology (fig. 21). Allowing for reuse of the timber and correlation with pottery spot-dates, the well was probably initially sunk in the early to mid 9th century. Finds relating to textile manufacture and ironworking were recovered, in addition to glass beads and a fire-blackened soapstone vessel. The latest feature in the activity sequence was the shallow ditch of a

Fig. 20. | *Photograph showing trench 3, with an east-west sondage taken to the surface of the Viking Age period (phase 2, 9th to the 11th century), showing the fire-shattered granite trackway (part in section, part in plan) and the metalled pathway leading from it to the well, with a timber lining dated to AD 746. The levelling of the slope of the sand spur as it extended towards the metalled waterfront and slipway can be seen in the lenses of dumps and dark deposits. Photo: C. Loveluck.*

narrow cultivated field strip, comprising part of a Medieval open-field system.

The discoveries from trench 4 also confirmed the expectations established by the survey results. Parts of at least two longhouses were revealed, along with nine *Grubenhäuser* of different sizes and dates, and several external hearths (fig. 22). Pottery spot-dates and vertical stratigraphic relationships show that the structures dated from the 6th/7th century to the 11th century, with longhouses and associated *Grubenhäuser* from the early part of the sequence being replaced by much larger, oval or sub-rectangular Viking Age *Grubenhäuser* (fig. 23). Again, evidence of textile manufacture was abundant. The residential and craftworking activities reflected in trench 4 were located approximately 70 m to the west of the longhouses, *Grubenhäuser*, fine metalworking and smithy sequence in trench 2, which was excavated in 2005. A large longhouse with bowed or 'boat-shaped' sides, dating from the late 6th/early 7th century, was located in turn approximately 50 m to the west of trench 4; it was partially excavated by Reno Fiedel in 2001. Together, they reflect a residential and artisan zone behind (and to the south of) the waterfront/harbour zone of the settlement; the large longhouse may reflect some social differentiation within the residential zone. Up the slope of a rise, to the south of the residential area, was the possible location of the cemetery.

Trench 5, the final trench to date, was indeed peripheral to the 5th to 11th century settlement. It contained sporadic pits of an early Iron Age date, including a ritual deposit of pottery, with Viking

Fig. 21. | *The excavated Viking Age well from phase 2 in trench 3 (probably 9th century; the dendrochronological date from the timber lining – probably reused – is AD 746), with an earlier retting pit/possible well to its north (to the right on the photograph). The remains of the plank-lined and metalled pathway can be seen in the upper right of the photograph. Photo: C. Loveluck.*

Fig. 22. | *View of buildings with posthole foundations and* Grubenhäuser *in trench 4. Photo: C. Loveluck.*

Fig. 23. | *One of the large oval* Grubenhäuser *from trench 4, dated to the late Viking Age on the basis of pottery and stratigraphic relationships. Photo: C. Loveluck.*

Fig. 24. | *Trench 5: view of early Iron Age pits, and close-up of the early Iron Age ritual deposit. Photo: C. Loveluck.*

Age pottery discovered on the surface to its east (fig. 24). The sporadic pits and their deposits also coincided with a rise in levels of manganese from the minor element analysis and a correspondingly very low level of phosphorus (fig. 19), suggesting the less intense occupation reflected by the pit deposits. A rise in levels of iron to the north of trench 5, towards the margins of the former waterway, may reflect the presence of bog iron in that area. As in trench 3, the latest features in trenches 2, 4 and 5 were shallow ditches defining the cultivated strips of a Medieval open-field system.

Current hypotheses on the biography of the settlement

In summary, the surveys and trial excavations to date have confirmed several zones of specific land-use within the settlement area at Stavnsager. The first zone comprised an area immediately behind an embankment or waterfront that seems to have lined the edge of the navigable watercourse. This 'port area' was occupied predominantly by small post-built and post-in-trench buildings, which were probably used for storage and exchange/trade activities. To the south of the waterfront and the trading zone were concentrations of longhouses and *Grubenhäuser*, the latter forming the majority.

This second zone seems to reflect a large population, which was probably involved in agriculture and craftworking. A probable cemetery was sited on the rise of a slope overlooking the waterway and fjord-edge settlement from the south. And finally, the western periphery of intensive activity within the 5th/6th to 11th century settlement was apparently confirmed, characterised by a zone of pits from the Pre-Roman Iron Age and a rise in manganese levels relative to phosphorous.

The various parts of the settlement were linked by route-ways, some of them metalled with fire-shattered granite; several wells and processing areas (including flax-retting pits) also structured settlement layout. The metal finds (found by metal detecting and ploughing) and the artefacts recovered from the *Grubenhäuser* clearly show that copper alloy casting, iron smelting and smithing and textile manufacture were undertaken on a significant scale. Combining the analysis of the survey and excavation data, along with the spatially plotted metal-detector finds, it is now possible to make preliminary suggestions about the nature of the settlement, and the transformation of its character and social networks, between the 5th and the late 11th century. Significantly, based on provisional indications, the extent of geographical contacts and the quantities of metal artefacts discarded do not reflect times when the structural character of the settlement was at its most impressive.

Just as the preliminary excavation evidence from trench 3 indicates two major transformations in the use of the waterfront come landing area, so the artefact evidence also suggests two major phases in the scale and nature of the maritime connectivity of the Stavnsager settlement. Between the 6th and 7th century, dress accessories and weaponry indicate contact networks around the western Baltic Sea, the North and Irish Seas and the English Channel. These objects include brooches from Sweden, an Anglo-Saxon sword pommel, a Frisian Domburg-type brooch, part of a Frankish square-headed brooch, and brooch fragments from Wales and Ireland (Høilund Nielsen 2009). They were discarded alongside votive objects, reflecting the presence of a likely pagan cult centre; weaponry and riding gear reveal the presence of a secular elite, and hack gold and metalworking demonstrate artisan and exchange activity (Fiedel et al. 2011).

From the later 8th century to the 11th century, however, while fine dress jewellery of regional types was still discarded, the quantities were smaller and evidence of long-distance contacts is much diminished. During this same period, the physical nature of the waterfront zone was at its most impressive, with a metalled slipway or harbour area and metalled trackways connected to it (Loveluck & Salmon 2011). In at least one instance, where a vertical stratigraphic relationship is discernible, the 700 m stone embankment along the edge of the former waterway also overlay Germanic Iron Age remains. Its creation may have been contemporary with the construction of the stone slipway or harbour area, and the metalled trackways. The imported artefacts that were present at this time reflect Baltic and North Atlantic maritime links, in the form of Islamic silver coinage, imported via the Russian river systems and Baltic sea-routes, and Norwegian soapstone vessels. Preliminary indications from the analysis of botanical remains from soil samples from this period indicate significant wheat consumption, though rye and barley were the main cereals grown in the vicinity of the settlement (Giorgi 2010). It is possible that these organic products constituted some of the main imports and exports from the harbour during the Viking Age.

By the mid to late 11th century, a further transformation occurred which seems to have resulted in a decline of the maritime orientation of the fjord-edge settlement at Stavnsager, coinciding with the expansion of large royally-sponsored port towns, such as Aarhus and Aalborg. The latter may have acted as a catalyst for the 'ruralisation' and the 'manorialisation' of the settlement elements in the vicinity of Stavnsager, manifested at Hørning, where a settlement was built on land that had been used as a cemetery. The development of a manorial centre here is probably reflected by the stave church, dated to the 1070s, and a large enclosure around it, which is evident from a gradiometer survey. All settlement activity on the fjord edge at

Stavnsager, below Hørning, seems to have ended in the late 11th century, after which the open-field system cut through all earlier remains.

Prospects for the future

The programme of systematic and superimposed surveys and excavations at Stavnsager has only just begun to shed light on the history of local transformations in this part of eastern Jutland, and their relationships to wider social and political developments in Scandinavia and northwestern Europe. Further finds are being discovered by metal detector and their locations plotted on a regular basis, thus constantly increasing the corpus of metal finds from the 100 ha artefact scatter. Tantalising questions still remain concerning the transformation of the settlement through time, and the identification of all the constituent elements of this poly-focal site. Confirmation of the existence of a cult-house during the 6th century is still awaited; investigation of the possible 'chieftain's' settlement focus, represented by the large, partially excavated longhouse dating from the later 6th/7th century, is a priority. More extensive work on the waterfront and port zone is also necessary, since integrated use of excavation evidence and GPR for predictive deposit modelling suggests a major man-made change in the topography near here during the 9th century (see Loveluck & Salmon 2011; Salmon this volume).

The combined survey, excavation and artefact evidence from Stavnsager to date, however, suggests a very stable settlement activity zone between the 6th and the 11th century, or at least a series of very stable nuclei within a wider zone of fluctuating activity, rather than a history of wholesale settlement shift. Such a provisional conclusion would accord with those of other detailed settlement studies of the mid to late 1st millennium AD in Denmark and England, where site formation processes have been analysed in detail (Holst 2004; Loveluck 2007; Powlesland 2000; Tipper 2004).

The exact nature of the activity sequence around Hørning Church is also yet to be established through excavation. On the basis of the excavations within Hørning Church by Krogh and Voss (1960-61), and gradiometer surveying immediately to the east of the church (2007), the original hypothesis was that activity proceeded from a 9th and 10th century burial ground to a focus on a stave church, which was constructed on top of a 30 m wide barrow (Krogh & Voss 1961). An enclosure encompassing the stave church and a wider space is evident from the gradiometer results (fig. 25), suggesting that Hørning could have comprised an 11th to 12th century manorial centre akin to that suggested at Lisbjerg, Jutland (Jeppesen & Madsen 1997). Targeted GPR survey, however, on a circular anomaly (a probable barrow) beyond the identified enclosure uncovered a more complex activity sequence (Loveluck & Salmon 2011; Salmon this volume). Below the remains of the mostly ploughed-out barrow, a large rectangular building was identified, approximately 20 x 10 m in size, with posthole foundations. If the barrow belonged to the 9th and 10th century cemetery, then either the building dates from a previous settlement phase, or it may have been part of a settlement adjacent to the burial ground that was subsequently encompassed by the 'space of the dead'.

This picture of discrete spaces for the living and for the dead, replaced by areas shared by both – with a linked church and cemetery from the late 11th century – is further supported by minor element distributions from the field to the east. Specific concentrations of phosphorous, manganese, iron and calcium (fig. 26) suggest intensive human action in the area around Hørning Church, beyond the bounds of the modern settlement. Indeed, the discovery of the building below the probable barrow suggests that a settlement focus at Hørning was contemporary with the fjord-edge settlement at Stavnsager. Only more extensive use of GPR in conjunction with excavation will confirm the hints provided by the different research methods used to date at Hørning.

The activities represented by scatters of metal finds located between the settlements at Stavnsager and Hørning are also, as yet, unknown. Finally, the relationship between Stavnsager and the Medieval sites at Moeskærgård and Hørning needs to be es-

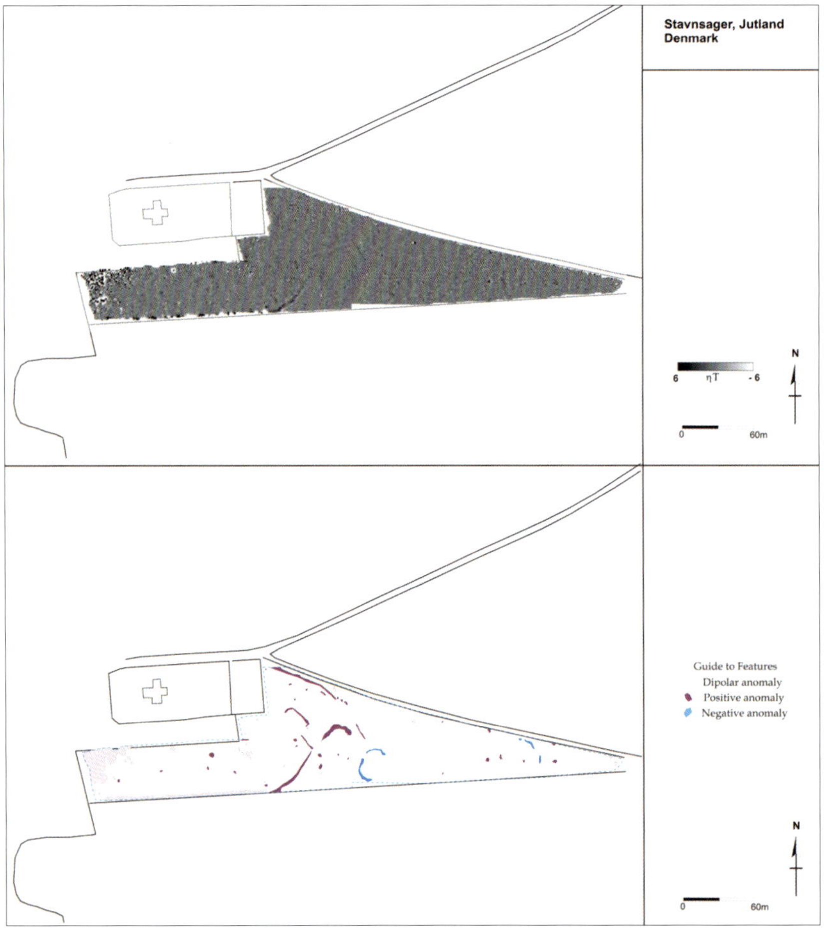

Fig. 25. | *Results of gradiometer survey to the east of Hørning Church, showing the enclosure surrounding the church and a probable associated settlement as well as circular features (possible barrows) to its east. After Strutt 2007.*

tablished more clearly. Currently, the hypothesis that Hørning represents the 11th century manorial centre of the vicinity is unproven, though 11th century riding gear and brooches from Stavnsager suggest people of some status were active, if not resident, at the settlement at that time. It is possible that the settlement focus at Moeskærgård represents the principal agricultural settlement that succeeded Stavnsager; if this were the case, it may still have been subordinate to Hørning in some way.

It is hoped that the programme of surveys and excavations can be continued in coming years to target further blocks of landscape within the 100 ha area in order to address some of the current unknowns. Fields adjacent to Moeskærgård are certainly available for analysis. It is also hoped that excavation can evaluate the current results of the surveys at Hørning to provide some absolute data on the chronology and nature of the wider activity sequence around the church. The integrated and superimposed evaluation methods also allow for and even necessitate a reflexive approach. For example, the gradiometer surveys and analyses of minor element distributions took measurements from specific depths, as they were geared to a macro-scale of the landscape/settlement survey. In the majority of cases these complementary methods did provide a good indication of the nature of archaeological features, cut into the subsoil, and of the use of space. Targeted excavations and GPR surveys demonstrated, however, that the depths of archaeological deposits, colluvial soils and the natural subsoil varied considerably in some areas: for example in the area of trench 3 and the waterfront, where the natural topography had been considerably altered. Hence, future application of different survey techniques will be tailored to our present understanding of deposits in the different settlement zones.

Excavation would not, by itself, have provided the evidence for the use of space in the different zones of the settlement currently investigated. This

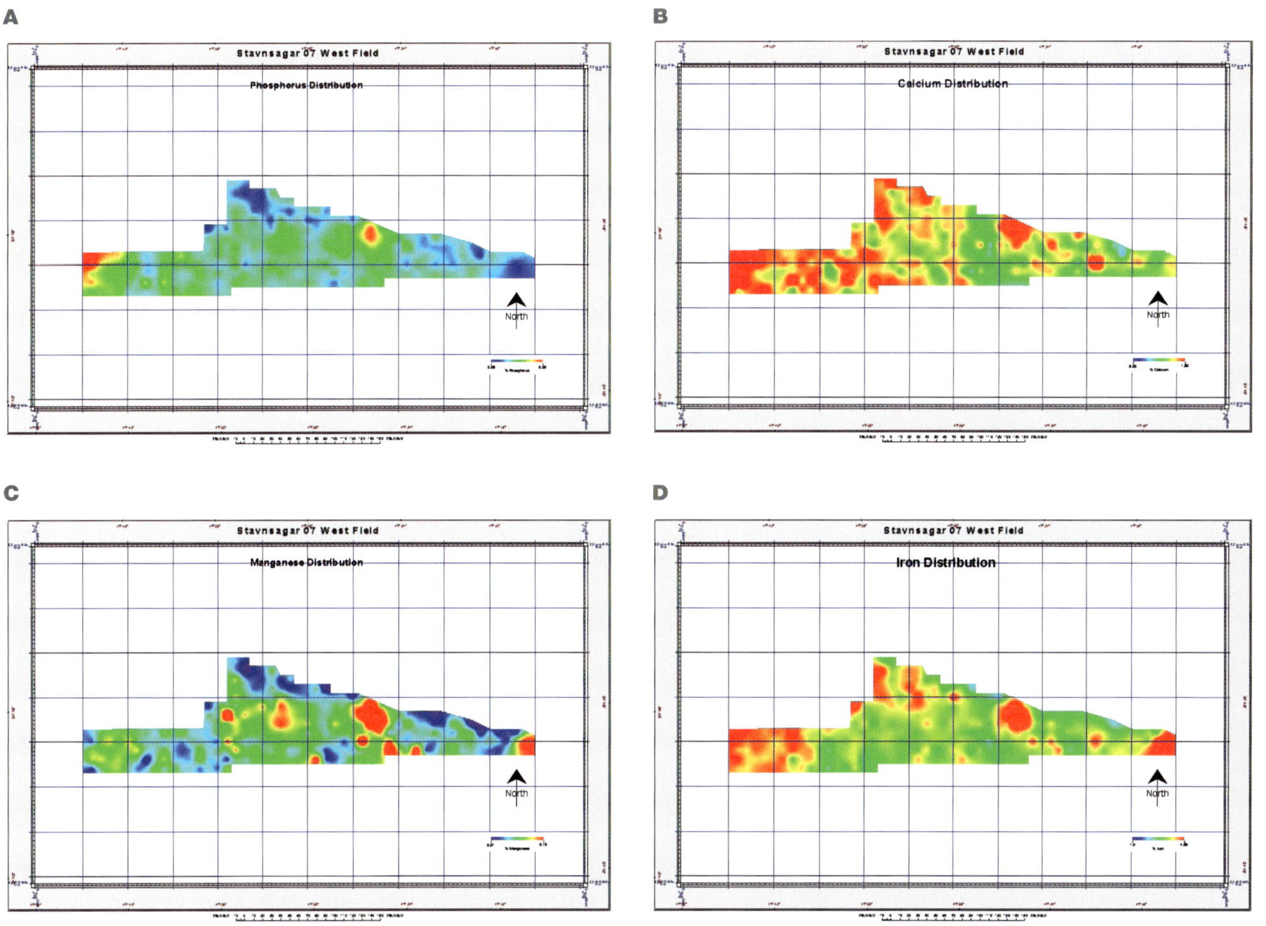

Fig. 26. | *Minor element distributions suggesting intensive human activity to the east of Hørning Church: a. phosphorous; b. calcium; c. manganese; d. iron. High concentrations of elements are shown in red, orange and yellow. P. Clogg.*

is particularly true in relation to the probable cemetery zone to the south of trench 1 (2005) and to the circular anomaly/barrow ditch overlying the building outside the enclosure at Hørning. The extent of modern plough damage to the probable cemetery zone on the brow of the slope overlooking the fjord-edge settlement indicates that any remains are suspended in the plough soil, so the only indicators of past use of space here are the high calcium and phosphorous 'fingerprints' and the distribution of dress accessories down the slope, in the direction of modern ploughing. Excavation would have removed these indicators in the 'topsoil.' It was also clear from the GPR survey at Hørning that the circular anomaly existed at a depth of only approximately 0.5 m, which would place it within the basal elements of the plough soil. That is to say, it may have been partially or fully destroyed by ploughing, though it could still produce gradiometer and radar signatures. Without prior knowledge of the existence of this circular feature, and its likely suspension in the lower element of the plough soil, normal removal of plough soil/topsoil prior to excavation would have destroyed it and limited our understanding of the changing use of space.

Finally, in conjunction with a more nuanced integrated survey strategy, it will be essential to create a representative sample of excavated assemblages on a sufficient scale, and from different settlement zones and deposit types, to confront current models of the character and development of settlements viewed as nodal points or 'central places' within the networks of the mid to late 1st millennium AD (Sindbæk 2007). Particular attention needs to be paid to the active processes governing deposit formation, artefact presence and preservation in certain zones, as a means of assessing the degree to which data from different areas is representative of the overall settlement or merely specific foci within it at different periods (Loveluck 2004). This is of particular importance given the emerging history of dynamic change within the settlement foci of Stavnsager-Hørning, which saw transformations in the nature of participants' lifestyles, networks and perspectives between the 5th and the 12th century AD.

Final conclusions

A number of concluding observations can be made on the value of question-led, superimposed strategies for the social analysis of settlements from later Prehistory and the Early Middle Ages in northern Europe. Firstly, integrated use of geophysical (magnetometry and resistivity) surveys in conjunction with analysis of minor element distributions can provide a representative and comprehensive 'baseline' level of archaeological evidence on settlement morphology and use of space on a landscape scale. This evidence base can be used to plan intensive, targeted methodologies for the analysis of the character of the occupational histories of sites. Such methods can include grid-based surface collection, when circumstances allow, and especially targeted excavations in different zones of settlements to confirm their physical structure, chronology, lifestyles and networks. Targeted use of ground-penetrating radar (GPR) has also demonstrated its value for predictive deposit modelling alongside excavation, and for clarification of stratigraphic sequences, sometimes without excavation (Loveluck & Salmon 2011; Salmon this volume).

Some of the survey results also have important consequences for our understanding of the dynamics of settlements and their populations during the mid to late 1st millennium AD. For example, the use of minor element distributions in conjunction with geophysics and excavation at Wilskerke and Stavnsager has demonstrated that these settlements were either totally stable between AD 600 and 1100, or at least that they possessed significant static foci during this period. This should caution very strongly against the application of 'shifting settlement' models of interpretation so often assumed in northern Europe for the 1st millennium AD. Where other detailed studies of site and deposit formation have been undertaken, the conclusions reached have also demonstrated very significant settlement stability.

There is also no doubt that survey strategies must be applied together with excavations on a sufficient scale, and post-excavation analysis in sufficient detail, if representative social analysis and interpretation is to be achieved. In the United Kingdom, for example, integrated surveys have often been applied without sufficient subsequent excavation. Large-scale excavation alone, however, does not hold all the answers either. As the results from Stavnsager illustrate, without the minor element, geophysical, GPR and metal-detector surveys, the cemetery zone at Stavnsager and the settlement and barrow sequence at Hørning would not have been recognised, as the remains would have been unknowingly removed in the topsoil prior to any excavation. Only with the combined use of the different techniques at our disposal, alongside appropriate conceptual frameworks to guide our questions, can we hope to gain a more comprehensive understanding of our ancestors and the spaces they inhabited.

Acknowledgements

Sincere thanks are extended to the following people and institutions for their support relating to the different projects discussed in this paper: the Rasmussen family, Moeskær; Kulturhistorisk Museum, Randers; the Danish Research Council for the Humanities (now called the Danish Council for Independent Research of Humanities); the Heritage Agency of Denmark (now called Danish Agency for Culture); the British Academy; the University of Nottingham; Dr Paul Johnson; Prof. David Hinton; the University of Southampton; the Province of West Flanders; the community of

Middelkerke, West Flanders; the Free University of Brussels (VUB); Dr Dries Tys; Danielle Feunteun; the Hatter Laboratory for Coastal and Harbour Archaeology; the Israel Science Foundation; and the Instituut voor het Archeologisch Patrimonium, Vlaanderen (IAP now VIOE).

Bibliography

Baeteman, C. 1999, The Holocene depositional history of the Ijzer palaeovalley (western Belgian coastal plain) with reference to the factors controlling the formation of intercalated peat beds. *Geologica Belgica*, 2: 1-2, 39-72.

Baeteman, C., D.B. Scott & M. Van Strydonck 2002, Changes in coastal zone processes at high-sea-level stand: a late Holocene example from Belgium. *Journal of Quaternary Sciences*, 17:5-6, 547-59.

Barker, D., T. Sly & K. Strutt 2005, *Netley Abbey: Topographic and geophysical survey report*, December 2005 (SREP 13/2005), Archaeological Prospection Services of Southampton.

Bintliff, J., M. Kuna & N. Venclova (eds.) 2000, *The future of surface artefact survey in Europe*. Sheffield.

Brooks, M. 2001, Shallows Farm, Hampshire: report on the investigative conservation of some iron objects funded by Winchester Museums Service. Unpublished report.

Buteux, S., V. Gaffney, R. White & M. Van Leusen 2000, Wroxeter hinterland project and geophysical survey at Wroxeter. *Archaeological Prospection* 7:2, 69-80.

Clark, A. 1996, *Seeing beneath the soil: prospecting methods in archaeology*. 2nd ed. London.

Clogg, P. & J. Taylor 2001, Multi-element soil analysis as an archaeological survey technique. In: A. Millard (ed.), *Archaeological Sciences 97. Proceedings of the conference held at the University of Durham 2nd-4th September 1997*. Oxford. 150-59.

Coates, R. 1989, *The place-names of Hampshire*. London.

Craddock, P.T., D. Gurney, F. Pryor & M.J. Hughes 1985, The application of phosphate analysis to the location and interpretation of archaeological sites. *The Archaeological Journal* 142, 361-76.

Crowson, A., T. Lane, K. Penn & D. Trimble 2005, *Anglo-Saxon settlement on the siltland of eastern England*. Sleaford.

Crowther, J. 1997, Soil phosphate surveys: Critical approaches to sampling, analysis and interpretation. *Archaeological Prospection* 4, 93-102.

Davies, G., P. Deckers, C. Loveluck & D. Tys, with K. Strutt & P. Clogg (forthcoming), Between the Frankish and North Sea worlds: settlement, exchange and identity in coastal Flanders, AD 400-1100.

Entwistle, J.A., P.W. Abrahams & R.A. Dodgshon 1998, Multi-element analysis of soils from Scottish historical sites. Interpreting land-use history through the physical and geochemical analysis of soil. *Journal of Archaeological Science* 25, 53-68.

Faber, E. (forthcoming), Report on the micro-analysis of archaeological deposits excavated at Stavnsager, east Jutland, 2005-2008. Unpublished assessment report, University of Nottingham.

Fiedel, R., K. Høilund Nielsen & C.P. Loveluck 2011, From hamlet, to central place, to manor. Social transformation of the settlement at Stavnsager, eastern Jutland, and its networks, AD 400-1100. *Neue Studien zur Sachsenforschung* 3, 161-76.

Francovich, R., H. Patterson & G. Barker (eds.) 2000, *Extracting meaning from ploughsoil assemblages*. Oxford.

Gaffney, V.L., C.F. Gaffney & M. Corney 1998, Changing the Roman landscape: the role of geophysics and remote sensing. In: J. Bayley (ed.), *Science in archaeology – an agenda for the future*. London.

Gaffney, C. & J. Gater 2003, *Revealing the buried past: geophysics for archaeologists*. Stroud.

Gerrard, C., with M. Aston 2007, *The Shapwick Project, Somerset. A rural landscape explored*. Leeds.

Gifford, C. 1997, An introduction to metal detecting and complementary activities at Breamore, Hampshire. *Avon Valley Archaeological Society Newsletter* 11.

Giorgi, J.A. 2010, The plant remains from Stavnsager (STAV08), north-east Jutland. Unpublished assessment report, University of Nottingham.

Hayes, P. & T. Lane 1992, *The south-west Fens*. Sleaford.

Høilund Nielsen, K. 2009, Stavnsager 400-1100: Weiler, Zentralort, Herrenhof. In: S. Brather, D. Geuenich, & S. Huth (eds.), *Historia archaeologica: Festschrift für Heiko Steuer zum 70. Geburtstag*. Berlin. 415-33.

Høilund Nielsen, K. & C.P. Loveluck 2006, Fortid og fremtid på Stavnsager – om de Britiske undersøgelser august 2005 og de foreløbige resultater. *Kulturhistorisk Museum Randers Årbog* 2006, 63-79.

Holst, M.K. 2004, The syntax of the Iron Age village. Unpublished PhD thesis. University of Aarhus.

Jackson, A. 2007, Archaeological soil analyses. In: C. Gerrard with M. Aston (eds.), *The Shapwick Project, Somerset. A Rural Landscape Explored*. Leeds. 183-200.

Jakobsen, P.R. & B. Hermansen 2007, Danmarks Digitale Jordartskort 1:25 000. Version 3.0. *Danmarks og Grønlands Geologiske Undersøgelse Rapport* 2007/84 [only on CD-Rom].

Jensen, S. 1985, Hvad 100 km læhegn gemte. *Mark og Montre* 1985, 49-54.

Jeppesen, J. & H.J. Madsen 1997, Trækirke og stormandshal i Lisbjerg. *Kuml* 1995-96, 149-71.

Jones, R. & M. Page 2006, *Medieval villages in an English landscape: beginnings and ends*. Macclesfield.

Kattenberg, A.E. & G. Aalbersberg 2004, Archaeological prospection of the Dutch perimarine landscape by means of magnetic methods. *Archaeological Prospection* 11, 227-35.

Keay, S., M. Millett, L. Paroli & K. Strutt 2005, *Portus: an archaeological survey of the port of Imperial Rome*. London.

Keay, S., G. Earl, S. Hay, S. Kay, J. Ogden & K. Strutt 2008, The potential of archaeological geophysics: the work of the British School at Rome in Italy. In: L. Orlando (ed.), *Geofisica per L'Archeologia: possibilità e limiti. Atti del Convegno Roma 10 Dicembre 2008*. Rome. 25-45.

Keay, S., G. Earl, S. Hay, S. Kay, J. Ogden & K. Strutt 2009, The role of integrated geophysical survey methods in the assessment of archaeological landscapes: the case of Portus. *Archaeological Prospection* 16:3, 154-66.

Krogh, K.J. & O. Voss 1961, Fra hedenskab til kristendom i Hørning. En vikingetids kammergrav og en trækirke fra 1000-tallet under Hørning kirke. *Nationalmuseets Arbejdsmark* 1961, 5-34.

Lane, T. with P. Hayes 1993, *Lincolnshire Survey: the Northern Fen-Edge*. Sleaford.

Lewis, C. 1997, Medieval settlement in Hampshire and the Isle of Wight. In: G. DeBor & F. Verhaege (eds.), *Rural settlements in Medieval Europe. Papers at the Medieval Europe Conference, Brugge 1997*. Zellik. 75-86.

Light, A., A.J. Schofield & S.J. Shennan 1994, The Middle Avon Valley Survey: a study in settlement history. *Proceedings of the Hampshire Field Club and Archaeological Society* 50, 43-102.

Loveluck, C. 2004, *Terres noires* and Early Medieval rural settlement sequences: conceptual problems, descriptive limitations and deposit diversity. In: L. Verslype & R. Brulet (eds.), *Terres noires-dark earth. Actes de la table ronde tenue à Louvain-la-Neuve les 9 et 10 novembre 2001*. Louvain-la-Neuve. 86-96.

Loveluck, C. 2007, *Rural settlement, lifestyles and social change in the later First Millennium AD. Anglo-Saxon Flixborough in its wider context. Excavations at Flixborough*. Vol. 4. Oxford.

Loveluck, C. & Y. Salmon 2011, Exploring an Early Medieval harbour and settlement dynamics at Stavnsager, Denmark: a geo-archaeological dialogue. *Antiquity* 85, 1402-17.

Loveluck, C. & D. Tys 2002, The development of the Medieval settlement pattern and landscape in coastal Flanders, AD 400-1500: the Leffinge pilot project. Unpublished report, University of Southampton.

Loveluck, C. & D. Tys 2006, Coastal societies, exchange and identity along the Channel and southern North Sea shores of Europe, AD 600-1000. *Journal of Maritime Archaeology* 1:2, 140-69.

Lyall, J. & D. Powlesland 1996, The application of high resolution Fluxgate Gradiometry as an aid to excavation planning and strategy formulation. *Internet Archaeology* 1. http://intarch.ac.uk/journal/issue1/lyall_index.html (accessed 15.10.2013).

Macphail, R.I. & J. Cruise 2001, The soil micromorphologist as team player. A multi-analytical approach to the study of European microstratigraphy. In: P. Goldberg, V.T. Holliday & C. Reid Ferring (eds.), *Earth Sciences and Archaeology*. New York. 241-267.

Munby, J. 1982, *Domesday Book: Hampshire*. Chichester.

Parry, S. 2006, *Raunds area survey. An archaeological study of the landscape of Raunds, Northamptonshire, 1985-94*. Oxford.

Potter, T.W. 1979, *The Changing landscape of South Etruria*. London.

Powlesland, D. 2000, *West Heslerton settlement mobility: a case of static development*. In: H. Geake & J. Kenny (eds.), *Early Deira – Archaeological studies of the East Riding of Yorkshire in the fourth to ninth centuries AD*. Oxford. 19-26.

Prevosti, M., K. Strutt & C. Carreras (forthcoming), *Ager Tarraconensis* project (right side of river Francoli) (PAT): geophysical surveys to identify rural Roman settlements typologies. In: *Changing Landscapes. Proceedings of the International Colloquium on Landscape Archaeology, 15th and 16th May 2008, held at Castelo de Vide, Portugal.* Bologna.

Rippon, S.J., M.H. Martin & A.W. Jackson 2001, The use of soil analysis in the interpretation of an early historic landscape at Puxton, Somerset. *Landscape History* 23, 27-38.

Roberts, B.K. & S. Wrathmell 2000, *An atlas of rural settlement in England.* London.

Rodwell, W. & E.C. Rouse 1984, The Anglo-Saxon rood and other features in the south porch of St. Mary's Church, Breamore, Hampshire. *Antiquaries Journal* 64, 298-325.

Rogerson, A., A. Davison, D. Pritchard & R. Silvester 1997, *Barton Bendish and Caldecote: fieldwork in southwest Norfolk.* Norwich.

Schofield, A.J. 1989, Understanding Early Medieval pottery distributions: cautionary tales and their implications for further research. *Antiquity* 63, 460-70.

Schofield, A.J. (ed.) 1991, *Interpreting artefact scatters: contributions to ploughzone archaeology.* Oxford.

Scollar, I., A. Tabbagh, A. Hesse & I. Herzog 1990, *Archaeological prospecting and remote sensing.* Cambridge.

Silvester, R.J. 1988, *The Fenland Project. No. 3. Marshland and the Nar valley.* Dereham.

Sindbæk, S.M. 2007, Networks and nodal points: the emergence of towns in Early Viking Age Scandinavia. *Antiquity* 81, 119-32.

Strutt, K. 2002, Breamore: Geophysical Survey Report February 2002. Unpublished survey report.

Strutt, K. 2004a, *Breamore settlement and landscape project: geophysical survey report March 2004* (SREP 2/2004). Archaeological Prospection Services of Southampton.

Strutt, K. 2004b, *St Michaels Priory, Breamore: geophysical survey report November 2004* (SREP 13/2004). Archaeological Prospection Services of Southampton.

Strutt, K. 2005, *The Breamore settlement and landscape project: geophysical survey report April 2005* (SREP 12/2005). Archaeological Prospection Services of Southampton.

Strutt, K. 2006, *Results of a geophysical survey at the site of Stavnsager, Jutland, Denmark, July-August 2005* (SREP 1/2006). Archaeological Prospection Services of Southampton.

Strutt, K. 2007, *Results of a geophysical survey at the site of Stavnsager, Jutland, Denmark, September 2007* (SREP 13/2007). Archaeological Prospection Services of Southampton.

Strutt, K. & S. Hay 2003, *Leffinge area settlement and landscape project: report on the geophysical surveys* (SREP 15/203). Archaeological Prospection Services of Southampton.

Strutt, K. & S. Keay 2008, The role of integrated geophysical survey methods in the assessment of archaeological landscapes: the case of Portus. In: R. Lasaponara & N. Masini (eds.), *Advances on remote sensing for archaeology and cultural heritage management.* Rome. 121-24.

Strutt, K., T. Sly & D. Barker 2004, *Portchester Castle: archaeological survey report*, May 2004 (SREP 1/2004). Archaeological Prospection Services of Southampton.

Tipper, J.B. 2004, *The Grubenhaus in Anglo-Saxon England: an analysis and interpretation of the evidence from a most distinctive building type.* Yeadingham.

Tys, D. 2003, Een middeleeuws landschap als materiële cultuur: de interactie tussen macht en ruimte in een kustgebied en de wording van een laatmiddeleeuws tot vroegmodern landschap – Kamerlings Ambacht, 500-1200/1600. 5 vols. Unpublished PhD thesis. Free University of Brussels (VUB).

Walker, R. 1992, Phosphate survey: method and meaning. In: P. Spoerry (ed.), *Geoprospection in the archaeological landscape.* Oxford.

Zimmermann, W.H. 1992, Die Siedlungen des 1. bis 6. Jahrhunderts nach Christus von Flögeln-Eekhöltjen, Niedersachsen. Die Bauformen und ihre Funktionen. *Probleme der Küstenforschung im südlichen Nordseegebiet* 19, 1-360.

The application of ground-penetrating radar (GPR) at Stavnsager, Denmark: Prospects and contributions

Yossi Salmon

In recent years there has been a growing trend towards the utilisation and assimilation of scientific tools and methods in archaeological projects in order to extend our ability to understand and interpret archaeological data. This multidisciplinary approach characterises the Stavnsager Archaelogical Project, directed by Reno Fiedel, Kulturhistorisk Museum Randers, Chris Loveluck, University of Nottingham, and Karen Høilund Nielsen. The Stavnsager site has been subjected to extensive investigation for almost two decades. Various geophysical and geochemical methods, such as magnetometry, electrical-resistivity and soil analysis, have been applied in combination with traditional archaeological excavation. The above research framework has allowed us to introduce the ground-penetrating radar (GPR) survey method into a relatively controlled environment and has consequently enabled us to examine several issues with respect to its application in the investigation of a later Iron Age site in eastern Jutland, Denmark.

The Stavnsager site covers the period from the end of the Roman Iron Age up to the early High Middle Ages (c. AD 400-1100). During this time, it served as a metal production centre and anchorage/landing site for maritime trade. Evidence from excavation and geophysical surveys indicates the presence of various settlement areas, including a village dating from the 5th to the 6th century, a longhouse from the late 6th or early 7th century and *Grubenhäuser* corresponding to most of the occupation sequence, as well as an undated stone embankment (Fiedel et al. 2011; Høilund Nielsen 2009).

Location and geomorphological background

The site is located in eastern Jutland, adjacent to a branch of the inner part of a large, now drained fjord system known as Kolindsund and Grund Fjord (fig. 1). The wetland areas marked correspond to those shown on maps from the late 19th century (Høilund Nielsen 2009; Loveluck et al. this volume). The modern landscape consists of low hilly terrain interspersed by wide valleys that would have been partly flooded, forming natural marine inlets, throughout most of prehistory. These valleys have gradually been returned to dry land as a consequence of post-glacial isostatic and eustatic processes and, during the last two centuries, as a result of intensive drainage of agricultural land. Stavnsager is situated to the south of a broad valley that may have provided navigable access to the sea until as late as the Viking Age. Today the valley is dry, with a series of interconnecting drainage channels along its entire length.

Three distinct sedimentary packages coincide with the geological and archaeological setting of the research area. The upper unit is a cultivated

Fig. 1. | *Location map showing Stavnsager and Hørning, eastern Jutland, Denmark.*

sandy/clayey soil varying in depth between 0.3 and 1.5 m, depending on the terrain and present-day agricultural activities. The lower unit is the subsoil, a melt-water till from the young moraine landscape, consisting mainly of sand with concentrations of gravel and, in some cases, boulders (Jakobsen & Hermansen 2007). Between these two layers, a third anthropogenic cultural layer can be distinguished, appearing mostly as a dark soil containing potsherds and charcoal. This unit is mainly cut into the subsoil and covered by the cultivated soil.

The application of ground-penetrating radar (GPR) in archaeology

Use of the GPR system makes it possible to distinguish between sedimentary layers, stones and a great variety of substances. The GPR data are acquired by transmitting pulses of radar energy into the ground from a surface antenna; this energy is then reflected by buried objects, features or bedding contacts back to the ground surface where it is detected by a receiving antenna. Surface radar antennas are moved over the ground along transections within a surveyed grid and a large number of subsurface reflections are collected along each transection. As radar energy moves through various materials, the velocity of the waves will change depending on the physical and chemical properties of the material through which they are travelling (Conyers 2004, 1-3).

Since the beginning of the 1990s, GPR has been employed as a geotechnical tool in the definition of lithological contacts, faults, bedding plans and joint systems in rocks (Baker 1991; Cook 1975; Deng et al. 1994), and soil scientists and hydrologists began to use the technique to investigate buried surfaces, soil units and the depth and nature of groundwater tables (Beres & Haeni 1991; Bristow & Jol 2003; Collins 1992; Smith et al. 1999). It was used sporadically in an archaeological context at several sites during the 1970s. However, the realisation that radar reflections measured in time could be defined in real depth proved to be a major advance for archaeology, and together with the introduction of spatial amplitude maps ('time slices') and 3D models, this brought about an increased use of GPR in archaeology during the 1980s (Conyers 2004, 19-20; 2010; Goodman et al. 1995).

The nature of the geo-archaeological evidence at Stavnsager

In 2008, the excavations and the geophysical and geochemical surveys were concentrated in two main areas on the cultivated arable land at Stavnsager and Hørning, both situated on rampart-shaped hills (fig. 2). The research area at Stavnsager has an extent of about 25.48 ha (c. 490 x 520 m) and is located about 150 m west of the farm Moeskærgård. The terrain is mainly plane with a moderate slope that becomes steeper near the edge of the drained fjord to the north (fig. 3). The Hørning area extends over about 6.37 ha (c. 130 x 490 m) and is located to the east of Hørning Church. It comprises plane terrain, with a slight and moderate slope towards the north and west (fig. 4). At Stavnsager, the depth of the topsoil is c. 0.6-0.7 m in the southern part of the area – as recorded in excavations carried out by the Nottingham University team – and about 1.3 m in the northern part, where an ancient wooden plank road was excavated by Kulturhistorisk Museum Randers. The depth of the topsoil at Hørning is estimated to be 0.5-1.3 m.

The relatively plane landscape at Stavnsager is a result of weathering processes active since the beginning of the Holocene period and continuous cultivation of the hilly moraine landscape, which has taken place in Jutland over the last six millennia (Jensen 1982, 5-7). Jensen's description of typical prehistoric remains in Denmark corresponds well with most of the archaeological finds at Stavnsager: 'It is important to realise that the vestiges of a typical prehistoric settlement in Denmark consist merely of the bottom layers of settlement. Preserved pavings, floor and hearths are rare. All such house traces have usually been removed by ploughing long ago. Potsherds and other object from the settlement are very few, as they have also been destroyed by ploughing. The "finds" are thus merely vague dark discolourations in the subsoil which represent the bottom of pits into which house posts were placed.' (Jensen 1982, 180).

Fig. 2. | *View of the areas surveyed in the vicinity of Hørning Church, facing west. Photo: C. Loveluck.*

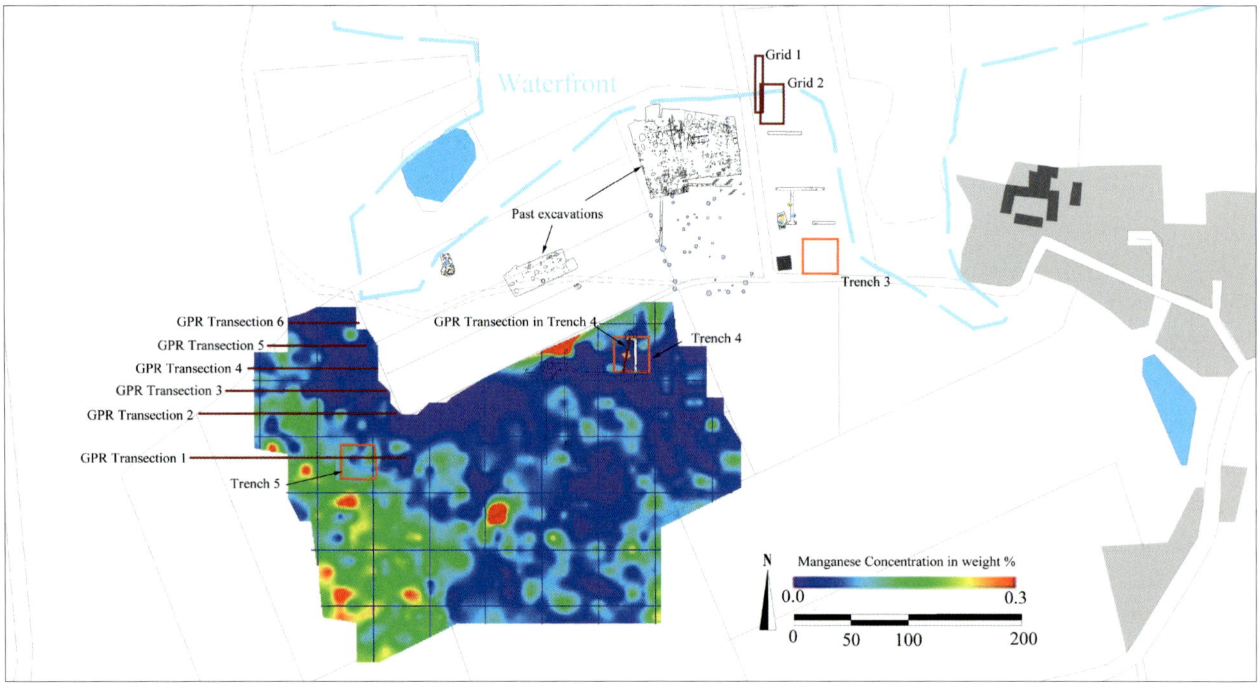

Fig. 3. | *Location map summarising all the research activities carried out at Stavnsager: GPR survey transections 1-6, grids 1 and 2 alongside excavation trenches 3, 4 and 5 – all from 2008; previous excavations; and a partial minor-element distribution plot showing a rise in levels of manganese at the western margins of the settlement – the latter was surveyed by P. Clogg.*

Preservation conditions may differ due to variations in the depth of the plough soil; thicker layers create better preservation conditions than thinner ones. Variation in depth is usually attributed to the action of levelling processes on the landscape, creating thicker deposits in the natural low-lying areas and relatively thin deposits on the tops of the hills (French 2003, 40-60). This depository nature allows us to reconstruct the paleogeography of the period when the site was inhabited. The primary questions in our present study were whether the 'dielectric contrast' between these 'vague dark discolourations' of the archaeological features and the virgin subsoil is strong enough to be distinguished by GPR, and whether the cultural layers from human activities

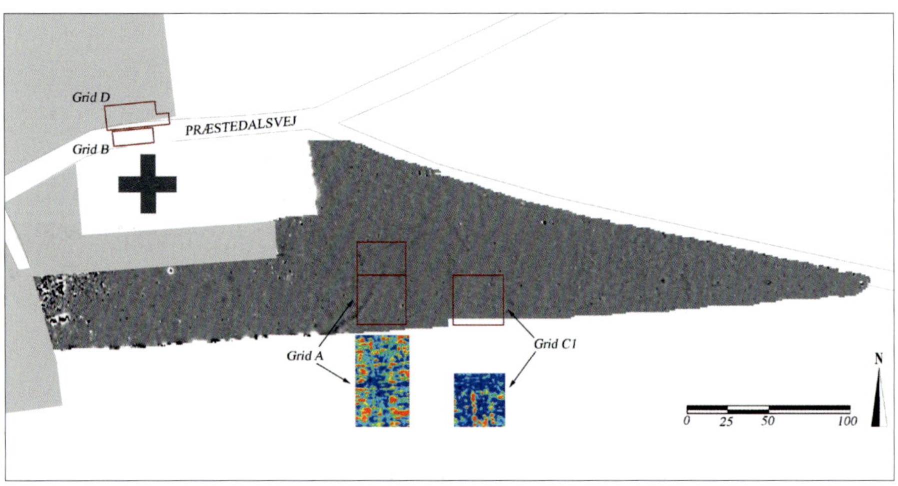

Fig. 4. | *Location of the GPR survey at Hørning; grid A, grid B, grid C1 and grid D are superimposed on the gradiometer survey results (obtained by C. Strutt). The latter show an oval feature crossing the eastern part of grid A from southwest to northeast and a ring-shaped feature in the centre of grid C1.*

can be discerned in areas with good preservation conditions.

Methodology

The survey was carried out using a GSSI SIR3000 pulse echo GPR system with two antennas of 400 MHz and 900 MHz and a survey cart. Three calibration procedures were employed before data acquisition in the field, gaining ons (zero nanosecond) offset corrections and trace stacking filtering. The calibration of the gaining procedure involved applying a set of gains in order to compensate for the natural attenuation of the wave energy as it travels through the subterrain. This procedure depends on the type of GPR system used. Some of the systems available do not require the application of gains, but the GSSI SIR3000 does. The second calibration procedure employed in the field, as well as during post-processing analysis, was correction of the ons offset. The ons offset is estimated on the basis of where the ground surface reflection is first recorded; it is a function of the different antenna designs as well as of the different characteristics of the transmitted pulse. The standard method of positioning the ons offset at the peak of the first positive amplitude in the trace (Yelf 2004) was used on the current data sets. The third calibration procedure involved the stacking filter, which averages the acquired set of traces into one trace. In the present project, this filter was applied only in a few cases where field conditions were poor due to electromagnetic interference from mobile telephone masts and electricity pylons. Whenever the stacking filter was applied, the number of traces averaged was noted.

Two types of velocity analysis were employed in this study: one using the Reflected Wave (RW) method during field data acquisition, the other used the point source reflection hyperbolas (APSRH) method, which was carried out in post-acquisition processing. The RW method involved placing a reflector (in the present case an iron pole) at a known depth and collecting a radar profile above it, thus measuring the wave velocity directly. The APSRH method, performed by computer software, generates a hyperbola that is adjusted to the acquired hyperbola generated from the ground, the geometry of which is a function of the average velocity of the material through which the radar energy has passed (Conyers 2004, 102-5; Leckebusch 2000; Lucius & Powers 2002). This method was used to calculate the coefficient reflectivity between the known archaeological features and the surrounding depositional units in order to assess the detection quality of the archaeological remains.

The interpretation of the archaeological data is largely dependent on an assessment of the size, shape and relative position of the archaeological features. It is possible to obtain this type of information by surveying an area with multiple GPR profiles at constant intervals within a defined grid. During post-processing, a spatial computer algorithm is applied to the acquired profiles. This slices and interpolates the data and creates amplitude maps/slices representing the amplitudes of the surveyed grid at a defined time/depth, termed a 'time slice' (Conyers & Goodman 1997; Goodman et al. 1995; 1998). These time slices, combined with elevation data, can be further interpolated into 3D models that can provide a better understanding of the results when compared with the known archaeological features in an area (Goodman 2009; Goodman et al. 2006).

The survey was conducted in three stages. The purpose of the first of these was to obtain a better understanding of the nature of the subterrain and its suitability for GPR survey. Three estimations had therefore to be made: of the penetration depth for the GPR system in the research area, of the ability of the GPR system to depict the archaeological features in the surrounding subterrain, and of the time to depth conversion rate. The three tasks were dealt with in two parts. The first part involved analysing the GPR profiles from known archaeological features using the RW and APSRH methods and comparing them to the other profiles. The second part involved studying the wave patterns reflected from known archaeological features, mainly *Grubenhäuser*, pits, hearths and postholes. The completion of the first stage created a basis for the interpretation of the GPR survey of areas that had not been excavated or exposed but had previously been partially surveyed by gradiometer and geochemical methods. In the second stage, a large area north of trench 5 was examined by surveying six east-west transections of 80-120 m in length in order to assess the archaeological potential of the field. The third stage involved conducting high-resolution 3D surveys of areas of high archaeological potential in order to delineate possible architectural features. In this stage, four areas were selected and analysed.

Results

Stage 1: Velocity analysis and transections on exposed archaeological features

Process: Before the acquisition gains were applied, ons offset correction was set and in some cases stacking filter was applied (five traces).

Post-process: ons offset correction and background removal filter were applied.

Description: Based on analyses of the subsoil and the nature of the archaeological evidence, our aims were to outline the difference between two types of typical subsoil, sandy sediment and gravel – both having been observed in the exposed excavation trenches at the time of the survey – and to delineate the archaeological features within them. A series of test transections were surveyed at selected locations with 400 MHz and 900 MHz radar antennas, conducting a velocity analysis based on the RW method. A metal bar was inserted to a depth of 0.54 m in a section of trench 5 just above the archaeological features. The reflections from the metal bar were clearly apparent in the radar reflection profile and a two-way travel time of 11.23 ns was measured (fig. 5a). The dielectric constant of this area and radar wave velocity were calculated using the following equation (Conyers 2004, 48):

$$K = \left(\frac{C}{V}\right)^2 = 9.717$$

Where: twt – two-way travel time = 11.23 ns
d – Depth = 0.54 m
V – Velocity of the material through which the radar passes
K – Relative dielectric permittivity (RDP)
C – Speed of light = 0.2998 ns/m

Fig. 5. | *The GPR velocity test at trench 5. (a) Reflection profile delineates the geological features and the metal test bar. (b) View of trench 5 facing west. Photo: C. Loveluck.*

The dielectric constant of the cultivated sandy layer (topsoil) was calculated at 9.7 RDP. A highly reflective gravel deposit was also observed which continued from the exposed trench into the cut (fig. 5b). In comparison to the other, less reflective depositional units in the surveyed trench the high reflections of the gravel deposit offered a good indication of a common geological feature in the area. The results of the post-processing APSRH analysis show that the dielectric constants of the different depositional units and archaeological features vary, but all fall in the range of 9-12 RDP. The analyses were also used as a basis for a velocity model to estimate the depth of the different buried features. The results show that the dielectric properties of the subterrain at Stavnsager were relatively low and provided a very suitable working environment for the penetration of radar.

The second part of Stage 1 involved running the GPR system on exposed archaeological features in order to examine the possibility of distinguishing between these and other depositional units. In this test we ran the GPR system with two antennas, 400 MHz and 900 MHz, over a line of exposed

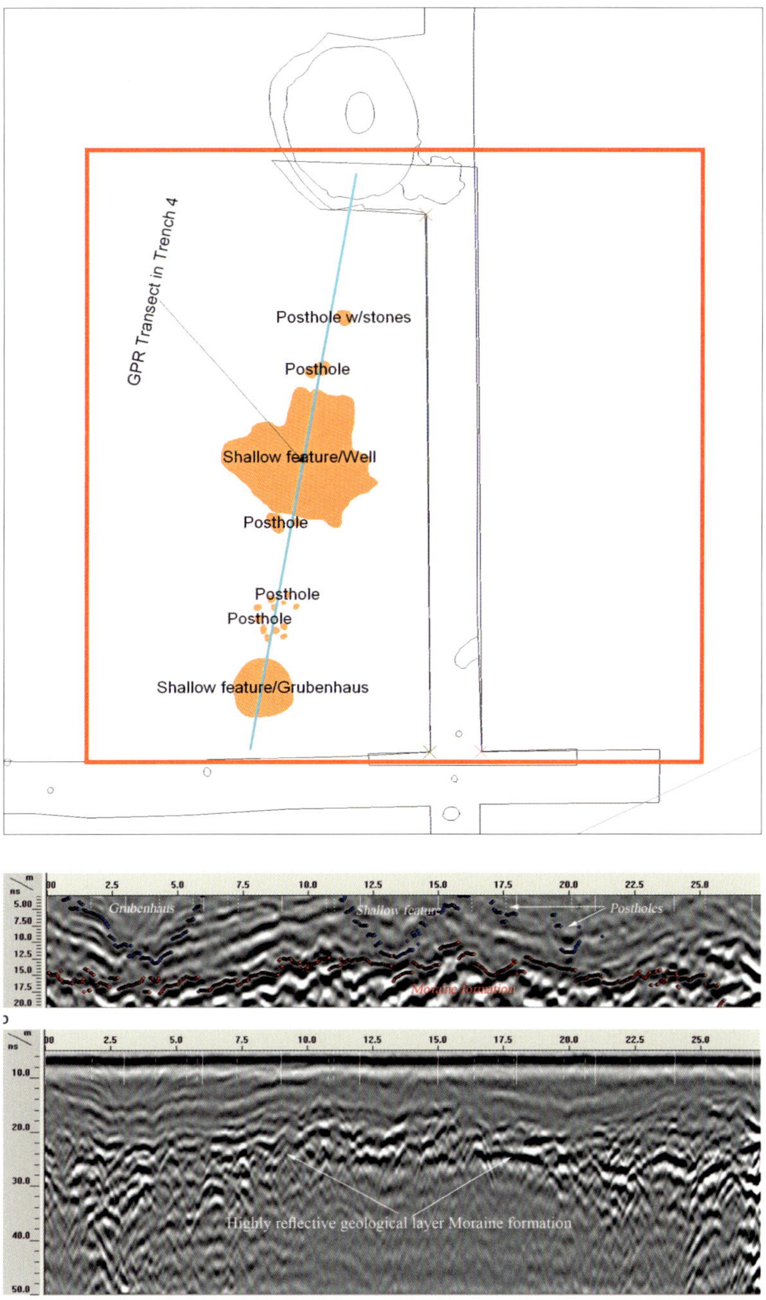

Fig. 6. | *GPR test transection inside trench 4. (a) Partial top plan of trench 4 showing archaeological features and the GPR transection line. (b) Reflection profile carried out with a 400 MHz antenna and a time window of 20 ns confirmed the presence of archaeological features. Post-processing involved ons offset correction and background remove filter. (c) The same transection in trench 4 carried out with a 400 MHz antenna using a time window of 50 ns. Post-process involved ons offset correction.*

features in trench 3 (fig. 6a). The results displayed in this transection reveal that a *Grubenhaus*, several postholes and an archaeological feature of unknown character were distinguishable, through different wave patterns, from the unit of the topsoil and from the surrounding subsoil (fig. 6b). The surrounding subsoil was found to consist of two clearly distinguishable depositional units: an upper, sandy and less reflective unit and a lower, highly reflective unit probably consisting of gravel (fig. 6c). The implementation of the APSRH method of velocity analysis showed that although the reflectivity coefficient of the topsoil, the subsoil and the anthropogenic cultural layer was relatively high, the calculated results for the dielectric properties of the known archaeological features appeared to vary. In most cases the coefficient of reflectivity was high, but sometimes it was very low. This means that even though radar penetration would be good and the resolution of the survey would be high, some archaeological features would remain undetected.

Stage 2: Transections in the vicinity of trench 5

In this stage, six transections oriented east-west were carried out in the vicinity of trench 5. They were done using the 400 Mhz and 900 Mhz antennas as described in the following table (see also figs. 3 and 4).

Process: Before the acquisition gains were applied, ons offset correction was set and in some cases stacking filter was applied (five traces).

Post-process: ons offset correction and background removal filter was applied.

This area has previously been subjected to geochemical survey, using energy-dispersive X-ray fluorescence for a range of minor elements. Of particular interest for the GPR survey was the role of phosphorous relative to manganese in the identification of the edge of intensive settlement activity (Loveluck et al. this volume). The phosphorous levels seemed to drop very significantly

Name	Length	Location	Description and results
Transection 1	188 m	Crossing oveTtrench 5. Described from E to W.	The first 30 m of the transection show an area that exhibits the same high reflection as gravel deposits noted above. Two possible archaeological features were noted in this deposit. On the stretch between 30-100 m there seemed to be no indications of archaeological activities. Towards the end of the transection, a possible Grubenhaus was noted.
Transection 2	174 m	Parallel to and 40 m north of Transection 1. Described from E to W.	The first 35 m show an area with possible archaeological features, while the rest of the transection shows no indications of these (fig. 7).
Transection 3	140 m	Parallel to and 20 m north of Transection 2. Described from E to W.	The first 14 m show possible archaeological features, while the rest of the transection shows no indications of these. However, there were some areas with high reflections, probably indicating virgin gravel deposits.
Transection 4	114 m	Parallel to and 20 m north of Transection 3. Described from E to W.	The first 35 m show an area with possible archaeological features, while the rest of the transection shows no indications of such.
Transection 5	87 m	Parallel to and 20 m north of Transection 4. Described from E to W.	The first 37 m show an area with possible archaeological features, while the rest of the transection shows no indications of these.
Transection 6	60 m	Parallel to and 20 m north of Transection 5. Described from E to W.	The first 38 m show an area with possible archaeological features, while the rest of the transection shows no indications of these.

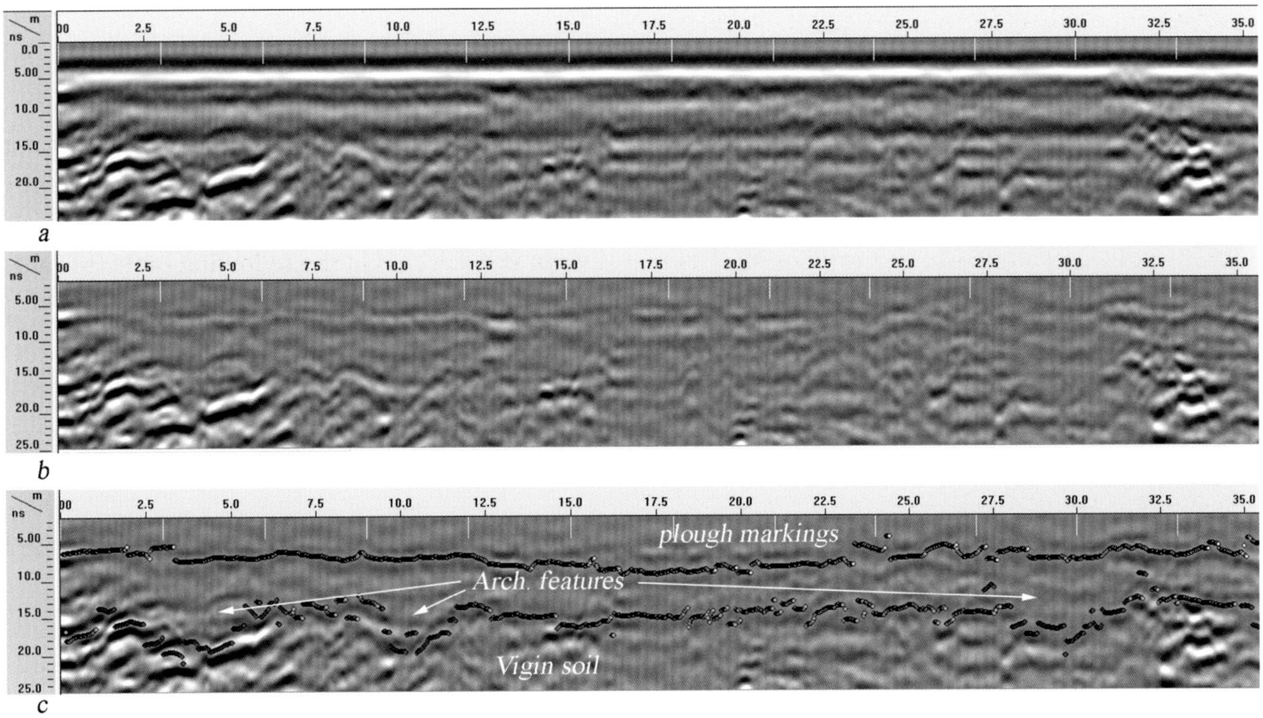

Fig. 7. | *The first 35 m of transection 2 east-west conducted using a 400 MHz antenna and a time window of 25 ns. (a) Raw data. (b) The same reflection profile as figure 6a after post-processing (ons offset correction and background removal filter). (c) The same reflection profile as figure 6b with interpretational notes pointing out the archaeological features.*

when manganese levels rose, especially on the western margins of the area, where metal artefacts have been retrieved (fig. 3; table 1). These results correspond with the results of the GPR findings. They pinpoint a number of locations in the eastern part of the surveyed area with possible archaeological features, while most of the western part seemed to be without any traces of archaeological activity. However, at the west end of transection 1, in an area beyond the perimeter of the geochemical survey, a possible *Grubenhaus* was noted that might indicate an additional area of settlement activity.

Stage 3: 3D survey of selected areas

The 3D survey grids for the selected areas were surveyed with multiple lines using the zigzag survey traverse method with a constant interval of 0.5 m. The transections were subsequently interpolated into time slices and 3D cubes. Where the topography sloped significantly, corrections for topography were applied using geodetic GPS elevation Data.

Process: All surveys were carried out using 400 MHz antenna in selected rectangular or square areas. Beforehand, the acquisition gains and ons offset correction were applied. In some cases stacking filter was also applied (five traces).

Post-process: ons offset correction and static correction was used for topography correction. The amplitude maps and the 3D models were created using an inverse distance interpolation procedure involving GPR-Slice software.

Grid A: Located southeast of Hørning Church, covering a level area of 30 x 50 m and oriented north-south. This area was selected on the basis of an elongated anomaly identified by the gradiometer survey (Strutt 2006). An analysis of the individual transections shows an area with pos-

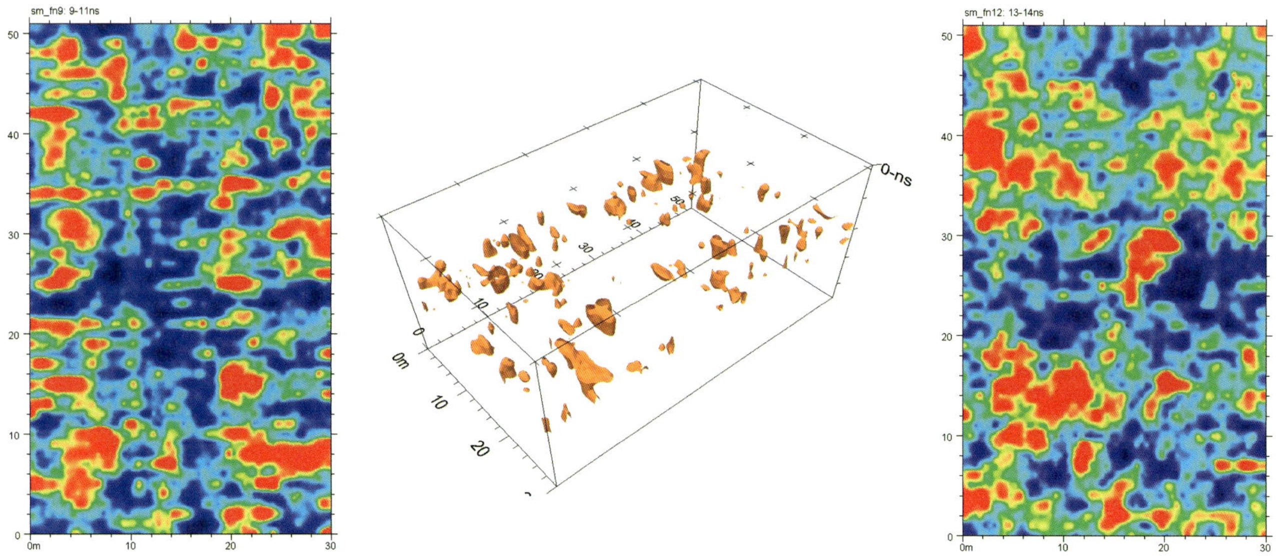

Fig. 8. | *The GPR survey of grid A. (a) Time slice of 11-13 ns showing possible archaeological features. (b) 3D isosurface representation of the archaeological features. (c) Time slice of 13-16 ns showing an elongated feature corresponding with part of an oval feature found by the gradiometer survey.*

sible small archaeological features, maybe postholes. In the amplitude maps from this area the time slice corresponding to c. 0.5 m below the surface showed possible features that, in shape and size, may correspond to multiple postholes. A few larger features were also noted at this depth (fig. 8a). The posthole-like features seem to line up forming two parallel rows oriented north-south and situated about 15 m apart (fig. 8b). In the time slice for c. 0.7 m below the surface, an elongated feature was detected that may correspond with the gradiometer-detected positive anomaly. The archaeological nature of these features is not entirely clear but could be resolved through further investigation.

Grid B: Located on the asphalt road called Præstedalsvej, immediately north of Hørning Church, covering an area of 10 x 25 m. The location of this survey area, as well as that of area D, was suggested by Reno Fiedel in order to locate possible features, for example burials or buildings, belonging to Hørning's early wooden church. The results showed no evidence of any archaeological features at this location.

Grid C1: Located southeast of Hørning Church, covering a level area of 30 x 30 m about 30 m east of grid A. This area was selected on the basis of a ring-shaped negative anomaly identified by the gradiometer survey (fig. 4). In the amplitude map and 3D model of this area, a large rectangular building oriented north-south, 20 m in length, between 8 m and 10 m in width and with posthole foundations, was clearly identified in the time slice for c. 0.75 m below the surface (figs. 9a and 9b). About 0.3 m above the building, traces of a circular feature appear to be delineated; these may correspond to the ring-shaped anomaly identified by the gradiometer. Since the anomaly was negative, it should be noted that this result is inconclusive (fig. 9c).

Grid D: This grid is the northern continuation of grid B, north of Hørning Church. It covers an area of c. 15 m x 40 m. The results reveal a feature with about 10 x 4 m of high reflection in the centre of the grid, very close to the surface. Analyses of the individual profiles reveal a 'ringing' effect extending down to the base of the profile which may indicate a high metal content. This corresponds with information received from the local inhabit-

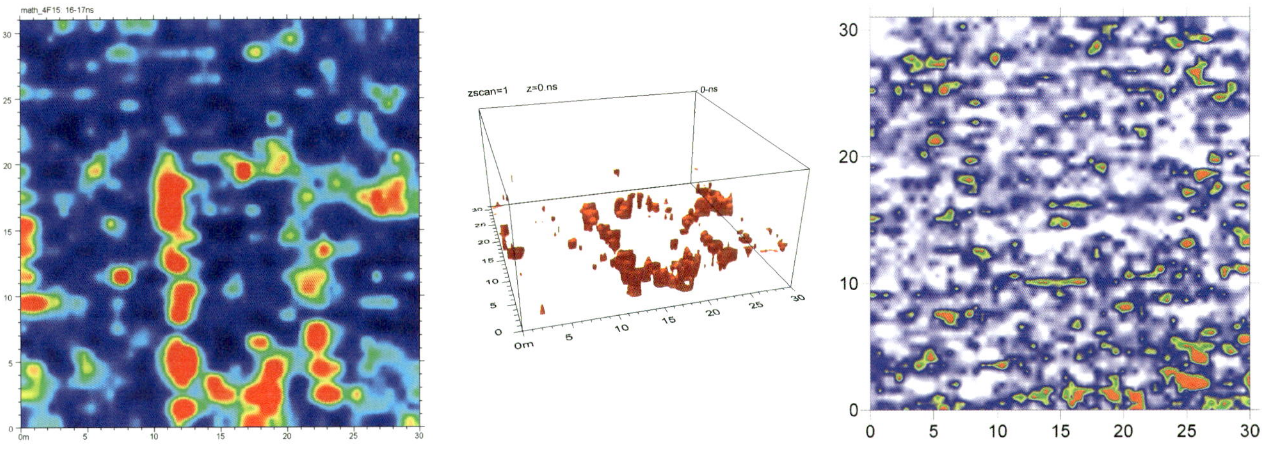

Fig. 9. | *The GPR survey of grid C1. (a) Time slice about 16-17 ns showing a possible archaeological structure. (b) 3D isosurface representation of the structure. (c) Time slice of 11-12 ns showing a ring-shaped feature corresponding with the ring-shaped negative anomaly detected by the gradiometer survey.*

ants, i.e. that the place once served as a dump for metal waste. The results showed no indication of archaeological features, but this could be due to masking by the 'ringing' effect.

The waterfront area: This is situated about 100 m northwest of trench 3, where the topography of Stavnsager is at its most varied. The area straddles part of the 700 m long stone embankment running east-west along the edge of the silted-up fjord (figs. 3, 10a and 10b). The surveyed area was laid out to cover an area of 50 x 30 m where the terrain changes from a steep slope into a flat zone (fig. 10c). Unfortunately, the flat area was covered with tall dense pasture vegetation which made it impassable with the GPR. We started from the southwest corner of the original grid, but after having surveyed 5 m eastwards, it was decided to move the location of the survey 25 m to the south, creating two overlapping grids: grid 1, 5 x 50 m in the west, and grid 2, 35 x 20 m in the east. The profiles of grid 1 and grid 2 show a slightly sloping reflection line, probably representing a sandy clayey surface about 0.75 cm below the surface (fig. 11a). This surface starts in the south of the surveyed area and continues about 20 m towards the north, where it ends just before the natural slope changes into flat terrain and where a c. 2 m stretch of highly reflective hyperbolas appears (fig. 11b). Beyond this area in the flatter lower terrain, the sandy clayey surface drops steeply until the end of the transection. This area depicted by the profiles can be interpreted as a fjord bank oriented east-west, bordered by a broad strip of stones and boulders. Its edge corresponds to the contour line for the waterfront of the silted-up fjord. Support for this interpretation can be found in the time slices and 3D models for grids 1 and 2, where an area of high reflection, oriented east-west, parallel and adjacent to the sandy clayey surface, can be observed about 0.75 m below the surface towards the north of the grid. In addition to this feature, several highly reflective features were noted in the southern part of grid 2, perhaps representing other possible archaeological features (fig. 11c).

Conclusions

On the basis of the pilot project at Stavnsager, it can be concluded that GPR with 400 MHz and 900 MHz antennas can be a useful tool for the archaeologist in locating and identifying buried archaeological features from at least the Germanic Iron Age in this specific environmental setting.

The results of the transection surveys show that the 400 MHz antenna detects natural geological

Fig. 10. | *The waterfront. (a) View of the surveyed areas north of trench 3. Photo: C. Loveluck. (b) Section of fire-shattered granite waterfront. Photo: R. Fiedel. (c) 3D model of the modern topography compiled from the micro-topography survey conducted by C. Briese using geodetic GPS.*

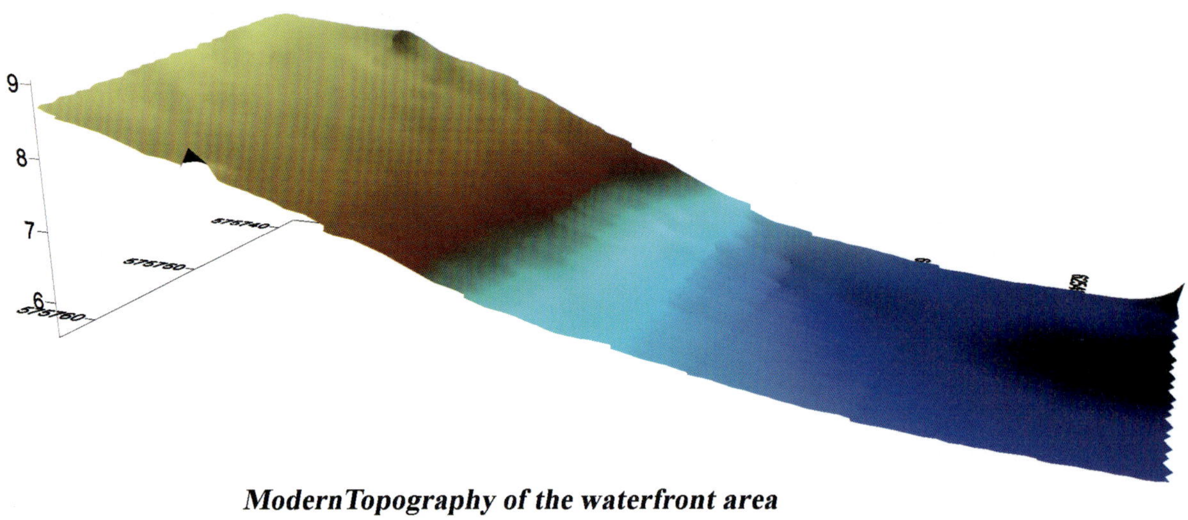

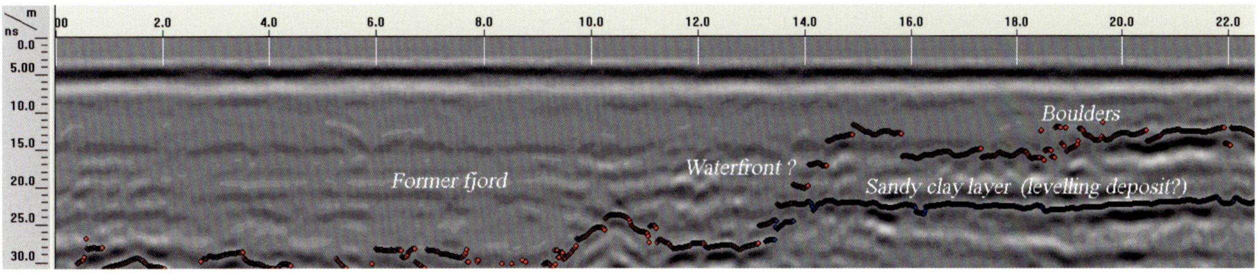

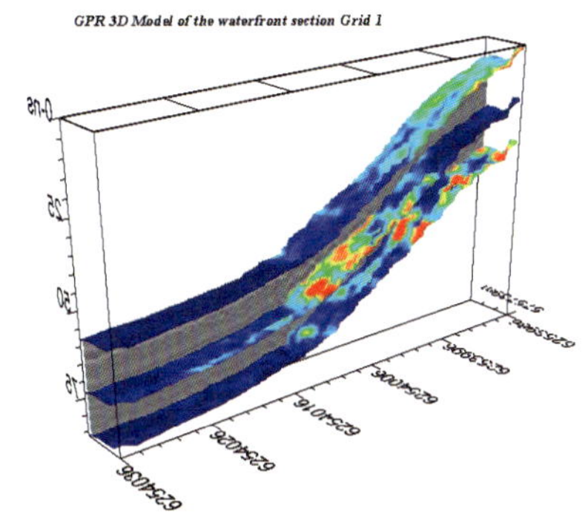

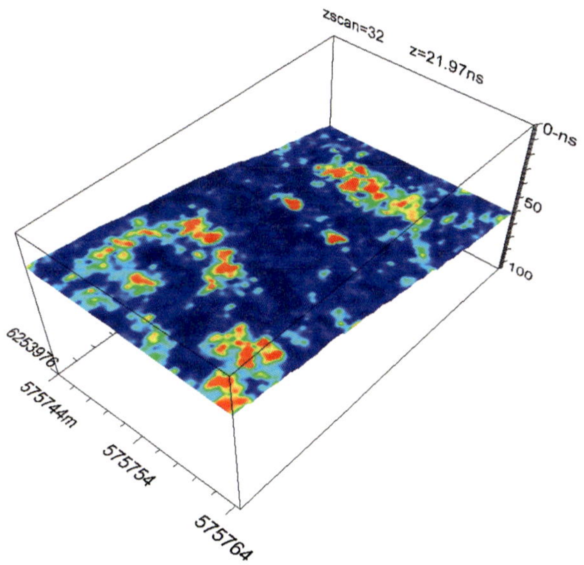

Fig. 11. | *The GPR survey of the waterfront. (a) GPR reflection profile showing the possible profile of the waterfront and deposits behind it. (b) 3D model showing the edge of the waterfront. (c) Time slice from grid 2 compiled with topographical data showing the waterfront edge and near vicinity with possible archaeological features.*

features and separates them from anthropogenic cultural layers and larger archaeological features such as *Grubenhäuser* and pits dug into the subsoil, but it fails to detect some of the postholes, whereas the higher resolution 900 Mhz antenna manages to detect smaller features including, in some cases, postholes. The penetration of the 900 MHz antenna also appeared to be surprisingly good in this specific geological environment as it also managed to detect the deeper highly reflective geological features below the site, despite its generally limited penetration energy. The results of the 3D grids showed that archaeological features such as *Grubenhäuser* and structures such as the lines of postholes and buildings, as seen in grids A and C1, respectively, were detectable. On the basis of the GPR results obtained in the present project, it can thus be concluded that the GPR method can be of valuable assistance in the investigation of areas of high archaeological potential like those seen at Stavnsager and Hørning Church.

A comparison between the gradiometer survey and the GPR gave some interesting results. It was noted that the large features detected by the gradiometer survey were also detected by GPR, although the negative anomalies were not very clear. In grid A at Hørning Church, the GPR survey delineated the approximate depth and volume of this feature. Several other features that were not detected in the gradiometer survey appeared to be detected by the GPR. A comparison of the results of the transections north of trench 5 and the energy-dispersive X-ray fluorescence survey also showed them to be compatible, giving a different perspective on human activity within the research area.

This integrated research approach, which combines geomagnetic, geochemical and GPR surveys with traditional archaeological excavations, has resulted in a comprehensive understanding of the past environmental setting and the geoarchaeological character and function of the Germanic Iron Age settlement at Stavnsager. The unique contribution of GPR lies in its flexibility to adjust the search scope and to examine the archaeological features in their geomorphological settings. This enables the archaeologist to study complex interdisciplinary issues such as the interaction between humans and their natural surroundings in an ever-changing environment.

Acknowledgements

Sincere thanks to the Israel Science Foundation for funding, and the Leon Recanati Institute of Maritime Studies, University of Haifa, for the permission to use their ground-penetrating radar equipment for the present research project. Many thanks are also due to Kulturhistorisk Museum Randers and the University of Nottingham for funding the GPR pilot project at Stavnsager. Sincere thanks to Reno Fiedel, Karen Høilund Nielsen and Chris Loveluck, the directors of the Stavnsager Archaeological Project, for the invitation to join the project. Thanks also Danielle Feunteun, Liv Stidsing Reher-Langberg and Christoph Briese for taking an active part in the fieldwork. Special thanks are due to Ragna Stidsing and Chris Loveluck for reading and editing this paper.

Bibliography

Baker, P.L. 1991, Response of ground penetrating radar to bounding surfaces and lithofacies variations in sand barrier sequences. *Exploration Geophysics* 22, 19-22.

Beres, L. & H. Haeni, 1991, Application of ground penetrating radar methods in hydrogeologic studies. *Groundwater* 29:3, 375-86.

Bristow, C.S. & H.M. Jol 2003, *Ground penetrating radar in sediments*. London.

Conyers, L.B. 2004, *Ground-penetrating radar for archaeology*. Walnut Creek, CA.

Conyers, L.B. 2010, Ground penetration radar for anthropological research. *Antiquity* 84, 175-84.

Conyers, L.B. & D. Goodman 1997, *Ground-penetrating radar: an introduction for archaeologists*. Walnut Creek, CA.

Cook, J.C. 1975, Radar transparencies of mines and tunnel rocks. *Geophysics* 40, 865-85.

Collins, M.E. 1992, Soils taxonomy: a useful guide for the application of ground penetration radar. In: P. Hänninen & S. Autio (eds.), *The proceedings of the fourth international conference on ground-penetrating radar: June 8-13, 1992. Rovaniemi, Finland*. Geological survey of Finland, special paper 16. 125-32.

Deng, S., Z. Zhengrong & H. Wang 1994, The application of ground penetrating radar to detection of shallow faults and caves. In: *The proceedings of the fifth international conference on ground penetrating radar, June 12-16, 1994, Kitchener, Ontario, Canada*. Waterloo, Canada. 1116-20.

Fiedel, R., K. Høilund Nielsen & C.P. Loveluck 2011, From hamlet, to central place, to manor. Social transformation of the settlement at Stavnsager, eastern Jutland, and its networks, AD 400-1100. *Neue Studien zur Sachsenforschung* 3, 161-76.

French, C.A.I. 2003, *Geoarchaeology in action: studies in soil micromorphology and landscape evolution*. London.

Jakobsen, P.R. & B. Hermansen 2007, Danmarks Digitale Jordartskort 1:25 000. Version 3.0. *Danmarks og Grønlands Geologiske Undersøgelse Rapport* 2007/84 [only on CD-Rom].

Goodman, D. 2009, *GPR-SLICE v7.0 Manual*. http://www.gpr-survey.com (accessed 02.03.2014).

Goodman, D., Y. Nishimura, H. Hongo & N. Higashi 2006, Correcting for topography and the tilt of ground-penetrating radar antennae. *Archaeological Prospection* 13:2, 157-61.

Goodman, D., Y. Nishimura, H. Hongo & O. Maasaki 1998, GPR-Amplitude rendering in archaeology. In: *The proceedings of the seventh international conference on ground penetrating radar, Radar Systems and Remote Sensing Laboratory, University of Kansas, May 27-31, 1998*. Lawrence, KS. 91-92.

Goodman, D., Y. Nishimura & J.D. Rogers 1995, GPR time slices in archaeological prospection. *Archaeological Prospection* 2, 85-89.

Høilund Nielsen, K. 2009, Stavnsager 400-1100: Weiler, Zentralort, Herrenhof. In: S. Brather, D. Geuenich, & S. Huth (eds.), *Historia archaeologica: Festschrift für Heiko Steuer zum 70. Geburtstag*. Berlin. 415-33.

Jensen, J. 1982, *The Prehistory of Denmark*. London/New York.

Leckebusch, J. 2000, Two and three dimensional ground penetrating radar surveys across Medieval choir: a case study in archaeology. *Archaeological Prospection* 7, 189-200.

Lucius, J., H., & M.H. Powers 2002, *GPR Data Processing Computer Software for PC*. Washington DC.

Smith, D. G., R.A. Meyers & H.M. Jol 1999, Sedimentology of an Upper Meso tidal (3.7 m) Holocene barrier, Willapa Bay, SW Washington, U.S.A. *Journal of Sedimentary Research, Section B: Stratigraphy and Global Studies* 69:6, 1290-96.

Strutt, K. 2006, *Results of a geophysical survey at the site of Stavnsager, Jutland, Denmark, July-August 2005* (SREP 1/2006). Archaeological Prospection Services of Southampton.

Yelf, R. 2004, *Where is true time zero?* In: *The proceedings of the tenth international conference on ground penetrating radar, Delft University of Technology, the Netherlands, June 21-24 2004*. Delft. 279-82.

Aerial archaeological survey of central places and other settlements: An evaluation of possibilities and limitations

Michael Vinter and Esben Schlosser Mauritsen

Aerial archaeology in Denmark: A brief introduction

Aerial photography is a non-destructive method of archaeological survey which, on the basis of differences in topography, soil colour or vegetation, can be used to locate and map archaeological sites. Buried ancient monuments that are invisible on the surface can become apparent in the vegetation in the form of increased or decreased plant growth. These traces are referred to, respectively, as positive or negative crop marks. The differences arise when crops are stressed as a result of drought. Consequently, they are seen primarily on the well-drained sandy soils of western and northern Jutland and appear most clearly in areas with uniform subsoil. Ever since the first attempts were made in the 1950s, aerial photography has produced impressive results with respect to archaeology, but it is only very recently that it has seen greater use in Denmark. Investigations conducted by the English pioneer, Prof. Dr J.K.S. St Joseph, beginning in the late 1960s, were of particular significance for aerial archaeology in Denmark. During the course of four summers, St. Joseph discovered more than a hundred new sites, of which several Iron Age sites have since acquired classic status in Danish archaeology (fig. 1). In the case of western Jutland, his work was followed up by Stig Jensen, Antikvarisk Samling Ribe and Lis Helles Olesen, Holstebro Museum, whereas this method has only seen sporadic application in other parts of Jutland and on the Danish islands (e.g. Eriksen & Olesen 2002).

During the course of the last five years, aerial archaeology has been applied across most of Jutland. The number of annual flying hours has, however, in most places been very modest. In Himmerland, 20 flying hours in 2007 and 2008, combined with archival studies and the examination of other aerial photographs, has resulted in a catalogue of 40 definite sites, to which may be added a similar number of uncertain classification. The great majority (75 %) represent villages and farmsteads dating from the Early Iron Age, while 20 % can be assigned to the Late Iron Age; these comprise two farmsteads and seven sites with *Grubenhäuser*.

In western Jutland, the ongoing research project *Fortiden set fra himlen* (An aerial view of the past), which began in 2008, has demonstrated the advantages of increasing the number of flying hours (Olesen 2011). Two years into the project, the number of photographed sites exceeded 560; these represent settlements, monuments etc., dating from the Bronze Age to the Middle Ages/Renaissance. In contrast to the situation in Himmerland, the ratio between Early and Late Iron Age sites is more even here. There is no doubt that a more balanced and representative picture is now available of the prehistoric reality of western Jutland, which can provide a foundation for more credible regional settlement and landscape studies. At the same time, it enables museums to improve their archival

Fig. 1. | Grubenhäuser *by the high-lying Vorde Church near Hjarbæk Fjord. Photo: Prof. St Joseph.*

checks and desk-based assessments prior to any construction work being initiated. Furthermore, aerial photographs can also be used for education, communication and scheduling casework.

Photo types and their application and availability

In general, a distinction can be made between two types of aerial photograph: oblique and vertical. Oblique photographs are most commonly taken at low altitude using a conventional camera, whereas vertical aerial photographs are taken from high altitude in continuous and overlapping series using specialised cameras. In an archaeological context, the former are often the most useful: They provide great richness of detail as it is possible to choose the camera angle and the lighting conditions, as well as precisely when the pictures are taken.

Vertical aerial photographs are taken with a

fixed high-quality camera mounted below the aircraft. As a rule, the images are taken from a relatively high altitude in series with a 60 % overlap between the individual photographs in order to obtain a stereographic effect. The scale varies between 1:4000 and 1:40 000. Since the middle of the 1980s, these photographs have been in colour. The first series providing national coverage is Basic Cover, which was created by the US Air Force in 1954 and is at a scale of 1:10 000. Hundreds of thousands of vertical aerial photographs are stored in several different archives (Olesen et al. 2011). The largest collections are with the Danish Geodata Agency (previously the Danish National Survey and Cadastre), and at the Danish Royal Library. Many series have now been scanned and made available online.[1] In general, the photographs were taken in spring which means that the visible features mainly represent large structures, for example barrows, field systems, cultural layers, ditches and anti-tank ditches; these are evident in the form of soil colour traces. Vertical aerial photographs can also reveal construction works and related activities that may have influenced the archaeological record or the landscape during the last 50 years.

A third source material is provided by the orthophoto series, which comprises geo-referenced mosaics of vertical aerial photographs. Contiguous orthophoto series of Denmark have been produced since 1995. Until recently, the orthophoto series did not differ from the earlier vertical aerial photographs. However, due to photography being conducted later and later in the year, as well as improved resolution and widespread drought conditions in early summer, it is now possible to observe detailed differences in the vegetation. As long as there are colour differences in the vegetation, it is possible in principle to see the same detail on a vertical photograph as on an oblique one.

Aerial archaeology and central places

Over the last 30 years, much research attention has been focused on metal-rich settlements dating from the Late Iron Age and Viking Age that are referred to collectively as 'central places'. This term covers elite settlements and specialised trading and craft sites, but there are a number of inherent problems with respect to its definition; this debate is dealt with elsewhere in these conference proceedings. In the present chapter, attention will be focused on the potential of aerial photography for investigating and seeking out magnates' residences, various production sites and trading places. As a point of departure, it can be said that this group of sites and monuments will be apparent as crop marks (i.e. vegetation traces) on a par with all other conceivable archaeological sites. The problem will be recognising whether these traces represent an actual specialised settlement, such as a production site or a magnate's residence. It is obviously difficult to detect gold or workshop waste from the air. This means that we must search instead for diagnostic settlement characteristics. For trade and production sites we must expect to find structures such as workshops and plot divisions, as well as accumulated cultural layers. At magnates' settlements we can expect to find striking structures in the form of great halls, an extraordinarily large farm croft or a palisade. The presence of a moat or a castle mound makes it easy to identify manors from the Middle Ages, but during the Late Iron Age and the Viking Age fortifications and defensive structures such as these are a rarity. Through excavation, robust demarcations of croft boundaries have been encountered in an elite context on several occasions. These include sites such as Lisbjerg Church, Kalmargården near Tissø and Jelling (Andersen 2009; Jeppesen & Madsen 1996; Jørgensen 2003). Most recently, a Viking Age rectangular farm croft enclosed within a palisade, rampart and moat was revealed at Erritsø. It should be eminently possible to find structures and sites of this type from the air.

Similarly, very few definite elite residences are known from the Late Iron Age and Viking Age in Denmark. None of these has to date been demonstrated by way of aerial photography but presumably it is only a question of time. Perhaps the only example so far of an elite residence or a great hall that has become apparent in the form of crop marks is the so-called 'house of glass' at Dejbjerg (Egeberg Hansen 1996). The traces on the vegetation were so clear that they were discovered on the ground and not from an aircraft.

A number of the elite settlements and the trading and production sites are characterised by thick accumulations of cultural material (cultural layers) and this should therefore also represent a useful indicator in the search for these settlements. However, certain problems are involved with recognising these layers. A posthole dug in a cultural layer will, due to the lack of contrast between the feature and its surroundings, be invisible to aerial photography. Conversely, sites with thick cultural deposits may be apparent through differences in soil colour. This is a familiar phenomenon on the island of Bornholm, where sites with significant accumulations of cultural deposits, such as Sorte Muld, are visible as dark-coloured areas in a ploughed field. It was on Bornholm that attempts were made to employ aerial archaeology in the search for sites of this type, and it has proved possible to delimit their lateral extent with the aid of vertical aerial photographs. Despite intensive efforts, however, no clear crop marks have been detected at these sites (M. Vennersdorf pers. comm.). It is a general paradox in aerial archaeology that the greater the occupation intensity of a given settlement the more it will obscure itself. A large number of postholes and other features in the same place will create their own background noise. A farmstead in a single phase will, by contrast, be immediately recognisable to any archaeologist.

Production sites are characterised first and foremost by *Grubenhäuser*, but they can also include a variety of pits related to textile, iron and comb production. Theoretically, it is difficult to make a morphological distinction between wells, pits of various types and *Grubenhäuser* seen from the air. *Grubenhäuser* do, however, have a tendency to appear as uniform in shape and size, whereas retting pits for example are often of markedly elongate form. The number of *Grubenhäuser* at individual sites varies from a small handful to several hundred. It is difficult, however, to determine whether a large number of *Grubenhäuser* are contempo-

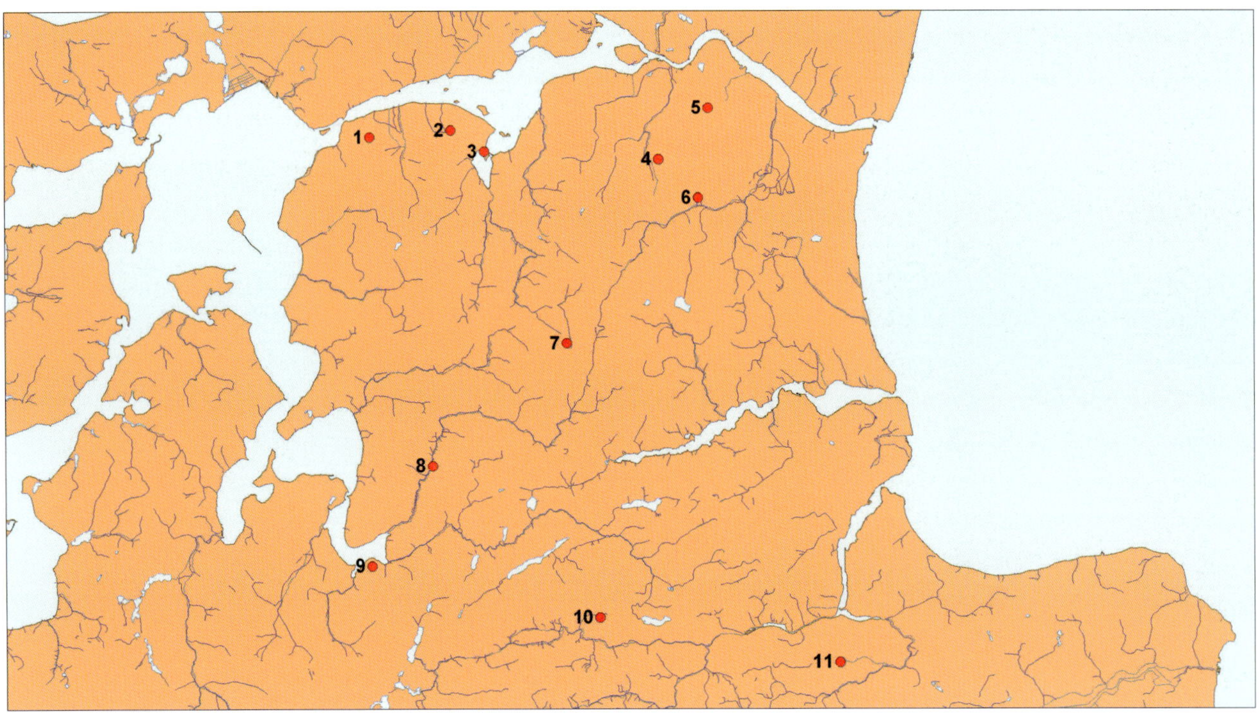

Fig. 2. | *Sites with* Grubenhäuser *on aerial photos of Himmerland and areas immediately to the south. 1. Næsborg Church, 2. Barmer, 3. Sebbersund, 4. Ferslev, 5. Postgården, 6. Flamsted, 7. Fyrkilde, 8. Torsgård, 9. Vorde Church, 10. Skjern Church, 11. Stavnsager.*

raneous, and thereby constitute an expression of a large-scale specialised production, or whether they merely represent ongoing replacement over a longer period of time. We must be content with the conclusion that the presence of *Grubenhäuser* indicates specialised production to some extent or other; *Grubenhäuser* are therefore useful objects to discover from the air. However, whether these represent a specialised production site or merely a more ordinary rural settlement can first be determined using other archaeological methods.

Focus on a region: Himmerland

Partly as a consequence of a recent aerial archaeological initiative, several new sites with *Grubenhäuser* have been discovered in recent years in Himmerland and areas immediately to the south. However, these sites, 11 in all, which lie scattered across the entire area, still represent a lower total than for western Jutland where there are estimated to be in excess of a hundred (fig. 2).

In general, only *Grubenhäuser* are visible, but in a few cases faint suggestions of post-built constructions are also apparent. The *Grubenhäuser* can be relocated almost every year, both by ordinary aerial survey and on orthophotos, but definite indications of actual longhouses continue to be absent. The few sites investigated on the ground include Stavnsager and Postgården, located to the southeast of Randers and Aalborg, respectively. Here, various archaeological investigations have documented the presence of both longhouses and metal artefacts in association with the *Grubenhäuser*. A crucial question in this respect is, however, whether the *Grubenhäuser* and longhouses are contemporary with one another or whether they represent different phases in the occupation and functional structure of these sites. At Stavnsager, the longhouses are thought primarily to date from the Early Ger-

Fig. 3. | Grubenhäuser *at Flamsted found on the orthophoto series from 2008. Note the marked green areas with better growing conditions. West of the road, they resemble filled-in palaeochannels, but in trial excavations to the east of the road, in the southern part of the field, they proved to overlie both a different, more clay-rich sandy subsoil and Neolithic cultural deposits. ©Scankort 2008. Published on www.degulesider.dk (accessed 15.10.2013).*

manic Iron Age, whereas the *Grubenhäuser* are from the Late Germanic Iron Age and the Viking Age. This is also thought to be the case at Bejsebakken near Aalborg (Høilund Nielsen & Fiedel 2001, 87; Nielsen 2002, 200). Most of the metal-detector finds from both these sites date from the Late Germanic Iron Age, and it seems accordingly that they should be related to the *Grubenhäuser* (Christiansen 2008, 111; Høilund Nielsen & Fiedel 2001, 79). At Postgården, neither the longhouses nor the hundreds of *Grubenhäuser* are securely dated but the metal-detector finds here also date primarily from the Late Germanic Iron Age. Apparently, a functional shift occurred at these sites, from an agrarian economy with some craft/specialised production in the Early Germanic Iron Age, to more specialised production in the Late Germanic Iron Age. The evidence is, however, still much too sketchy for it to be said that this is a general feature of the sites with *Grubenhäuser* in Himmerland.

The other sites, such as Skjern by Nørre Å, Torsgård by Simested Å, Flamsted by Lindenborg Å and Barmer by Vær Å, have several features in common. All are located relatively far from the coast, between 7 and 20 km, but immediately alongside larger rivers that may have been navigable during the Late Iron Age. Both Torsgård and Barmer lie close to abandoned churches, while the site at Skjern lies adjacent to an existing Medieval church and a Medieval castle mound. All are situated so far from existing villages that they would probably not have been located without aerial photography. The sites at Barmer and Skjern have not yet been investigated in further detail but an intensive metal-detector survey is expected to be carried out at the former in the future.

The site at Flamsted is located on a sandy point that extends out into the wide Lindenborg river valley. Here, in 2008, c. 40 *Grubenhäuser* could be observed on an orthophoto. Nordjyllands Historiske Museum carried out a minor trial excavation on a very limited part of the area in the autumn of 2009 (T.T. Christiansen pers. comm.). At the same time, a metal-detector survey of the site was conducted.

Fig. 4. | *Areas surveyed by metal detector at the Torsgård site. Stars denote detector finds and circles* Grubenhäuser *visible on aerial photographs. E.S. Mauritsen.*

Fig. 5. | *Torsgård, by the river Simested Å, photographed on 3rd July 2007. The* Grubenhäuser *lie on a sandy promontory surrounded on three sides by wetlands. Directly west of the river lies the site of the abandoned church at Mindrup. Photo: M. Vinter.*

The trial excavations confirmed the presence of several *Grubenhäuser*. The site also contained traces of settlement in the form of cooking pits, minor ditches and postholes from a settlement that was not evident on the aerial photograph. The intensive metal-detector survey gave a negative result. So far, the site must be considered as an agrarian settlement with specialised production (fig. 3).

The situation is rather different at Torsgård, which lies some distance up the river Simested Å in western Himmerland. Its position in the landscape, as based on historical maps from the late 19th century, is very similar to that of Flamsted, i.e. on a sandy point surrounded by wetlands on three sides. The aerial photographs reveal c. 80 *Grubenhäuser* but no traces of longhouses. Reconnaissance and metal-detector surveys at the site carried out by the authors of this chapter revealed a picture of a production site with both metal-working and an agrarian economy. On the surface lay numerous quern stones, a loom weight and a fair amount of pottery, whereas the plough soil contained around 50 metal artefacts in the form of bronze and lead fragments as well as a number of brooches. The latter comprised a gilt rectangular disc brooch, a small tortoise brooch and a Lamb of God brooch. Together, they extend over a period of 400 years, from c. AD 600 to 1000, and therefore bear witness to this site's long period of use. Torsgård must also be considered as an agrarian settlement with specialised production. However, in contrast to Flamsted, the economy here was probably supplemented by metalworking. Flamsted and Torsgård are excellent examples of how aerial photography cannot stand alone but must be supplemented by other methods. From the air, the two sites appeared identical. It was only when surface reconnaissance and metal-detector survey became involved that it was possible to begin to differentiate between them (figs. 4 and 5).

Mapping of a local settlement landscape: The example of Föhr

One of the great advantages of aerial archaeology is that it is capable of mapping archaeological structures over large areas. This can be done using significantly fewer resources than any other method of investigation and, as already mentioned, it is 100 % non-destructive. A detailed mapping of large areas does, however, require a broad time frame due to varying growth conditions and crops from year to year.

Fig. 6. | *Crop marks in pastureland at Wrixum on Föhr, August 2006. Photo: E.S. Mauritsen.*

An example of what can be achieved within a delimited area is provided by the results obtained from the North Frisian island of Föhr. Here, *Fortiden set fra himlen*, in cooperation with Archäologisches Landesamt Schleswig-Holstein, has carried out annual aerial surveys with the aim of creating a total archaeological photo-map of the island from the air (Mauritsen et al. 2009). Previously, knowledge of the settlement development on Föhr was mostly limited to the period between the 5th and the 7th/8th centuries AD (Kersten & La Baume 1958, 97ff). Only a few archaeological excavations have been carried out here in recent times, and the perception of a gap in the island's occupation history during the Late Iron Age had not changed to any notable degree. For this particular period, it is possible with some justification to refer to the island as an archaeological terra incognita. This view was changed fundamentally by the first reconnaissance flight on 18th August 2006.

Following an exceptionally dry summer, extensive areas showing crop marks could be observed over large areas of the geestland. The majority of the traces were found at Wrixum, on the northern margin, but large sites were also observed on the island's south coast at Nieblum, Witsum and Hedehusum. The observations were dominated by substantial feature types such as *Grubenhäuser*, wells, a few ring ditches and large, irregular ditch systems. The latter extended over several hundred metres, while other ditch systems surrounded what must be presumed to be farmsteads. Post-built constructions were virtually absent. To a certain extent this is due to the observations having been made in grass, which is a less informative 'crop' than barley or wheat, for example. This constitutes a dating problem, but the presence of *Grubenhäuser* places at least some of the activity in the area in the period AD 200-1100.

On the German side, attention since the discoveries has been directed towards the settlement traces at Wrixum (fig. 6). As these cover an area of more than 60 ha, a total investigation is not feasible. Instead, part of the area has been subjected to metal-detector surveys, followed by geophysical surveys. The detector surveys, with the exception of a single silver dirhem and a piece of hack gold, gave a surprisingly poor result. This may be due to poor soil conditions for the preservation of metals more vulnerable to corrosion. It is surprising that not even a single fragment of a bronze brooch has been found on a site with so many documented traces of habitation. The geomagnetic survey, however, was more productive. It revealed at least three three-aisled longhouses, which can be dated to the Late Roman Iron Age or Early Germanic Iron Age. Furthermore, the buildings appear to have stood in direct association with a part of the many ditch features. The

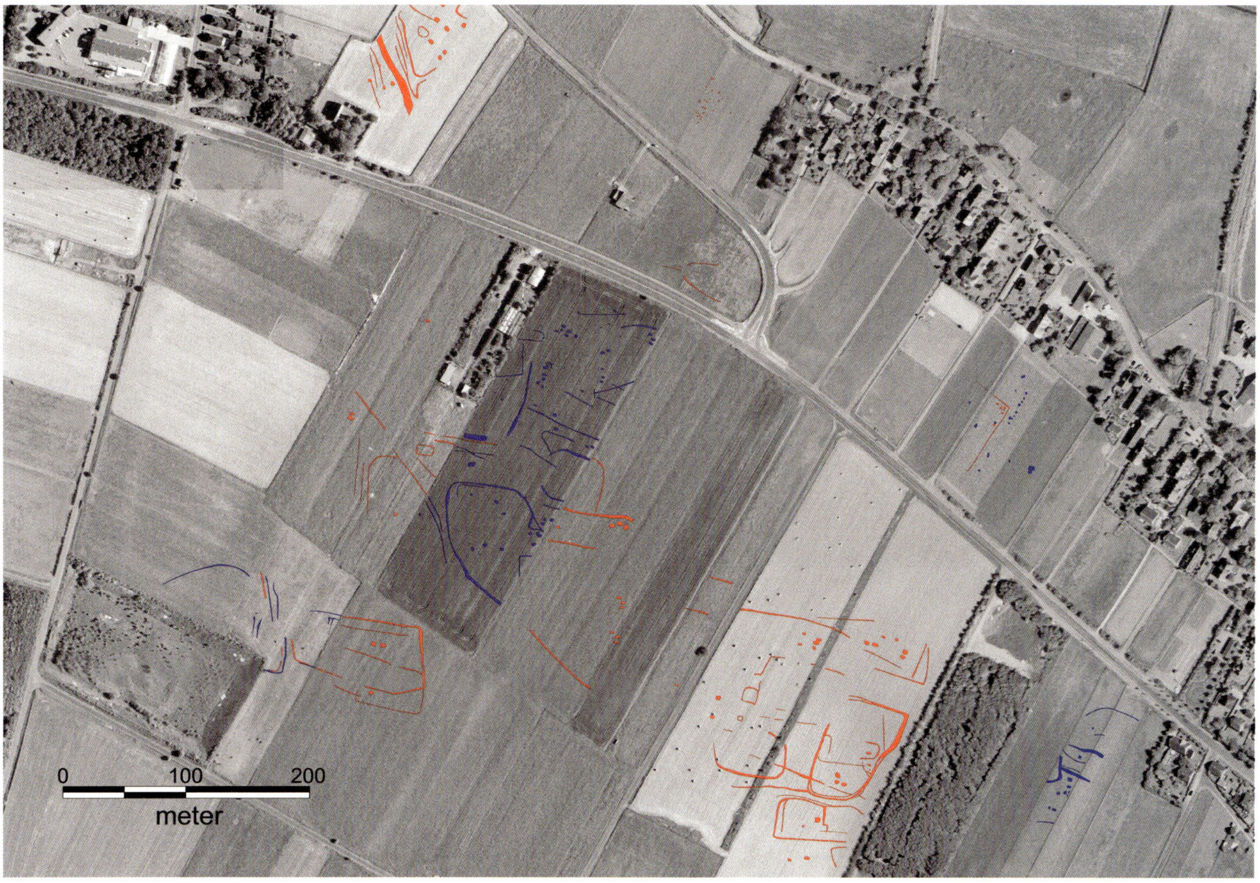

Fig. 7. | *Interpretation of photogrammetrically-corrected oblique photos of the area around Wrixum on Föhr. Crop marks noted in 2006 are shown in red; traces noted in 2008 are shown in blue.*

longhouses are remarkable in having lengths in excess of 50 m, suggesting a certain social status in the settlement.

The flights in 2008 and 2009 did not increase the number of known sites on Föhr to any significant degree, but they added detail to our knowledge of them as well as demonstrating that they extended over larger areas than was previously thought. It can be maintained with some justification that a reasonably accurate picture has now been drawn of the settlement areas on the geestland of Föhr. The investigation demonstrates the advances that can be made with limited time and resources. In total, less than five hours of flying time was expended over the island, and the results provide an optimal basis for further investigations of an entire prehistoric settlement landscape even before the first turf is cut (fig. 7).

Aerial archaeology as a basis for further investigation

Known elite, craft and trading sites are rarely located in places where urban development or similar activities will lead to investigations through the planning process and ordinary rescue excavation activity. A research-funded total investigation will in most cases be impossible for economic reasons. Even when it is possible to map large parts of a site by way of aerial photography, many unanswered questions will unavoidably remain. A manageable solution to this problem can therefore be to undertake limited and targeted excavation. Using aerial-archaeological mapping, particularly interesting 'key areas' may be identified in advance.

In *Fortiden set fra himlen*, an integrated part of the project has been to evaluate selected sites with respect to development of the aerial-archae-

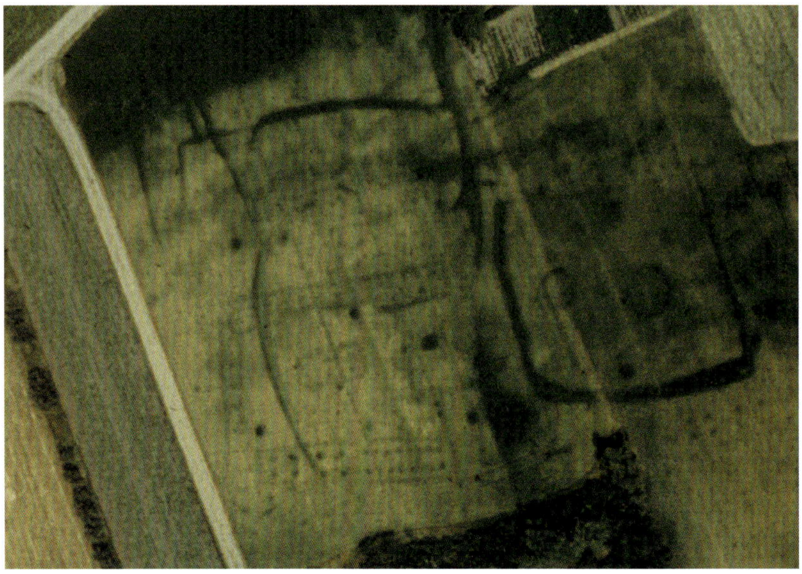

Fig. 8. | *Oblique photo of Vesterager, taken in 1992. The photo has been turned and the original shooting direction is from the left. Photo: P. Eriksen.*

ological method through targeted excavations. One of the sites currently being investigated is Vestager, near Stadil Fjord in western Jutland. It is not a central place, but the project provides an example of how follow-up investigations can be approached at all sites, and what they can contribute in the way of new information (figs. 8 and 9). The site was discovered in 1992 and comprises longhouses and a so-called *sadeltagshegn* (the farmyard area alongside the fence is covered by a pitched roof) dated to AD 400-500. Two small ring ditches and a number of presumed boundary ditches were also observed. It had previously been suggested that the ditches may have been dug in the Middle Ages and that the ring ditches could perhaps be associated with animal pens (Eriksen & Olesen 2002, 57ff).

As repeated flights did not provide any answer to this question, it was decided in 2009 in cooperation with Ringkøbing-Skjern Museum to carry out a minor excavation. Its aim was to date and determine the function of the ring ditches and the other ditches as well as to evaluate the representativity of the observations made from the aerial photographs. Accordingly, a trench was laid out with the intention of exposing part of the ditches and one of the ring ditches. Not surprisingly, the subsoil at Vesterager was found to be pure sand, in which the archaeological features stood out as darker brown fill. The ring ditch, when exposed, proved to be surprisingly modest in its dimensions – just 35 cm wide and 30 cm deep. No grave or artefacts were encountered that could securely determine the age and function of this feature. The boundary ditches could, however, be very securely linked to the Iron Age settlement; one of the ditches started at the corner of a building. From the aerial photographs it could be seen that this was probably also true of the eastern gable of the longhouse. The boundary ditch thus enclosed a farmyard measuring c. 27 x 27 m. It is worth noting that the excavation did not result in any significant changes to the interpretation based on the aerial photography. No buildings, wells or ditches were found that were not already known – and this was despite the fact that the topsoil layer was c. 50 cm deep, which is relatively thick according to western Jutish norms. These findings are surprising as previous investigations of a Viking Age site at Staby Church, also in western Jutland, had demonstrated that the traces revealed in advance by crop marks only constituted the 'tip of the iceberg' with respect to the actual archaeological structures present (Eriksen et al. 2009, 243f). It is not possible to determine exactly what is present at a given site solely on the basis of aerial photography. The observations may be representative, but they may also be very much

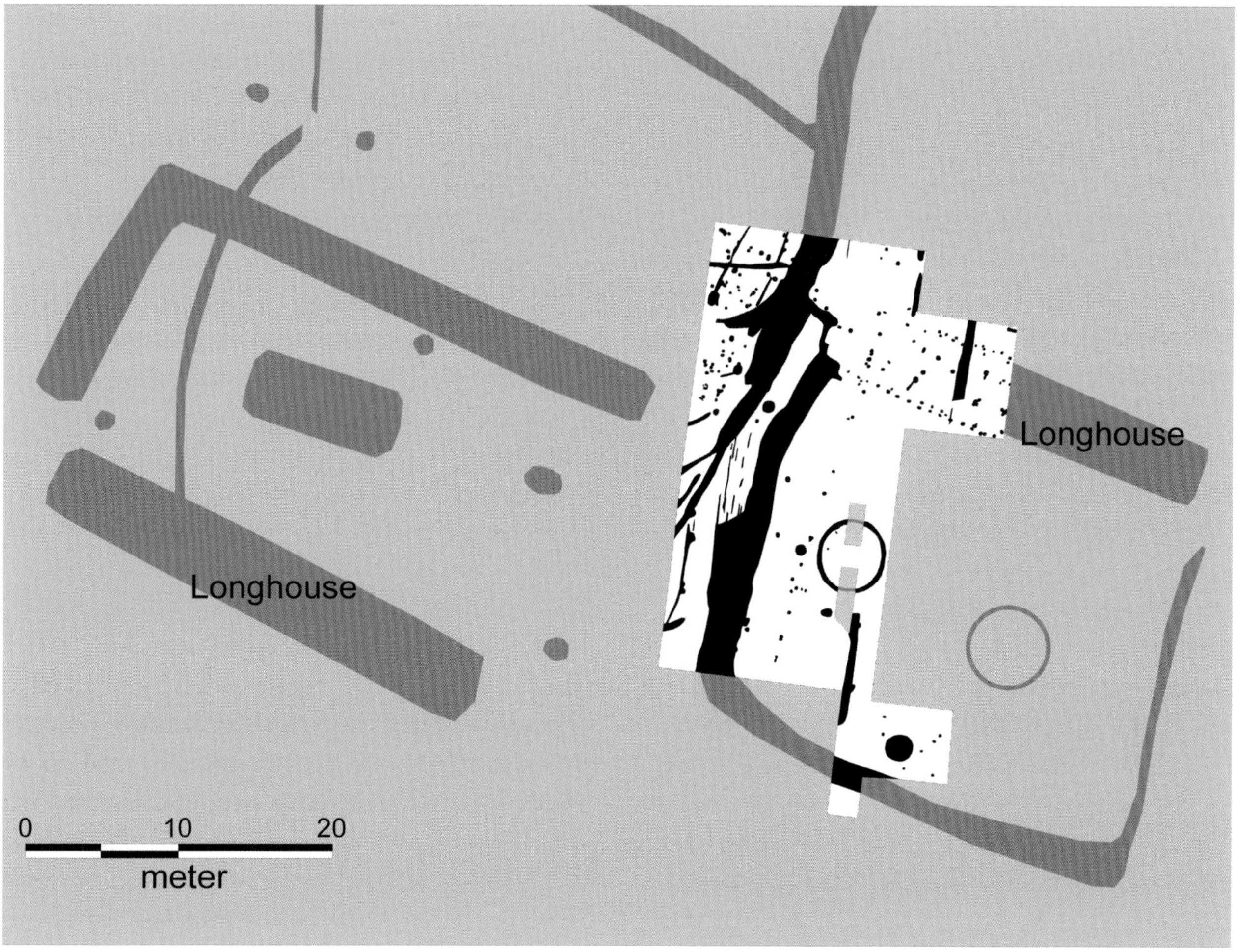

Fig. 9. | *Rough photogrammetric outlining of an oblique photo from 1992 (cf. fig. 8), compared with the excavation trench of 2008.*

the opposite. A targeted and delimited investigation will in most cases be required in order to determine the degree of representativity of the crop marks at a given site.

Conclusion

An attempt has been made here to outline a picture of how aerial archaeology can be applied in searches for and research into sites and monuments which have been given the term 'central places'. The great advantage of aerial archaeology is that it provides us with a view down into the ground even before we have unpacked our spade and trowel. Through aerial surveys and studies of series of vertical photographs it is possible, even with limited resources, to search and map large areas. That said, the method also has a series of inherent limitations. As has been discussed above, it can be difficult to identify elite, workshop/craft and trading sites alone on the basis of their crop marks. The problem is particularly acute with respect to metal-rich sites, for example, which are of course defined on the basis of a particular artefact category. Instead, it is necessary to exploit other diagnostic characteristics such as numerous *Grubenhäuser*, great hall buildings and fences around the farmsteads which, in contrast to artefacts, are recognisable from the air.

As has also been shown, aerial-archaeological investigations can be productively incorporated into settlement and landscape archaeology studies, whether these relate to a region such as Himmerland or a small island in the Wadden Sea, as was the case with Föhr. A new aerial-archaeological discovery or a much more extensive mapping exercise can both provide valuable starting points for further investigations. Finally, it should be emphasised that crop marks cannot stand alone in the assessment of a given site. The representativity of these traces can vary greatly from site to site.

Danish aerial archaeology has had a long and slow beginning. There is, however, still the prospect that the method will win a much greater role in the archaeology of the future. The availability on the internet of a number of aerial photographs – both new and old series – has made it possible to practice this discipline at the computer screen. At the same time, the number of aerial photo-reconnaissance flights executed by professional archaeologists has increased markedly within the last five years. There is every reason to believe that aerial archaeology will result in many new, exciting and remarkable discoveries in the future.

Bibliography

Andersen, S.W. 2009, Bautasten og kæmpehegn. *Skalk* 2009:2, 11-15.

Christiansen, T.T. 2008, Detektorfund og bebyggelse. Det østlige Limfjordspmråde i yngre jernalder og vikingetid. *Kuml* 2008, 101-43.

Egeberg Hansen, T. 1996, Et jernalderhus med drikkeglas i Dejbjerg, Vestjylland. *Kuml* 1993-94, 211-37.

Eriksen, P. & Olesen, L.H. 2002, *Fortiden set fra himlen. Luftfotoarkæologi i Vestjylland.* Holstebro.

Eriksen, P., T. Egeberg, L.H. Olesen & H. Rostholm 2009, *Vikinger i vest. Vikingetiden i Vestjylland.* Højbjerg.

Høilund Nielsen, K. & R.A. Fiedel 2001, Stavnsager – spredte glimt af et jernaldersamfund gennem mere end 700 år – fra 400 til 1100 e. Kr.f. *Kulturhistorisk Museum Randers Årbog* 2001, 71-89.

Jeppesen, J. & H.J. Madsen 1996, Trækirke og stormandshal i Lisbjerg. *Kuml* 1995-96, 149-71.

Jørgensen, L. 2003, Manor and market at Lake Tissø in the sixth to eleventh centuries: The Danish 'productive' sites. In: T. Pestell & K. Ulmschneider (eds.), *Markets in Early Medieval Europe: trading and productive sites, 650-850.* Macclesfield. 175-207.

Kersten, K. & P. La Baume 1958, *Vorgeschichte der nordfriesischen Inseln. Die vor- und frühgeschichtlichen Denkmäler und Funde in Schleswig-Holstein, Band IV: Die nordfriesischen Inseln Amrum, Föhr und Sylt (Kreis Südtondern).* Neumünster.

Mauritsen, E. S., M. Segschneider & T. Wunderlich 2009, Siedlungsprospektion mit Luftfotografien und Geomagnetik. *Archäologische Nachrichten aus Schleswig-Holstein* 15, 20-23.

Nielsen, J.N. 2002, Bejsebakken, a central site near Aalborg in northern Jutland. In: B. Hårdh & L. Larsson (eds.), *Central places in the Migration and Merovingian periods: papers from the 52nd Sachsensymposium, Lund, August 2001.* Stockholm. 197-213.

Olesen, L.H. 2011, An aerial view of the past – aerial archaeology in Denmark. In: D.C. Cowley (ed.), *Remote sensing for archaeological heritage management. Proceedings of the 11th EAC heritage management symposium, Reykjavík, Iceland, 25-27 March 2010.* Brussel. 275-82.

Olesen, L.H., H. Dupont & C. Dam 2011, *Luftfotos over Danmark. Luftfotoserier i private og offentlige arkiver.* Holstebro.

Notes

1 Vertical aerial photographs: http://flyfotoarkivet.dk (accessed 18.10.2013). Ortho series: http://kort.arealinfo.dk (accessed 18.10.2013).

Central places from a scientific perspective: From geophysics to micro-morphology

Peter Hambro Mikkelsen and Tatiana Smekalova

In this chapter the term 'central place' will be understood as defining a locality yielding metal-detector finds which, in number and composition, elevate it above the level of an ordinary village, where there would often be no metal finds of significance. At such productive sites archaeologists will uncover remains of activities that extend above and beyond those found at a normal agrarian settlement, though they must be presumed to vary from settlement to settlement. By taking a scientific approach to the archaeological evidence, it is possible in many cases to obtain complementary information about the activities that took place at a settlement site. This approach can include everything from the application of geophysical survey methods to demonstrate the extent of activities, to the morphological or chemical analysis of the find material. In the following, we will provide some examples of approaches that could prove advantageous in the archaeological process.

The agrarian settlement

It is important to be aware of the fact that the great majority of activities for which we find evidence at archaeological sites had their basis in an agrarian society. Figure 1 is a depiction of rural working life in the 18th century; many fundamental agricultural tasks remained on the whole unchanged between the Iron Age and this time. In excavations of 'normal' agrarian settlements, it is the archaeological remains from these tasks which – if they leave behind any physical traces – are found. Accordingly, when investigating productive sites, it is important to have an idea of the range of potential variation in

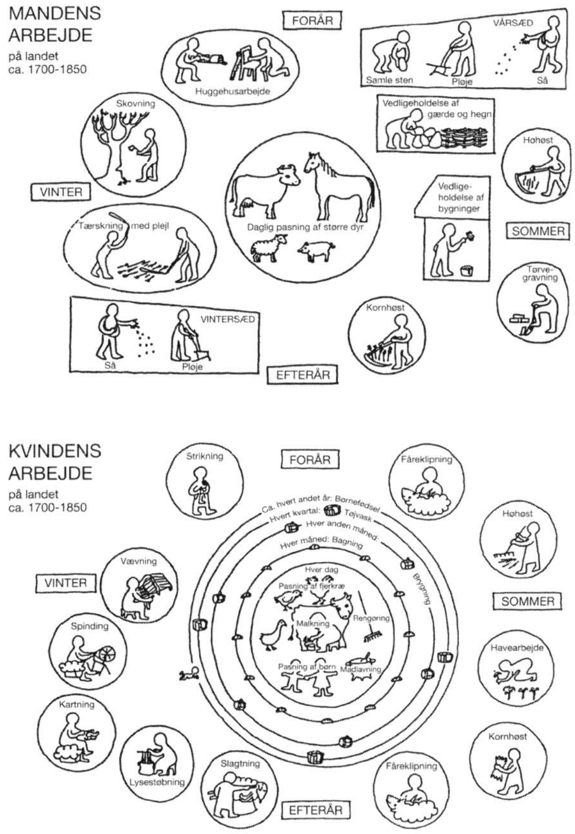

Fig. 1. | *Illustration of manual tasks in rural settlements, c. AD 1750. After Mikkelsen & Nørbach 2003.*

how different tasks can appear at the sites that have *not* produced metal finds. In the following, a couple of examples are given with reference to some of the aspects that can distinguish a normal agrarian settlement from a metal-yielding settlement.

Settlement-related differences

An important consideration in understanding these different settlement environments is their physical position in the landscape. Is it conceivable that productive sites had different relationships with watercourses, fords, major road junctions, trading sites and fortified sites from agrarian settlements? A site's location is obviously crucial to its ability to exploit the surrounding landscape, not just in terms of a subsistence economy, including access to fishing and suitable land for cultivation, but also with regard to the availability of raw materials such as wood/timber and bog iron ore. Seen from a prehistoric viewpoint, settlements may, as a rule, be presumed to have been self-sufficient in food. Consequently, a landscape analysis is naturally included in any calculation of the potential a given site has for meeting this requirement. In this respect, it is important to include an investigative method such as pollen analysis, as heavy human impact on the landscape will be reflected in the pollen spectra. For example, an increased proportion of cultivated land will have a decisive effect on the route followed by pollen in reaching the sediment layers on a lake bed. The less woodland there is in an area, the greater the distance pollen grains can be transported through the air without becoming trapped.

The occurrence of a particular craft activity can also be imagined to have been of significance for the local resource scenario. Will the massive amount of iron extraction which took place in southwestern Jutland during the 4th and 5th centuries AD be evident in pollen diagrams? The great demand for wood for extraction of the iron must have left its mark on the landscape.

If a production site can be seen to have had the functions of a trading place, it is possible that imports of wares and goods were necessary to its production. These imports may have been commodities that external traders brought with them as raw materials, semi-manufactures or finished products. Furthermore, an actual trading site would have required a greater amount of food than could be obtained locally– especially if it was of a more permanent character. It is therefore conceivable that there were imports of regional and exotic foodstuffs. There is an example of an over-regional import from the ring fortress of Fyrkat, where a large find of charred grain is interpreted as having been imported from the area immediately south of the Baltic (Helbæk 1977; Robinson 1991).

It is also possible that ritual and religious manifestations took place at these productive sites, and their roles as local or regional power centres were essential to the locations of such settlements. To characterise Haithabu merely as a productive site would not be doing it justice. It was clearly a special trading place which, solely on the basis of its fortifications and size, must have had a political significance extending far beyond that apparent at other settlements.

Finding a site

It is no great secret that the recent enormous increase in records of productive sites is due to the introduction of the metal detector. But neither is it any secret that the occurrence of a large number of metal objects does not in itself lead to the mounting of an excavation. Finds of metal items in the plough soil do not, in isolation, justify an archaeological investigation if the site is not threatened by development. As a consequence, the only way of determining the extent of a potential site is, in many cases, simply to discover where the metal finds cease to turn up.

An obvious way of obtaining further information about these sites is to employ geophysical survey methods: Explained very briefly, the basic apparatus – a magnetometer – functions by measuring differences in the earth's magnetic field. When the subsoil has been displaced in prehistoric or historical times, for example by the construction of a *Grubenhaus*, hearth or iron-smelting furnace, this

Fig. 2. | *Fieldwork. Photo: P. Hambro Mikkelsen.*

creates a local disturbance in the earth's magnetic field. The magnetometer will register the changes brought about by these activities as anomalies, thereby producing a signal that can be identified (Smekalova et al. 2008) (fig. 2). The great advantage of this method is that there is no need to excavate in order to gain an overview of the site and no damage is caused to any potential archaeological remains. In the following, a brief presentation will be given of magnetometer surveys of sites based primarily on the occurrence of *Grubenhäuser*.

Magnetic survey proved to be a very effective method for the investigation of Viking Age *Grubenhäuser*, which are numerous at settlements in southwest Jutland. In 2004-05, three such settlements were surveyed: Henne Kirkeby, Nørre Farup and Snæum Kirke, all in southwest Jutland. They are all situated on the first elevated area back from the sea, on the banks of rivers or fjords, so they had good maritime links. It is interesting that these settlements are also all close to churches that are only slightly later in date than the settlements themselves. Magnetic surveys of these settlements revealed strong local anomalies resulting from different *Grubenhäuser*. Many of these represented workshops. Depending on the nature of the workshop, the magnetic signals from the *Grubenhäuser* were either weaker (weaving workshops) or stronger (smithies and metal-casting workshops). At Henne Kirkeby, magnetic surveys revealed more than 330 *Grubenhäuser* situated on both sides of a street over a distance of more than 500 m (fig. 3).

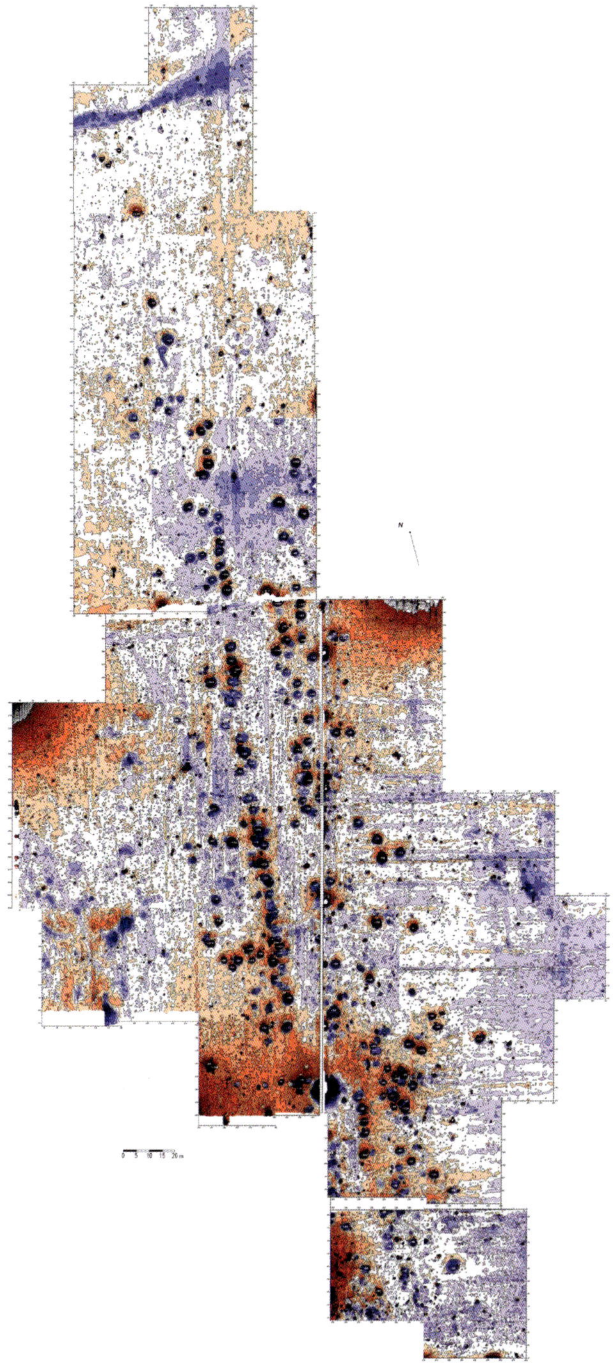

Fig. 3. | *Magnetic map of Henne Kirkeby, from the 2004-06 surveys. After Smekalova et al. 2008.*

A small number of magnetometer surveys have been carried out at Gudme on Funen, in an area where many archaeological investigations have taken place over a number of years. The surveys focused on an Iron Age environment comprising a series of linked and continually occupied settlements. The site is characterised by good conditions for preservation, and the remains of the farmsteads in several phases and enclosed within fences appear to be reasonably intact beneath the soil. This extended area constitutes a large and exceptional central place dating from the Late Roman and Germanic Iron Age. In 2008, a minor magnetometer survey was carried out there, its most important result being the discovery of an area with a concentration of local anomalies that could indicate the presence of archaeological features. A clear difference could be seen between the character of the magnetic field in the northern part of the plot (anomalies present) and the southern part (almost no anomalies) (fig. 4).

With the aid of magnetic survey, it was possible to identify an area showing the greatest concentration of strong local anomalies. These could result from pits back-filled with magnetic material relating to 'high temperature' industry at the site. The eastern, western and northern boundaries of the site were not established. The settlement appears to continue further in these directions.

A final example of the application of magnetometer survey moves a little outside the subject of productive sites. It is, however, of great relevance to demonstrate the method's potential, both with respect to revealing distribution boundaries and, even more specifically, regarding the selection of features and structures worth the time, money and energy required for investigation. In the beginning of the 1970s, sand and gravel quarrying at Rønninge Søgård on northeast Funen led to the discovery of Bronze Age cooking pits distributed across a large area. In 2007, the area around the gravel quarry was subjected to magnetometer survey. This proved to be a very effective, rapid and non-destructive method for the investigation of a site with this type of feature. At Rønninge, the survey showed that the cooking pits were organised in different ways in two distinct parts of the site. The westernmost area had been destroyed by a gravel pit. The total number of cooking pits revealed by the survey was about 470 (fig. 5).

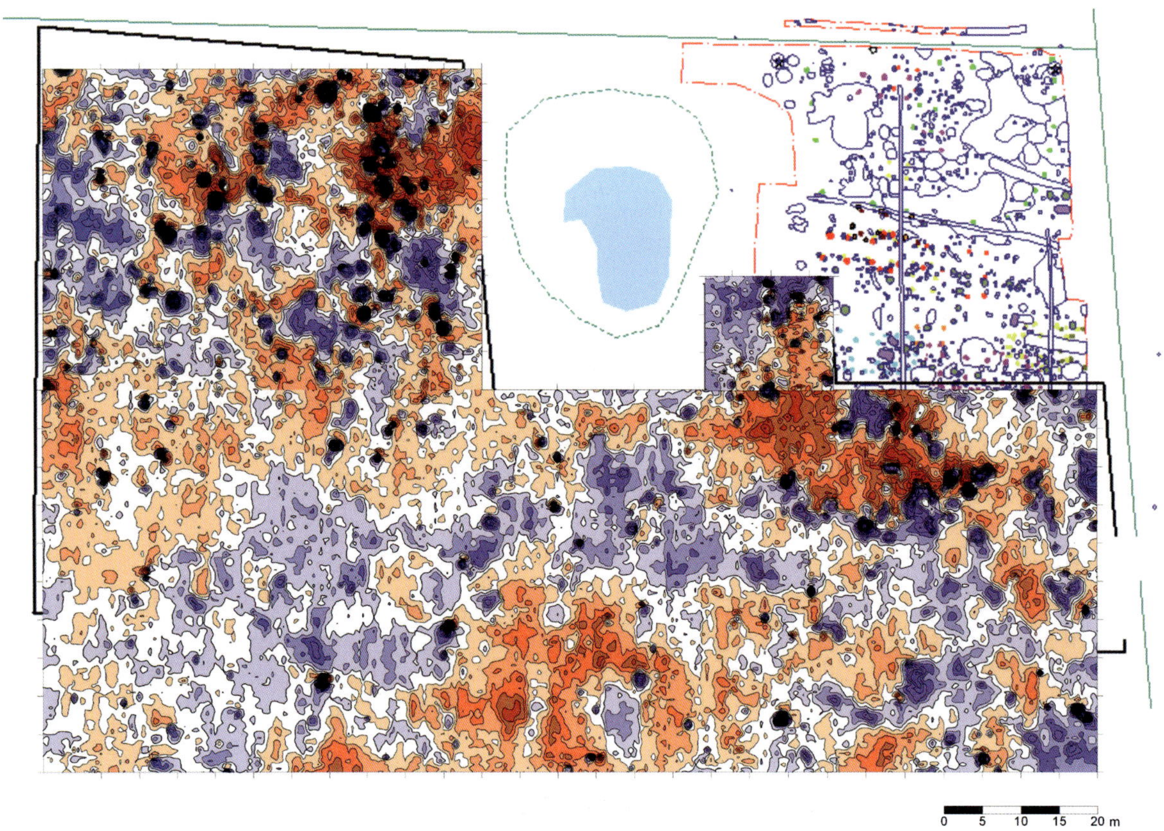

Fig. 4. | *Magnetic and interpretation map of Gudme. After Smekalova et al. 2008.*

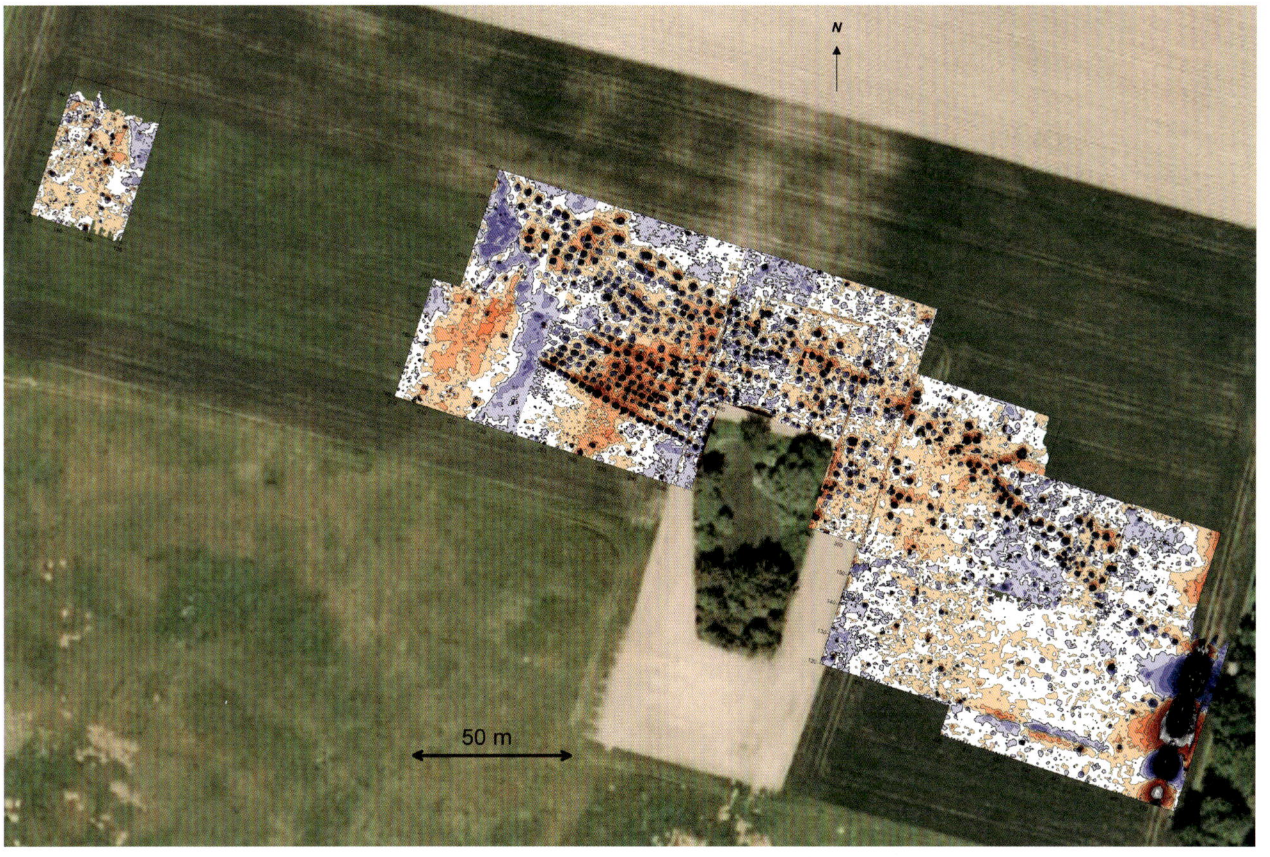

Fig. 5. | *A large number of cooking pits revealed by magnetometer survey at Rønninge Søgård. After Smekalova et al. 2008.*

On the basis of the survey data, it is possible to select which cooking pits should be investigated further – for charcoal analysis, for example, or the removal of material for radiocarbon dating – and then to make the argument for preserving the remaining features for posterity.

The plough soil

Normal practice in the archaeological investigation of productive sites, following the presence of metal objects in the plough soil being established, is to remove the plough soil mechanically in order to obtain an overview of the types of structures and features present at the site in question. Beneath the plough soil there can either be an intact preserved cultural layer (or layers), direct contact with the subsoil, or features such as postholes or *Grubenhäuser*.

Unfortunately, plough soil is usually ignored. Many metal detectorists discriminate against iron in their searches and, as a consequence, only artefacts made of other metal types are found and no true picture of the quantity of iron present at a site is obtained. This discrimination against iron is easily understandable, given how much metal has been thrown out into fields in modern times, but it still introduces a bias in the material.

It is not solely the occurrence of iron in the plough soil that is a problem. The investigations at Gudme have clearly demonstrated that significant quantities of metal finds of gold, silver and bronze are present on the surface of the fields and that corresponding metal finds occur beneath the soil, in addition to glass fragments, glass beads and remains left by craft activities, which can all contribute information about the site.

An example was provided by investigations at Sorte Muld on Bornholm (Klindt-Jensen 1957). The actual excavation here resulted in the recovery of a very limited number of fish bones, 13 in total. This led Klindt-Jensen to conclude that marine resources had not been exploited nutritionally at the site. When, many years later, gold foil figures were found at Sorte Muld, it became necessary to wet-sieve the soil in order to ensure their recovery. In the process, many thousands of fish bones were also recovered together with other types of finds. The application of wet-sieving was accordingly crucial for the result – and the technique is also now required practice by archaeozoologists, because without the very small bones the evidence value of the bone assemblage is limited. Marine resources now appear to have constituted a larger part of the diet at Sorte Muld than was previously thought.

Wet-sieving is a very important methodical approach for plough soil – and obviously also for cultural layers and the fills of features and structures. Wet-sieving is also preferable to dry-sieving, as it is much easier to overlook finds in the latter. The mesh size should of course be carefully considered; too small an aperture leads to the process being difficult and slow, in which case it is advantageous to take smaller samples and wet-sieve finely.

Excavation of structures and features

If we take as our point of departure a *Grubenhaus* as a representative of a feature type, we may begin by stating that a large number of activities took place in these buildings – including some that cannot be detected today. As an archaeologist, one is limited both by the type of excavation methods that can be applied and by the investigative methods that have been developed – and can be afforded. A distinction should be made here between research excavations, which generally have greater resources, and 'normal' excavations, where there are often difficult financial choices to be made that will determine which investigations are carried out.

If the finds recovered during actual excavations are excluded, it is wet-sieving and flotation that have produced the new finds during the course of the past two decades. Flotation leads primarily to the recovery of charred material such as charcoal, grain and weed seeds, but other material can also be discovered in the heavy residue of the sample. Another simple low-technology method is the use of a strong magnet to quickly reveal the presence of iron scale and other magnetic material in the archaeological layer – this material is often so small or in such poor condition that it would not be found by wet-sieving.

A number of other investigative methods become impossible as soon as the fill and the basal layer formed during the functional period of a *Grubenhaus* are removed. One example is pollen analysis. Pollen studies are normally considered as significant for the interpretation of developments in the landscape, but they can also be used to show human activity in a particular area (Enevold 2013). Accordingly, threshing activities and other kinds of processing food will leave a characteristic signature in an over-representation of certain pollen types in the pollen spectra. There are also other less well-known approaches to soil studies, including the analysis of the occurrence of starch grains and phytoliths. Both of these material types reveal something about the use of plant material and, in contrast to pollen, they represent stationary material which – under normal circumstances – does not become significantly redeposited.

Another investigative method involves the sampling and analysis of soil micro-morphology. A block of soil is carefully cut out from a soil section and impregnated with epoxy resin, and then cut into very thin slices. These are then ground down to a thickness of about 30 μm. Examination of the sample in a transmitted light microscope allows scientists to register the components that make up the actual stratigraphy. It is possible to see layers formed of very small particles, for example, of charred material, organic remains or other applied material. The use of this type of investigation has resulted in clear evidence of the occurrence of a solid layer of phytoliths in a *Grubenhaus* in Esbjerg.[1] Originally, there was a very thick layer of organic material here, probably straw. A normal excavation would simply have removed the material.

The scientific perspectives

It is immediately obvious that only a small proportion of the investigative methods available are currently being applied to productive sites. In the following, a series of examples addressing different questions will be highlighted in order to draw attention to a few of the many aspects in need of study.

These perspectives are to some degree linked to the three basic conditions under which the artefacts are found: plough soil, cultural layer(s) and postholes, wells and other feature types.

The plough soil

Plough soil primarily preserves inorganic and charred organic remains. The finds will have been displaced from their original context but are, even so, relevant to an understanding of what has taken place in the area.

The cultural layer(s)

This layer and the information held within it have been created by processes that took place in situ. However, a cultural layer may very well have been exposed to influences such as bioturbation. Similarly, ploughing in the past – or another activity in the area – can bring about some degree of contamination. Cultural layers deposited in hollows or cut features such as pits and *Grubenhäuser* have, in general, been afforded greater protection and therefore present opportunities to obtain more information that can be related directly to a particular activity.

Postholes, wells and other feature types

Metal-casting: Excavations at Holstebro in northwestern Jutland have demonstrated the occurrence of amber and/or resin in connection with bronze casting.[2] In the investigation of a *Grubenhaus* complex at Henne Kirke, amber and/or resin were found in several *Grubenhäuser*.[3] An analysis should be carried out of the presumed amber in order to ascertain whether it is simply resin that after many years in the soil now resembles amber. In addition to wet-sieving and flotation techniques used to recover these materials, it also seems obvious to investigate casting moulds for traces of resin. The use of resin is known from modern-day traditional bronze casters in India, where it is mixed with wax used for the models. The wax becomes more stable by being mixed with the resin, and this allows the production of more advanced wax models.[4]

Textile production: Finds of loom weights are interpreted as an indication of textile production, but as a rule it is impossible to gain any further information about this production. The close association between occurrences of loom weights and *Grubenhäuser* suggests an extensive production of, for example, sails for ships. But if the loom, and with it the loom weights, was removed before the *Grubenhaus* was abandoned, there will be no direct recognisable traces of this production. However, in weaving experiments it has become apparent that unfired loom weights lose some of their surface when, as part of the process, they clash together; with time a layer of clay particles is formed on the floor beneath the loom. It must be possible to find such layers of unfired clay by way of micromorphological investigation.[5]

Smithing: The use of strong magnets will quickly demonstrate any presence of hammer scale or other metallic material in basal or fill layers. If hammer scale is present in the basal layer, it is important to record its distribution and abundance in order to be able to establish the layout and organisation of the blacksmith's workshop (Joutijaarvi et al. 2005).

Agriculture: Agriculture can be investigated with respect both to pollen in wells, which can provide an impression of developments in the landscape, and to charred grain and weed seeds recovered from postholes and burnt-down *Grubenhäuser*. For example, a large quantity of rye grains was found in Aarhus together with a woven basket of willow withies. The basket was probably used in sieving the grain in a *Grubenhaus*, which then burned down.[6] Archaeobotanical analysis of the grain and weed seeds can contribute information on agrarian practices, for example sowing season, field weeds, efficiency of processing and the size of cereal grains (Mikkelsen & Nørbach 2003).

Conclusion

The productive sites have great potential relative to the application of scientific methods before, during and after an excavation. Many different kinds of analysis are available, and it is therefore important for the excavator to rank, in order of priority, the investigative methods to be used at a given location.

There is no doubt that scientific methods are becoming increasingly involved in archaeology in Denmark. This is a result of, among other things, the Heritage Agency of Denmark, (now called the Danish Agency for Culture) providing the opportunity, right from the budget-design phase, to incorporate these types of investigation into a project. We may thus secure as much information as possible from the archaeological features and structures which, through the process of excavation, will be exposed to total destruction. The gathering of information about prehistoric activities must include all aspects of science – we owe this to our prehistoric forefathers, to our contemporaries, who can see the results in our museums, and not least to our descendants, who will not have the opportunity to repeat our excavations.

Bibliography

Enevold, R. 2013, Pollen studies of textile material from an Iron Age grave at Hammerum, Denmark. *Journal of Archaeological Science* 40, 1838-44.

Helbæk, H. 1977, The Fyrkat grain. A geographical and chronological study of rye. In: O. Olsen & H.W. Schmidt (eds.), *En jysk vikingeborg. 1. Borgen og bebyggelsen.* København. 1-41.

Jouttijärvi, A., T. Thomsen & A.S.A. Moltsen 2005, Værkstedets funktion. In: M. Iversen et al. (eds.), *Viborg Søndersø 1018-1030. Arkæologi og naturvidenskab i et værkstedsområde fra vikingetid.* Højbjerg. 297-320.

Klindt-Jensen, O. 1957, *Bornholm i folkevandringstiden og forudsætningerne i tidlig jernalder.* København.

Mikkelsen, P.H. & L.C. Nørbach 2003, *Drengsted. Bebyggelse, jernproduktion og agerbrug.* Højbjerg.

Robinson, D.E. 1991, Plant remains from the Late Iron Age/ Early Viking Age settlement at Gammel Lejre. *Journal of Danish Archaeology* 10, 191-98.

Smekalova, T.N, O. Voss & S.L. Smekalov 2008, *Magnetic surveying in archaeology.* Højbjerg.

Notes

1 Oral communication from PhD student Nina Nielsen, Aarhus University. The study will be published in her thesis.

2 Oral communication from archaeologist Malene Nyman, Skive Museum.

3 Oral communication from museum curator Lene B. Frandsen, Varde Museum.

4 Oral communication from Arvid Ramsbøl, Reconstruction Department, Moesgård Museum.

5 Oral communication from PhD student Lone Gebauer, University of Copenhagen.

6 The contents are presently being analysed in the Department of Archaeological Science and Conservation, Moesgård Museum.

Museums referred to in the papers

Name until 2009	Present name	Home page	In English
Vendsyssel Historiske Museum	Vendsyssel Historiske Museum	www.vhm.dk	Vendsyssel Historical Museum
Nordjyllands Historiske Museum	Nordjyllands Historiske Museum	www.nordmus.dk	The Historical Museum of Northern Jutland
Lindholm Høje Museet	Nordjyllands Historiske Museum	www.nordmus.dk	The Historical Museum of Northern Jutland
Skive Museum	Museum Salling, Krydsfelt Skive	www.museumsalling.dk	Museum Salling
Holstebro Museum	Holstebro Museum	www.holstebro-museum.dk	Holstebro Museum
Ringkøbing-Skjern Museum	Ringkøbing-Skjern Museum	www.levendehistorie.dk	Ringkøbing and Skjern Museum
Kulturhistorisk Museum Randers	Museum Østjylland	www.museumoj.dk	East Jutland Museum
Moesgård Museum	Moesgård Museum	www.moesmus.dk	Moesgård Museum
Varde Museum	Museet for Varde by og omegn	www.vardemuseum.dk	Varde Museum
Esbjerg Museum	Sydvestjyske Museer	www.sydvestjyskemuseer.dk	Southwest Jutland Museums
Antikvarisk Samling Ribe	Sydvestjyske Museer	www.sydvestjyskemuseer.dk	Southwest Jutland Museums
Odense Bys Museer	Odense Bys Museer	museum.odense.dk	Odense City Museums
Svendborg og Omegns Museum	Øhavsmuseet, Arkæologi Sydfyn	www.ohavsmuseet.dk	Museum of Southern Funen and Islands
Nationalmuseet	Nationalmuseet	natmus.dk	National Museum of Denmark
Roskilde Museum	Roskilde Museum	www.roskildemuseum.dk	Roskilde Museum
Museet Færgegården	Roskilde Museum. Frederiksund Museum, Færgegården	www.roskildemuseum.dk	Roskilde Museum
Kalundborg Museum	Museum Vestsjælland	museumvestsjaelland.dk	West Zealand Museum
Vordingborg Museum	Museum Sydøstdanmark, Danmarks Borgcenter	www.museerne.dk	Museum Southeast Denmark and the Danish Castle Centre

List of authors

Torben Trier Christiansen	Aarhus University, Department of Culture and Society, Section for Medieval and Renaissance Archaeology, Moesgård Allé 20, 8270 Højbjerg, DK.
Philip Clogg	Durham University, Archaeological Artefacts Forensic Analysis Centre, Dawson Building, Department of Archaeology, South Road, Durham DH1 3LE, UK.
Andres Sigfried Dobat	Aarhus University, Department of Culture and Society, Section for Prehistoric Archaeology, Moesgård Allé 20, 8270 Højbjerg, DK.
Per Ethelberg	Museum Sønderjylland, Arkæologi Haderslev, Dalgade 7, 6100 Haderslev, DK.
Claus Feveile	Østfyns Museum, Vikingemuseet Ladby, Vikingevej 123, 5300 Kerteminde, DK.
Reno Fiedel	Fjordvej 7, 8950 Ørsted, DK.
Mads Kähler Holst	Moesgård Museum / Aarhus University, Department of Culture and Society, Section for Prehistoric Archaeology, Moesgård Allé 20, 8270 Højbjerg, DK.
Jens G. Lauridsen	Museet for Varde By og Omegn, Kirkepladsen 1, 6800 Varde, DK.
Christopher Loveluck	University of Nottingham. Department of Archaeology, University Park, Nottingham, NG7 2RD, UK.
Esben Schlosser Mauritsen	Ringkøbing-Skjern Museum, Arkæologi Vestjylland, Bundsbækvej 25, 6900 Skjern, DK.
Peter Hambro Mikkelsen	Moesgård Museum, Moesgård Allé 20, 8270 Højbjerg, DK.
Karen Høilund Nielsen	Byagervej 160, 1 mf, 8330 Beder, DK.
Yossi Salmon	The Leon Recanati Institute for Maritime Studies, The Sir Maurice and Lady Irene Hatter Laboratory for Coastal and Harbour Archaeology, University of Haifa, 199 Aba Khoushy Ave. Mount Carmel, Haifa, IL.
Torben Sarauw	Nordjyllands Historiske Museum, Algade 48, 9000 Aalborg, DK.
Martin Segschneider	Archäeologisches Landesamt Schleswig-Holstein, Brockdorff-Rantzau-Strasse 70, 24837 Schleswig, DE.
Tatiana Smekalova	Moesgård Museum, Moesgård Allé 20, 8270 Højbjerg, DK.
Ernst Stidsing	Museum Østjylland, Stemannsgade 2, 8900 Randers C, DK.
Kristian Strutt	University of Southampton, Faculty of Humanities, Avenue Campus, Highfield Road, Southampton, SO17 1BF, UK.
Jens Ulriksen	Roskilde Museum, Munkebro 2, 4000 Roskilde, DK.
Michael Vinter	Moesgård Museum, Moesgård Allé 20, 8270 Højbjerg, DK.
Sidsel Wåhlin	Vendsyssel Historiske Museum, Museumsgade 3, 9800 Hjørring, DK.